SYNTACTIC THEORY A
ACQUISITION OF ENGLIS

SYNTACTIC THEORY AND THE ACQUISITION OF ENGLISH SYNTAX

THE NATURE OF EARLY CHILD GRAMMARS OF ENGLISH

Andrew Radford

BASIL BLACKWELL

Copyright © Andrew Radford 1990

First published 1990

Basil Blackwell Ltd
108 Cowley Road, Oxford. OX4 1JF, UK

Basil Blackwell, Inc.
3 Cambridge Center
Cambridge, Massachusetts 02142, USA

British Library Cataloguing in Publication Data

A CIP catalogue record for this book is available from the British Library

Library of Congress Cataloging in Publication data

Radford, Andrew.
    Syntactic theory and the acquisition of English syntax: the nature of early child grammars of
English/Andrew Radford.
        p.   cm.
    Includes bibliographical references.
    ISBN 0–631–16357–3—ISBN 0–631–16358–1 (pbk.)
    1. English language – Syntax. 2. Children – Language. I. Title.
PE1369.R34 1990   90-418
425—dc20   CIP

Typeset in 10½/12 pt Ehrhardt
by TecSet Ltd, Wallington, Surrey
Printed in Great Britain by T. J. Press Ltd, Padstow, Cornwall

Contents

Preface

This book is concerned with the grammar of children's speech during the period when they first come to string words together in systematic patterns to form elementary phrases and clauses – a stage variously referred to in the acquisition literature as 'telegraphic speech', 'early patterned speech', 'early grammatical speech', and 'early multi-word speech'. According to Goodluck (1989), children typically enter this phase of grammatical development at around 20 months of age, and progress to a more advanced (and more adult-like) stage of development at around 24 months of age.

Why devote a whole book to such a short period in the child's linguistic life? The answer is that this particular period in the child's grammatical development is of paramount importance for any attempt to construct a theory of language acquisition, since it represents the first point at which we have clear evidence that the child has begun to develop a grammar of the language being acquired. By detailed study of the initial grammars developed by children, we may hope ultimately to be able to shed light on the fundamental questions which any theory of language acquisition must seek to address – viz. the extent to which children's initial grammars are shaped by innate linguistic principles, the point at which different principles become operative, and the ways in which the relevant principles interact with the child's linguistic experience. The data used as the empirical basis of this study comprise a corpus of more than 100,000 utterances of the spontaneous speech of young children between one-and-a-half and three years of age. The contents of this book are essentially a synthesis of ideas which I have presented over the past five years in lectures on child language acquisition both in my (former) home university of Bangor, and in visiting lectures at the following other universities:

1984: Cambridge, Fez, Malaga, Rabat, Reading, York
1985: Essex
1986: Essen, Essex, Genova, Pavia, Reading
1987: Essen, Manchester, Newcastle, Reading, Utrecht, Tübingen, York
1988: London (Philological Society)
1989: Deusto, Essen, Kent, Manchester, Vitoria

In the hope of making the book intelligible to as wide an audience as possible (particularly to readers who are afflicted by aggravated arboriphobia), I have attempted to simplify the exposition by avoiding excessive use of unnecessary technical apparatus and jargon. I have also included introductory material aimed both at syntacticians who have little familiarity with acquisition research, and at psycholinguists who have little familiarity with recent work in syntactic theory (not to mention students who have little familiarity with work in either field!).

There are a number of people whom I would like to thank for their invaluable help with the acquisition research which led up to the publication of this book. Special thanks are due first and foremost to dozens of my former undergraduate and postgraduate students who allowed themselves to be dragooned into patiently pursuing many of the reluctant heroes of this toddlers' tale with microphone and portable recorder, and extracting from them countless hours of toddler talk: I am sure that they will have forever imprinted on their memories the joy of finally completing a 50-page phonetic transcription of the unintelligible utterances of some uncooperative urchin, followed by the agony of having the transcription returned with hundreds of transcription errors marked in humiliating red ink!

I am likewise grateful to a number of people who made helpful comments on an early draft of the manuscript, and/or who kindly sent me drafts of their own research papers. These include Michelle Aldridge (Bangor), Martin Atkinson (Essex), Bob Borsley (Bangor), Memo Cinque (Venice), Harald Clahsen (Düsseldorf), Helen Goodluck (Ottawa), Eithne Guilfoyle (McGill), Dick Hudson (University College London), Barbara Lust (Cornell), Brian MacWhinney (Carnegie-Mellon), Leslie Milroy (Newcastle), Christer Platzack (Lund), Luigi Rizzi (Geneva), Tom Roeper (Amherst), Neil Smith (University College London), Virginia Valian (Hunter College New York), and Jurgen Weissenborn (Max-Planck-Institut, Nijmegen).

In addition, I should like to express my gratitude to the Leverhulme Trust for providing me with a generous grant to assist my research into the acquisition of noun phrases (i.e. the research reported on in the relevant parts of chapters 3 and 4).

Finally, I should like to thank my wife Khadija for patiently recording and transcribing the speech of many of the heroes and heroines of this developmental drama – and for not recording the comments made by the villain of the piece (= me) when the word-processor greedily gobbled up whole portions of the text!

Andrew Radford
Essex

1

Aims and Approaches

At around the age of one-and-a-quarter years, children are typically at the 'one-word stage' in the acquisition of their mother tongue – i.e. at the stage where their utterances comprise single words spoken in isolation. As a representative example of the child's speech production at this stage, consider the following dialogue between Allison Bloom at age 16 months 3 weeks and her mother (from Bloom 1973: 163):

(1) ADULT: Where's the little man who rides the car?
    CHILD: *Gone* (gesturing 'gone')
    ADULT: Who rides the car?
    CHILD: *Gone* (gesturing 'gone')
    ADULT: Is he gone?
    CHILD: *There* (walking towards bag)
    ADULT: See if you can find him
    CHILD: *Away* (looking into bag)
    ADULT: Where is he?
    CHILD: *Gone* (gesturing 'gone')
    ADULT: Is he gone?
    CHILD: *There!* (reaching into bag and pulling out man)

It is traditionally supposed that children's speech at the one-word stage has no syntactic structure whatever: thus, Bühler (1922: 55) characterizes one-word speech as 'asyntactic', and in a similar vein Stern (1928: 51) remarks that at the one-word stage 'Speech elements so far show no understanding of grammar'. Recent researchers have reached a similar conclusion (cf. e.g. Atkinson 1985: 294, Greenfield et al. 1985: 234, and Peters 1986: 313 for analogous remarks). If this is so, then the obvious conclusion to draw is that at the one-word stage, the words used by young children have phonological and semantic properties, but as yet have no syntactic properties. Because their words lack syntactic properties at this stage, children are unable to combine words into larger structural units (i.e. phrases or clauses) in any *productive* way.

However, between the ages of one-and-a-half and two years, children start to combine words together in systematic patterns which suggest that they have begun to master the basic principles of grammar (i.e. phrase- and sentence-formation) in the native language they are acquiring. For example, some six months after producing the single-word utterances in (1) above, Allison Bloom (at age 22 months) produced multi-word utterances such as those in (2) below:

(2)   (a)   Man drive truck. Baby drive truck. Baby doll ride truck. Pig ride. Baby Allison comb hair. Baby eat cookies. Mommy eat cookie. Baby open door. Mommy open. Horse tumble.
      (b)   Get Mommy cookie. Eat apple juice. Eat Mommy cookie. Open can. Open box. Pour Mommy juice. Put away Allison bag. Get toys. Get diaper. Open box. Help cow in table. Sit down. Put on. Build tower.
      (c)   Eating Mommy cookie. Wiping baby chin. Peeking Mommy. Peeking lady. Standing up. Walking around (Allison Bloom at age 22 months)

Such utterances exhibit morphosyntactic characteristics which suggest the emergence of *grammar* in Allison's speech at this stage: the clues which lead us to this conclusion are partly morphological (viz. the use of the plural +*s* and gerund +*ing* inflections), and partly syntactic (e.g. the fact that subjects are consistently positioned before, and complements after, their associated Verbs).

Allison's utterances in (2) are typical of a child at the stage of development which we shall refer to here as *early child English* (variously referred to in more general terms as 'early patterned speech', 'early multi-word speech', 'early grammatical speech' and 'telegraphic speech'). Her utterances appear to be organized in accordance with systematic grammatical principles (suggesting the development of a rudimentary grammar), but are very different in character from the corresponding adult sentences. Viewed from an adult perspective, early child English has an apparently *elliptical* character, in that various key constituents appear to be 'missing': for example, Allison's speech at this stage is characterized by the absence of possessive *'s*, the present/past tense inflections +*s*/+*d*, auxiliaries such as *will/can/do* etc., and determiners such as *a/the*, together with the sporadic omission of subjects, objects, and prepositions. Brown and Fraser (1963) note that in this respect, early child English bears an obvious superficial resemblance to the kind of English used by adults in sending telegrams (= *telegraphic* English), where nonessential constituents are omitted. As Brown and Bellugi note (1964: 311): 'One does not send a cable reading; "My car has broken down and I have lost my wallet: send money to me at the American Express in Paris", but rather "Car broken down; wallet lost; send money American Express Paris." ' The fact that adult telegraphese seems to have much the same elliptical character as childese (i.e. the language of young children at the 'early patterned speech' stage) led Brown and Fraser to draw an intuitively appealing (though potentially misleading) analogy between the two, and to characterize early child English as essentially *telegraphic* in nature.

Thus, in the course of a few months, children progress from the *agrammatical* (i.e. grammar-less) single-word stage illustrated in (1) above to the early *grammatical* ('telegraphic') stage illustrated in (2) at which they appear to have developed rudimentary grammars. The central question with which we shall be concerned in this book relates to how, when, and why children develop their initial grammars, and what is the nature of these initial grammars. More specifically, we shall attempt to answer the questions set out in (3) below:

(3)   (i)   At what point can the child be said to have developed an initial *grammar* of the language being acquired?

(ii)   How and why does the transition from *agrammatical* to *grammatical* speech come about?

(iii) What are the various stages of grammatical development which children go through, and what are the defining characteristics of each stage?

(iv)   To what extent are early child grammars the product of innate knowledge, and to what extent are they the product of linguistic experience?

The ultimate goal of any developmental psycholinguist must be to develop a Theory of Language Acquisition which provides principled answers to these (and many other) key questions.

There are two approaches to the task of developing a theory of language acquisition found in the relevant linguistic literature – one involving the study of *adult grammars*, the other involving the study of *child grammars*. The first (adultocentric) approach is primarily associated with the work of Chomsky and his followers, and concentrates on the attempt to answer question (3)(iv). Chomsky argues that detailed work on the grammars of a wide range of different adult languages over the past two decades has led to the conclusion that the grammars of all natural (= human) languages share a common 'core' of deep-seated universal properties: the attempt to characterize this set of universal properties has become known as the study of 'Universal Grammar' (i.e. the search for a universal theory of the nature of the grammars of natural languages). To be rather more precise, Chomsky argues that the grammars of all languages comprise a series of inter-related components, called *modules*. Each such module deals with a specific aspect of the linguistic properties of grammars. For example, the *categorial* module is concerned with the principles which regulate the categorial constituent structure of phrases and sentences; the *transformational* module is concerned with the principles governing the nature and application of movement rules; the *bounding* module is concerned with the principles which determine why certain grammatical processes are *bounded*, in the sense that they can only apply within a limited domain, and cannot go beyond certain bounds; the *case* module is concerned with the principles governing the morphosyntax of case-marked forms such as *I/me/my*; the *theta* module is concerned with the nature of the semantic relations between predicates and arguments, and thus tells us (e.g.) that in 'John killed Mary', *John* fulfils the theta (= thematic) role of AGENT and *Mary* that of PATIENT of *killed*; and the *binding* module specifies the conditions under which one expression can *bind* another, and thus tells us for example that in a sentence like 'Fred says that Bill hurt himself', *himself* can only be bound by (i.e. interpreted as referring back to) *Bill* and not *Fred*. It would not be appropriate to go into further details about the nature and interaction of these various modules here: for a book-length introduction to this topic, see Cook (1988). It may well be that not all the modules are operative in all grammars of all languages: for example, there is some recent research suggesting that there is no *transformational* module operating in certain types of language (e.g. Japanese).

Thus, Chomsky claims, all grammars of all (adult) languages comprise parallel systems of *modules* interconnected in complex ways. However, the 'common core' of universal properties shared by the grammars of different languages range far beyond the mere fact that every grammar of every natural language contains a similar system of interconnected modules. Chomsky argues that there are deep-seated similarities between languages in respect of the precise form of each of the individual modules which make up the overall grammar, so that (e.g.) the *case module* of the grammar of English will be similar in form to the *case module* of the grammar of an apparently completely different language such as Arabic. The word 'similar' here is of particular significance: it would obviously be fatuous to claim that all natural language grammars contain a set of *identical* modules, since this would imply that the only difference between languages would be in the set of morphemes (i.e. stems and affixes) which they contain. Thus, our theory has to allow for the fact that there will be some variation in the precise form of a given module from one language to another.

Chomsky has maintained that this type of intramodular variation is 'within fixed limits' (Chomsky 1977: 75). The task of the linguist in seeking to define the 'limits' within which a given module varies from one grammar to another is to determine the set of *parameters of variation* between a given module in one grammar and its counterpart in other grammars. Thus, the goal of Universal Grammar is to determine what the universal *principles* are which are common to all natural language grammars, and at the same time to determine the *parameters of variation* within which grammars vary from one language to another. For example, we might argue that the case modules of English and (Classical) Arabic share the universal property that a transitive preposition assigns case to (i.e. determines the case of) a (pro)nominal which it governs (e.g. its object), but differ in respect of the particular case assigned (objective case in English, and genitive case in Arabic). This approach has given rise to what is generally known as a *principles-and-parameters* model of Universal Grammar.

Now, if it is indeed the case that there are deep-seated similarities between the grammars of different languages (characterizable in terms of a universal system of *principles and parameters*), then the obvious question we have to ask is why this should be so. Chomsky has argued that the 'core properties' of Universal Grammar which languages share are of such an abstract nature that they are not 'learnable' simply on the basis of exposure to the kind of *linguistic experience* (= speech input) which the child receives. He therefore concludes that these 'universal properties' of language must be part of the child's genetic endowment, and that children are born with an innate knowledge of Universal Grammar (i.e. of the system of *principles and parameters* that determine the form of natural language grammars). If this is so, then it clearly has important implications for the nature of the language acquisition process: more precisely, it would vastly reduce the complexity of the acquisition task which children face. We should then expect that those principles of language which are invariant across languages will not have to be 'learned' by the child, since they will be part of the child's genetic endowment: on the contrary, all that the child has to 'learn' are those grammatical properties which are subject to parametric variation across languages. Moreover, the child's learning task will be further simplified if it turns out (as has been suggested in recent research) that the values which a parameter can have fall within a narrowly specified range, perhaps characterizable in terms of a series of binary choices: cf. the suggestion by Piattelli-Palmarini (1989: 3) that 'each [parameter] can be "set" on only one of a small number of admissible values (for many linguistic parameters there seem to be just two such possible values)'. For example, we might suppose that one of the linearity (i.e. word-order) parameters along which languages vary concerns whether they normally position *heads* either before or after all their *complements*. There would then be two classes of languages: (i) *head-first* languages like English which normally position (e.g.) a head verb like *give* before all its complements (cf. '*Give* the book to Mary'), and (ii) *head-last* languages like Japanese which normally position a head Verb like *ageru* 'give' after all its complements (cf. 'Sono hon-o Mary-ni *agenasai*', literally 'The book Mary-to give'). This would exclude the possibility of there being any language in which (e.g.) some head verbs always precede their complements, and others always follow them.

Now, if the relevant parameter can have only one of two values (so that a language is either consistently head-first or consistently head-last), then Universal Grammar (UG) will genetically endow the child with this knowledge, so that the child's acquisition task is reduced to the relatively simple one of selecting the parametric value appropriate for the language he is acquiring, on the basis of his linguistic experience (i.e. on the basis of the speech input he receives). This simplified parameter-setting conception of the child's acquisition task has given rise to a metaphorical acquisition model in which the child is visualized as having to 'set' a series of switches in one of two positions (up/down) – each such switch representing a different parameter (the relevant 'switch' in the case we are discussing here determining the relative order of heads and their complements, so that e.g. *up* = head-first, *down* = head-last).

The *principles-and-parameters* model of acquisition (which Chomsky arrives at on the basis of detailed study of the nature of *adult* grammars) obviously has important implications for the study of child language development. Let us make the familiar assumption that the child's syntactic development can be characterized in terms of a succession of grammars G_1, G_2, G_3...G_A, where G_1 represents the child's initial grammar, G_2 represents the next grammar developed by the child, G_3 the next (and so on), and G_A represents the adult grammar which the child finally comes to acquire: thus, G_1...G_{A-1} are *child grammars*, and G_A is the 'mature' adult grammar. Now, if Chomsky is right in positing genetic constraints on the form of natural language grammars (so that grammars can vary, but only within genetically predetermined limits), then it would seem to follow that we should expect child grammars to be cast in the same (genetic) mould as adult grammars, and thus to show evidence of being constrained by the same system of principles and parameters as adult grammars. However, it is important to note that *maturational* factors may complicate this picture. For it may well be (as suggested by Chomsky 1981: 9), that certain universal principles are genetically programmed to come into operation only at a specific point in the child's linguistic maturation: this would imply that such principles would be inoperative in the earliest child grammars, and become operative only when the child reaches a given point of maturation (in much the same way that the physiological changes associated with puberty come about only at a certain point of development).

The parameter-setting model of acquisition brings a number of interesting questions in its wake – in particular, the following two:

(4) (i) At what point in the child's development do specific parameters come 'on line' (= become available to be set)?
     (ii) How are the relevant parameters set when they come 'on line'?

There would seem to be two different answers which we might envisage for question (4)(i). One is that all parameters are 'on line' immediately (because UG genetically endows the child with the relevant set of parameters), and hence become (potentially) available to be set from the very earliest stages of the child's grammatical development (though particular parameters may not be set immediately because of experiential difficulties in determining the appropriate settings). A second (*maturational*) view is that different parameters might be (genetically) programmed to come 'on line' at different stages of maturation; this would mean that a given parameter would not be available to be set prior to the relevant point of maturation.

Once a given parameter comes 'on line', it becomes potentially available to be set – but then the question arises as to how it is set (cf. question (4)(ii)). One possibility (suggested in recent work by Nina Hyams, 1986, 1987a, 1987b, 1988, 1989) is that Universal Grammar might predetermine a fixed 'initial' value for a given parameter: the learner's task would then be to determine whether this genetically specified initial value is appropriate for the language he is acquiring; if not, he has to 're-set' the parameter accordingly (this in effect leads us towards a *parameter-resetting* model of acquisition, rather than a *parameter-setting* one). Under this view, a given parameter would be 'preset' (by UG) immediately it comes 'on line'. However, an alternative possibility might be that even when a given parameter comes 'on line' it will remain *unset* (and so inoperative) until such time as the child has accumulated sufficient linguistic experience to arrive at a provisional setting of the relevant parameter: on this view, there might be some delay between a parameter coming 'on line', and being 'set'.

Without doubt, the *principles-and-parameters* model has had an enormous impact on the direction of language acquisition research in the past decade. However, in an obvious sense, the model provides more questions than answers, so that its contribution might be seen as methodological rather than empirical. For example, the model itself makes no precise predictions about the nature of early child grammars: instead, we have the rather vague suggestions that some parameters (which?) may remain unset until the child has accumulated sufficient linguistic experience (How much? when?), and that maturational factors (of what kind?) may retard the operation of other parameters (which? for how long?). Moreover, there is very far from being a general consensus among linguists about the nature and function of parameters, with the consequence that 'The theoretical status of parameters is unclear at the moment' (De Haan and Tuijnman 1988: 119). It seems clear, then, that the questions which we asked in (3)(i–iii) and (4) above about the emergence and nature of early child grammars cannot be resolved by consideration of *adult grammars*, but instead require us to make a detailed study of the child's developing syntactic competence.

The term *competence* is defined by Chomsky (1965: 4) as denoting 'the speaker-hearer's knowledge of his language' – though it should be noted that all reference to linguistic 'knowledge' in our discussion here should be construed as being to *tacit* (i.e. subconscious) and not to *explicit* (i.e. conscious) knowledge; wherever the need arises to avoid confusion, we shall enclose terms like 'know(ledge)' and 'aware(ness)' within quotation marks in order to indicate that they are being used to denote tacit rather than explicit knowledge. Since we are interested in characterizing the nature of early child grammars, the obvious question to ask is what kind of data we can collect which will give us an insight into the nature of the child's developing syntactic competence (i.e. the child's *tacit* syntactic knowledge). There are two types of study which might provide us with relevant data: (i) *experimental* studies, and (ii) *naturalistic* studies. Let's briefly compare the two approaches.

Over the past few years, there have been an increasing number of interesting experimental studies of the acquisition of particular aspects of syntax – see, for example, the various papers on the acquisition of anaphors and pronominals in the anthologies edited by Tavakolian (1981) and Lust (1986, 1987). Experimental studies offer obvious advantages and disadvantages. The main advantage is that a properly designed experiment enables the experimenter to control specific variables, and thereby avoid 'accidental gaps' in the data: but the main disadvantage is that experimental studies by their very nature tend to be relatively narrow in scope (e.g. they focus on the acquisition of one specific type of item or construction), and so cannot offer a broader perspective on the child's overall linguistic development: cf., for example, Roeper's (1987: 315) remark that in experimental work, 'The data is often uninterpretable because it's too narrowly focussed, and then often leads to an understatement of children's abilities'. An added problem is that (as Painter 1984: 36 notes) 'Children...in their first year or two of life... make very unsatisfactory laboratory subjects'. In consequence, experimental procedures have to be elaborate and time-consuming, and are all too often relatively unsuccessful. Illustrative of the problems involved are the following remarks by Lila Gleitman (1989: 36) on conducting a *selective looking* experiment with two-year-old subjects: 'It is tedious in the extreme to set up (requiring the preparation of movies, etc.), takes hordes of infants to carry out (for some scream or sleep or worse, and have to be removed from the premises; and only a few trials can be presented even to the more docile infants), and yields probabilistic results...'. Similar problems in conducting experimental studies of very young children's linguistic competence are reported in Brown and Bellugi (1964), Benedict (1976), Rodgon (1976), Pinker (1984), Fletcher (1985), and Lalleman (1988).

A conventional alternative to experimental studies are *naturalistic studies*: typically, these involve collecting and analysing a *corpus* (i.e. sample) of children's 'free-speech' (to use a term borrowed from Miller et al. 1981: 21). The corpus is collected by making videotape or audiotape recordings of a child's spontaneous speech behaviour in a natural setting (e.g. at home) where the child is in conversation with someone he is familiar with and talks freely to (e.g. his mother). The resultant recordings are then transcribed and analysed: it is particularly important that both an orthographic *and a phonetic* transcription of the child's speech are kept, since an accurate phonetic transcription of the child's speech is an essential safeguard against the imaginative excesses and adultocentricity of the transcriber (it is quite remarkable how many different orthographic interpretations inexperienced transcribers can give to a mere schwa, which often gets transliterated into orthographic form as some specific item such as 'he', or 'can', or 'my', etc.). There are numerous additional common-sense precautions which have to be taken when collecting and transcribing the corpus: cf. for example the guidelines outlined in Miller et al. 1981: 9–16, and Crystal 1986: 20–9.

The main advantage of using naturalistic speech samples is that (with talkative subjects, at any rate!) they generally yield a large number of examples of a wide range of linguistic phenomena, so enabling the linguist to build up a reasonably comprehensive picture of the child's *overall* linguistic development at a given stage. On the other hand, there are also some drawbacks to using naturalistic speech samples, of which I shall mention only two here. The first is that the linguist cannot in any way 'control' the data he gets, so that in some instances there will be 'accidental gaps' in the data, or too few examples of a particular phenomenon to make a proper analysis of it (of course, the larger the overall corpus, the less the danger of 'accidental gaps'). The second is that a naturalistic corpus does not yield *introspective* well-formedness judgements of the type the linguist typically relies upon in analysing adult speech (e.g. by asking informants whether such-and-such a sentence is grammatical, etc.). However, it probably has to be conceded that very young children are not able to verbalize any 'linguistic intuitions' which they may have – hence the fact that numerous studies have reported a complete failure to elicit consistent linguistic judgements from young children; cf. the remark by Gleitman, Gleitman and Shipley (1974: 140) that 'So far no-one has found a little child who gives stable judgments on his own primitive language' (and cf. also parallel observations by Brown and Bellugi (1964: 15), McNeill (1966: 23), Brown (1970: 72–3), and Schaerlaekens (1973)). Thus, if the absence of introspective child data is a consequence of the linguistic immaturity of child subjects, it should not be regarded as a limitation intrinsic to naturalistic (rather than other types of) studies of early child speech. It should also be remembered that in the structuralist era, a corpus was the 'standard' method of collecting data even for the analysis of adult language; hence the observation by Harris (1951: 12) that 'Investigation in descriptive linguistics consists of recording utterances in a single dialect and analysing the recorded material.'

Given the relatively broad scope of the enquiry here (which, as we shall see shortly, covers a wide variety of different aspects of early child syntax), the present work is based entirely on a corpus of naturalistic speech samples. The study is restricted to monolingual children acquiring English as their first language, for two reasons. Firstly, the syntax of the target system (= adult English) is relatively well understood, given the enormous amount of published theoretical and descriptive work on English; this obviously facilitates comparisons between the child's system at a given point, and the adult target system. Secondly, in order to minimize the 'accidental gaps' problem alluded to above, a naturalistic study needs to be based on an extensive corpus of utterances: in the case of the present study, this is provided in part by a sizeable corpus of naturalistic speech samples collected by my students over the past seven years, in part by the transcripts of the survey of 60 preschool children conducted by Gordon Wells at the University of Bristol in the early 1970s, and in part by examples and transcripts of early child English cited in the existing published literature. Taken together, these provide a relatively large data-base comprising more than 100,000 early child English utterances. It clearly would not have been practicable for me to attempt to collect a similar-sized corpus for other languages – even for languages in which I could claim some descriptive competence (viz. French and Italian). And to have collected a 'small' corpus of French or Italian data (say a dozen or so samples of each) would have meant that the conclusions about the acquisition of French or Italian resulting from the study would have owed more to wishful thinking than to objective analysis. I take it as self-evident that real progress in understanding the nature of language acquisition is more likely to come from an in-depth analysis of the acquisition of one relatively well understood class of phenomena in one relatively well understood language, than from a number of superficial studies of acquisition in a variety of languages whose structure is less well understood. The obvious drawback to a monolingual developmental study, however, is that any Theory of Language Acquisition must ultimately seek to explain the acquisition of *all* human languages, not just the acquisition of English.

The corpus collected by my students over the past few years includes cross-sectional samples of the speech of the following children at the ages indicated, in months (since we are concerned here with early child English, I have excluded all samples of children over 30 months of age):

(5)   Sean 17; Stefan17; Helen 18; Lucy 20; Hayley 20; Allison 21; John 22; Leila 23; Claire 23; Chrissie 23; Leigh 24; Domenico 24; Anne 24; Anna 24; Michael 24; Lucy 24; Angela 25; Adam 26; Alex 26; Becky 26; Rebecca 26; Thomas 26; Laura 26; Elizabeth 26; Robert 26; Sarah 26; Heather 26; Samantha 27; Katy 28; Emma 28; Melanie 28; Jonathan 28; Michelle 29; Joel 29; Esther 29; Alistair 30; Vimbai 30; Ruth 30; Matthew 30

It also includes longitudinal samples of the speech of the children specified in (6) below (ranked in order of age at the start of the first recording; ages indicated are in months and – where more than one recording was made in a given month – weeks):

(6)   Daniel 15, 19.0, 19.1, 19.2, 20.0, 20.1, 20.2, 20.3, 21.0, 21.2,
            21.3, 22.0, 22.1, 22.2, 22.3, 23.0, 23.2, 23.3, 24.0, 24.1,
            24.2, 24.3, 25, 25.1, 25.2, 26
        Dewi 15, 17, 18, 19, 20, 25
        Paula 18, 23
        Elen 19, 20
        Stephen 19, 20,
        Bethan 20, 21.0, 21.1
        Jem 21, 23, 24, 26, 27, 28, 29, 30
        Jenny 21, 22, 23, 24, 25, 26, 27, 28
        Angharad 22, 23
        Holly 23, 24
        Hannah 26, 27, 28, 30
        Lisa 27, 29

Each sample is in the form of an audiotape recording of 45 minutes duration made on a Marantz Superscope audio recorder, and has been transcribed both phonetically and orthographically. The recordings and initial phonetic transcriptions were made by my students, with all phonetic transcriptions subsequently corrected by me. Although phonetic transcriptions have been made of all child utterances in the corpus, for typographical convenience only orthographic transcriptions of child data will generally be used in the text here.

The second source of data used here are examples and transcripts taken from published studies of early child English. Included in the illustrative data cited are examples of the speech of the children specified in (7) below (the source publication being identified in parentheses):

(7)   Adam 28 (Brown and Fraser 1963)
        Allison 16, 19, 20, 22 (Bloom 1973)
        Andrew 19–23 (Braine 1963)
        Claire 24.0, 24.2, 24.3, 25.1, 25.2, 25.3, 26.0 (Hill 1983)
        Dory 1.24, 1.26, 1.30, 1.34, 1.40, 1.42 years (Gruber 1973)
        Eric 19, 20, 22, 23, 25, 26 (Bloom 1970)
        Eve 25 (Brown and Fraser 1963)
        Gia 19, 20, 22, 23, 25, 27 (Bloom 1970, Bloom et al. 1975)
        Helen 20, 21, 24, 26 (Ede and Williamson 1980)
        Jonathan 23, 24 (Braine 1976)
        Kathryn 21, 22, 24 (Bloom 1970, Bloom et al. 1975)
        Katie 22, 23 (Greenfield et al. 1985)
        Kendall 22, 23 (Bowerman 1973)
        Richard 22 (Bruner 1983)

Stephen 23–24 (Braine 1963)
Stevie 25 (Braine 1973)
Susan 22, 24 (Ervin-Tripp 1964, Miller and Ervin 1964)

In nearly all cases, the relevant data have been published in orthographic form only. Where data included in the text are taken from published sources, the name of the child involved is marked by a prefixed asterisk, and the source can then be identified from the list in (7).

The third source of data used here are transcripts from the Bristol University survey directed by Gordon Wells, and conducted in the early 1970s. This includes orthographic transcripts of recorded samples of the children specified in (8) below, at the ages indicated (although the recordings in the case of the children specified in (8)(b) and (c) continue at three-monthly intervals up to the age of 42 months, only the transcripts of children aged 30 months or less have been taken into account here, for the reason given earlier; subscripts are used to distinguish different children with the same name):

(8) (a) $Amanda_i$, $Amanda_j$, Amy, $Andrew_i$, $Andrew_j$, Anna, Anthony, Brendan, Darren, Emma, Gary, Hannah, Glenn, Helen, Jane, Joanna, Johanna, Kate, Kathrine, Lee_i, Lee_j, Lee_k, Lisa, $Louise_i$, $Louise_j$, Lucy, Mandy, Mark, Mary, Michelle, Morag, $Neil_i$, $Neil_j$, $Paul_i$, $Paul_j$, $Paul_k$, $Rachel_i$, $Rachel_j$, Richard, Rowena, $Samantha_i$, $Samantha_j$, Sandra, Sarah, Thomas, Timothy, Toby, $Tracey_i$, $Tracey_j$, Zoe [15 months]

(b) Benjamin, Darren, Geoffrey, Gerald, Jonathan, Martin, Neil, Tony [15, 18, 21, 24, 27, 30 months]

(c) Abigail, Betty, Debbie, Ellen, Elspeth, Frances, Gary, Gavin, Harriet, Iris, Jack, Jason, Laura, Lee, Nancy, Neville, Olivia, Penny, Rosie, Samantha, Sean, Sheila, Simon, Stella [18, 21, 24, 27, 30 months]

Throughout the text, I have used a prefixed + sign to identify children from the Bristol survey. However, I have cited relatively few examples from the Bristol corpus here, partly in order to avoid copyright problems, partly because of the obvious 'gaps' in the picture of a child's early language development which result from sampling at three-monthly intervals, partly because of the lack of a proper phonetic transcription, and partly because the transcripts of the children at the earlier stages of development which interest us here often contain insufficient exemplars of a given child's speech for any reliable analysis to be made.

Thus, the approach adopted in this study is a *naturalistic* one, based on a substantial corpus of spontaneous speech data. However, the use of a naturalistic corpus raises the obvious question of what aspects of the information provided by the corpus we focus on. Naturalistic recordings of child speech typically will yield data both about *comprehension* (i.e. the range of structures which a child appears to comprehend), and about *production* (i.e. the range of structures which the child is capable of producing). Thus, the question arises as to whether we should use *comprehension* or *production* data in assessing the child's syntactic competence. In principle, both types of data can serve as useful potential sources of information about child competence. However, it is important to note the point made by Fletcher (1985: 208) that neither the child's ability to comprehend a particular utterance, nor his ability to produce it, necessarily provides us with any evidence of specific syntactic knowledge on the child's part. We can illustrate the point that comprehension need not entail syntactic knowledge in terms of the following fictitious dialogue between mother and child:

(9)   ADULT: Who did Fido bite?
        CHILD: Daddy

From the fact that the child replies correctly to his mother's question, we might reasonably infer that he has understood the question (or at any rate, understood enough of it to be able to answer it appropriately). But what kind of (tacit) knowledge is this understanding based on? Now, it might seem reasonable to suppose that in order to answer the question correctly, the child will require three distinct types of knowledge: (i) *semantic* (he needs to know the meaning of the words); (ii) *pragmatic* (he needs to be able to relate the particular sentence to a particular situation); and (iii) *grammatical* (he needs to be able to *parse* the sentence, and identify the grammatical function of each of its constituents e.g. to identify which is the subject, which the object, etc.). Indeed, we might suppose that quite detailed grammatical knowledge is required in order for the child to be able to understand the sentence: e.g. the child must be able to work out that *who* is an interrogative pronoun which functions as the direct object of *bite*, *did* is a past tense auxiliary, *Fido* is a subject nominal, and *bite* is a transitive verb; and that in wh-questions, auxiliaries are inverted with their subject, and interrogative phrases are positioned in front of the auxiliary...and so on. Thus, if we follow this line of reasoning, then the child's one-word reply to the question asked by his mother in (9) conceals an immense amount of 'covert' syntactic knowledge.

But now consider an alternative analysis, on which the child's understanding of the sentence reflects only semantic and pragmatic competence, and does not presuppose syntactic competence. On this second analysis, the child needs no syntactic knowledge to be able to answer a question such as that in (9). Let us suppose that the child has minimal semantic knowledge, and knows the meaning of the words *who*, *Fido*, and *bite*, but does not know the meaning of *did*. More particularly, let's suppose that he knows that *who* asks for the identity of some person, that *Fido* refers to the family pet, and that *bite* is a particularly painful two-place predicate involving X sinking his teeth into Y. Let's also suppose minimal pragmatic knowledge on the part of the child: i.e. let's assume that he has observed that dogs sometimes bite humans, but that humans never bite dogs; and let's also assume that the child's stored memory of experiences includes the rather vivid memory of Fido biting daddy earlier on in the morning, when daddy accidentally (?) trod on his tail. Given this minimal semantic and pragmatic knowledge (and no syntactic knowledge), it is clearly a simple enough task for the child to infer that *who* is the logical subject and *Fido* the logical object of *bite*. Even if the child does not understand the meaning of *did*, the uniqueness of the event (assuming that Fido only bit daddy on one occasion) means that any specification of time reference is communicatively redundant. Once the child has been able to reconstruct the propositional content of his mother's utterance on the basis of the semantic and pragmatic evidence available to him, it is clearly a simple enough matter for him to reply correctly.

The moral of this canine anecdote is that the child's apparent comprehension of a question such as 'Who did Fido bite?' does not necessarily tell us anything about his syntactic competence, since the child *could* in principle respond correctly to such a question without being able to assign a full syntactic description to it. Thus, the mere fact that a child seems to 'understand' a sentence (as judged by his ability to produce an appropriate response to it) cannot by itself be taken as providing any evidence of syntactic knowledge. It is not, of course, that comprehension data cannot in principle be used as a source of evidence for grammatical knowledge: rather, if we are to use comprehension data in this way, we need to be able to factor out those aspects of 'understanding' which are attributable to semantic and pragmatic competence, and those aspects which are due to the child's syntactic ability to parse a given type of structure correctly. Of course, this can be done (albeit with difficulty) in carefully controlled experimental situations: however, it is virtually impossible to determine the relative roles played by these two types of knowledge in naturalistic speech samples. For this reason, naturalistic studies of syntactic competence tend not to place great weight on comprehension data: the general consensus is that 'Comprehension tasks seem to tap syntactic competence much less directly than production tasks' (Flynn and Lust 1980: 41, n.5).

However (as noted by Fletcher 1985), similar problems can beset the use of *production* data as a potential source of evidence of grammatical competence. The very fact that a child *produces* a particular utterance clearly cannot be taken as indicating grammatical knowledge. For example, many children have a repertoire of what Miller et al. (1981: 25) call 'routines' (e.g. nursery rhymes, song fragments, commercial jingles, etc.): however, it seems clear that 'memorised routines in particular may not be characteristic of the child's spontaneous constructions' (ibid.). For example, the fact that a child is able to invert the italicized sequence in ritually reciting 'Baa-baa black sheep, *have you* any wool...?' could hardly be taken as conclusive evidence that the child has mastered the syntax of subject–auxiliary inversion.

For much the same reason, it is often argued that *formulaic* or *semiformulaic* utterances cannot be taken as a reliable source of evidence of syntactic competence, on the grounds that they are not fully productive structures, and are thus not purely categorial in nature. A *formulaic* utterance is one in which a given sequence of words (or morphemes) occurs only in a specific combination in the child's speech, and where no part of the utterance can be replaced productively by other items. An example of such a formulaic utterance is provided by Greenfield et al. (1985: 242): in relation to their subject Kate at age 22–23 months, they note that 'In response to either the doorbell or the phone ringing, she would call out [*agedit*] (gloss: I'll get it) as she ran to answer it. None of these four potentially separable adult morphemes (*I will get it*) had yet occurred individually.' Thus, *agedit* was a purely formulaic utterance in Kate's speech: this in turn means that we could not in principle use such an utterance as evidence that Kate had mastered the syntax of nominative pronouns like *I*, or of modal auxiliaries such as *will*.

Analogous problems are posed by *semiformulaic* utterances. Examples of such utterances are provided by Klima and Bellugi (1966: 201): they note that the earliest types of wh-questions produced by the children they studied comprised either formulaic utterances such as *Whatsthat?*, or semiformulaic utterances of the form (10) below:

(10)   (a)   What NP doing?
        (b)   Where NP go?

The structures in (10) contain three constituents, but in each case the first and last constituents are invariable (in the sense that they contain a specific lexical item not replaceable by other similar items), and only the middle constituent is variable (in the sense that a variety of different Noun Phrases can occur in the relevant position, so that the children produced utterances such as: 'Where *milk* go?', 'Where *horse* go?', etc.). Thus, the structures in (10) are not purely categorial in nature, but rather are partly lexical (in the sense that only specific lexical items can occur in two of the three positions), and partly categorial (in the sense that any appropriate NP can occur in the middle position). Clearly we must be wary of using formulaic or semiformulaic utterances as sources of evidence about the nature of the structural (i.e. categorial) knowledge which the child may have: for example, it would not be legitimate to infer from semiformulaic utterances of the schematic form (10)(a) (i.e. utterances such as 'What cowboy doing?', etc.) that the children 'know' that *what* is a wh-pronoun, and have developed a syntactic rule positioning wh-constituents clause-initially.

A particular problem arises over child speech production which is (potentially) wholly or partly *imitative* in nature (i.e. utterances where a child appears to be repeating part or all of something previously said by someone else in the child's presence). At first sight, it might seem as if imitative speech should be discounted entirely as a source of evidence about child competence, since imitative speech might be thought to be the product of mimicry abilities (and thus represent parrot-like repetition of a phonological string to which the child may assign no grammatical description). Thus, when a child produces a perfect imitation of an adult structure, we cannot be sure whether this is a true reflection of the child's syntactic competence, or simply a 'blind imitation' which reflects little more than the child's mimicry abilities. Much more significant, therefore, are *imperfect imitations* of adult speech produced by young children, since these can more plausibly be taken to be genuine exemplars of the child's own speech – i.e. cases where, in attempting to repeat an adult utterance, children produce their own counterpart of the adult utterance. For example, Brown and Fraser (1963: 73) noted (*inter alia*) that children who have not yet acquired Determiners like *the* will systematically omit determiners in imitations of adult model sentences: thus, when asked to imitate 'Read *the* book', both Eve at 25 months and Adam at 28 months said simply 'Read book', omitting the italicized determiner (and so suggesting that children productively imitate only those items whose grammar they have acquired). In much the same vein, McNeill (1966: 69) notes that a child asked (eight separate times) to repeat the model sentence *Nobody likes me* on each occasion produced the form *Nobody don't like me*. Similarly, Braine (1971) notes that a child who was asked 'Can you say *the other spoon?*' replied '*Other one spoon*'. And Slobin (1979: 96) notes that when asked to repeat the question 'Where can I put them?' Adam replied with 'Where I can put them?'. Such examples suggest that when a child produces imperfect imitations of adult speech, he is not simply blindly repeating unprocessed sound-sequences, but rather is 'processing heard speech according to his own inner structures' (Slobin 1979.). But if imitative speech is indeed processed through the child's grammar, it can clearly provide us with a valuable source of evidence about the nature of the child's competence (at least in the case of *imperfect imitations*). However, *perfect imitations* provide a more problematic source of evidence: thus, since we cannot in principle exclude the possibility that perfect imitations may indeed simply be 'blind repetitions', clearly common sense dictates that we treat the evidence provided by such utterances with caution. Where imitative speech shows precisely the same characteristics as spontaneous speech, it seems safe to make use of it; but where imitative speech results in utterance types which are totally unrepresentative of the child's sponta-neous speech production, it is obviously wise not to rely on such data.

Overall, in analysing a child's speech production, we clearly need to discount 'stereotype sentences', 'set expressions', and 'blind imitations' (i.e. utterances in which a child repeats an adult model sentence verbatim, but shows no evidence of being able to produce a similar type of sentence in his spontaneous speech production). It seems reasonable to suppose that we can only take a child's production of a particular structure to reflect syntactic knowledge when the structure is used *productively* – that is when the child uses the same structure with a variety of different lexical items in each position in that structure. Thus (to return to our earlier canine anecdote), if a child simply blindly repeats 'Who did Fido bite?' after his mother (but shows no evidence of being able to produce related wh-questions in his spontaneous speech), we would clearly not consider this to be proof of syntactic competence. But by contrast, if a child is able to produce a whole range of similar questions (so that alongside 'Who did Fido bite?', he also produces interrogatives such as 'What can daddy do?', 'Where will mummy go?', 'How can I mend it?' etc., thereby demonstrating that the utterance is not a rote-learned 'set expression', or a 'blind imitation' of a parental model sentence), then it seems reasonable to infer that he must indeed have a high level of syntactic knowledge in order to be able to produce that kind of structure. For example, if the child systematically preposes auxiliaries like *did* but not nonauxiliary verbs like *bite* in direct questions, it is reasonable to infer that he tacitly knows that *did* is an auxiliary, but that *bite* is a nonauxiliary verb.

Because of the nature of naturalistic data samples, data from the child's speech *production* generally give a more reliable indication of the existence of some level of syntactic competence than do data from speech comprehension. It is relatively easy (with a large enough corpus) to demonstrate from speech production data that a child is using a particular construction *productively*; by contrast, it is remarkably difficult to establish from naturalistic data which aspects of a child's comprehension might be due to semantic/pragmatic knowledge, and which to purely grammatical knowledge. For this reason, most (though not all) of the evidence we rely on here in attempting to model the grammatical competence of young children will be drawn from child speech *production* data.

To summarize: in (3) and (4) above, we raised a number of questions concerning the nature of early child grammars of English: we then went on to discuss the kinds of evidence which might offer us some insight into the earliest stages of the syntactic competence of very young children, suggesting that the most fertile source of evidence would be data from young children's *spontaneous speech production*, and we gave details of the corpus of naturalistic child speech samples used as the empirical basis of the present study. Having collected our corpus, the next process is to analyse the relevant data, and attempt to use it to answer the questions posed in (3) and (4) above, that is, to determine the point at which children can be said to have developed grammars, and to identify the characteristics of early child grammars.

Given the postulate made by Chomsky in *Aspects of the Theory of Syntax* (1965: 55) that grammatical operations are 'necessarily *structure-dependent* in that they manipulate substrings only in terms of their assignment to categories', it follows that a necessary prerequisite for the development of a grammar is the development of a system of grammatical *categories*. Thus, we might seek to approach the question of the point at which children develop grammars in terms of the question: 'At what point do we have evidence that children have developed a formally differentiated set of grammatical categories?' This is a question which we turn to answer in the next chapter.

2

Categorization in Early Child English

At the end of the previous chapter, we suggested that one of the earliest clues to development of grammars in early child speech would be the development of grammatical categories. If this is so, then the obvious question to ask is at what point we have empirical evidence that children have begun to develop such a system of grammatical categories. The traditional view (dating back to works such as Stern 1928) is that the child's early grammatical development can be divided up into the following four main stages:

(1) (i)   0–12 months: prelinguistic stage
     (ii) 12–18 months: single-word stage
     (iii) 18–24 months: early multi-word stage
     (iv) 24–30 months: later multi-word stage

The *prelinguistic* stage is the period before the development of the child's first words; the *single-word* stage is the period during which children's utterances comprise a single word spoken in isolation; the *early multi-word* stage is the point at which children begin to string two, three or four words together to form productive syntactic structures; the *later multi-word* stage is the point at which structures of five, six, or seven words in length start to become productive.

We can illustrate the progression between these four different stages in terms of the following (hypothetical) examples of what a child called Jane might say at each of the relevant stages while reaching out for an apple in front of her:

(2) (a) *Oogh* [prelinguistic stage]
     (b) *Apple* [single-word stage]

(c) *Jane want apple* [early multi-word stage]
(d) *I want to have an apple* [later multi-word stage]

At the prelinguistic stage, all Jane produces is a prelinguistic vocalization (i.e. a grunt!); at the single-word stage, she simply names the object requested; at the early multi-word stage, she is able to form a simple proposition of the form *subject + verb + object*; at the later multi-word stage, she has a more elaborate sentence structure showing evidence of the acquisition of so-called *function words* – e.g. the pronoun *I*, the infinitival particle *to*, and the determiner *a*.

Given our suggestion that the development of a system of grammatical categories provides the most obvious indication that children have developed initial grammars of the language they are acquiring, the natural question to ask is at which of the four stages outlined in (1) above *categorization* takes place. I take it as self-evident that it is unlikely to take place at the *prelinguistic* stage. Moreover – as we shall see – there is abundant evidence that child speech during the *one-word* stage is inherently *acategorial* (i.e. non-categorial) in nature, and that only at the *early multi-word* stage do children enter a *categorial* phase of development.

The *prelinguistic* stage is characterized by the appearance of *babbling* (see Ingram 1989: 83–138 for an overview of research into the child's development during this stage). Towards the end of the babbling period, children begin to develop a language-specific phonology, identifying and producing segments of the target language, and combining them into (sequences of) 'nonsense' syllables such as /ma/, /wa/, /ba/, etc.: at this stage, these syllables are just 'sound patterns' (i.e. sequences with relatively consistent phonological and phonotactic properties, but with no semantic or grammatical properties) and thus don't in any sense represent 'words'. The next major stage (the *single-word stage*) occurs when (at around one year of age) the child begins to segment utterances into recurrent sequences, and to associate particular sound-sequences with particular concepts, so developing his first lexical items (i.e. first words) – for example when the child comes to realize that the sequence /kat/ denotes a friendly furry feline. At this point, the child has begun to develop elementary words: that is, simple form–meaning complexes. Of course, young children frequently mis-segment utterances into words, so resulting in (what from an adult perspective are) *mislexicalizations*. What is of more interest from our point of view, however, is that there is no reason to suppose that the child's words at this single-word stage (viz. between one and one-and-a-half years of age) have any grammatical properties. If this is so, then it means that the earliest words produced by young children have relatively stable phonological and semantic properties, but no categorial properties. For example, the word 'cat' for a typical child at the one-word stage might have a relatively constant phonological form /kat/ (perhaps variously realized as [kat], [kak], [ka], etc.) and a relatively constant meaning (so that it is used to denote purring pussies): but if the child's speech is *acategorial*, then the child would have no tacit awareness of the categorial properties of the word (viz. that it is a common count noun).

A simple analogy with second language acquisition might make it clearer just what it means to suggest that the child's speech at the single-word stage is *acategorial* in nature. An English tourist who (ad)ventures on a brief you-can-do-it-in-a-week package tour of Italy will acquire during his week's stay a suntan, a tummy bug (from all that oily food) and a rudimentary repertoire of Italian words. He may, for example, learn that you're supposed to say 'Permesso' when pushing past someone in a crowded space; that you say 'Scusi' to apologize for pinching the wrong bottom; that you say 'Grazie' to express gratitude, and 'Prego' to acknowledge such an expression of gratitude; that you say 'Arrivederci' to bid farewell to someone...and so on. At this *single-word* stage, the tourist's rudimentary vocabulary is entirely *acategorial*: all he 'knows' is that these are words used in specific situations for specific communicative functions; but he has no (tacit) 'awareness' of the grammatical status of such words. So, for example, he will not realize that 'Permesso' is a passive participle form of the irregular third conjugation verb *permettere*, and thus corresponds to the English passive participle 'permitted'; that 'Scusi' is a third person singular subjunctive form of the first conjugation verb *scusare* (used as an addressee-imperative in formal speech styles), and thus corresponds to the English imperative 'Excuse!'; that 'Grazie' is the plural form of a first declension feminine noun *grazia*, and thus corresponds to English 'Thanks'; that 'Prego' is a first person present tense indicative form of the first conjugation verb *pregare*, and thus corresponds to the English 'I beg'; or that 'Arrivederci' is a compound of the preposition *a* 'to', a contracted assimilated form *r* of the definite article *(i)l* 'the', a verbal prefix *ri* 'again', a contracted infinitive form of the second conjugation verb *veder(e)* 'to see', and a first person plural direct object clitic pronoun *ci* 'us' (so that the whole expression could be glossed on a morpheme-by-morpheme basis as 'to + the +re + see + us'). Our casual tourist will be blissfully unaware of all these grammatical complexities: he has simply learned these forms as unanalysed wholes, and uses them without any knowledge of their grammatical status. Thus, whereas 'arrivederci' is arguably a five-morpheme sequence for an Italian native speaker, for the tourist it is a 'set phrase', and hence a single-morpheme *amalgam* (in the sense of MacWhinney 1978). The tourist's words are nothing more than simple form–meaning (i.e. phonological–semantic) associations, lacking categorial status. Indeed, we might argue that his one-word utterances at this stage have phonological and pragmatic properties (the tourist knows in what situation you use the word, and for what communicative purpose), but neither syntactic *nor even semantic* properties (i.e. the tourist doesn't really know what the words 'mean', he just knows how to use them in a given situation).

It seems reasonable to suppose that (in some ways) the young child is just like our linguistically naive tourist: that is, he can communicate with words, but although these words have constant phonological, pragmatic, and (perhaps) semantic properties, they lack grammatical properties, and hence are purely *acategorial* in nature. There seems to be general agreement in the recent child language literature that this is so. Thus, Maratsos (1982: 248) remarks that there is 'no good reason to credit children with having captured formal categories such as "noun" and "verb" in their early speech'. This view is supported by Greenfield et al. (1985: 234), who remark that 'A consensus is growing among researchers that the initial achievements in language acquisition, especially prelingually and during the one-word period, are primarily pragmatic and semantic': similarly, Atkinson (1985: 294) comments: 'The arguments are convincing that no case can be made for the one-word child having access to a system of syntactic representation'; and in the same vein, Berman (1988: 51) remarks that 'Language production at the one-word phase and during the period of initial word-combinations is largely "agrammatical".'

However, the general assumption that early child speech is acategorial obviously raises the question: 'At what point do we have empirical evidence that *categorization* has taken place in child speech, and that children have developed a system of grammatical categories?' This question in turn raises an even more fundamental question of principle, relating to the kinds of empirical evidence we can bring to bear in order to decide whether a child's speech at a given age is categorial or acategorial. In trying to answer this question of principle, it may be useful to bear in mind the kind of grammatical criteria which linguists employ in order to decide what system of categories is employed in the grammar of an adult language. These are of two main kinds: (i) morphological, and (ii) syntactic. We'll look at each of these types of criteria in turn, and see if we can use them to determine the categorial status of early child speech (see Valian 1986 and Radford 1988a for a more detailed discussion of categorization criteria).

The relevant morphological evidence for assigning words to categories concerns the fact that certain types of *inflection* (i.e. grammatical ending) attach only to words belonging to a specific category: for example, plural +*s* attaches only to nouns in English, and gerund +*ing* only to verbs. Of course, the suggestion that inflectional properties provide an essential source of evidence about categorial status is in no sense a novel one: cf. the remark by Hyams (1989: 224) that 'Children are sensitive to inflectional morphology and...this information is used by the child in determining category membership'. Using morphological evidence, we can say that we have clear evidence that a given child has acquired a given category once the child starts to acquire one or more of the inflections which attach to items belonging to that category – provided always that he is using the relevant inflections *productively* (i.e. attaching them to a wide range of stems, and not just using them in rote-learned 'set expressions'), *selectively* (e.g. attaching noun inflections only to noun stems and never to any other kind of stem), *contrastively* (e.g. attaching a plural inflection only to plural forms and not to singular forms), and *appropriately* (i.e. using an inflection only in contexts where it is required). In saying that evidence for categorization comes from the *acquisition* of inflectional morphemes, I am tacitly presupposing a distinction between *acquisition* and *mastery* this distinction needs to be elaborated upon. I shall assume that a sufficient condition for the *acquisition* of a particular inflection is that the inflection should be productively used in such a way that it is *only* attached to an appropriate category of stems (so that a noun inflection such as plural +*s* is only attached to noun stems); by contrast, a more demanding condition for *mastery* of a particular inflection is that the inflection should be productively used in such a way that it is *always and only* attached to an appropriate class of stems in an appropriate context. What this means in practical terms is that if a child sometimes attaches the plural +*s* inflection to a given noun in a plural context (e.g. says 'two doggies') and sometimes does not (e.g. also says 'two doggy'), but never attaches plural +*s* to any kind of word other than a noun (hence never to an adjective, so that we don't have **'two *cuddlies* doggies' – the asterisk here being used to denote a non-occurring form), then this in itself is sufficient to demonstrate *acquisition* of the plural +*s* inflection, though not *mastery* of it. By contrast, in order to demonstrate mastery of the plural +*s* inflection, we need to show that the child *always* uses the plural form *doggies* in a plural context, and hence always says *two doggies* and never *two doggy. Of course, since 'always' is a criterion which makes no allowance for *execution* errors (e.g. sporadic errors in phonological execution attributable to children's problems in articulating word-final consonants, or consonant clusters), it might seem reasonable to weaken the 'always' criterion for mastery to an 'almost always' criterion: thus we might posit that a sufficient condition for a child to demonstrate mastery of an inflection is to attach it only to appropriate stems, and to use it in at least 90% of the contexts where it would be obligatory in adult speech (so that mastery of plural +*s* would require the child to produce structures such as *two doggies* at least 90% of the time, and structures like *two doggy* no more than 10% of the time): and indeed, a 90% threshold has widely been adopted in the acquisition literature (following Brown 1973); in our terms, this 90% threshold would serve as a measure of (a specific level of) *mastery*, not as a measure of (the fact of) *acquisition*.

The obvious question to ask at this point is why we should assume that acquisition of inflections can provide us with evidence of categorization, rather than imposing the stronger requirement that only mastery of inflections is sufficient to justify postulating that the child has developed a set of grammatical categories. One answer is that the occurrence of overgeneralized forms like *two mans* and *two peoples* in early child speech is generally taken as very strong evidence that children 'know' that +*s* is a noun inflection (and, by extension, that they 'know' that *man* and *people* are nouns). However, although forms like *mans* and *peoples* demonstrate acquisition of the plural +*s* morpheme, they clearly do not demonstrate mastery of it (for the obvious reason that the resulting forms are ungrammatical in adult English). For reasons such as these, we shall assume that acquisition (rather than mastery) of inflectional morphemes is sufficient to provide us with evidence of categorization.

In addition to *morphological* evidence from the acquisition of inflections, we can also make use of *syntactic* evidence in attempting to determine the categorial status of words in adult English. The vast majority of the relevant syntactic evidence is *distributional* in nature, and relates to the ways in which words can be combined together to form phrases and sentences. For example, we conclude that *boy* is a noun because it can be combined with a preceding determiner (as in 'the boy'), but that *follow* is not a noun, because it cannot combine in the same way (*'the follow'); conversely, we can conclude that *follow* is a verb since it can serve as the complement of the infinitive particle *to* ('to follow'), whereas *boy* cannot (*'to boy'). Thus, in order to establish whether a given group of words forms a category in child speech, we might seek to determine whether those words share the same *distribution* (i.e. occur in the same range of phrase or clause positions). If we could demonstrate that children have divided words into a small number of different distributional classes in this way, then this would provide us with *direct* syntactic evidence that the children concerned have begun to develop a system of grammatical categories.

However, while direct distributional evidence provides us with a useful technique for investigating the system of categories used by children who have already reached the 'multi-word speech' stage, at which they are systematically combining words into productive structures (typically from around the age of one-and-a-half years on), such a technique cannot in principle be applied to children at the one-word stage (roughly, between one and one-and-a-half years of age), because they are not yet combining words together to form productive syntactic structures. Of course, the very absence of systematic word combinations at the one-word stage might in itself lead us to follow Atkinson (1985: 298) in maintaining that this provides conclusive evidence that the child has not yet developed a system of grammatical categories: cf. his remark (ibid.) that 'As there is no word-combination at the one-word stage, there is no syntax.' However, this may be a somewhat premature conclusion. After all, it might be that what the child is doing at the one-word stage is observing and analysing adult speech, and assigning the words in his vocabulary to grammatical categories on the basis of their perceived morphosyntactic properties in adult speech. It might also be that psychological/ physiological immaturity limits the child to producing utterances only one word in length at this stage, so that his (tacit) categorial knowledge isn't reflected in the production of word combinations. Bearing in mind this alternative possibility, we clearly need to explore techniques which will provide us with *indirect* syntactic evidence of whether (or not) children at the one-word stage have begun to develop a system of grammatical categories. But what kind of techniques can we use?

One type of indirect distributional evidence which we could in principle use is the *completion* technique, used successfully by a number of psycholinguists to study the child's grammatical development (the best known example of this being Berko's (1958) *wug* test, in which children were asked to complete sentence sequences such as: 'Here is a *wug*. Now there are two of them. There are two . . .'). This technique involves examining the child's ability to complete a phrase or sentence begun by someone else with an appropriate word. Sequences of this type are by no means uncommon in children's conversations with adults, where an adult will start a phrase or sentence and wait for the child to complete it. Typical examples of completion sequences taken from a single 45-minute recording of Jem at age 21 months in conversation with his mother are given in (3) below (in each case the initial incomplete phrase or sentence is produced by his mother, and Jem's response is italicized):

(3)   (a)   What's that? A big green... *Pencil*
      (b)   Where do we go in Beaumaris? We go to the... *Slides*
      (c)   Mummy's reading a... *Book*
      (d)   And there's a little... *Pussycat*
      (e)   He's smelling the... *Flower*
      (f)   He's got a lovely red... *Balloon*
      (g)   Where did it pop? On your... *Tummy*

Since the only categorially appropriate way of completing the adult's phrase or sentence with a single word in each of the examples in (3) is to use a noun, we might suppose that since Jem can systematically and consistently correctly complete such sequences with a categorially appropriate word (= a noun), he must have tacit categorial knowledge (with the caveats noted in the next paragraph) – i.e. he must 'know' that the italicized words are nouns. Thus, in principle, there is no reason why we should not use the completion technique to determine whether the child at the one-word stage has 'covert' categorial knowledge or not.

However, it is important to acknowledge that there are a number of potential pitfalls in applying the completion technique to the analysis of early child speech. For example, we clearly have to exclude sentence-completions which involve *routines* such as the following (from Bloom 1970: 228):

(4)   ADULT: Baa-baa black sheep, have you any...
      CHILD: Wool (*Allison 20)

We also have to be wary of using the technique in contexts where there are strong pragmatic clues to the nature of the missing word – as in the following (hypothetical) scenario:

(5)   ADULT: *(pointing to picture of Noddy's car in book)*
               Noddy drives a big red...
      CHILD: Car

That is, we cannot ignore the possibility that the child may simply be responding to the picture of the car, or to the mother's ostensive gesture (perhaps interpreting her pointing gesture as a request to name the object being pointed to), rather than responding to the syntactic form of the mother's utterance.

There may also be a second type of indirect syntactic evidence which we can use in order to determine the categorial status of children's earliest speech (at the one-word stage). The relevant technique involves looking at the answers which children give to wh-questions (i.e. to questions introduced by a wh-word such as *who/what/where* etc.). However, there is an important qualification to be made here – namely that the relevant technique relates to the *phrasal* rather than *clausal* responses which children give to wh-questions. We can illustrate the difference between the two types of response in terms of the dialogue in (6) below: speaker B can reply to speaker A's question either by using a full clause (= a *clausal* response), or by simply using a phrase (= a *phrasal* response):

(6)   SPEAKER A: What did you buy?
       SPEAKER B: I bought a new dress (*clausal* response)
                  A new dress (*phrasal* response)

The core assumption underlying the use of the wh-question-answering technique is that specific wh-words require a phrasal response which is both *semantically* and *categorially* appropriate to the type of question asked. For example, from a semantic viewpoint, a *who*-question requires as its reply an expression which specifies the identity of one or more human beings; while from a categorial point of view, a *who*-question requires a phrasal response which has the categorial status of a *nominal* constituent. We can illustrate these constraints on what is an appropriate reply to a *who*-question in terms of the following question–answer paradigm:

(7)   SPEAKER A: Who were the secret police looking for?
       SPEAKER B: Westerners/Outsiders (human nominal)
                  Him (human nominal proform)
                  !Trains (inanimate nominal)
                  !This (inanimate nominal proform)
                  *Outside (prepositional)
                  *Western (adjectival)

(We use ! to indicate a response which is semantically inappropriate, and * to indicate a response which is categorially inappropriate.) Thus, a phrasal response to a *who*-question is an appropriate answer to the question only if the response has the syntactic status of a nominal constituent, and has the semantic property that it denotes a human being.

Rather more complex are *where*-questions. From a semantic point of view, the response required is an expression which specifies the location of some entity. However, the required categorial status of the response varies according to the precise form of the *where*-question. In its *prepositional* use (i.e. when used as the object of a preposition), *where* allows either a nominal or a prepositional response: e.g.

(8)   SPEAKER A: Where have you just come from?
       SPEAKER B: The station (locative nominal)
                   There (locative nominal proform)
                   From the station (prepositional locative)
                   Mary (nonlocative nominal)
                   Very distant (locative adjectival)

But in its *prepositionless* use (i.e. when not used as the object of a preposition), *where* requires a prepositional response: e.g.

(9)   SPEAKER A: Where is the key?
       SPEAKER B: Under the mat (prepositional locative)
                   There (prepositional locative proform)
                   !For Mary (nonlocative prepositional)
                   *The mat (locative nominal)

Examples such as these suggest that both semantic *and categorial* knowledge are required in order to be able to provide appropriate phrasal responses to wh-questions.

More complex still are *what*-questions. In its most frequent use, *what* requires a response which has the semantic property that it specifies the identity of some entity (generally, though not necessarily, a non-human one), and the categorial property of being a nominal: e.g.

(10)   SPEAKER A: What can you see through the binoculars?
       SPEAKER B: Mountains (inanimate nominal)
                   Nothing (inanimate nominal proform)
                   Girls in bikinis (human nominal)
                   *On the mountain (prepositional)
                   *Very pretty (adjectival)

But questions of the form 'What...do?' are rather more complex, in that they also allow a verbal expression as an appropriate answer – provided that the expression is semantically appropriate (e.g. it denotes an action), and morphologically appropriate (in that the morphology of the verb matches that of *do*): cf.

(11)   SPEAKER A: What on earth are you *doing*?
       SPEAKER B: *Hiding/*Hide/*Hidden* (gerundive verb)

(12)   SPEAKER A: What shall I *do?*
       SPEAKER B: *Hide/*Hiding/*Hidden* (=infinitival verb)

(13)   SPEAKER A: What has he done?
       SPEAKER B: *Hidden/*Hide/*Hiding* (= perfective verb)

Thus, we see that considerable *grammatical* competence is required in order to answer a *what*-question.

Overall, then, we see that the ability to give appropriate phrasal replies to wh-questions requires both categorial and semantic knowledge. Accordingly, we might seek to use children's phrasal responses to wh-questions to test whether they are 'aware' of the requirement for phrasal replies to wh-questions to be categorially appropriate, and (more generally still) whether they have a tacit awareness that different words belong to different categories, even as early as the one-word stage. This is not, of course, in any sense a 'novel' technique; on the contrary, it is one frequently used in assessing children's categorial competence: see, for example, the remark by Bowerman (1973: 11) that 'Information about the child's knowledge of constituent structure is contained in his responses to parental wh-questions.' Naturally, obvious common-sense precautions have to be taken in using the technique – ignoring question–answer routines, ignoring answers which may be prompted by pragmatic cues (e.g. interpreting a pointing gesture as a request to name the object pointed at), and so on.

All in all, we see that there are (at least) four different types of question which we might ask in order to determine the categorial status of early child speech:

(14)   (i)   Is the child productively attaching specific inflections to appropriate classes of words?
       (ii)   Is the child combining words together in ways which suggest that different words belong to different distributional classes?
       (iii) Does the child provide categorially appropriate responses to completion sequences?
       (iv)   Does the child provide categorially appropriate phrasal responses to wh-questions?

Having isolated four criteria which we can use to determine the categorial status of early child speech, the next step is to see what results our four criteria yield when we apply them to typical samples of early child speech. At what stage do we have evidence that *categorization* has indeed taken place in child speech? For the sake of concreteness, we'll take as our data sample the four transcripts of the spontaneous speech of Allison Bloom at ages 16, 19, 20 and 22 months contained in Lois Bloom's (1973) book *One Word at a Time*: these transcripts have the obvious advantage of having been published in a 'classic' work on early child speech, and of being familiar to a wide audience – hence readily accessible.

In all four transcripts, Allison's speech output largely comprises words which (if analysed in adult terms) would seem to belong to the four major categories of noun, verb, preposition, and adjective: thus, we find (what in adult terms would be) nouns such as *baby, mommy, man, cookie, pig, cow, horse, car, chair, juice*, etc., together with (what in adult terms would be) Verbs such as *tumble, cover, help, turn, scrub, climb*, etc., and (what in adult terms would be) prepositions like *down, up, off, on*, and *over*, plus (what in adult terms would be) adjectives such as *big, small, dirty*, and *clean*. However, while the categorial status of such words as nouns, verbs etc. is relatively clear-cut in adult speech, it cannot be assumed that such items have any specific categorial status in Allison's speech at any or all of the relevant stages: rather, this is a matter which needs to be established empirically, by using criteria such as those listed in (14) above. We shall argue that these criteria lead us to the conclusion that Allison's transcripts at 16 and 19 months show no sign of the onset of categorization, and that only in the two later transcripts (at 20 and 22 months) do we have clear evidence that Allison has developed a formally differentiated set of grammatical categories.

Let's consider first of all the properties of Allison's transcripts at 16 and 19 months which lead us to conclude that her speech at this point is acategorial in nature. From a *morphological* point of view, a crucial argument in support of this conclusion comes from the fact that there is simply no trace of productive use of inflections either at 16 or at 19 months: for example, there are no occurrences of the noun plural $+s$ inflection, or of the verbal $+ing$ inflection. Indeed, the only potentially inflected form is *gone*. Now, while *gone* in adult speech would be the perfective participle form of the verb *go*, it cannot be analysed as an inflected form of *go* in Allison's speech at this stage, for the simple reason that she is not using *go* at all (so that *gone* is probably best analysed as an uninflected stem form). Thus, there is no evidence of the acquisition of any inflections, and in consequence no morphological evidence that Allison's speech is *categorial* at this stage.

But what of the relevant syntactic (i.e. distributional) evidence? This yields very much the same results as the morphological criterion. At 16 months, we find that Allison is clearly at the one-word stage and appears to have no productive word combinations. Much the same is also true at 19 months, where once again we find largely single-word utterances, and only a couple of potential phrases ('over there' and 'big baby'). Thus, since there is no evidence of systematic word combinations at 16 or 19 months, there is thus no direct distributional evidence that categorization has yet taken place. So, we have no *direct* morphological or syntactic evidence that categorization has taken place by 16 or 19 months. But what of *indirect* evidence? Unfortunately, the completion technique proves of little practical use, given that we find only one such sequence (from the transcript at 16 months), viz.

(15)   ADULT: This is for...(pouring juice into another cup)
       CHILD: *Mama*

Although Allison responds with what would appear to be a categorially appropriate word (i.e. a potential noun), it is clear that one 'correct answer' cannot in principle be taken as indicative of underlying categorial competence (i.e. of the ability to *consistently* supply categorially appropriate responses in sentence completion tasks); moreover, we have to bear in mind that (15) may be a *routine* mother–child exchange.

A more promising source of indirect syntactic evidence may come from Allison's responses to wh-questions, since each transcript contains a couple of dozen such question–answer interactions between mother and daughter. Now, it is certainly true that Allison produces a number of 'correct answers' to simple wh-questions, where rich contextual clues enable her to infer what is an appropriate answer. However, it is equally clear that where 'contextual clues' are insufficiently rich, she frequently produces categorially inappropriate answers, as the responses in (16) below indicate; in these examples, the question is asked by her mother, and Allison's reply is italicized (the number in parentheses indicates her age in months):

(16)   (a)   What do you hear? (as telephone rings) – *There* (16)
       (b)   What do you want? – *Away* (16)
       (c)   What's that? – *There* (19)
       (d)   What is it? – *Small* (19)
       (e)   What's this? – *Small* (19)
       (f)   What should I do? – *Baby* (16)
       (g)   What are you doing? – *Truck* (19)
       (h)   Who rides the car? – *Gone* (16)
       (i)   Who says bow wow? – *Home* (19)
       (j)   Who's Bob? – *Home* (19)

(k)   Where's the girl? – *Girl* (16)
(l)   Where's Dada? – *Dada* (16)
(m)   Where will the truck go? – *Brrmmm* (19)
(n)   Where's the pig? – *Big* (19)

There seems little point in commenting on the nature of the categorial errors Allison makes in her answers. Suffice it to say that the data in (16) provide no evidence that Allison is 'aware' that *what/who* questions are appropriately replied to by a (pro)nominal expression of some kind, *what...do* questions by a verbal constituent, and (prepositionless) *where* questions by a prepositional constituent. Thus, given that Allison appears not to have mastered the categorial constraints on phrasal responses to wh-questions, the obvious conclusion is that we have no evidence that categorization is under way in her speech.

Overall, then, there seems little evidence that Allison has developed a formally differentiated set of word categories at either 16 or 19 months. However, the picture presented by the transcripts of Allison's speech at ages 20 and 22 months is a very different one. We find an expansion in the range of (apparent) nouns, verbs, prepositions, and adjectives being used: but much more significantly, we begin to find the emergence of inflected forms. Thus, in the transcript of Allison's speech at 20 months, we see the emergence of the +*ing* verb inflection, so that the form *wiping* occurs eight times (alongside the uninflected form *wipe*), *coming* occurs three times, and *running* occurs twice: we also find the plural noun *children*. At 22 months, we find an even larger range of inflected forms. The gerund inflection +*ing* is now more widely used, so that we find *squeezing* used four times (alongside *squeeze*), *eating* (alongside *eat*), *wiping, peeking, standing,* and *walking* used twice, and *shaking, chewing,* and *screaming* used once each. We also find the regular noun plural inflection +*s* being used: thus, the form *cookies* occurs four times (alongside *cookie*), and the form *toys* occurs 3 times (alongside *toy*). So, from a purely morphological point of view, it would seem that we start to have clear evidence that categorization has taken place in Allison's speech from around 20 months.

Moreover, direct syntactic evidence leads us to the same conclusion. At 20 months, we begin to see the emergence of systematic word combinations which look very much like noun phrase structures in utterances such as *baby cup, baby doll, baby Allison, dirty diaper, more juice,* and *mommy juice* (= 'mommy's juice'). We also find potential verb phrase structures such as *walk rain, walk school, buy store, sit down,* and *lie down.* By 22 months, we see a more extensive range of (what appear to be) noun phrase structures, including *dump truck, green cup, tiny cow, daddy cow, more apple juice, chocolate chip cookie,* and a vastly increased range of (what appear to be) verb phrases, such as *comb hair, get diaper, open can, open box, help baby, get toys, eat cookies, eating mommy cookie, wiping baby chin, get mommy cookie, pour mommy juice, put away Allison bag, ride truck again, drink apple juice again, help cow in table,* etc. Thus, our direct distributional evidence yields parallel results to the morphological evidence: both sets of evidence point to the onset of categorization in Allison's speech by 20 months.

But what of indirect distributional evidence? The completion technique once again proves unsuccessful, since there are no such sequences in either transcript. By contrast, there are quite a number of question–answer sequences in both transcripts, and these would appear to suggest that Allison has begun to acquire categorial constraints on phrasal responses to wh-questions, since she generally supplies categorially appropriate phrasal answers to the wh-questions which her mother puts to her, as we see from the examples in (17) below (where the initial question is asked by her mother, and Allison's response is italicized):

(17)   (a)   Who came to school with Mommy today – *Allison* (20)
       (b)   Who's going uptown? – *Baby...doll* (20)
       (c)   What do we need for the diaper? – *Pin* (20)
       (d)   What are you wearing? – *Dress* (22)
       (e)   What did Mommy do? – *Spill* (20)
       (f)   What should mommy do? – *Help cow in table* (22)
       (g)   What are you doing? – *Wiping* (20)
       (h)   What are you doing? – *Shaking* (22)
       (i)   Where's school? – *There* (20)
       (j)   Where's the tiny cow? – *Right here* (22)
       (k)   Where are the cookies? – *In bag* (22)

The fact that she relatively consistently answers *who/what*-questions with a nominal, *what...do(ing)*-questions with a verbal constituent, and (prepositionless) *where*-questions with a prepositional constituent (or proconstituent) suggests that at this point she has become (tacitly) 'aware' of categorial constraints on question-answering, and thus leads us to the conclusion that her speech is by now *categorial* in nature. At this point, there would seem to be at least four distinct categories in Allison's speech – nouns (which have the morphological characteristic that they take the plural +*s* inflection), verbs (which have the morphological characteristic that they take the gerund +*ing* inflection), adjectives (which are uninflected and can premodify a noun within a noun phrase), and prepositions (which are also uninflected, but cannot serve as nominal premodifiers within noun phrases).

Thus, the balance of the evidence from the four transcripts of Allison Bloom's spontaneous speech suggest that categorization is well under way by the age of 20 months. Of course, the obvious question to ask is whether Allison is a typical child, or whether she is more or less advanced than other children of her age. Comparative evidence would suggest that categorization takes place in most children's grammars somewhere between the ages of one-and-a-half and two years. For example, we find abundant evidence that the noun plural inflection +*s* is beginning to be used productively during this period, as examples such as the following illustrate (where the pluralized noun is italicized):

(18) (a) *Legs. Shoes. Bottles* (Helen 18)
      (b) *Shoes* off. *Flowers. Wellies.* (Elen 19)
      (c) *Socks. Wheels. Glasses* (*Helen 20)
      (d) Shake *hands.* ə need *shoes.* Man sit *blocks* (*Eric 20–21)
      (e) *Shapes* in. *Shapes* gone. *Dogs. Birdies* flying. *Stones. Wheels* (Bethan 21)
      (f) Want *crayons.* Dirty *boots. Coats. Slides. Chips.* Touch *heads.* More *bubbles. Cups* back (Jem 21)
      (g) *Beaks. Slippers. Bats. Carses* [= 'cars'] (+Benjamin 21)
      (h) *Walkies. Sweeties. Letters. Weebles* (John 22)
      (i) *Boots* gone. *Numbers* (Angharad 22)
      (j) More *nuts.* Mommy *shirts* hot. Coffee *noodles. Raisins.* Make *arms.* Go *slides* (*Kathryn 22)
      (k) More *lights.* Kendall *presents* (*Kendall 22–23)
      (l) *Stones. Biscuits. Castles. Tablets. Vases. Sweeties. Shoes. Fat legs. Numbers. Burgers. Red wheels* (Leila 23)
      (m) *Moo-cows.* Not go *shops. Drinks. Cakes. Balloons* go up (Claire 23)
      (n) Get *sweets.* For *boys. Feets. Ears. Fingers* (Domenico 24)
      (o) *Boots. Ducks. Hens. Shoes* (Anne 24)
      (p) Big *cats.* Small *cats.* Short *cats.* Night-night *peoples* (*Claire 24)

The fact that plural +*s* is being used productively at this stage is indicated by the occurrence of overgeneralized plural forms such as *carses, feets,* and *peoples.*

Further support for the claim that children have begun to categorize words at this point in their development comes from the fact that they begin to make more and more productive use of the verb inflection +*ing*: e.g.

(19)   (a)   Baby *talking. Reading* book (Hayley 20)
        (b)   *Coming* to rubbish. *Dipping. Going* round. Joey *eating. Riding. Digging.* Doggy *barking* (Bethan 20–21)
        (c)   *Eating* cereal (*Eric 20)
        (d)   *Going* down slide. *Breaking* stick. Wayne *sitting* on gate. *Peeling* apple. (Daniel 20–21)
        (e)   Lois *coming. Helping* Mommy. *Making* train (*Kathryn 21–22)
        (f)   Kimmy *running.* Phil *running.* Pam *running. Writing* book. Kendall *crying* there (*Kendall 23)
        (g)   Man *taking.* Not today *shopping* (Claire 23)
        (h)   *Hiding. Singing. Playing* (Leigh 24)
        (i)   *Riding* bicycle. *Writing* house. Daddy *sleeping* bed. Mamma *rocking* (*Claire 24)

During the same period, we also find examples of verb forms which would be analysed in adult speech as containing the V-inflection perfective +*n*: cf.

(20)   (a)   Daddy *gone* (Paula 18)
        (b)   *Gone* (Elen 19, Lucy 20, Hayley 20, *Allison 22)
        (c)   *Broken* truck (Dewi 20)
        (d)   Blanket *gone.* Geraint *gone.* Stick *gone* (Bethan 20)
        (e)   Baby *gone.* Nana *gone.* Postman Pat *gone* (Jenny 21)
        (f)   *Broken.* Wayne *taken* bubble. Stick *gone.* Wayne *gone.* (Daniel 21)
        (g)   Rocks...*broken* (*Kendall 22)
        (h)   Biscuit *gone.* Hammer *gone.* Car *gone* (Angharad 22)
        (i)   Jem *drawn* with Daddy pen. Mummy *thrown* it (Jem 23)
        (j)   That *broken* (Claire 23)
        (k)   Bunny *broken* foot (*Claire 24)

Obviously, the limited amount of data we have here makes it impossible to be sure whether there is any evidence of acquisition of the perfective +*n* inflection at this stage (it is quite possible that the italicized items in (20) might be misanalysed as monomorphemic stem forms). However, evidence from the productive use of the nominal +*s* and verbal +*ing* inflections suggests that categorization is well under way between the ages of one-and-a-half and two years. This evidence is entirely consistent with the findings reported in the literature on the acquisition of inflectional morphemes. For example, the classic study by De Villiers and De Villiers (1973a) shows some productive use of plural +*s* even in the youngest children in the sample (Zoe at 16 months, Faryl and Jessica at 19 months, and Hannah and Joshua at 21 months), and likewise some productive use of gerund +*ing* (indeed, 100% correct use by Zoe at 16 months and Hannah at 21 months).

The evidence from longitudinal studies suggests that once categorization begins in the child's grammar, it spreads fairly quickly through the child's lexicon: for example (as we saw earlier), once Allison Bloom acquires the verbal +*ing* inflection (at around the age of 20 months), she very soon comes to attach it to a wide range of verb stems, so that her transcript at age 22 months shows forms such as *squeezing, eating, wiping, peeking, standing, walking, shaking, chewing,* and *screaming*. The rapid spread of categorization may suggest that children formulate *lexical redundancy rules* which inter-relate the various grammatical properties of items. Such redundancy rules may also inter-relate different categorial uses of the same item (e.g. accounting for the fact that items like *brush* and *comb* can function either as nouns or as verbs): the existence of such rules is suggested by the phenomenon of *categorial overextension* in child speech. We can illustrate this phenomenon (from the speech of more advanced children) in terms of examples such as those in (21) below (from Clark 1982: she identifies the children only by their initials):

(21)   (a)   Mummy *trousers* me (DH 27, talking about getting dressed)

(b)   The buzzer is *buzzering* (EB 27, when the stove timer went off)

(c)   I'm *souping* (S 28, eating soup)

(d)   You have to *scale* it first (S 28, wanting to have some cheese weighed)

(e)   *Rocker* me, mommy (J 30, seated in a rocker)

(f)   *Pillow* me! (J 30, asking a teacher to toss a pillow at him during a mock pillow fight)

(g)   I *broomed* her (S 31, having hit his baby sister, explaining what made her cry)

(h)   Daddy's *rugging* down the hall (S 32, hearing his father using the vacuum cleaner in the hall)

(i)   I'm *lawning* (S 33, playing with a toy lawnmower)

(j)   Don't *broom* my mess (S 35, not wanting his mother to sweep his room)

    (k)   He's *keying* the door (S 36, watching a man opening a door with a key)

    (l)   Make it *bell* (RG 36, wanting a bell to be rung)

    (m) Is it all *needled?* (S 38, asking if the pants his mother is mending are ready)

What the children are doing here is extending an item which functions solely as a noun in adult speech to use as a verb. Why should this be? One answer would be to suppose that having observed the dual categorial status of items like *brush* and *comb*, the children formulate a redundancy rule to the effect that 'Any noun denoting a concrete entity can be used as a verb for talking about a state, process, or activity associated with that entity' (Clark 1982: 417): this rule is then overextended to nouns to which it is inapplicable in adult speech, so resulting in sentences such as those in (21) above. Other patterns of categorial overextension are reported in Clark (1981).

Given the speed at which the process of categorizing items in the child's vocabulary is completed once under way, it is conceivable that children may make use of more powerful redundancy rules which enable them to deduce the categorial properties of items from their semantic properties – though this seems to me to be a purely empirical question. Suggestions which can be interpreted in this light are to be found in Grimshaw 1981, Macnamara 1982, Pinker 1982, 1984, 1987, and Elliott and Wexler 1986. For example, Pinker (1984: 40) claims that 'The categorization of words can be inferred from their semantic properties': more specifically, he claims that children will use semantically based redundancy rules to categorize items denoting objects as nouns, items denoting actions as verbs, items denoting attributes as adjectives, and items denoting spatial relations as prepositions. This initial (semantically based) categorization of items provides a provisional analysis which is adopted only if not contradicted by morphosyntactic evidence. Pinker argues that such an analysis is justified (in part) by the fact that 'children's first nouns appear universally to refer to physical objects, their first verbs to actions, adjectives to attributes' (1984: 57). In much the same spirit, Lebeaux (1988: 44) suggests that grammatical categories may be derived from cognitive categories: cf. his remarks that

> Grammatical categories, while ultimately fully formal in character, are nonetheless 'centered' in the cognitive categories, so that membership in the latter acts as a marker for membership in the former: a noun phrase is the canonical grammatical category corresponding to the cognitive category 'thing'; a verb (or verb

phrase) is the canonical grammatical category corresponding to the cognitive category 'action'...and so on.

In a similar vein, Elliott and Wexler (1986) propose that Universal Grammar genetically endows the child with a set of *Feature Realization Principles* which derive the subcategorial features of items from their conceptual features.

There are, however, a number of problems which beset any attempt to derive grammatical categories from semantic, conceptual, or cognitive categories. Many of the claims made in this respect are so vague and sweeping that they have little empirical content (they tend to have the ring of a politician's manifesto – promising much, but ultimately achieving little!). Even where specific proposals are made, they rarely seem to stand up to close scrutiny. For example, the only specific Feature Realization Principle proposed by Elliott and Wexler (1986) is one to the effect that any item carrying the conceptual feature [+INDIVIDUAT-IVE] will be assigned the subcategorial feature [+COUNT]; a redundancy rule will then specify that [±COUNT] is a subcategorial feature of nouns. However, if this principle is part of Universal Grammar (and hence part of the child's biological endowment), we should expect to find that the very earliest utterances produced by children show evidence of mastery of the count/noncount distinction in nouns. But the evidence presented in Brown and Bellugi (1964) would seem to challenge this hypothesis. They argue that the earliest use of determiners by Adam and Eve showed that they had not mastered the count/noncount distinction: for example, Adam and Eve combined the indefinite article *a* not only with singular count nouns (as in *a coat*), but also with mass nouns (so producing forms such as *a celery* and *a dirt*), with proper nouns (giving rise to forms like *a Becky* and *a Jimmy*), and with plural count nouns (hence forms such as *a hands* and *a shoes*). Equally relevant here is the observation by Slobin (1966: 140) that in children acquiring Russian as their native language, 'the distinction between mass and count nouns is not stabilised until age 8'. Such data clearly call into question the empirical validity of the assumptions made by Elliott and Wexler – as indeed does the experimental work on the acquisition of the mass/count distinction cited below (p. 44). It would seem as if the case for claiming that categorial or subcategorial distinctions in early child speech are rooted in semantic or cognitive categories is – for the time being, at least – 'not proven' (to borrow a term from the Scottish legal system).

In this chapter, we have argued at some length that the earliest (one-word) utterances produced by young children are *acategorial* in nature. Using a variety of different types of criteria (based on the morphological and distributional properties of words in child speech on the one hand, and on children's responses to sentence-completion and question-answering tasks on the other), we concluded that we begin to have evidence that children have developed a formally differentiated set of categories during the early multi-word speech period, at around the age of 20 months (±20%) (though – as with all aspects of early child language development – we have to allow for considerable individual variation between children in respect of the age at which they attain a given stage). We argued that the relevant categories developed by young children at this stage are purely formal (grammatical) constructs, and that early child syntax is organized in terms of *grammatical classes* and *grammatical relations*. Thus, we have supposed that (once they reach the categorial stage of development at around 20 months) children's vocabulary items are assigned to grammatical classes such as noun/verb/adjective/preposition, and are combined into larger structures (phrases and clauses) in terms of grammatical relations. One relevant type of grammatical relation is what Chomsky (1986b) refers to as *categorial selection* (= c-selection, more traditionally known as *subcategorization*); using this terminology, we might say that a verb like *want* c-selects a nominal or clausal complement ('I want *a new car*', 'I want *you to buy a new car*'). On this view, when a young child forms (productive) utterances such as 'Want red car', 'Want Teddy', 'Want Mummy', 'Want orange sweetie', etc., he is combining a verb *want* with a noun phrase *red car/Teddy/Mummy/orange sweetie*, and is thereby showing evidence of 'knowing' some of the c-selection properties of *want* – viz. that *want* allows a noun phrase complement. The child is thus showing evidence of acquisition of grammatical classes and grammatical relations (provided that 'Want red car' is a productive structure in which *want* can be replaced by a variety of other Verbs, and *red car* can be replaced by a variety of other noun phrases).

However, although we have assumed here that early child speech is organized in terms of grammatical classes and grammatical relations, it should be pointed out that a number of developmental psycholinguists (particularly in the early 1970s) rejected this view, and argued instead that the child's earliest word combinations are organized entirely in terms of *semantic classes* and *semantic relations*. This led to a variety of claims in the acquisition literature to the effect that young children initially develop 'semantically based grammars' – cf. suggestions along these lines made in Schlesinger (1971, 1982), Bowerman (1973), Brown (1973), Braine (1976), Gleitman (1981), and Macnamara (1982). Within this approach, children's early patterned speech was seen as the output of semantically based 'formulae' or 'schemata' such as those illustrated in (22) below (where capitals are used to denote semantic classes):

(22)
Schema	*Example*
AGENT + ACTION	Adam write
ACTION + PATIENT	Change diaper
AGENT + ACTION + LOCATIVE	Adam fall toy
ACTION + GOAL + PATIENT	Give doggie paper
ACTION + PATIENT + LOCATIVE	Put doggie window
ENTITY + LOCATION	Ball on table
ATTRIBUTE + ATTRIBUTANT	Red ball
POSSESSOR + POSSESSED	Mommy shoe

Under this alternative *semantic* analysis of early patterned speech, formal grammatical categories (like noun, verb, adjective, and preposition) were claimed to play no part whatever in accounting for the child'ss early word combinations. 'Grammatical' categories (it was claimed) emerge only at a later stage of development, perhaps as a result of maturational factors (Gleitman 1981 suggests that the principles of grammatical categorization come 'on line' only at a specific point of maturation, resulting in a change from semantically based grammar to a morphosyntactically based grammar – a change which she regards as analogous to that of the tadpole's transformation into a frog).

It seems to me, however, that there is strong empirical evidence against the claim that children's early patterned speech is organized purely in terms of *semantic* classes. Part of the evidence which falsifies this claim is *morphological* in nature. As we saw earlier, from the very beginnings of productive multi-word combinations in English (at around 20 months of age), we find children beginning to make productive use of the plural +*s* inflection, and the gerund +*ing* inflection. If children's word-classes at this stage are semantically (rather than grammatically) based, then we should expect to find (e.g.) that each such inflection would be attached only to a specific semantic class of expressions (e.g. plural +*s* might be attached to AGENT words, and gerund +*ing* to ACTION words). However, such predictions are entirely false. As we can see from the data presented earlier, plural +*s* attaches to *nouns* irrespective of their (presumed) semantic function – i.e. whether they are AGENTS (as in (18)(e) '*Birdies* flying'), PATIENTS (cf. (18)(f) 'Touch *heads*'), LOCATIVES (cf. (18)(d) 'Man sit *blocks*'), GOALS (cf. (18)(m) 'Not go *shops*'), or whatever. And any suggestion that +*ing* might be an inflection which attaches to ACTION words would seem to be falsified by the fact that there are no reported examples of children attaching +*ing* to action prepositions like *up/down* or action adjectives like *naughty* (so that while children say 'Baby up' while climbing onto a chair, and 'Baby naughty' while misbehaving, they do not say *'Baby upping', or *'Baby naughtying'): on the contrary, +*ing* is an inflection which children attach *only* to verbs (as examples such as (19) above illustrate clearly). Much the same point is made by Maratsos et al. (1979) and Maratsos (1981): they note that when (at around 26 months) children begin to acquire the past tense morpheme +*ed*, they unerringly attach it to verbs (even to stative verbs not denoting actions, resulting in overgeneralized forms such as *thinked/feeled/knowed*), never to non-verbal ACTION predicates like the adjective *naughty* (so that we don't find children saying *'He *naughtied* all the time'). Contrary to what we would expect if children were operating with semantically based word classes, they make very few categorial morphological errors (i.e. errors involving attaching a given type of inflection to the wrong category) – a fact noted by Smith (1933), Cazden (1968), Brown (1973), Maratsos and Chalkey (1980), Maratsos (1982, 1988), Berman (1988), Levy (1988), and many others. Evidence from studies of the acquisition of other types of inflection leads to the same conclusion, namely that the child's inflectional morphology works on the basis of the assignment of words to *grammatical categories* (not semantic classes): for example, it has been argued (e.g. by MacWhinney 1978, Karmiloff-Smith 1979, and Levy 1983) that children rely on grammatical rather than semantic cues in the acquisition of the gender properties of nouns (though see also the evidence presented by Mulford 1985). And Hyams (1986) argues that agreement inflections in the speech of young children acquiring Italian are associated with grammatical rather than semantic classes.

An additional problem faced by proposals for 'semantically based child grammars' is that they provide no satisfactory account of certain aspects of the *structure* and *distribution* of words and phrases in early child speech. For example, in (22) the sequence 'Ball on table' is described as an instance of the semantic schema ENTITY + LOCATION. However, this sequence is ambiguous in early child speech as between a nominal structure (paraphraseable as 'The ball which is on the table'), and a (verbless) clausal structure (paraphraseable as 'The ball is on the table'): in the nominal structure, *on table* functions as an adnominal adjunct to the noun *ball*, while in the clausal structure, *on table* has a predicative function, in that it is being predicated of the subject noun *ball*. Both types of prepositional structure (adnominal and predicative) occur in early child speech, as illustrated by the bracketed structures in the following examples (and many more similar examples which we shall give in later chapters):

(23)   (a)   [Stephen *in school*] (Jem 23) [predicative]
       (b)   Want [sweetie *in bag*] out (Daniel 24) [adnominal]

In the first example here, *in school* is used as a predicate, so that the overall bracketed structure is a (verbless) clause, paraphraseable as 'Stephen is in school'; but in the second example, *in bag* functions as an adjunct to the noun *sweetie*, so that the overall bracketed structure is a noun phrase (paraphraseable as 'the sweetie which is in the bag'), not a clause. However, while the two structures can easily be differentiated in terms of their different grammatical (nominal or clausal) structures (in ways which will become clear in the next chapter), it is not obvious how the two would be differentiated in terms of semantic schemata like (22), since both appear to be instances of the ENTITY + LOCATIVE schema.

Thus, one problem posed by the 'semantic schemata' approach is that it provides no obvious way of handling the fact that a single 'schema' may correspond to more than one syntactic structure. However, a second problem posed by the analysis is precisely the converse – namely that there are cases where word combinations which are analysed as different types of schema correspond to a single constituent type (i.e. cases where word combinations which are assigned different semantic structures by schemata such as those in (22) turn out to have essentially the same syntactic distribution). For example, if 'Red ball' is analysed as an example of an ATTRIBUTE + ATTRIBUTANT pattern, and 'Mommy shoe' is analysed as an example of an entirely distinct POSSESSOR + POSSESSED pattern, how do we account for the fact that these two different patterns have the same distribution in early child English, and hence (e.g.) both can occur as the object of a verb like *want*? It might seem that we can overcome the problem by a simple terminological change, analysing the relevant structures as instances of ATTRIBUTE + ENTITY, and POSSESSOR + ENTITY respectively; we could then claim that both types of expression are in some sense ENTITY expressions, and for this reason have essentially the same distribution. However, any such proposal seems to me to be tantamount to recognizing that the relevant sequences have a hierarchical, endocentric (i.e. headed) structure, and thus in effect have a *syntactic* structure: this becomes clearer if we replace the term ENTITY by its grammatical counterpart 'noun', and the term 'ENTITY expression' by its obvious counterpart 'noun phrase'. In other words, what we are really doing is nothing more illuminating than attaching new (allegedly semantic) labels to old (strictly grammatical) constructs.

An additional problem faced by proposals for 'semantically based child grammars' is that there is some experimental evidence that the combinatorial classes with which children operate are determined by the child on the basis of grammatical (e.g. distributional) criteria rather than semantic criteria. Experimental evidence produced by Katz, Baker and Macnamara (1974) and replicated by Gelman and Taylor (1983) suggests that some children as young as 17 months use distributional evidence to infer the categorial status of nonsense words. Likewise, Gordon (1985) reports that experimental evidence relating to the acquisition of nonsense words by young children leads to the conclusion that children rely primarily on grammatical rather than semantic cues in acquiring the mass/count distinction. Gathercole (1985) presents experimental data in support of a parallel conclusion that 'children begin learning the mass–count distinction...not as a semantic one, but as a morphosyntactic (distributional) distinction' (ibid: 411). And Gleitman (1989) argues that children infer the semantic properties of items from their morphosyntactic properties, rather than the converse.

Perhaps the most convincing distributional evidence of all that children's earliest word-classes are based on traditional grammatical categories such as noun/verb/adjective/preposition comes from the evidence (which we shall present in the next chapter) of a compelling cross-categorial symmetry in the way that children combine nouns with other constituents to form noun phrases, combine verbs with other constituents to form verb phrases, combine prepositions with other constituents to form prepositional phrases...and so on. The resulting cross-categorial structural symmetry (which we shall illustrate in detail in due course) provides a powerful argument for positing that early child utterances have a well-defined syntactic structure, and are organized on the basis of a small number of grammatical classes and grammatical relations.

It is perhaps important at this juncture to clarify an essential point of principle. What we are claiming here is that early child English shows evidence of the development of a set of categories and structures which are purely *formal* (i.e. grammatical, or morphosyntactic) in nature. However, the claim that early child syntax is organized in terms of grammatical classes and relations should not be misinterpreted as implying that semantic relations have no part to play in early child grammars (whatever that might mean). We can illustrate this point in terms of the following (hypothetical) example of an early child utterance:

(24)   Pussies chasing birdies

By claiming that an utterance such as (24) has a *grammatical* structure in which *pussies* and *birdies* are nouns, and *chasing* is a verb, we are not in any sense denying that there are also semantic (i.e. *thematic*) relations holding between the constituents concerned – e.g. that *pussies* is the AGENT and *birdies* the PATIENT of *chasing*. What we are claiming, however, is that relevant aspects of the morphosyntax of such sentences (e.g. the question of the kind of words which the plural +*s* and gerund +*ing* inflections can be attached to) are determined by the *grammatical* rather than the *thematic* properties of such constituents: e.g. plural +*s* doesn't attach to the thematic class of AGENTS, but rather to the syntactic class of *nouns*; and gerund +*ing* doesn't attach to the semantic class of ACTION predicates, but rather to the syntactic class of *verbs*.

We might go further and argue that precisely because syntactic structure and thematic structure are independent (though inter-related) levels of representation, there is no conflict whatever between the claim that early child sentences have a syntactic structure, and the claim that they have a thematic structure. More specifically, we might suppose that the earliest structures produced by young children are *categorial-thematic* structures, i.e. structures in which constituents have both a categorial and a thematic function. For example, we might argue that an utterance such as (24) above would be a verb phrase (or verbal small clause) with the simplified structure (25) below:

(25)

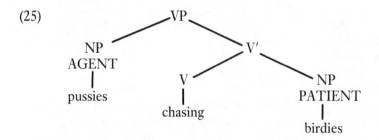

(25) clearly has a categorial structure (in that each constituent is assigned a specific categorial status indicated by the category labels VP, V', V, and NP). However, it also has a thematic structure, in that each constituent (other than the overall VP itself) has a specific thematic function: the V *chasing* assigns the thematic role PATIENT to its NP complement *birdies*; and the V-bar *chasing birdies* assigns the thematic role AGENT to its subject NP *pussies*. We might interpret grammars incorporating

semantic schemata such as those in (22) above as implicitly claiming that all structures produced by young children at this stage are *thematic*, in the sense that every child constituent theta-marks or is theta-marked by any sister constituent which it has. (25) would be a *thematic* structure in this sense, since V theta-marks the sister NP to its right, and V-bar theta marks the sister NP to its left: conversely, each NP is theta-marked by its sister (that sister being V in one case, and V-bar in the other); the overall VP is not assigned a theta-role, since it has no sister constituent.

It may well be that the purely thematic function of constituents in early child grammars determines their categorial status. Abney (1987) suggests that thematic constituents typically belong to 'lexical' categories (nouns, verbs, adjectives, prepositions and their projections), whereas *nonthematic* constituents belong to 'functional' categories (determiners, auxiliaries, complementizers and their projections). If this were so, the claim that early child sentences are purely thematic structures would lead us to expect that the earliest utterances produced by young children would have a purely *lexical* categorial structure – i.e. would comprise (projections of) the four primary lexical categories noun, verb, adjective, and preposition. We might then suggest that children's structures at this stage would typically have the canonical form (26) below (simplified in various ways, such as by ignoring potential adjuncts, and by ignoring the possibility that all constituents of XP other than the head X may be optional):

(26)

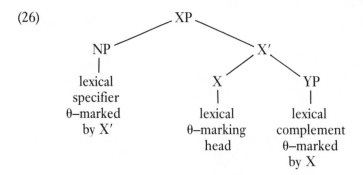

If this is so, then it follows that the earliest structures produced by young children are *lexical-thematic* structures (i.e. structures in which all constituents belong to lexical categories, and in which all sister constituents are thematically inter-related). This is the central hypothesis which we shall put to the empirical test in the course of our book.

However, a brief technical footnote is in order at this point.

We have noted Abney's (1987) suggestion that it is lexical categories which have thematic properties. However, the inter-relationship between categorial status and thematic status is more complex than this, for two reasons. On the one hand, there are some lexical categories which do not theta-mark their sisters: for instance, a single-bar constituent headed by a 'raising' predicate like *seem/likely*, or by a passive participle like *thought* does not theta-mark its sister (subject) constituent; hence, in a sentence such as:

(27)   *The enemy* seems to be thought likely to **destroy the city**

the italicized subject *the enemy* is theta-marked by the the bold-printed V-bar **destroy the city**, not by (any projection of) the passive participle *thought* or the raising predicates *likely* and *seems*. On the other hand, the converse also seems to be true, namely that some functional categories may theta-mark their sisters: for example, Chomsky suggests in *Barriers* (1986b: 20) that modal auxiliaries may theta-mark their complement VPs (though it is generally assumed that single-bar projections of modals do not theta-mark their subject specifiers, since in all uses modals permit nonthematic subjects like existential *there*, as illustrated by modal *may* in a sentence such as 'The government has decreed that there may not be any further street demonstrations without a court order'). Accordingly, we might (rather more carefully) say that a given word-level category X is *thematic* just in case X theta-marks any sister complement it has, and its X-bar projection theta-marks any sister subject specifier it has: conversely, X is *nonthematic* if X has a nonthematic complement, or a nonthematic specifier, or both. It would then follow that *only* (but not *all*) words belonging to lexical categories are thematic: functional constituents would always be nonthematic (e.g. modals would be nonthematic in that they have thematic complements, but nonthematic subject specifiers), and some lexical constituents would also be nonthematic (e.g. 'raising' and 'passive' predicates likewise have thematic complements but nonthematic subjects). It would also be the case that nominal arguments are theta-marked only by lexical, not by functional constituents.

One of the predictions which follows from the *lexical-thematic* analysis proposed here is that all constituents in early child English will have a purely *lexical* categorial status, so that children at this stage will make no productive use of *functional* constituents at all. This is a claim which we shall put to the empirical test in the next chapter, where we address the crucial question: 'What is the nature and range of the earliest system of grammatical categories developed by young children?'

3

Lexical Category Systems in Early Child English

The evidence which we presented in the previous chapter suggests that children begin to develop an initial system of categories somewhere around the age of 20 months (±20%). However, the obvious question to ask at this point is: 'What is the nature of this initial system of categories?' What we shall argue here is that the earliest categories acquired by young children are *lexical* categories – a hypothesis compatible with the *lexical-thematic* analysis of early child sentences suggested at the end of the previous chapter. We shall also claim that only three or four months later (typically around the age of 24 months, ±20%) do we begin to find evidence of the acquisition of *functional* categories. If this is so, we can distinguish three major stages in the development of the categorial component in the child's grammar, viz:

(1)   (i)   *precategorial* stage
        (ii)   *lexical* stage
        (iii) *functional* stage

The *precategorial stage* is the period of one-word speech when categorization has not yet taken place in child grammars, so that children's utterances at this stage have no categorial structure. The *lexical* stage is characterized by the acquisition of a set of lexical word categories and their phrasal projections. The *functional stage* is characterized by the acquisition of functional word categories and their phrasal projections. Given that the developmental model presented here presupposes familiarity with the distinction between *lexical* and *functional* categories and with the term *projection*, by way of background information we shall provide a brief outline of some of the assumptions about category systems which we are making here.

The system of categories for adult English which we shall presuppose here is essentially that adopted in recent versions of *X-bar Syntax* (cf. Radford 1988a for an introduction to the relevant concepts and terminology): more specifically, we shall adopt the system of categories used in Chomsky's (1986b) *Barriers* monograph, modified in the light of more recent work by Abney (1987) and others. Within this framework, there are assumed to be four primary *lexical* categories in (adult) English – viz. nouns (= N), verbs (= V), prepositions (= P), and adjectives (= A), with adverbs being analysed as a subclass of adjectives (for the reasons set out in Radford 1988a: 138–41). Lexical categories have the property that they have a very large membership; for example, there are dozens of Prepositions in English, and thousands of nouns, verbs, and adjectives. By contrast, functional categories (sometimes referred to as 'nonlexical' or 'grammatical' categories) have a very much more restricted membership, usually comprising no more than a handful of members. There are three functional categories which will be of interest to us here. The first are *determiners* (= D) – a class traditionally assumed to contain items such as those italicized in (2) below, and having the function of introducing (more precisely, specifying the referential or quantificational properties of) noun phrases such as those bracketed below:

(2)　(a)　Don't trust [*a/the/this/that* foreign bank]
　　　(b)　Does he have [*some/any/no/much* money]?

The second are *Complementizers* (= C) – that is, complement-clause introducing particles: for example, in (3) below, the bracketed clause is a *complement clause* in that it functions as the complement of the bold-printed head verb/adjective; since the italicized particles have the function of introducing the bracketed complement clauses, they are known as *Complementizers*:

(3)　(a)　I **know** [*that* you must be tired]
　　　(b)　I'm **anxious** [*for* you to meet my mother]
　　　(c)　I really **wonder** [*whether* he will turn up]
　　　(d)　I somehow **doubt** [*if* he will tell the truth]

The third major type of functional category is the constituent which Chomsky in his (1986b: 3) *Barriers* monograph labels as I. The class of I constituents includes the infinitival particle *to*, as well as the class of inflected modal auxiliaries, i.e. items such as *will/would, shall/should, can/could, may/might*, etc. which are inflected for tense in the sense that the first member of each pair is morphologically a present tense form, and the second member a past tense form carrying the past tense $+d/+t$ inflection. The category label I thus serves as a convenient abbreviation for both infinitival and inflected forms. One of the reasons for positing that infinitival *to* and inflected modal auxiliaries belong to the same category of I constituents is that they occupy the same internal position within the clause, as we see from examples such as (4) below:

(4)　　(a)　I'm anxious that [the president *should* approve it]
　　　　(b)　I'm anxious for [the president *to* approve it]

Thus, given this analysis, an I constituent can be either finite (and so contain e.g. an inflected modal auxiliary like *should*), or nonfinite (and so contain the infinitival particle *to*).

Recent work on category systems has suggested that all word categories can be *projected* (i.e. 'expanded') into higher-level phrasal categories in symmetrical ways. The core assumption of the X-bar model is that any word category X (where X = noun, verb, preposition, complementizer, etc.) can function as the head of a phrase and be projected into the corresponding phrasal category XP by the addition of up to three different kinds of 'modifier'. Thus, X can be projected into a 'small' X-phrase called an X-(single)-bar (= X′) by the addition of one or more *complements*; the resultant X-bar can in turn be (recursively) projected into another X-bar by the addition of an *adjunct* of some kind; and this X-bar can be further projected into an X-double-bar (= X″ = XP = full X-phrase) by the addition of a *specifier* of an appropriate kind. Given these assumptions, we can say that phrases in English have the schematic structure (5) below:

(5)　　[$_{X''}$ specifier [$_{X'}$ adjunct [$_{X'}$ [$_{X}$ head] complement/s]]]

(where the head X is a word category of some kind, and where complements, adjuncts, and specifiers are themselves full phrasal constituents). Although simplified somewhat for expository purposes, the generalized X-bar schema in (5) will suffice as a (somewhat idealized) representation of the canonical structure of phrases in adult English.

The central assumption of recent X-bar work is that *all* word categories are projectable in precisely symmetrical ways. It follows from this that not only lexical categories (V, N, A, P), but also *functional* categories (D, C, I) are projectable into single- and double-bar constituents. We can illustrate this cross-categorial projection symmetry between lexical and functional categories in adult English in terms of an example such as (6) below:

(6)   They probably will each bitterly criticize the other

For the sake of brevity, we shall consider only how the verb *criticize* and the auxiliary *will* are projected into higher-level constituents. In accordance with the schema in (5), the V *criticize* is projected into a V-bar by the addition of the following nominal complement [*the other*]; the resulting V-bar [*criticize the other*] is projected into a further V-bar by the addition of the adverbial adjunct *bitterly*; the V-bar thereby formed [*bitterly criticize the other*] is then projected into a V-double-bar (i.e. a full verb phrase) by the addition of the quantificational specifier *each*, so forming the VP [*each bitterly criticize the other*]. Some evidence that this sequence is indeed a phrasal constituent comes from the fact that it can be preposed (in an appropriate discourse setting, e.g. after a sequence such as 'He said that they would each bitterly criticize the other, and...'): cf.

(7)   *Each bitterly criticize the other*, they probably will

Given these assumptions, the VP concerned will have the simplified structure (8) below:

(8)   [$_{VP}$ each [$_{V'}$ bitterly [$_{V'}$ [$_{V}$ criticize] the other]]]

and it should be clear that (8) conforms to the generalised X-bar schema presented in (5) above.

Consider now how the modal auxiliary *will* is projected into higher-level constituents. Since *will* is inflected for tense (its past tense counterpart being *would*), we might follow the notational practice in Chomsky's (1986b) *Barriers* monograph and assign it the category label I (with I in this case denoting an inflected modal auxiliary). We can then say that the I constituent *will* is projected into I-bar by the addition of the following verb phrase complement in (8); the resulting I-bar [*will each bitterly criticize the other*] is then further projected into another I-bar by the addition of the adverbial adjunct *probably*; and the resulting I-bar [*probably will each bitterly criticize the other*] is in turn projected into an I-double-bar (= I″ = IP = Inflection Phrase) constituent by the addition of the pronominal specifier *they*, so that the overall clause in (6) has the simplified structure (9) below:

(9) [$_{IP}$ They [$_{I'}$ probably [$_{I'}$ [$_{I}$ will] [$_{VP}$ each bitterly criticize the other]]]]

Once again, it should be clear that the structure in (9) conforms to the generalized X-bar schema in (5).

The key assumption in recent work that functional categories are projectable has important implications for the analysis of nominal and clausal constituents such as those bracketed in (2–4) above. It has led to suggestions (in work by Stowell 1981, Koopman 1984, Chomsky 1986b, Fukui 1986, Hellan 1986, Abney 1987, Fassi–Fehri 1988, and Grosu 1988) that such constituents are projections of head functional categories. What the 'functional head' analysis means in more concrete terms is that the bracketed nominal constituents in (2) above would be analysed as projections of the head italicized D constituent, and thus have the status of DP (= Determiner Phrase) constituents. Similarly, it means that the bracketed clausal constituents in (3) above would be analysed as projections of the head italicized C constituent, and thus have the status of CP (= Complementiser Phrase) constituents. In the same way, the bracketed clausal constituents in (4) above will be analysed as projections of the head italicized I constituents, and thus will have the status of IP (= Inflection Phrase) constituents. Given these assumptions, the bracketed constituents in the (a) examples in (2–4) above would have the respective (simplified) structures indicated in (10) below: it should be noted that for the sake of expository simplicity we shall adopt the conventional practice throughout this book of omitting constituents (particularly single-bar constituents) not central to the discussion at hand;

(10)   (a)   [$_{DP}$ [$_D$ *a/the/this/that*] [$_{NP}$ foreign bank]]
        (b)   [$_{CP}$ [$_C$ *that*] [$_{IP}$ you must be tired]]
        (c)   [$_{IP}$ [$_{DP}$ the president] [$_I$ *should*] [$_{VP}$ approve it]]

Such an analysis is theoretically desirable for two main reasons: firstly, it extends the range of *projectable* categories from lexical to functional categories, so resulting in complete cross-categorial symmetry in the projection system found in adult grammars; and secondly, it enables clauses (formerly analysed as *exocentric* structures with no head) to be analysed as *endocentric* (= headed) structures which are projections of head C and I constituents. Thus, the DP/CP/IP analysis enables us to propose a maximally constrained model of constituent structure in which (i) all word categories are projectable, and (ii) all higher-level (i.e. phrasal or clausal) constituents are endocentric projections of a corresponding head word-level category.

Given that both lexical and functional categories are projectable in parallel ways, the obvious question to ask is what differences there are between them. Abney (1987: 64–5) argues that the distinction between *functional* and *lexical* categories is rooted in Universal Grammar: more particularly, he argues that functional categories have the following (putatively universal) characteristics which differentiate them from lexical categories:

(11)   (a)   'Functional elements constitute closed ... classes
       (b)   Functional elements are generally phonologically and mor-phologically dependent. They are generally stressless, of-ten clitics or affixes, and sometimes even phonologically null
       (c)   Functional elements permit only one complement, which is in general not an argument. The arguments are CP, PP, and ... DP. Functional elements select IP, VP, NP
       (d)   Functional elements are usually inseparable from their complement
       (e)   Functional elements lack ... 'descriptive content'. Their semantic contribution is second-order, regulating or con-tributing to the interpretation of their complement. They mark grammatical or relational features, rather than pick-ing out a class of objects.

An additional differentiating property is that only items belonging to *lexical* categories are thematic, whereas all items belonging to *functional* categories are nonthematic (in the technical sense defined at the end of chapter 2). Perhaps because functional items do not assign theta-roles to their specifiers, both the head position and the specifier position in a functional category system (CP, IP, DP) can be left underlyingly empty. This in turn means that both the head and specifier positions within a functional category system may be filled *transformationally* (i.e. by a constituent moving into the relevant position from some other position).

The possibility of transformationally filling the head and/or specifier positions within a functional category system can be illustrated by paradigms such as the following (the relevant structures are simplified in a variety of ways, for ease of exposition):

(12)   (a)   We mustn't let [$_{VP}$ *the enemy* [$_V$ destroy] the city]
       (b)   [$_{IP}$ *the enemy* [$_I$ will] [$_{VP}$ *e* [$_V$ destroy] the city]]
       (c)   [$_{CP}$ [$_C$ *Will*] [$_{IP}$ the enemy [$_I$ *e*] [$_{VP}$ e [$_V$ destroy][$_{NP}$ the city]]]]
       (d)   [$_{CP}$ *Which city* [$_C$ will] [$_{IP}$ the enemy [$_I$ *e*] [$_{VP}$ e [$_V$ destroy] *e*]]]

In (12)(a), the DP *the enemy* functions as the subject (i.e. specifier) of a lexical category (the verb *destroy*) and is assigned a thematic role (e.g. AGENT) by the verb (more accurately, by the V-bar *destroy the city*). In (12)(b), by contrast, the DP *the enemy* has moved out of its underlying position as specifier of the bracketed VP, into its superficial position as specifier of the bracketed IP: as a result of this movement, the specifier position within the VP becomes *empty* (here designated as *e*, an empty category which is the trace of the moved italicized DP). In (12)(c), we see the result of an additional movement, whereby the modal *will* moves from the head I position of IP into the head C position of CP, so leaving the head I position within IP empty (= *e*). In (12)(d), we find that the italicized DP *which city* (which must originate as the complement of the bracketed VP in order to receive the PATIENT theta-role which *destroy* assigns to its complement) has moved into the specifier position within CP, leaving the complement position within the bracketed VP empty (= *e*). More precisely, (12)(d) involves three separate movements: (i) movement of *will* from the head I position of IP to the head C position of CP; (ii) movement of *the enemy* from the specifier position in VP to the specifier position in IP; and (iii) movement of *which city* from the complement position in VP into the specifier position in CP. Thus, the possibility of transformationally filling the head and specifier positions in functional category systems is amply illustrated by examples such as (12)(d).

Having given a brief outline of the range of lexical and functional category systems found in adult English, we can now return to consider the question which we posed at the beginning of this chapter, relating to the range of category systems found in early child grammars of English (viz. in children roughly between one-and-a-half and two years of age). What we shall argue here is that the categorial component of early child grammars of English is purely *lexical* in character, in that children at the initial stage of categorisation develop lexical category systems (more specifically, an N-system, V-system, P-system, and A-system), but no functional category systems (viz. no D-system, C-system, or I-system).

The obvious question to ask at this point is what empirical evidence there is in support of the claim that the earliest categorial systems developed by young children are purely lexical in nature. Before we turn to look in detail at the evidence provided by our own corpus, we shall first review some of the existing published studies which provide suggestive evidence in support of this conclusion. Part of the relevant evidence comes from early studies of the *imitative speech* produced by young children (either experimentally or spontaneously). As we noted in our brief discussion of imitative speech in chapter 1, it has generally been hypothesized that children can only *consistently* imitate correctly those items whose morphosyntax they have acquired, and that they will omit other items. In this connection, it is interesting to note the following attempted imitations of adult model sentences produced by the children specified at the ages (in months) indicated:

(13)   (a)   ADULT: Mr Miller will try
             CHILD: *Miller try* (*Susan 24, from Ervin-Tripp 1964)

       (b)   ADULT: I will read the book
             CHILD: *Read book* (*Eve 25, from Brown and Fraser 1963)

       (c)   ADULT: I can see a cow
             CHILD: *See cow* (*Eve 25, from Brown and Fraser 1963)

The items which are successfully imitated by the children all belong to lexical categories – viz. the verbs *try*, *read*, and *see*, and the nouns *Miller*, *book*, and *cow*. The items which are omitted by the children arguably all belong to functional categories: these include the I constituents *will* and *can*, and the D constituents *a* and *the*. They also include two further potential D constituents, namely the pronoun *I* (Abney 1987: 281–4 argues that personal pronouns are D constituents), and the title *Mr* (titles might be argued to function as determiners for proper names in English). The fact that the children concerned successfully imitate lexical but not functional categories suggests that they have acquired a set of lexical categories at this stage, but no functional categories. This in turn suggests that the earliest stage in children's development of a categorial system is a *lexical* stage at which they have developed a set of lexical categories, but no functional categories.

Supporting evidence for these conclusions comes from published naturalistic studies of children's spontaneous speech production. For example, if we turn to the transcript (in Bloom 1973) of Allison Bloom's speech at age 22 months (i.e. two months or so after categorization has taken place in her grammar), we find that her vocabulary comprises items which can arguably be categorized as in (14) below:

(14)   NOUNS: baby, mommy, doll, horse, cow, pig, hair, knee, back, chair, table, box, can, cup, truck, school, diaper, skirt, dress, blouse, crumb, cookie(s), toy(s), children

       VERBS: comb, drink, eat, get, open, spill, ride, tumble, help, wait, pull, build, sit, wiping, standing, peeking, eating, walking, squeezing

       PREPOSITIONS: in, on, out, down, up, away, around

ADJECTIVES: green, yellow, big, tiny, funny, empty, sharp

Thus, the set of word-level categories which Allison appears to have acquired comprises the four primary lexical categories N, V, P and A. There is simply no evidence that Allison at this stage has acquired any functional categories at all: her transcript contains no potential determiners (hence there is no occurrence of *a/the/this/that/some/any*, etc.), no potential complementizers (hence no clause-introducing particles like *that/for/whether/if*), and no potential I constituents (e.g. no inflected modals like *will/would*, etc. and no infinitival *to*). Thus, published studies of both imitative and spontaneous speech produced by children would seem to lend plausibility to the suggestion that the earliest grammars developed by young children acquiring English as their mother tongue have a purely *lexical* categorial system. It should be noted that this hypothesis is in no sense a novel one: there have been numerous equivalent suggestions in the traditional acquisition literature which might be reinterpreted in these terms (cf. e.g. Guillaume 1927, McCarthy 1954, Brown and Fraser 1963, Brown and Bellugi 1964, Ervin-Tripp 1973: 231, and Bowerman 1973: 25), as well as more recent suggestions along similar lines within an X-bar framework (cf. e.g. Radford 1985, 1986, 1988b, Abney 1987: 64, Guilfoyle and Noonan 1988, Lebeaux 1988, Kazman 1988, etc.).

If our *lexical* analysis of early child grammars of English is along the right lines, then we should expect to find that all phrasal and clausal constituents in early child English are purely lexical structures, in the sense that they are projections of a head lexical category formed by combining that head lexical category with complement/adjunct/specifier phrases which are themselves projections of other head lexical categories. Conversely, we should also expect to find that there are no *functional* structures in early child English – i.e. no structures which contain (projections of) head functional categories. We shall organize our defence of this central thesis of our book along the following lines. In the remainder of this chapter, we shall argue that at the earliest stage of their categorial development (viz. typically at around the age of 20–23 months, $\pm20\%$) children develop lexical category systems, and thus develop an N-system, V-system, P-system, and A-system; in chapters 4–8, we shall argue that children during this period have no D-system, C-system, or I-system in their grammars; in chapter 9, we shall argue that early child grammars; also lack *nonthematic* constituents; and in chapter 10 we consider possible explanations for why early child grammars are purely *lexical-thematic* in nature, and the implications of this for the development of a Theory of Language Acquisition.

Accordingly, we begin in this chapter by arguing that children at the initial stage of their categorial development have begun to develop lexical category systems, and thus 'know' how to project nouns, verbs, prepositions and adjectives into the corresponding phrasal categories. It seems reasonable to suppose that once we begin to find evidence (of a kind which we presented in the previous chapter) that children have developed lexical word categories, we will also begin to find parallel evidence that they have developed the corresponding phrasal categories as well. There are two reasons for thinking this. One is that a large part of the evidence on which children rely in categorizing words is distributional in nature – i.e. is based on the ways in which word categories are projected into phrase categories by being combined with other categories: from this point of view, then, we should expect the principles of *categorization* and *projection* to come into operation simultaneously in child grammars (since projection is itself an inherently categorial process by which higher-level categories are formed from lower-level ones).

The second reason for supposing that projection is mastered hand-in-hand with categorization is universalist in nature. The obvious structural symmetry between the different category systems in English (the V-system, the I-system, etc.) seems so deep-seated that it is inconceivable that it could be an accidental property of English: rather, it seems more likely that the symmetry represents an inherent 'design feature' of natural language. If this is so, then we should expect to find that the basic structural (i.e. constituency) relations implicit in the schema (5) are universal: i.e. that complements universally have the function of expanding a head (zero-bar) word category into a single-bar constituent, that adjuncts universally have the function of (recursively) expanding a constituent of a given type (e.g. N-bar) into another constituent of the same type, and that specifiers universally have the function of expanding a single-bar constituent into a double-bar constituent. This conclusion gains support from the fact that these basic X-bar assumptions have led to insightful descriptions of the syntax of a wide range of constructions in a wide range of different languages, such as Arabic (Fassi Fehri 1988), Dutch (Hoekstra 1984), French (Kayne 1984), Hebrew (Borer 1984), Hungarian (Horvath 1985), Italian (Burzio 1986), Quechua (Lefebvre and Muysken 1988), Spanish (Jaeggli 1982)... and so on and so forth. We might therefore follow Brown, Cazden and Bellugi (1968: 392) in concluding that grammatical configurations 'are to the child what nut-burying is to the squirrel'.

However, it has to be admitted that the cross-linguistic situation is by no means clear. The most obvious challenge to the assumption that constituency relations are universal is posed by supposedly *nonconfigurational* languages. For example, in a language like Navaho, the arguments of predicates may be syntactically affixed to the verb, rather than projected into a hierarchical syntactic structure (cf. Saito 1985). It may even be that there are a further class of languages which might be termed *weakly configurational*. For example, if Fukui (1986) is correct in positing that Japanese has no specifiers (in the sense defined earlier), and Rouveret (1989) is correct in supposing that Welsh likewise has no specifiers, then it follows that the range of structurally distinct constituent types will vary from one language to another (e.g. languages like English would draw a structural distinction between specifiers and adjuncts, but languages like Japanese and Welsh would not). If this were so then it would follow that one of the parameters which the child acquiring a language would have to set would be a *configurationality* parameter: this would determine whether the language is *strongly configurational* (e.g. projects specifiers, complements and adjuncts into structurally distinct positions), *weakly configurational* (e.g. projects complements into a different structural position from non-complements, but makes no structural distinction between adjuncts and specifiers), or *nonconfigurational* (i.e. makes no structural distinction between different classes of non-head constituents, e.g. specifiers, complements, and adjuncts).

It might seem at first sight as if the existence of such a configurationality parameter would undermine any suggestion that constituency relations are universal. However, this is not necessarily so, since constituency universals could be reformulated as *implicational* universals (in the sense of Greenberg 1966, or Hawkins 1983). Thus, UG might specify (e.g.) that

> 'If a language is nonconfigurational, it will project all nonhead constituents as sisters of their heads; if a language has a configurationally distinct class of adjuncts, these will serve to (recursively) project a given constituent X^n into another constituent X^n of the same categorial status; if a language has a configurationally distinct class of specifiers, these will have the configurational status of daughters of the maximal projection X^m of the head X, and sisters of a non-maximal projection X^{m-1}.'

Given this view, then constituency relations would indeed be universal, in the sense that if a given language L has a structurally distinct class of specifiers, the hierarchical position occupied by specifiers in L will be determined by UG. However, there seems little point in speculating further about the configurationality parameter: its uncertain status can be illustrated by the debate in the published literature about the (non-)configurational status of Japanese: thus, Hale (1981, 1982, 1983) and Farmer (1984) argue that Japanese is a *nonconfigurational* language; Fukui (1986) argues that it is *weakly configurational* (in that it has no distinct class of specifiers); and Gunji (1987) – working within a different framework – in effect assumes that it is *strongly configurational* (i.e. that it has a structurally distinct class of specifiers). In order to avoid becoming ensnared in a tangled web of configurationality, we shall assume that if there is indeed a configurationality parameter, young children acquiring English come to 'realize' at a very early age that English is a *strongly configurational* language (perhaps as a consequence of its relatively fixed word order, etc.)

An additional class of parameters which children will have to set are *linearity* parameters – that is, parameters which determine the linear ordering of constituents. As we noted in chapter 1, it is abundantly clear that the relative linear ordering of heads, complements, adjuncts, and specifiers will vary from one language to another. For example, in English (and many other languages) heads generally precede their complements; however, there are also languages in which heads follow their complements, as illustrated by the Korean examples in (15) below:

(15)   (a)   Moonul dateora
               Door close (= 'Close the door!')

        (b)   byunhwa-edaehan kalmangul
               change-for desire (= 'desire for change')

In the English translation of the examples in (15), we see that the head verb *close* precedes its complement *the door*; the head noun *desire* precedes its complement *for change*; and the head preposition *for* precedes its complement *change*: thus, English consistently positions heads before complements, and so might be said to be a *head-first* language. By contrast, we find precisely the opposite ordering in Korean. More specifically, the head verb *dateora* follows its complement *moonul*; the head noun *kalmangul* follows its complement *byunhwa-edaehan*; and the head preposition *edaehan* follows its complement *byunhwa* (and so might more appropriately be called a *postposition*). Since Korean consistently positions heads *after* their complements, it might be said to be a *head-last* language. Given that English is head-first and Korean is head-last, it is clear that the relative ordering of heads and complements is one linearity (i.e word-order) parameter along which languages will differ.

It should be noted, however, that word-order variation between languages falls within narrowly circumscribed limits: there are no languages in which (e.g.) some head verbs are positioned before their complements and others after, and no languages in which (e.g.) verbs which take two complements are systematically positioned between the two complements. This suggests that word-order variation between languages is heavily constrained: for example, the head/complement parameter would appear to be a binary parameter allowing only two (unmarked, i.e. 'normal') settings (head-first or head-last). In much the same way (although we shall not illustrate this here), languages also vary with respect to whether they position *adjuncts* to the right or left of the single-bar constituents to which they are adjoined, and similarly vary with regard to whether they position specifiers as the leftmost or rightmost constituents of their containing phrases. It would seem likely that all word-order parameters allow for strictly binary choices, so that in mastering the relative ordering of constituents within a given structure in a given language, the child will in essence have to set the value of the following three parameters:

(16)   (i)   *head* parameter: head-first or head-last
       (ii)   *adjunct* parameter: adjunct-first or adjunct-last
       (iii) *specifier* parameter: specifier-first or specifier-last

It should, of course, be pointed out that this is a vast oversimplification of a complex set of phenomena (e.g. sometimes both choices are permitted, particularly in the case of adjuncts, with syntactic and/or stylistic factors determining the preferred setting in specific contexts), but it will suffice for expository purposes. It should also be noted that recent theoretical work has attempted to derive what appear to be simple word-order parameters from more abstract theoretical principles, relating to the canonical directionality of government (cf. e.g. Kayne 1984, Hoekstra 1984), case-marking (cf. e.g. Stowell 1981, Chomsky 1981, Travis 1984, and Fassi Fehri 1988), theta-marking (cf. e.g. Koopman 1984 and Travis 1984), or predication (cf. Travis 1984). Much of the relevant work is highly technical in nature, and it would lead us too far astray to attempt to discuss it here.

What we are suggesting is that since the ordering of constituents varies from language to language, the child will be faced with the acquisition task of determining from his linguistic experience (e.g. the adult speech which he hears around him) the appropriate setting for each of the word order parameters in (16). However, if each of the relevant linearity parameters involves a binary choice, then the acquisition task for the child will be a relatively simple one: indeed, this is all the more so as minimal linguistic experience would be required in order to set each of the relevant parameters. For example, given that parameters are categorially based, once a child is able to parse an utterance such as 'Close the door!', he will be able to infer from the fact that the verb *close* in English precedes its complement *the door*, that *all verbs* in English precede their complements (since Universal Grammar excludes the possibility that some verbs may precede and others follow their complements). If we further assume that (in the unmarked case, i.e. 'normally') a given parameter has the same value across categories, then the child will also be able to hypothesize that not just verbs, but all other categories (adjectives, nouns, prepositions, etc.) likewise precede their complements in English. Thus, the task of setting word order parameters is one which requires minimal linguistic experience.

If our reasoning here is along the right lines, then it follows that the task facing the child in learning how to project word categories into phrase categories may ultimately reduce to the relatively trivial one of setting a few directionality (i.e. ordering) parameters. Furthermore, if (as we have suggested) these parameters involve simple binary choices which can be made on the basis of minimal linguistic experience, then we should expect to find evidence that the basic projection schema for English (5) is acquired at a very early age indeed.

Thus, we have two reasons for thinking that the principles of *projection* will come into operation at the same stage of development as the principles of *categorization*. The first is that projection is itself an inherently categorial process by which head categories are combined with other categories to form phrasal categories, so that projection is an indissoluble part of categorization. The second is that Universal Grammar endows the child with an innate knowledge of the principles of projection, and leaves him only the relatively trivial acquisition task of determining the *directionality* of the various projection parameters (i.e. the relative ordering of heads, complements, adjuncts, and specifiers). This leads us to hypothesize that once we have evidence that children have developed the four primary lexical word categories N, V, P and A, we will also find evidence that they 'know' how to project them into the corresponding phrasal categories NP, VP, PP and AP, and thus have developed an N-system, V-system, P-system, and A-system. We shall argue here that this prediction is entirely correct.

We shall begin by arguing that children, from the very onset of categorization, 'know' how to project N into NP, and have thus developed a relatively complex N-system. From a very early age indeed, we find that children seem to 'know' how to project N into N-bar by the addition of a following nominal complement, so resulting in [Noun + complement] structures such as those bracketed in (17) below:

(17)   (a)   [*Cup* tea] (= 'a cup of tea', Stefan 17)
       (b)   [*Bottle* juice] (= 'a bottle of juice', Lucy 20)
       (c)   [*Picture* Gia] (= 'a picture of Gia', *Gia 20)
       (d)   Want [*piece* bar] (= 'I want a piece of the chocolate bar', Daniel 20)
       (e)   Have [*drink* orange] (= 'I want to have a drink of orange', Jem 21)
       (f)   Want [*cup* tea] (Jenny 21)
       (g)   [*Cup* tea] ready (John 22)
       (h)   [*Picture* Kendall]. [*Picture* water] (= 'a picture of Kendall/water', *Kendall 23)
       (i)   Blue [*ball* wool] (*Jonathan 23)
       (j)   [*Drink* water] (= 'a drink of water', Paula 23, *Jonathan 24)
       (k)   [*Colour* crate] (= 'The colour of the crate', Anna 24).
       (l)   [*Colour* new shoes] (= 'The colour of my new shoes', Anna 24)

Such structures are by no means common at this stage, but I assume that this is an 'accidental' lexical gap attributable to the fact that most of the nouns in the child's early vocabulary are concrete nouns which do not take complements. Structures like (17) show the complement consistently positioned after the italicized head noun, so suggesting that the head/complement parameter is correctly set at its appropriate head-first value very early indeed (as we predicted). An additional point of interest about child nominals such as (17) is the fact that they show no use of the preposition *of* which would be required before the complement in adult English: if we analyse adult *of* here as a nonthematic constituent and perhaps a *functor* (cf. the relevant discussion in the next chapter), then the fact that the child omits *of* is clearly consistent with our overall hypothesis that children at this stage have developed purely lexical-thematic structures, and have not yet acquired the grammar of functional or nonthematic constituents.

If we posit that children 'know' how to project head nouns into N-bar constituents from a very early age, the obvious question to ask next is whether they also 'know' how to recursively project N-bar constituents into other N-bar constituents by the addition of an appropriate kind of *adjunct* phrase. Given that (in the adult English target system) an N-bar such as [*cup of tea*] can be projected into a further N-bar by the addition of a preceding adjectival adjunct such as *hot*, and given that the resultant N-bar [*hot cup of tea*] can then be further expanded into another N-bar by the addition of another preceding adjectival adjunct such as *nice* so resulting in the N-bar [*nice hot cup of tea*], we might wonder whether children at this stage have acquired the syntax of nominal adjuncts (i.e. of attributive adjectives).

There seems to be abundant evidence that children do indeed 'know' at a very early age that adjectives can be used to premodify nominal constituents, as the following examples illustrate (where the premodifying adjective is italicized):

(18)   (a)   *Nice* book. *Good* girl. *Blue* bead (Paula 18)
        (b)   *Blue* dress. *Red* dress (Hayley 20)
        (c)   *Naughty* boy. *Big* teddy (Bethan 20)
        (d)   *Red* slide. *Big* puss (Lucy 20)
        (e)   *Dirty* diaper (*Allison 20)
        (f)   *Dirty* soap. *Black* hair (*Kathryn 21)
        (g)   *Green* cup. *Tiny* cow (*Allison 22)
        (h)   *Bad* boy (John 22)

This is generally a (potentially) productive process at this stage, as the following examples illustrate (the examples in (19)(a) being taken from a single 45-minute recording of Jem at age 21 months, and those in (19)(b) being taken from Braine 1976: 32):

(19)   (a)   *Blue* pen. *Brown* horsey. *Black* hair. *Orange* hair. *Yellow* book. *Green* tree. *Nice* fire. *Big* castle. *Big* ball. *Big* car. *Big* potato. *Big* pen. *Big* cup. *Big* 'O'. *Little* 'P'. *Little* cup. *High* mountain. *High* castle. *Hot* bath. *Naughty* cow. *Naughty* man. *Bad* pen. *Bad* man. *Honest* man. *Nice* lady. *Dirty* boots (Jem 21)
        (b)   *Big* plane. *Big* book. *Big* car. *Big* stick. *Big* rock. *Big* ball. *Big* chicken. *Big* lamb. *Big* dog. *Big* bread. *Big* tower. *Big* duck. *Little* stick. *Little* rock. *Little* ball. *Little* plane. *Little* lamb. *Little* key. *Little* duck. *Little* bread. *Red* car. *Blue* car. *Green* car. *Red* block. *Blue* block. *Blue* ball wool. *Green* light. *Hot* light. *Hot* stick. *Hot* pipe. *Clean* diaper. *Old* carrot (*Jonathan 23)

It seems reasonable to suppose that the italicized adjective in such examples functions as an adjunct to a following N-bar which generally comprises simply a head N, but in the case of the example 'blue *ball wool*' comprises a head N *ball* and a following complement *wool*.

Of course, if attributive adjectives do function as nominal adjuncts in early child speech, then we should expect to find that they can be recursively *stacked* in front of the nominals they modify: and indeed children do seem to be 'aware' of the possibility of stacking multiple adjectives in front of nominals at an early age, as the following examples illustrate:

(20) (a) *Big heavy* book. *Big heavy* boat (Jem 21)
      (b) *Little yellow* one. *Nice yellow* pen. *Nice heavy* book. *New green* bubbles. *Nice clean new* bed (Jem 23)
      (c) *Nice little* chicken (Chrissie 23)
      (d) *Nice new* smarties. *Nice new* ball (Jem 24)
      (e) *Nice little* pussycat (Lucy 24)

This is a phenomenon which is 'predicted' by the adjunct analysis (under which an attributive AP recursively expands an N-bar into another N-bar).

An obvious question to ask, however, is what empirical evidence there is that the nominals to which attributive adjectives are adjoined are N-bar constituents (rather than e.g. simple N constituents). Part of the relevant evidence comes from *one*-pronominalization facts. We might suppose that a child overhearing a simple conversation such as:

(21) SPEAKER A: Feel like making me a *cup of coffee?*
      SPEAKER B: A black *one?*
      SPEAKER A: No, A white *one*

should be able to infer that the proform *one* can have as its antecedent a [Noun + complement] sequence like *cup of coffee*, and conclude that *one* functions as an N-bar proform.

Now, from a very early age indeed, children use attributive adjectives to premodify the N-bar proform *one*, as the following examples illustrate:

(22) (a) *Yellow* one (Paula 18)
      (b) *Big* one (Bethan 20)
      (c) *Fat* one (Lucy 20)
      (d) *Dirty* one (+Neil 21)

(e)   You got *yellow* one (Angharad 23)
(f)   *Red* one (Lucy 24)

It seems reasonable to suppose that children 'realise' that *one* can be used to replace a whole N-bar such as *cup of coffee*, but cannot simply replace the head N *cup* (cf. **I'd like a black *cup/*one* of coffee'). Moreover, they also seem to 'know' that a nominal together with a premodifying attributive AP also functions as an N-bar, and so can serve as the antecedent for *one*. The evidence for claiming this comes from sequences such as the following:

(23)   (a)   ADULT: Here's a *tiny bar of chocolate*
             CHILD: Do you want to have that *one*? (Heather 26)
       (b)   I'll get *new car* for him. I've got *one* in my postbag (Heather 26)
       (c)   That's a *brown eye*. Another *brown eye*. No, that *one* (Sarah 26)

Although these examples are from children at a more advanced *functional* stage of grammatical development, they suggest that at a very early age, young children 'know' that *one* can refer to N-bar sequences like *tiny bar of chocolate*, *new car*, or *brown eye*. What is much more significant, however, is proform evidence relating to NPs containing more than one prenominal AP. In this regard, consider the evidence provided by the following 'replacement sequence', produced by Jem at age 23 months:

(24)   Nice *yellow pen*, nice *one* (Jem 23)

Braine (1971) argues that (as if rehearsing structural paradigms) children frequently produce sequences of two or more parallel structures in which a given constituent in the first structure is replaced by an equivalent constituent in the second: he calls these 'replacement sequences'. What Jem appears to have done in (24) is replace the italicized sequence *yellow pen* by the proform *one*, so suggesting that the sequence *yellow pen* is an N-bar constituent: but this is precisely what the analysis of attributive APs as N-bar adjuncts would lead us to expect (since *pen*, *yellow pen*, and *nice yellow pen* would all be N-bar constituents under the adjunct analysis).

   Of course, what data like (24) tell us is that very young children seem to 'know' that in sequences where two attributive APs are used to premodify a nominal, the second AP forms an N-bar together with the following nominal. But the adjunct analysis predicts that the overall sequence of both APs together with the nominal also forms an N-bar, and so can serve as the antecedent of the N-bar proform *one*. Hence, the obvious question to ask is whether we have any empirical evidence from child speech that children are 'aware' of this. The answer is that indeed we do have such evidence, from exchanges such as the following:

(25)   ADULT: Ah! *Nice little chicken*!
        CHILD: Stroke that *one* (Chrissie 23)

The very fact that Chrissie appears to use the proform *one* to refer back to the whole italicized sequence of two attributive APs and a head nominal suggests that she is 'aware' that attributive APs are N-bar adjuncts which recursively expand one N-bar into another (it has to be admitted, of course, that the evidence is equivocal to the extent that it is not possible to 'prove' that the antecedent of *one* is not *little chicken* or simply *chicken*; nor indeed is it possible to prove that *one* isn't being used in a deictic fashion, without any linguistic antecedent, to refer directly to the chicken).

It goes without saying that any analysis of child syntax based on naturalistic speech samples is bound to be grossly *underdetermined* by the data (firstly because we often have insufficient data to draw firm conclusions, and secondly because the evidence provided by the data which we do have is often equivocal). However, there seem to be reasonable empirical grounds for supposing that attributive APs have the status of N-bar adjuncts in early child English, and that the child correctly sets the *adjunct parameter* from the very start (so that attributive adjectives unerringly precede the nominals they modify).

Although we have so far confined our discussion of N-bar adjuncts here to adjectival premodifiers, a second potential source of adjuncts are *nominal* premodifiers such as the italicized expressions in (26) below:

(26)   (a) *biscuit* box (Dewi 18)
        (b) *milk* lorry (Elen 19)
        (c) *bubble* liquid (Daniel 20)
        (d) *animal* book (*Gia 20, holding book about animals)
        (e) *money* box (+Samantha 21)
        (f) *teddy* bear; *dustbin* man (Bethan 21)
        (g) *beach* ball; *pussy* cat (Jem 21)

(h) *tiger* book; *bear* book; *puppy* book; *baby* book (= book about babies); *bread* book (= book about making bread); *jewelry* pin; *party* hat; *coffee* cake; *cottage* cheese (*Kathryn 21–22)
(i) *apple* juice; *grocery* store; *chocolate chip* cookie (*Allison 22)
(j) *chocolate* biscuit; *chocolate* sweet; *golf* ball (Daniel 23)
(k) *Christmas* tree (Jem 23)
(l) *wine* gum; *sweetie* gum (Leigh 24)

If we were to analyse the italicized nominal premodifiers in (26) in much the same way as we analysed attributive adjectivals, then we might suppose that the italicized expressions are NPs which function as N-bar adjuncts. This would then mean that both APs and NPs can function as N-bar adjuncts in early child English.

However, an alternative analysis of nominal premodifiers would be to posit that the overall expressions containing them are *compound nouns* of the following schematic form:

(27) $[_N [_N \text{modifier}] [_N \text{head}]]$

where the right-hand N is the head, and the left-hand N is the premodifier. The *compound* analysis in (27) would amount to analysing the premodifier as a noun which functions as an adjunct to the head noun. One of the predictions made by such an analysis is that nouns can be recursively compounded with other nouns: and the expression *chocolate chip cookie* in (26)(i) would appear to bear out this prediction – at least, if we assume that it is a trimorphemic compound of the form:

(28) $[_N [_N [_N \text{chocolate}] [_N \text{chip}]] [_N \text{cookie}]]$

A second prediction made by the *compound noun* analysis is that none of the nouns in the compound would be replaceable by *one*, since *one* is an N-bar proform, and each of the nouns in the compound has the status of N, not of N-bar. It is true of my own data (and is true of the data reported in the literature, as far as I am aware) that we do not find compound nouns containing *one* (e.g. we don't find that compound nouns such as *beach ball* have pronominal counterparts such as *beach one). In this respect, nominal premodifiers contrast sharply with adjectival premodifiers, since the latter (but not the former) can be followed by *one* (e.g. *new car* has the pronominal counterpart *new one*, as we have already seen). Of course, given the *underdeterminacy* problem posed by naturalistic studies, it is not possible to prove that this is a systematic rather than an accidental gap – but the evidence is suggestive.

A third prediction made by the compound noun analysis is that adjectival premodifiers will always be positioned before nominal premodifiers (so that children would be predicted to say *big beach ball*, but not **beach big ball*). Empirical support for this claim comes from utterances such as the following:

(29)   *big* teddy bear (Jem 21)

where the adjectival premodifier *big* precedes the nominal premodifier *teddy*. Of course, a single example is a grossly inadequate basis from which to generalize (and reflects once again the obvious problem of underdeterminacy). However, in default of evidence to the contrary, I shall assume that [Noun + Noun] sequences in early child speech are compound nouns, but that in [Adjective + Nominal] sequences, attributive adjectives function as N-bar adjuncts (so that the nominal which they premodify has the status of an N-bar).

Having argued that children at the initial stage of their categorial development (typically in the age-range 20–23 months, ±20%) 'know' how to project N into N-bar by the addition of a following nominal complement, and likewise 'know' how to recursively project N-bar into a further N-bar by the addition of a preceding adjectival adjunct, the obvious question which it remains for us to ask is whether they likewise 'know' how to project an N-bar into a full NP by the addition of a preceding specifier phrase. It has frequently been suggested in relation to adult grammars that possessor phrases (i.e. phrases denoting possessors) universally function as nominal specifiers (underlyingly, at least). If this is so, then we might conjecture that this is part of the 'innate knowledge' with which Universal Grammar endows the child: this in turn would lead us to expect that children would 'know' that possessors function as nominal specifiers which serve to expand N-bar into NP. In the light of this conjecture, it is interesting to note that we find numerous examples of possessive structures in early child English, as illustrated by the examples below (where the possessor NP is italicized):

(30)   (a)   *Mummy* [car]. *Mummy* [tea]. *Daddy* [hat] (Stefan 17)
         (b)   *Mummy* [coat]. *Daddy* [shoe] (Daniel 19)
         (c)   *Dolly* [hat]. *Mommy* [key]. *Lamb* [ear]. *Gia* [eyes] (*Gia 19-20)
         (d)   *Hayley* [dress]. *Hayley* [book] (Hayley 20)
         (e)   *Baby* [cup] (*Allison 20)
         (f)   *Claire* [pencil] (Alison 21)
         (g)   *Nana* [key] (Daniel 21)

(h)   *Tiger* [tail]. *Sheep* [ear]. *Kathryn* [sock] (*Kathryn 21)
(i)   *Big teddy bear* [supper]. *Baby* [supper]. *Baby* [feet]. *Jem* [chair]. *Mummy* [box] (Jem 21)
(j)   *Dewi* [party]. *Mummy* [bag]. *Mummy* [key] (Daniel 23)
(k)   *Nicola* [man] [= 'Nicola's boyfriend'] (Claire 23)
(l)   *Kendall* [rocking chair]. *Kimmy* [bike]. *Kendall* [pail]. *Kimmy* [pail]. *Kendall* [turn]. *Papa* [door] (*Kendall 23)
(m)   *Teddy* [colour] (Lucy 24)
(n)   *Mommy* [chair]. *Mommy* [shoe]. *Claire* [pencil]. *Claire* [eye] (*Claire 24)

Given the assumption that possessors are (underlyingly) specifiers, the most likely analysis of the data in (30) would be to posit that the italicized possessive phrase functions in each case as the specifier of the bracketed nominal (which we might suppose to have the status of an N-bar comprising a head noun without a complement).

If possessive phrases have the status of specifiers expanding N-bar into NP in early child English, then it follows (from our earlier assumptions) that they will precede attributive adjectives (since these function as N-bar adjuncts and thus are contained within N-bar). Some empirical evidence that this is in fact the case comes from examples such as the following:

(31)   (a)   *Mummy* [blue dress] (Hayley 20)
       (b)   *Daddy* [new car] (John 22)

The relative position of possessive and adjectival prenominal modifiers is thus entirely as predicted. More generally still, if the analyses presented here are along the right lines, then it would seem that even by the age of one-and-three-quarters, young children 'know' that N-bar can be projected into NP by the addition of a preceding possessive specifier, and that they unerringly set the specifier parameter at the specifier-first value appropriate for English. The systematic absence of possessive *'s* in structures such as (30) and (31) is a feature which we will comment on in detail in the next chapter: suffice it to note for the time being that if *'s* is analysed as a *functor*, then its absence follows from our overall hypothesis that the earliest utterances produced by young children involve purely *lexical* structures which lack functional categories.

From all the evidence we have presented here, there seems little doubt that at the very earliest stage of their categorial development, children have developed a complex N-system, and thus 'know' how to form compound nouns, how to project N into N-bar by the addition of a following complement, how to recursively project N-bar into N-bar by the addition of a preceding adjectival adjunct, and how to project N-bar into NP by the addition of a preceding possessive specifier. Not surprisingly, we find parallel evidence that they have also developed a V-system. Thus, children at a very early age seem to 'know' how to project V into V-bar by the addition of a following complement, so forming V-bar structures such as those bracketed in the examples below (where the head V is italicized):

(32) (a) Paula [*play* with ball]. [*Open* box]. [*Go* in]. [*Get* out] (Paula 18)

(b) [*Want* Teddy]. [*Want* money]. [*Want* coat]. [*Want* drink]. [*Want* bubble]. [*Want* down]. [*Want* in]. [*Want* out]. [*Open* door]. [*Have* money] (Daniel 19)

(c) Hayley [*draw* boat]. [*Sit* down]. [*Want* Lisa]. [*Turn* page]. [*Reading* book]. [*Want* duck]. [*Want* boot] (Hayley 20)

(d) [*Coming* to rubbish]. [*Go* in]. [*Get* out]. Bethan [*sit* down]. [*Gone* out]. [*Going* round]. [*Getting* out]. [*Come* off] (Bethan 20–21)

(e) [*Touch* heads]. [*Cuddle* book]. [*Want* crayons]. [*Want* malteser]. [*Open* door]. [*Want* biscuit]. [*Bang* bottom]. [*See* cats]. [*Sit* down] (Jem 21)

(f) Baby Allison [*comb* hair]. Baby [*eat* cookies]. [*Get* Mommy cookie]. [*Open* can]. [*Wiping* baby chin]. [*Pour* Mommy juice]. [*Peeking* Mommy]. [*Get* toys]. [*Open* box]. Baby doll [*ride* truck]. [*Help* baby]. [*Get* diaper]. [*Standing* up]. [*Help* cow in table]. [*Sit* down]. Man [*drive* truck]. Baby [*open* door]. [*Walking* around] (*Allison 22).

The fact that the complement is consistently positioned after the head verb provides obvious corroboration of our suggestion that the head/complement parameter is correctly set at an early age.

Given that children have begun to master the syntax of verbal complements at this stage, an obvious question to ask is whether they have likewise mastered the syntax of verbal adjuncts. One possible source of adjuncts are adverbials such as *more* and *no(t)*: it may well be that these function as V-bar adjuncts in structures such as (33) below:

(33) (a) Gia [*more* read book]. [*More* write] (*Gia 20)

(b) [*More* read]. [*More* sing]. [*More* walk] (*Andrew 19–23)

(c)   Man [*no* go in there]. Kathryn [*no* fix this]. Kathryn [*no* like celery] (*Kathryn 22)

Thus, *more* in (33)(a) and (b) may serve as an adjunct to the V-bar constituents [*read book*], [*write*], [*read*] and [*sing*] which follow it (though other possibilities might be envisaged, e.g. that *more* is analysed as a verb like *want*): likewise, *no* in (33)(c) might be analysed as an adjunct to the V-bars [*go in there*], [*fix this*], and [*like celery*] (but might alternatively be a verb). If this is so, then it means that children have begun to acquire a (restricted) class of V-bar adjuncts at this stage. An additional point of interest is the fact that the *adjunct-first* order found in verb phrases such as (33) parallels the same order found in noun phrases such as (18–20), thereby highlighting the apparent symmetry in the various categorial systems developed by young children.

Given the evidence presented above that children (by the age of one-and-three-quarters or so) have begun to acquire the syntax of verbal complements and adjuncts, the remaining question which we need to address is whether or not we have parallel evidence that they have likewise begun to acquire the syntax of verbal *specifiers*. It seems reasonable to hypothesize that Universal Grammar identifies for the child the nature and function of specifiers: for example, we might suppose that UG determines that the specifiers of lexical categories are their *subjects*. If this is so, then it follows that the specifier of a V-bar constituent (comprising a head V and any complements it may have) will be the subject of the V-bar. This in turn might lead us to suggest that early child clauses such as those in (34) below should be analysed as verb phrases in which the italicized subject NP functions as the specifier of the bracketed V-bar:

(34)   (a)   *Paula* [play with ball]. *Daddy* [gone] (Paula 18)
        (b)   *Hayley* [draw boat]. *Baby* [talking] (Hayley 20)
        (c)   *Bethan* [want one]. *Bethan* [sit down]. *Geraint* [gone]. *Blanket* [gone] (Bethan 20)
        (d)   *Mommy* [push]. *Mommy* [pull]. *Lois* [coming]. *Kathryn* [want raisin]. *Machine* [make noise] (*Kathryn 21)
        (e)   *Daddy* [come]. *Daddy* [coming]. *Helen* [ride] (*Helen 21)
        (f)   *Baby Allison* [comb hair]. *Baby* [eat cookies]. *Mommy* [eat cookie]. *Mommy* [open]. *Baby* [ride truck]. *Horse* [tumble]. *Man* [drive truck]. *Baby* [drive truck]. *Baby* [open door] (*Allison 22)
        (g)   *Kendall* [sit]. *Kendall* [read]. *Daddy* [hide]. *Daddy* [write]. *Kimmy* [bite]. *Horse* [run] (*Kendall 22)

Given this assumption, a child clause such as (34)(f) *Baby eat cookies* would have the structure:

(35)   [$_{\text{VP}}$ [$_{\text{NP}}$ Baby] [$_{\text{V'}}$ [$_{\text{V}}$ eat] [$_{\text{NP}}$ cookies]]]

(cf. the parallel assumption made by Guilfoyle and Noonan 1988). The subject NP *baby* would then be analysed as the specifier of the V-bar [*eat cookies*], and accordingly would serve the structural function of expanding the V-bar into a full verb phrase (the resultant verb phrase being in effect a verbal clause). Such an analysis would be in keeping with the widespread assumption in recent work on adult grammars that the subjects of verbs must originate as V-bar specifiers in order to receive an appropriate theta-role from the relevant V-bar (cf. e.g. Hoekstra 1984, Sportiche 1988, Kuroda 1987, Fassi Fehri 1988, and many others).

In the same way as we have evidence that young children in the initial stages of categorization develop an N-system and a V-system, we likewise have evidence that they develop a P-system. Thus, they clearly 'know' from a very young age that P can be projected into P-bar by the addition of a following complement, as examples such as (36) below illustrate (where the P-bar constituents are bracketed, and the head P is italicized):

(36)   (a)   Paula play [*with* ball]. [*In* there], mummy. Put [*in* there]. Go [*in* there]. Hat [*on* baby] (Paula 18)
        (b)   Sit [*on* Teddy] (Dewi 18)
        (c)   [*In* there] (Elen 19)
        (d)   [*In* water]. [*In* bag]. Mouse [*in* window]. [*In* there]. Put [*in* there] (Hayley 20)
        (e)   [*Round* here]. Coming [*to* rubbish]. [*In* there]. [*Out* there]. [*Up* there]. [*Over* there] (Bethan 20–21)
        (f)   [*In* bag]. Baby [*down* chair]. Help cow [*in* table] (*Allison 22)
        (g)   [*In* there]. Want get [*out* cot]. Go [*in* there]. Push [*in* there]. Lots [*in* here]. Telephone [*in* there]. Not [*in* there]. Gone [*down* there]. [*To* mirror]. (Angharad 22)
        (h)   [*Without* shoe]. Pee [*with* potty]. Peep [*in* key hole]. Stephen [*in* school]. Go [*to* nice lady]. Jem draw [*on* carpet]. Jem draw [*on* box] (Jem 23)

It is surely significant that we find the same *head-first* order in P-bar structures as in the V-bar and N-bar structures which we looked at earlier (suggesting an obvious cross-categorial symmetry). Moreover, we find a few sporadic examples of prepositional adjuncts (i.e. P-bar adjuncts) at around the same period: cf. examples such as the following (where the adjunct is italicized):

(37) (a) [*Right* down] (*Eve 18)
      (b) Go [*right* down] (Leila 23)
      (c) Her go [*back* in] (Jem 23)
      (d) Got it [*right* in] (Michael 24)

Once again, we find the same *adjunct-first* order as we observed earlier in the child's V-system and N-system.

   Given the evidence that children have begun to master the syntax of prepositional complements and adjuncts at this stage, we might wonder whether they have likewise mastered the syntax of prepositional speci- fiers as well. One possible source of these can be found in clausal constructions such as the following, where the italicized NP would appear to function as the subject of the bracketed prepositional predi- cate, the overall [subject + predicate] structure forming a *prepositional clause* (in the sense that a child utterance such as 'Book on table' resembles the (similarly verbless) prepositional clauses found in adult languages such as Arabic or Russian, and corresponds to an English clause such as 'The book is on the table'):

(38) (a) *Doggy* [down] (+Olivia 18)
      (b) *Mouse* [in window] (Hayley 20)
      (c) *Coat* [off]. *Coat* [on]. *Paper* [off]. *Crayon* [under] (Bethan 20–21)
      (d) *Top* [on] (Lucy 20)
      (e) *Lorry* [out]. *Daddy* [away]. *Mummy* [away] (Jem 21)
      (f) *Wayne* [in bedroom] (Daniel 21)
      (g) *Bubble* [on dungaree] (Daniel 21)
      (h) *Dolly* [in]. *Nut* [off]. *Nut* [out]. *Lid* [on] (*Helen 21)
      (i) *Bear* [in chair] (+Gerald 21)
      (j) *Plates* [out] (*Richard 22, wanting to get plates out of cupboard)
      (k) *Lid* [off] (Angharad 22)
      (l) *Hat* [off]. *Santa head* [off]. *Head* [on]. *White sweater* [off]. *White sweater* [on]. *Salt* [on]. *Scarf* [off]. *Sleeves* [up]. *Red shoe* [up] (*Susan 22)
      (m) *Baby* [down chair]. *Diaper* [out]. *Skirt* [on]. *Blouse* [on]. *Truck* [outside]. *Cow* [out] (*Allison 22)

(n)   *'Frigerator* [on]. *Slipper* [on]. *Mommy* [in]. *Shoe* [off]. *Hat* [on]. *Lotion* [away]. *Ear* [outside]. *Kendall* [down] (*Kendall 22–23)

(o)   *Clock* [on there]. *Light* [up there]. *Kitty* [down there]. *Cover* [down there]. *Boot* [off]. *Light* [off]. *Pants* [off]. *Shirt* [off]. *Papa* [away] (*Andrew 18–23)

(p)   *Stephen* [in school]. *Top* [on] (Jem 23)

(q)   *Teaparty* [up there]. *That* [down there]. *That* [on] (Claire 23)

(r)   *Dolly* [on horsey]. *Mess* [on legs] (Daniel 23–24)

(s)   *Shoes* [on]. *Hat* [on]. *Socks* [on] (*Jonathan 23–24)

(t)   *Pixie* [outside]. *Daddy* [in there]. *Mummy* [in there] (*Claire 24)

If we posit that the specifiers of lexical categories are (underlyingly) their subjects, we might suppose that in child prepositional clauses such as (38) above the italicized subject NP serves as the specifier of the bracketed P-bar predicate. If this is so, then a child prepositional clause such as (38)(b) *Mouse in window* would be analysed in the manner indicated in (39) below:

(39) $[_{PP} [_{NP} \text{Mouse}] [_{P'} [_{P} \text{in}] [_{NP} \text{window}]]]$

with the NP *mouse* functioning as the subject and specifier of the predicative P-bar [*in window*].

It might at first sight seem rather strange that *clausal* structures like those in (38) should be analysed as *phrases*. However, within Chomsky's *Barriers* system of categories there is no real distinction between clauses and phrases, since all clauses are analysed as phrases – viz. as phrasal projections of a head word-level category. For example, 'Ordinary Clauses' (in the sense of Radford 1988a) are analysed as CP (= complementizer phrase) constituents, i.e. as phrasal projections of a head complementizer constituent. Likewise, 'Exceptional Clauses' (in the sense of Radford 1988a) are analysed as IP (= inflection phrase) constituents, hence as phrasal projections of a head inflection constituent. Similarly, 'Small Clauses' are analysed (following Stowell 1981) as phrasal projections of a head lexical category, so that a Small Clause with a prepositional predicate would be analysed as a prepositional phrase, i.e. as a phrasal projection of a head preposition. Given these assumptions, the various types of clause bracketed in the examples in (40) below:

(40)   (a)   I consider [that John is over the limit]
      (b)   I consider [John to be over the limit]
      (c)   I consider [John over the limit]

would be analysed as phrases with the following (simplified) structure:

(41)   (a) $[_{CP}$ $[_{C}$ that] John is over the limit]
      (b) $[_{IP}$ John $[_{I}$ to] be over the limit]
      (c) $[_{PP}$ John $[_{P}$ over] the limit]

Thus, the Ordinary Clause bracketed in (40)(a) would be analysed as a complementizer phrase (CP) in (41)(a), the Exceptional Clause bracketed in (40)(b) would be analysed as an inflection phrase (IP) in (41)(b), and the (prepositional) Small Clause bracketed in (40)(c) would be analysed as a prepositional phrase in (41)(c). It follows that, within the framework adopted here, all *clauses* are reanalysed as *phrases*: thus, in saying that the child clauses in (38) are prepositional phrases, what we are in effect saying is that they have much the same internal constituent structure as adult prepositional Small Clauses like that bracketed in (40)(c).

Given that children have relatively well developed N-, V- and P-systems at this stage, we might expect to find evidence that they have developed an equally complex A-system. However, the evidence that they 'know' how to project A into A-bar by the addition of a following complement is decidedly sparse: in fact, I have only one example in my corpus of an [Adjective + Complement] structure produced by a child under two years of age, namely:

(42)   You be [*good* to me], mummy! (Holly 23)

There are a number of factors which might account for the comparative rarity of [Adjective + Complement] structures in early child English. One is that the first adjectives acquired by young children (viz. items like *big/small*, *hot/cold*, *good/bad*, *nice/naughty*, *clean/dirty*, *red/yellow/green* etc.) are adjectives which (in adult speech) either never take complements, or do so only rarely. A second factor may be that many adjectival complements are prepositional phrases headed by an idiosyncratic (hence unpredictable and difficult to learn) preposition (e.g. 'keen *on*...', 'proud *of*...', 'cross *with*...', etc.). A third factor may be that prenominal attributive adjectives never permit complements (cf. *'a proud *of his achievements* athlete').

However, we have rather more substantial evidence that children have begun to master the syntax of A-bar adjuncts at this stage. From a very early age, we find children using expressions such as *very*, *too*, *bit*, *no*, etc. as adjuncts to adjectival constituents, as examples such as the following illustrate:

(43)   (a)   [*Very* good] (Bethan 21)
        (b)   Sausage [*bit* hot]. [*No* good] (Jem 23)
        (c)   [*Very* good] (Paula 23)
        (d)   [*Very very* naughty] (Chrissie 23)
        (e)   [Very *nice*] mouse. David [*too* small] (Holly 23)

Indeed, examples such as (43)(d) *very very naughty* seem to suggest that even very young children are 'aware' of the possibility of recursively stacking (or perhaps iterating) adjectival adjuncts. Given the evidence that children have begun to acquire the syntax of adjectival complements and adjuncts at this stage, a natural question to ask is whether they have likewise acquired the syntax of adjectival specifiers as well. One possible source of adjectival specifiers can be found in clausal constructions such as the following, where the italicized NP would appear to function as the subject of the bracketed adjectival predicate, so that the overall [subject + predicate] structure forms an *adjectival clause* (similar in structure to the verbless adjectival clauses found in adult languages like Ilocano, but having much the same interpretation as adult English copula clauses of the form *DP is AP*):

(44)   (a)   *Geraint* [naughty] (= 'Geraint is naughty', Bethan 20)
        (b)   Lisa [naughty] (Hayley 20)
        (c)   *Hand* [cold]. *Fire* [hot] (Elen 20)
        (d)   *Bow-wow* [asleep] (Stephen 20)
        (e)   *Wayne* [naughty] (Daniel 21)
        (f)   *Man* [empty] (*Allison 21)
        (g)   *Mommy* [busy]. *Baby* [busy] (*Kathryn 21)
        (h)   *Cup tea* [ready]. *Potty* [dirty] (John 22)
        (i)   *Girl* [hungry]. *Daddy* [hungry]. *Mommy* [hungry]. *Boy* [hungry] (*Kathryn 22)
        (j)   *Apple* [cold]. *Light* [hot] (*Eric 22)
        (k)   *Doggie* [sleepy]. *Hair* [wet] (*Kendall 22–23)
        (l)   *Sausage* [bit hot] (Jem 23)
        (m)   *Joelle* [silly] (Leila 23)
        (n)   *Claire* [full] (*Claire 24)
        (o)   *Shirt* [wet]. *Shoe* [wet] (*Jonathan 24)

It seems likely that child clauses with adjectival predicates such as those in (44) above can be analysed as adjectival phrases in which the italicized NP functions as the specifier of the bracketed A-bar predicate. If this is so, then an adjectival clause such as (44)(l) *Sausage bit hot* would have the skeletal structure (45) below:

(45)   [$_{AP}$ [$_{NP}$ Sausage] [$_{A'}$ [$_{NP}$ bit] [$_{A'}$ [$_A$ hot]]]]

where the NP *sausage* functions as a subject specifier expanding the A-bar *bit hot* into the full adjectival phrase (i.e. adjectival clause) *Sausage bit hot*. In this respect, the child's structure (45) would resemble an adult adjectival Small Clause such as that bracketed in (46) below:

(46)   I found [*the sausage a bit hot*]

Under the analysis of Small Clauses in Stowell (1981) (whereby Small Clauses are taken to be phrasal projections of a head lexical category, so that adjectival Small Clauses are analysed as adjectival phrases, i.e. APs), the bracketed adjectival Small Clause in (46) would be analysed as having the following structure:

(47)   [$_{AP}$ [$_{DP}$ the sausage] [$_{A'}$ [$_{DP}$ a bit] [$_{A'}$ [$_A$ hot]]]]

Thus, the child's adjectival clause (45) would have essentially the same structure as the adult adjectival Small Clause (47) – the one major difference being that young children (because their grammars lack functional categories) use lexical NPs in contexts where adults use functional DPs (so that we have *sausage* in place of *the sausage*, and *bit* in place of *a bit*).

To summarize: we have abundant empirical evidence that in the initial phase of categorization, children develop an N-system, a V-system, a P-system, and an A-system. They thus have a full set of lexical category systems, and 'know' how to project the four primary lexical categories N, V, A, and P into the corresponding single-bar and double-bar constituents. What is quite remarkable (and inescapable) is the striking structural symmetry in these various category systems: in each case, a head category X can be combined with a following complement to form an X-bar; this X-bar in turn can be (potentially recursively) combined with a preceding adjunct to form another X-bar; and the resulting X-bar can be combined with a preceding specifier to form an X-double-bar. What all of this suggests is that young children at this stage have developed a category-neutral X-bar schema of the generalized form (48):

(48)   [$_{X''}$ specifier [$_{X'}$ adjunct [$_{X'}$ [$_X$ head] complement/s]]]

and (48) is clearly identical to the 'basic' schema for adult English which we outlined in (5) above.

However, before we conclude our discussion in this chapter, let us first dispose of two rather different types of objection to the analysis proposed here. The first relates to the question of *productivity*: thus, we might object that the actual set of word combinations found in any corpus of child speech is far more restricted, far more item-specific, and (hence by implication) far less symmetrical than the generalized X-bar schema in (48) would imply. Braine (1976: 66) is implicitly presenting an argument of this kind when he objects to analysing [verb + nominal] structures (e.g. *see* + nominal, *want* + nominal, *have* + nominal, *eat* + nominal, etc. structures) in early child speech as instances of a common structural pattern – i.e. (in our terms) as instances of a V-bar constituent comprising a head verb and an NP complement. His objection is based on the fact that each nominal complement of each verb has a 'specific semantic content' – for example, the nominal object of *eat* is restricted to being an expression of 'oral consumption' (Braine 1976: 67). The overall implication is that since different (classes of) verbs allow different semantic classes of nominal objects, there is no reasonable sense in which the various [verb + nominal] combinations can be said to be instances of a common structural pattern involving a unitary class of object expressions (i.e. NPs). What are we to make of this kind of objection to our symmetrical X-bar analysis of early child syntax?

The answer to this is that the objection is entirely misplaced. Chomsky (1986a: 86) argues that there are two different types of properties which determine the range of expressions which can function as the complement of a given head, namely (i) the *c-selection* (*c* = categorial) properties of the head, and (ii) the *s-selection* (*s* = semantic) properties of the head. The c-selection properties of the head determine the range of syntactic categories which can function as complements of the head; while the s-selection properties of the head determine the semantic function of the complement. Thus, the fact that different verbs permit a different (semantic) range of complements tells us only that the verbs concerned have different s-selection properties, not that they have different c-selection properties. We can make our discussion here more concrete by considering the following contrast in adult English:

(49)   (a)   John wrote *a poem/!a banana*
         (b)   John ate *a banana/!a poem*

(! here is used to indicate semantic anomaly.) The fact that the verbs *write* and *eat* allow different semantic classes of complements clearly does not undermine the claim that in categorial terms both *write* and *eat* select DP complements. The more general point being made here is that the fact that two (or more) predicates may have different s-selection properties does not prevent them from having the same c-selection properties. Since the only selectional properties of items which fall within the scope of the X-bar schema in (48) are their c-selection properties, arguments relating to the s-selection properties of items are in principle irrelevant to any discussion of the categorial constituent structure of utterances. The question of what range of different NPs children use as the complement of a verb like *eat* is clearly not a *syntactic* one; it is partly a question of *semantics* (determined by what meaning a given child ascribes to *eat*), partly a question of *pragmatics* (determined by the child's experience of the edibility of different objects in the world), and partly a question of *vocabulary* (determined by whether or not the child has a sufficient range of vocabulary items to describe all the objects that he knows are edible). Since such (s-)*selection restrictions* (as they are traditionally known) are inherently semantic/pragmatic in nature, they cannot (in principle) be used as the basis of an argument relating to the categorial structure of a given type of phrase or sentence.

A second way in which we might seek to undermine the generalized X-bar schema presented in (48) is by questioning the assumption that there is cross-categorial symmetry and stability in the relative linear ordering of different types of constituent in early child English. The symmetry assumption would lead us to expect that children never make significant word order errors in acquiring English: and indeed the stability of word order in early child English is frequently commented on in the acquisition literature. For example, Brown (1973: 156) comments that 'The violations of normal order are triflingly few'; and in a study of seven American children, Ramer (1976) noted that the percentage of word order errors made by the children ranged from 0% to 3.8%. However, it should also be noted that the acquisition literature has occasionally revealed examples of structures in early child English which might appear to challenge this hypothesis. For example, Bloom (1970: 87) reports that Gia at age 19 months produced the following example of [Object + Verb] structure (where the presumed object is italicized):

(50)   *Balloon* throw (*Gia 19, dropping a balloon as though she were throwing it)

Similarly, Miller and Ervin (1964) report Susan at age 22 months as saying:

(51)   *Book* read (*Susan 22)

Likewise, Brown, Cazden and Bellugi (1968) report the following examples of apparent [Object + Verb] structures in Adam's speech (at an unspecified age):

(52)   *Paper* find. *Paper* write. *Daddy suitcase* go get it

But they note that 'These are the only exceptions in thousands of well-ordered sentences' (ibid: 392).

How are we to interpret such problematic (albeit rare) apparent counterexamples to our claim that the earliest single-bar structures developed by young children consistently show head-first order? Bloom (1970: 88) suggests that we should analyse such structures not as examples of [Object + Verb] structures, but rather as examples of [Topic + Verb] structures: thus, she suggests that the immediate adult counterpart of Gia's utterance *Balloon throw* in (50) above would be:

(53)   The *balloon*, I *throw* it

(the child's counterpart retaining only the italicized items belonging to lexical categories, omitting functional categories, including the prenominal determiner *the*, and the pronominal determiners *I* and *it*). In an adult structure such as (53), it seems likely (given the arguments in Radford 1988a: 530-3) that [*the balloon*] is a dislocated nominal, base-generated as an adjunct to the clause [*I throw it*]. We might accordingly propose to analyse the italicized 'objects' in examples such as (50–52) above as dislocated NPs base-generated as adjuncts to a verbal Small Clause (i.e. a VP). If we further posit (following Hyams 1986) that 'missing arguments' in early child English are instantiations of the null pronominal *pro* (which can be thought of informally as a covert counterpart of overt pronominals such as *I/you/he/she/it*, etc.), then we might suppose that (50) would have the structure (54) below:

(54)   [$_{VP}$ [$_{NP}$ Balloon] [$_{VP}$ *pro* [$_V$ throw] **pro**]]

where *pro* is a null pronominal, and where the first (italicized) *pro* designates the 'understood' null subject/specifier of the VP (and so corresponds to the adult overt pronoun *I*), and the second (bold-printed)

pro designates an understood null resumptive pronominal complement of the verb *throw*, interpreted as coreferential to the dislocated NP *balloon* (and so corresponds to the adult overt pronoun *it*). Such a *dislocation* analysis is by no means implausible, given Gruber's (1967) observation that dislocation structures such as *Car, it broken* are sometimes found in early child speech; moreover – as we shall see in chapter 8 – 'covert' subjects and objects are frequent in early child English. What adds additional plausibility to the dislocation analysis is the occurrence of the overt resumptive pronoun *it* in the last example in (52). If we adopt the dislocation analysis, we thereby dispose of a potentially troublesome set of apparent counterexamples to the claim that there is a striking cross-categorial symmetry in the internal constituent structure of the earliest (lexical) category systems developed by young children.

The most important conclusion to emerge from our discussion in this chapter is that the initial grammars formulated by young children show clear evidence of the acquisition of a well developed set of symmetrical lexical category systems, in that young children at the relevant stage (typically between the ages of 20 and 23 months ±20%) seem to 'know' how to project head nouns, verbs, prepositions and adjectives into the corresponding single-bar and double-bar categories, by the addition of appropriately (and symmetrically) positioned complements, adjuncts, and specifiers. This very fact constitutes the first part of our evidence in support of our hypothesis that the earliest category systems developed by young children acquiring English as a first language are purely *lexical* in nature. The second part of the evidence (presented in chapters 4–8) will aim to show that (by contrast) there are no functional category systems in early child grammars of English – hence no D-system, no C-system, and no I-system. We begin our presentation of the second part of the evidence in the next chapter, where we argue that early child nominals are characterized by the absence of a determiner system.

We conclude this chapter with a brief technical footnote. Our discussion here has assumed that heads can be 'expanded' into higher-level constituents by the addition of three different types of constituent – viz. *specifiers*, *complements*, and *adjuncts*. It should be noted, however, that there have been a number of recent attempts to reanalyse (at least some types of) *adjuncts* as heads taking phrasal (XP) complements. For example, Abney (1987) suggests that attributive adjectives should not be treated as nominal adjuncts, but rather as heads taking noun phrase complements. In more concrete terms what he suggests is that in a phrase such as:

(55)   a hot cup of coffee

the adjective *hot* is not an adjunct to the N-bar *cup of coffee*, but rather is the head of the expression *hot cup of coffee*, this expression having the status of an AP comprising the adjective *hot* and an NP complement *cup of coffee* – as represented in a simplified form in (56) below:

(56)   [$_{DP}$ [$_D$ a] [$_{AP}$ [$_A$ hot] [$_{NP}$ [$_N$ cup] of coffee]]]

He further posits an *Inheritance Principle* whereby the AP inherits the categorial status of its NP complement, so that the overall expression *hot cup of coffee* becomes an NP by inheritance (hence the fact that it can serve as the complement of a determiner like *a*).

Within the spirit of the 'adjuncts-as-heads' analysis, we might similarly suppose that adverbs like *completely* should not be taken to be adjuncts to V-bar, but rather as head A constituents taking a VP complement: under this analysis, a VP such as that italicized in (57):

(57)   The bombs may *completely destroy the city*

would have the simplified structure (58) below:

(58)   [$_{AP}$ [$_A$ completely] [$_{VP}$ [$_V$ destroy] the city]]

We might then posit that the AP inherits the VP-hood of its complement, so that the overall expression *completely destroy the city* becomes a VP by inheritance (hence the fact that it can serve as the complement of an I constituent like *may*).

The obvious implication of the adjuncts-as-heads analysis is that by reanalysing adjuncts as heads, we may be able to eliminate the class of adjuncts from Universal Grammar, so that syntactic structures may ultimately be reducible to combinations of heads, specifiers, and complements. It should be emphasized that it is by no means clear that this goal is attainable (see Radford 1989 for a discussion of problems posed by the attempt to eliminate the class of adjuncts from the theory of grammar). However, what is more important for our present purposes is that any such reanalysis of (e.g.) prenominal attributive adjectives as heads rather than adjuncts in no way undermines the central conclusion which we have reached in this chapter, namely that the initial grammars of English formulated by young children show clear evidence of the acquisition of a well developed set of symmetrical lexical category systems. For the sake of expository consistency, we shall adopt the well-established *adjunct* analysis here (though it is a simple enough matter to reformulate our conclusions in terms of the rival *adjuncts-as-heads* analysis).

4

Absence of a Determiner System in Early Child English

In the previous chapter, we put forward the hypothesis that the fundamental defining characteristic of the categorial component in early child grammars of English is the acquisition of lexical category systems, and the concomitant nonacquisition of functional category systems. In this chapter, we intend to test this hypothesis by looking at the syntax of the earliest nominal structures produced by young children acquiring English as their first language. If our *lexical* analysis of early child grammars of English is along the right lines, then we should expect to find that nominals in early child English are purely *lexical* structures, in the sense that they are projections formed by combining a head lexical category (= a noun) with complement/adjunct/specifier phrases which are themselves projections of other head lexical categories, so that early child nominals entirely lack functional categories of any kind. More specifically, our hypothesis would predict that the earliest nominal structures produced by young children are *indeterminate* (in the technical sense that they entirely lack a determiner system), so that the child's counterpart of adult determiner phrases are simple noun phrases (cf. the parallel claim made by Guilfoyle and Noonan 1988). If this is so, then it follows that early child nominals are purely *lexical* projections of a head N into NP, and lack further *functional* projections of NP into DP.

Perhaps the most obvious piece of evidence in support of this claim is the fact that children use *indeterminate* nominals (i.e. nominals lacking a D-system) in contexts where adults would require *determinate* nominals (i.e. nominals containing a D-system). This can be illustrated by the spontaneous speech data in (1) below:

(1)   (a)   Where *helicopter?* Here *helicopter.* Where *bee?* Where's *green car?* Got *bee.* Got *bean.* Open *door* (Stefan 17)

(b) Paula *good girl* (= 'Paula is a good girl'). *Ribbon* off. Paula want open *box* (Paula 18)

(c) Open *door*. Want *ball*. Want *car* (Stephen 19)

(d) *Coat* off. *Nappy* off. *Orange*, please (Elen 19)

(e) Hayley draw *boat*. Turn *page*. Reading *book*. Want *duck*. Want *boot* (Hayley 20)

(f) *Blanket* gone. *Stick* gone. *Finger* there (Bethan 20)

(g) *Top* on. Read *book* (Lucy 20)

(h) *Dog* barking. Got *lorry*. *Paper* off. *Yellow crayon* there. Want *ball* (Bethan 21)

(i) *Lorry* out. Cuddle *book*. Bang *bottom* (Jem 21)

(j) Open *can*. Open *box*. Eat *cookie*. Get *diaper*. Build *tower*. Hurt *knee*. Help *cow* in *table*. *Horse* tumble. *Man* drive *truck*. *Pig* ride. *Diaper* out. *Napkin* out (*Allison 22)

(k) Wayne in *garden*. Want *tractor*. Want *sweet*. Want *chocolate biscuit*. Want *orange*. Want *coat*. Daddy want *golf ball*. *Lady* get *sweetie* now. Where *car*? Where *bike*? Where *tractor*? *Tractor* broken (Daniel 23)

In each of these examples, the italicized child nominal is headed by a singular count noun, and would therefore require a premodifying determiner such as *a*, *the*, *my*, etc. in adult speech; but the child's nominal is indeterminate in every case, thus suggesting that the children in question have not yet developed a determiner system.

The same pattern (of children consistently using NPs in contexts where adults require DPs) shows up even more clearly in children's responses to *what*-questions: the data in (2) below are a mere handful of the hundreds of examples of question–answer sequences of this type in my corpus (the first part of each utterance is a question asked by an adult, and the child's subsequent response is italicized):

(2) (a) What's this? – *Telephone* (Paula 18)

(b) What's this? – *Spoon* (Paula 18)

(c) What's this? – *Balloon* (Dewi 18)

(d) What do you want? – *Biscuit* (Dewi 18)

(e) What's that one? – *Chick* (Stephen 19)

(f) What is it? – *Bird* (Stephen 19)

(g) What's that? – *Tree* (Elen 19)

(h) What's this here? – *Banana* (Elen 19)

(i) What are we looking for, Dewi? – *Bird* (Dewi 20)

(j) What do we need for the diaper? – *Pin* (*Allison 20)

(k) What's this? – *Carrot* (*Helen 20)

(l)   What's daddy built for you? – *Castle* (*Helen 20)
(m)   What's the lady got? – *Mouse* (Hayley 20)
(n)   What is it? – *Sock* (Hayley 20)
(o)   What's Noddy riding in? – *Tractor* (Bethan 20)
(p)   What's this? – *Train* (Bethan 20)
(q)   What are you doing with the brush? – *Butterfly* (Lucy 20)
(r)   What's that? – *Truck* (Bethan 21)
(s)   What's this? – *High chair* (Bethan 21)
(t)   What's this that mummy's drawing? – *High mountain* (Jem 21)
(u)   What's that in there? – *Big ball* (Jem 21)
(v)   What do you want? – Want *cup* (Daniel 23)
(w)   What's that? – *Train* (Daniel 23)
(x)   What's that? – *Good book* (Leigh 24)
(y)   What's that one? – *Naughty cow* (Leigh 24)
(z)   What have you got on there? – *Frog* (Anne 24)

In each case, the child's reply contains a nominal headed by a singular count noun – whereas the adult counterpart of such utterances would require the nominal to be premodified by a determiner such as *a*, *the*, etc.: once again, the natural conclusion to draw from the relevant data is that children use NPs in contexts were adults require DPs.

The same pattern (viz. adult DP = child NP) also shows up in child speech which is wholly or partly *imitative*. Thus, in contexts where adults produce a determinate DP, this is consistently imitated by children as an indeterminate NP – as the following sequences indicate (the bold-printed nominal is the adult DP, and the italicized nominal is the child's NP imitation):

(3)   (a)   Did you drop **your tea**? – Drop *tea* (Stefan 17)
        (b)   Is there **a baby** in there? – *Baby* (Stefan 17)
        (c)   You want **the top** off? – *Top* off (Helen 18)
        (d)   Has he got **any legs**? – *Legs* (Helen 18)
        (e)   This is **a kitten** – *Kitten* (Dewi 18)
        (f)   Teddy's in **the boot** – *Boot* (Dewi 18)
        (g)   Is it **a duck** or a chick? – *Duck* (Stephen 19)
        (h)   Is that **a drum**? – *Drum* (Dewi 19)
        (i)   Did you go down **the slide**? – *Slide* (Dewi 19)
        (j)   That's **a bag**, look – *Bag* (Elen 20)
        (k)   Mummy will take **the nut** off – *Nut* out (*Helen 21)
        (l)   You were playing in **the water** – In *water* (Hayley 20)
        (m)   That's **a goat** – *Goat* (Hayley 20)

(n)   Tell him he's **a naughty boy** – *Naughty boy* (Bethan 20)
(o)   That's **a cup** – *Cup* (Lucy 20)
(p)   Paint **a rabbit** – *Rabbit* (Lucy 20)
(q)   It's **a brush, a hairbrush** – *Brush* (Daniel 22)
(r)   That's **an apple**, that one – *Apple* (Daniel 22)
(s)   That's **a hippo** – *Hippo* (Leigh 24)
(t)   It's **the sun** – *Sun* (Leigh 24)

If we make the conventional assumption that children can consistently imitate only those items whose morphosyntax they have mastered, then the fact that they systematically imitate adult DPs as NPs would seem to suggest that they have not yet developed a D-system of their own.

There is a further source of evidence which we can look to in order to seek corroboration for our claim that early child nominals are indeterminate (in the sense that they lack a D-system). Recent work (e.g. Fukui 1986) has suggested that the genitive *'s* morpheme in English functions as a head determiner constituent. Given this assumption, a nominal such as:

(4)   the enemy's destruction of the city

might be analysed as having the (simplified) superficial structure indicated in (5):

(5)   [$_{DP}$ the enemy [$_D$ *'s*] [$_{NP}$ destruction of the city]]

in which the following NP [*destruction of the city*] functions as the complement of the head genitive determiner *'s*, while the preceding DP [*the enemy*] functions as its specifier. At first sight, it might seem implausible to suggest that a *clitic* morpheme (i.e. a morpheme which ends up attached to another word) such as genitive *'s* could function as a head determiner. However, recall the claim by Abney (1987: 64–5) that 'Functional elements are ... often clitics'; and indeed there are many languages in which the counterpart of the English determiner *the* is a clitic (e.g. Arabic, Romanian, Swedish, etc.). Moreover, English has a number of clitic I constituents (including the *'ll/'d* allomorphs of *will/would*) which similarly cliticize to their specifiers (cf. structures such as *He'll resign*). Thus, the analysis of genitive *'s* as a (clitic) determiner is by no means implausible.

However, while (5) may be an adequate representation of the superficial syntactic structure of (4), there is some reason to suppose that it cannot be an adequate representation of its underlying structure. The reason is that we need to ensure that *the enemy* is assigned an appropriate theta-role (that of AGENT) by the N-bar *destruction of the city*. Clearly *the enemy* cannot be assigned a theta-role by genitive *'s* if we hold to the general assumption that determiners do not assign (or transmit) theta-roles. The obvious conclusion is that *the enemy* must be theta-marked by the N-bar *destruction of the city*. However, if we further assume (following Chomsky 1988b: 17) that 'theta-marking must be internal to the projection of the theta-marking head', then it is clear that in order to be theta-marked by *destruction of the city*, the DP *the enemy* must originate within the immediate maximal projection of the head noun *destruction*. Since it is clearly the 'subject' of *destruction*, then if we assume that Universal Grammar determines that subjects occupy the structural position of specifiers, it follows that *the enemy* must originate within the bracketed NP in (5), as its specifier. Given these assumptions, the underlying structure of (5) will be along the lines of (6) below:

(6)   [$_{DP}$ [$_D$ *'s*] [$_{NP}$ the enemy [$_N$ destruction] (of) the city]]

(If we were to follow the analysis in Chomsky's *Knowledge of Language* (1986a: 192), we might suppose that *of* is not present in the underlying structure, though this is a matter of no immediate consequence for our present discussion.) The corresponding superficial structure (5) is then derived from the underlying structure (6) by movement of the DP *the enemy* from the specifier position within NP into the empty specifier position within DP, in the manner indicated schematically in (7) below:

(7)   [$_{DP}$ [$_D$ *'s*] [$_{NP}$ *the enemy* [$_N$ destruction] (of) the city]]

Current work suggests that this movement is 'forced' by the requirement that DPs (like *the enemy*) must be assigned *case*. If functional categories (specifically D and I) can assign case leftwards to their specifiers in adult English, but lexical categories cannot assign case to their specifiers, then it follows that the DP *the enemy* can only receive case if it moves out of the specifier position within the bracketed NP in (7) into the specifier position within DP in (5); it will then be assigned genitive case by the Determiner *'s* in (5). If *'s* is a nominal *enclitic* (i.e. a morpheme which must be suffixed to a nominal), then an additional factor 'forcing' *the enemy* to move to the left of the Determiner *'s* is the need to provide a suitable 'host' for *'s* to encliticise to (thereby avoiding violation of a constraint which requires affixes to be attached to an appropriate host).

If the genitive *'s* morpheme is indeed a head determiner constituent, and if we are correct in hypothesizing that early child nominals lack a D-system, then we should expect to find that when children are at the *lexical* stage of their categorial development, their counterpart of adult genitive DP structures will show no evidence of acquisition of the genitive *'s* morpheme. This prediction is borne out by the fact that children at this stage do not attach the genitive *'s* suffix to possessor nominals: see, for example, the examples in (8) below (familiar from the previous chapter), where the possessor nominal is italicized:

(8) (a) *Mummy* [car]. *Mummy* [tea]. *Daddy* [hat] (Stefan 17)
     (b) *Baby* [car]. *Betty* [car]. *Mummy* [car]. *Betty* [chair]. *Joanne* [tea] (+Betty 18)
     (c) *Mummy* [coat]. *Daddy* [shoe] (Daniel 19)
     (d) *Dolly* [hat]. *Mommy* [key]. *Lamb* [ear]. *Gia* [eyes] (*Gia 19–20)
     (e) *Hayley* [dress]. *Hayley* [book] (Hayley 20)
     (f) *Baby* [cup] (*Allison 20)
     (g) *Claire* [pencil] (Alison 21)
     (h) *Nana* [key] (Daniel 21)
     (i) *Big teddy bear* [supper]. *Baby* [supper]. *Baby* [feet]. *Jem* [chair]. *Mummy* [box] (Jem 21)
     (j) *Nicky* [money] (+Abigail 21)
     (k) *Lois* [scarf]. *Kevin* [snoopy] (*Gia 22)
     (l) *Dewi* [party]. *Mummy* [bag]. *Mummy* [key] (Daniel 23)
     (m) *Nicola* [man] (= 'Nicola's boyfriend' Claire 23)
     (n) *Katie* [turn] (= 'Katie's turn', *Katie 23)
     (o) *Kendall* [rocking chair]. *Kimmy* [bike]. *Kendall* [pail]. *Kimmy* [pail]. *Kendall* [turn]. *Papa* [door] (*Kendall 23)
     (p) *Teddy* [colour] (Lucy 24)
     (q) *Mommy* [chair]. *Mommy* [shoe]. *Claire* [pencil]. *Claire* [eye] (*Claire 24)

Moreover, this pattern (of *s*-less possessives) is a productive one, as abundant examples in the published literature attest: citing just two works for illustrative purposes, the examples in (9)(a) below are examples (from Bloom 1970) of uninflected possessor nominals in Kathryn's speech at 21 months, while the data in (9)(b) (from Braine 1976) are similar examples from the transcript of Jonathan at age 24 months:

(9)   (a)   *Mommy* haircurl(er). *Mommy* cottage cheese. *Mommy* milk.
              Mommy hangnail. *Mommy* vegetable. *Mommy* pigtail. *Mommy*
              sock. *Mommy* slipper. *Kathryn* sock. *Kathryn* shoe. *Wendy*
              cottage cheese. *Baby* cottage cheese. *Cat* cottage cheese.
              Jocelyn cheek. *Baby* milk. *Tiger* tail. *Sheep* ear (*Kathryn 21)
       (b)   *Daddy* coffee. *Daddy* shell. *Mommy* shell. *Andrew* shoe.
              Daddy hat. *Elliot* juice. *Mommy* mouth. *Andrew* book. *Daddy*
              car. *Daddy* chair. *Daddy* cookie. *Daddy* tea. *Mommy* tea.
              Daddy door. *Daddy* book. *Mommy* book. *Daddy* bread. *Elliot*
              cookie. *Elliot* diaper. *Elliot* boat. *Daddy* eat (= 'Daddy's
              food'). *Daddy* juice. *Mommy* butter. *Daddy* butter (*Jonathan
              24)

Likewise, none of the children reported on in the studies by Brown
(1973) and De Villiers and De Villiers (1973a) made productive use of
genitive *'s* at this stage. Thus, it would seem that we have abundant
empirical evidence that children at this point in their development have
not acquired the genitive determiner *'s*. This in turn is consistent with
our more general suggestion that such children have not yet acquired a
D-system, and thus are at a purely *lexical* stage in their categorial
development. These early lexical structures produced by young children
might be said to be *thematic* structures in the sense that they directly
encode the thematic relations between a head lexical category and its
arguments, in so far as all theta-marked arguments of a given head noun
are superficially contained within its maximal projection (i.e within the
immediately containing NP). Thus, in some respects, the superficial
syntactic structures produced by the child reflect (the lexical core of) the
underlying structures of the corresponding adult nominals.
      What data such as (8) and (9) suggest is that whereas possessor
nominals are underlyingly specifiers of NP but have to move into the
specifier position within DP in order to get case in adult English, in early
child English by contrast, possessor nominals are both underlyingly and
superficially positioned as specifiers of NP. Why should this be? What we
are suggesting here is that this is correlated with the fact that nominals
(including possessor nominals) have the status of case-marked DPs in
adult English, but the status of caseless NPs in early child English. We
can illustrate this correlation in terms of the following contrast between
adult and child possessive structures:

(10)   (a)   *the lady*'s cup of coffee (adult)
        (b)   *lady* cup coffee (child)

The (italicized) possessor phrase *the lady* has the status of DP in the adult English example (10)(a), while its child counterpart *lady* in (10)(b) is arguably a simple NP (the fact that the child's nominal lacks the referential determiner *the* and the possessive determiner *'s* suggests that the nominal has no D-system, and hence has the status of NP rather than DP). Let us suppose (essentially following Abney 1987) that one of the licensing requirements for DPs is that they require *case* and hence can only occur in *case-marked* positions: more specifically, in order for a DP to be well-formed, it must occur in a position where it can be assigned case by an appropriate case assigner. Given our assumption that possessor phrases originate as nominal specifiers, then the possessive DP *the lady* in (10)(a) will originate as the specifier of the N-bar *cup of coffee*, so that the (simplified) structure underlying (10)(a) will be:

(11) $[_{DP}$ $[_D$'s$]$ $[_{NP}$ *the lady* $[_{N'}$ $[_N$ cup$]$ of coffee$]]]$

However, since *the lady* is a DP, and since DPs require case, the italicized possessor phrase cannot remain in the specifier position of NP (since this is a *caseless* position, i.e. a position to which no case is assigned), but rather must move into a *case-marked* position. Since the specifier position within DP is a case-marked position (given that the determiner *'s* case-marks its specifier to the left), the case requirement is satisfied by movement of *the lady* from the specifier position within NP into the specifier position within DP, so resulting in the superficial structure (12) below:

(12) $[_{DP}$ *the lady* $[_D$'s$]$ $[_{NP}$ *e* $[_{N'}$ cup of coffee$]]]$

(where *e* marks the empty specifier position within NP which results from movement of the italicized possessor phrase into the specifier position within DP). Thus, this movement of the possessive DP satisfies the case requirement on DPs (and also satisfies the requirement for the enclitic *'s* to have a host to attach to).

If (following Abney 1987) we assume that case is an intrinsic property of DPs, then it seems reasonable to suppose that if children have no D-system, they will likewise have no case-system: this in turn will lead us to expect that wherever adults use case-marked DPs, children will use caseless NPs. Now, if early child nominals are caseless NPs, then it follows that there will be no case constraints on the distribution of these nominals in early child English – i.e. no requirement for child nominals in caseless positions to be moved into case-marked positions.

In the light of these assumptions, let us return to consider the underlying structure of an NP such as (10)(b) *lady cup coffee*. Given our assumption that possessor phrases like *lady* originate as nominal specifiers, it follows that the structure underlying (10)(b) will be along the lines of (13) below:

(13)   [$_{NP}$ *lady* [$_{N'}$ [$_N$ cup] coffee]]

The overall structure [*lady cup coffee*] is arguably an NP rather than a DP (since there is no *'s* determiner), and the italicized possessor nominal *lady* is likewise arguably an NP (since it lacks the determiner *the*). Although the possessor nominal *lady* is in a caseless position (since nouns like *cup* are not direct case assigners), this does not lead to violation of any case principle, since the relevant requirement is for DPs (not NPs) to carry case. Thus, whereas the adult possessor phrase has the superficial status of a moved case-marked DP functioning as a specifier within a containing DP, the child possessor phrase by contrast has the status of a base-generated (unmoved) caseless NP occupying the specifier position within a containing NP. This reinforces our overall suggestion that children use caseless NPs in contexts where adults require case-marked DPs.

If we are correct is supposing that case is an inherent property of the D-system, then we should expect to find that there will be no case-system operating in child grammars until such time as the D-system has been acquired. This in turn would lead us to predict that children at the lexical stage of development (when they have no D-system) will show no evidence of having acquired the case-marking mechanisms which operate to assign case to DPs in adult grammars. Some support for this claim comes from the fact that children at this stage fail to use the 'dummy' (i.e. nonthematic and semantically empty) case-marking preposition *of* to introduce noun complements, as we see from (13) above, and from examples such as those in (14) below (familiar from the previous chapter):

(14)   (a)   [*Cup* tea] (= 'a cup of tea', Stefan 17)
        (b)   [*Bottle* juice] (= 'a bottle of juice', Lucy 20)
        (c)   [*Picture* Gia] (= 'a picture of Gia', *Gia 20)
        (d)   Want [*piece* bar] (= 'I want a piece of the chocolate bar', Daniel 20)
        (e)   Have [*drink* orange] (= 'I want to have a drink of orange', Jem 21)

(f)   Want [*cup* tea] (Jenny 21)

(g)   [*Cup* tea] ready (John 22)

(h)   [*Picture* Kendall]. [*Picture* water] (= 'a picture of Kendall/ water', *Kendall 23)

(i)   Blue [*ball* wool] (*Jonathan 23)

(j)   [*Colour* crate] (= 'The colour of the crate', Anna 24)

(k)   [*Colour* new shoes] (= 'The colour of my new shoes', Anna 24)

(l)   [*Drink* water] (*Jonathan 24)

In adult English, nouns cannot directly case-mark their complements, so that the bracketed NP in a structure such as:

(15)   *a [$_{NP}$ piece *the bar*]

would be ungrammatical, since the italicized DP complement [*the bar*] would fail to be assigned case by its head noun *piece* (in violation of the requirement that DPs require case). Instead, the 'dummy' preposition *of* must be used to introduce the complement, as in:

(16)   a [$_{NP}$ piece **of** *the bar*]

(Given that *of* has no independent semantic or thematic content, we might argue that it has the status of a *functor* here, in the sense that it is an item with a purely 'grammatical' function.) Since prepositions assign case to their complements, use of the 'dummy' preposition *of* in a structure such as (16) enables the DP [*the bar*] to be assigned case, and so to satisfy the requirement that DPs must carry case. However, the fact that children have not acquired the syntax of the 'dummy' case-assigner *of* at this stage (as shown by its systematic absence in [Noun + complement] structures such as (14) above) indicates that the case principles which determine the superficial form of nominal structures in adult English are not yet operative in their grammars: in more general terms, it indicates the lack of a case-system in early child grammars of English. There would seem to be an obvious correlation between the absence of the dummy case-marker *of* in a child nominal such as *piece bar* in (14)(d), and the absence of the determiners *a* and *the* required in the adult counterpart '*a* piece **of** *the* bar' – i.e. between the absence of a case system on the one hand, and the absence of a determiner system on the other. If case is posited to be an inherent property of the D-system, then this correlation can obviously be accounted for in a principled way.

There is a further way in which we can 'test' the suggested correlation between the absence of a determiner system in early child grammars, and the absence of a case system. The constituents most systematically inflected for case in adult English are personal pronouns such as *I/me/my*, *we/us/our*, *he/him/his*, and *they/them/their* (all of which have distinct nominative/objective/genitive case forms). Interestingly, Abney (1987) – adapting an earlier analysis by Postal (1970) – argues on entirely independent grounds that personal pronouns are pronominal determiners (i.e. pronouns which occupy the head D position of DP, hence having the status of pro-D constituents). More specifically, Abney maintains that just as *a* functions as a determiner in expressions such as *a transformational grammarian*, so too does the pronoun *we* in expressions like *we transformational grammarians*. Such an analysis would provide an obvious way of accounting for the fact that in many varieties of (northern British) English, the personal pronoun *them* can be used not only *pro*nominally, but also *pre*nominally (so that *them books* corresponds to the standard form 'those books'). Moreover, it may well be that the analysis of pronouns as determiners has developmental plausibility, since (older) children in the initial stages of acquiring pronouns are often reported to use pronouns both pronominally and prenominally: for example, Brown and Bellugi (1964) report utterances such as *Mommy get it ladder*, and Braine (1976) reports utterances such as *Have it egg*; one possible interpretation of such data is that the pronoun *it* here is being used as a *pre*nominal – rather than a *pro*nominal - determiner (though of course other interpretations are possible, e.g. an analysis in which the nominal is a dislocated constituent, and the pronoun has a reprise function). At any rate, what is important from our point of view is that the analysis of pronouns as determiners would lead us to expect that if early child grammars contain no determiner system and (consequently) no case system, then young children at the lexical stage of their categorial development will show no evidence of having acquired the morphosyntax of case-marked pronouns (i.e. of pronouns overtly inflected for case).

In this connection, it is interesting to note the observation by Bloom et al. (1978) that many young children at this stage have a *nominal* style of speech which is characterized by their non-use of case-marked pronouns such as *I/you/he/she/we/they* etc.: cf. the parallel remark by Bowerman (1973: 109) that in the first stage of their grammatical development 'Seppo and Kendall used no personal pronouns at all'. We can illustrate this nominal speech style from the transcript of the speech of Allison Bloom at age 22 months provided in the appendix to Bloom (1973: 233–57), since Bloom et al. (1978: 237) report that Allison's NPs at this stage were 'exclusively nominal'. Of particular interest to us is the fact that Allison used nominals in contexts where adults would use pronominals. For example, in conversation with her mother, Allison uses the nominal expressions *baby*, *baby Allison*, or *Allison* to refer to herself (where an adult would use the first person pronouns *I/me/my*), as we see from the examples in (17) below:

(17) (a) *Baby Allison* comb hair. *Baby* eat cookies. *Baby* eat cookie. *Baby* eat. *Baby* open door. *Baby* drive truck. *Baby* ride truck. *Baby* down chair
      (b) Help *baby*
      (c) *Allison* cookie. Put away *Allison* bag. *Baby* cookie. *Baby* diaper. *Baby* back. Wiping *baby* chin (*Allison 22)

The adult counterparts of Allison's sentences would contain (in place of the italicized nominal) the nominative pronoun *I* in (17)(a), the objective pronoun *me* in (17)(b), and the genitive pronoun *my* in (17)(c); but Allison's utterances in each example contain only an uninflected nominal. Similarly, Allison also uses the nominal *Mommy* to address her mother in contexts where adults would use the second person pronouns *you/your*, as the following examples illustrate:

(18) (a) *Mommy* open. *Mommy* help. *Mommy* pull. *Mommy* eat cookie
      (b) Peeking *Mommy*. Get *Mommy* cookie. Pour *Mommy* juice
      (c) Eat *Mommy* cookie. Eating *Mommy* cookie. *Mommy* lap (*Allison 22)

Thus, in place of the italicized nominal in (18), an adult would use the nominative/objective pronoun *you* in the (a) and (b) examples, and the genitive pronoun *your* in the (c) examples. But Allison systematically avoids the use of definite pronouns. Now, if definite pronouns function as pronominal determiners, then the fact that children like Allison have not acquired definite pronouns at this stage would clearly lend further empirical support to the claim that such children have not yet acquired a D-system. The fact that children are using nominals in (what in adult terms are) pronominal contexts would suggest that they are using simple NPs in contexts where adults require DPs: and indeed, the fact that the genitive determiner *'s* is systematically omitted in examples such as (17)(c) and (18)(c) lends further credence to the claim that the nominal constituents developed by young children at this stage have the status of indeterminate NPs which lack a D-system (and hence lack a case system). No doubt the case morphology of definite pronouns is one of the factors which make them particularly difficult for children to acquire.

Thus, the fact that children at this stage have not acquired referential determiners such as *a/the/this/that* etc., or the genitive determiner *'s*, or case-marked pronominal determiners such as *I/me/my* provides us with strong evidence that early child nominals are purely lexical in character, and so contain no functional D-system. We have already suggested that the nonacquisition of a D-system in early child speech would seem to be correlated in an obvious way with the nonacquisition of the morphosyntactic (i.e. case) properties associated with the D-system. However, if children have no D-system at this stage, then we should also expect to find that they have not yet acquired the *semantic* properties of the adult D-system (i.e. they do not 'know' how certain semantic properties are syntactically encoded in the adult D-system). In this connection, we might note the claim by Abney (1987) that one of the essential semantic functions of the determiner system in adult English is to specify referential properties of nominals and pronominals (cf. e.g. the distinction between '*a* dog' and '*the* dog', or between pronominal determiners such as *I* and *you*). Given our central hypothesis that children have not mastered the grammar (i.e. morphology, syntax, and semantics) of the D-system at this stage, we should expect to find that they do not 'know' what referential properties are carried by determiners (either prenominal determiners such as *a/the* etc. or pronominal determiners such as *I/you/he* etc.). The fact that children make no productive use of prenominal determiners at this stage, and typically make no productive use of pronominal determiners (*I/you/he* etc.) either would seem to provide some (albeit weak) support for the claim that children are not 'aware' of how the relevant referential properties are encoded in the D-system, given that *avoidance* is a strategy which children resort to in order to mask incompetence.

However, there is also additional evidence which leads to the same conclusion. Young children seem unaware of the fact that (non-vocative) nominals in adult speech (other than those containing a first or second person pronominal determiner, e.g. *we/you linguists*) are not used to refer to the speaker or addressee, but rather are only used to refer to some third person. The intrinsic third person reference of such nominals can be illustrated by paradigms such as the following:

(19)   Psychologists claim that **(most) linguists** take *themselves/*
        **ourselves/*yourselves* too seriously

The fact that only a third person plural reflexive form (*themselves*) can be used to refer back to the bold-printed nominal **(most) linguists** provides us with empirical evidence that such nominals are inherently third person forms in adult English. However, young children seem to show no 'awareness' of the third person reference of nominals: part of the evidence for claiming this comes from the fact that they frequently use their own names in self-reference, as exemplified by sentences such as (17) above and (20) below (where the italicized nominal represents the name of the speaker):

(20)   (a)   *Hayley* draw boat (Hayley 20)
        (b)   *Bethan* sit down (Bethan 20)
        (c)   *Helen* ride (*Helen 21)
        (d)   *Jem* draw (Jem 21)
        (e)   *Kathryn* like celery (*Kathryn 22)
        (f)   *Jem* put back. *Jem* draw orange. Mummy smack *Jem* (Jem 23)
        (g)   *Kendall* bite. *Kendall* bark. *Kendall* swim. *Kendall* break. *Kendall* turn page (*Kendall 23)
        (h)   *Domenico* on lorry (Domenico 24)
        (i)   Where *Claire* pencil? *Claire* full. *Claire* picture (*Claire 24)
        (j)   *Betty* clip hair. *Betty* touch head (+Betty 24)

Children's lack of awareness of the intrinsic third person reference of nominals is also illustrated by the fact that they use nouns to refer to addressees, as in the examples in (18) above and (21) below (where the italicized noun refers to the person being addressed):

(21)   (a)   *Lady* do. *Lady* draw (Jem 21)
        (b)   *Mommy* busy. *Mommy* push. *Mommy* pull (*Kathryn 21)
        (c)   *Lady* help (Daniel 22)
        (d)   *Mummy* sit down. *Mummy* take top off. *Mummy* cry (Jem 23)
        (e)   Want *Mummy* do (Anna 24)

Indeed, the following examples show both speaker and addressee being referred to by nouns:

(22)   (a)   *Mommy* pick-up...*Kendall* ('You pick me up', *Kendall 23)
        (b)   *Mummy* smack *Jem* ('You smack me', Jem 23)

The fact that children are using nouns to refer both to the speaker and to the addressee indicates that they have not mastered the restriction that nominals in adult English are typically used only for third person reference: more generally still, it is an indication that children at this stage have not mastered the referential properties of nominals.

But why should this be? One plausible answer is to suppose that relevant (third-person) referential properties of nominals are determined by their D-system in adult English: thus, the adult counterpart of 'Lady do' would be '*The lady* will do it', where *the* (like *this* and *that*) might be argued to function as a third person determiner (cf. Abney 1987: 282 for a suggestion along these lines): and we might similarly suggest that expressions such as 'Mummy' and 'Daddy' (and indeed all proper names) in adult English are DPs headed by a third person determiner which is null in English, but may overtly surface as the counterpart of the third person determiner *the* in other languages (cf. Italian *il babbo*, literally 'the daddy'). However, if we suppose that early child nominals are simple NPs with no D-system, then it follows that there will be no person restrictions on the referential properties of early child nominals (since these person restrictions are associated with a functional D-system not yet acquired).

It may well be that not just the *person* properties of (adult) nominals, but also their *binding* (i.e. coreference) properties have not been acquired by children at the lexical stage of their development. Some suggestive evidence pointing in this direction comes from examples such as the following:

(23)   (a)   *Kendall* see *Kendall* (= 'I can see myself', *Kendall 23, looking at a picture of herself)
        (b)   *Betty* touch head...touch *Betty* head (+Betty 24)

In adult grammars, nominals such as 'Kendall' are arguably DPs headed by a determiner which is null in English, but can surface as the counterpart of *the* in other languages. Such nominal DPs have referential properties which require them to be *free* – i.e. interpreted as referentially independent – in adult English (see Chomsky 1986a for an attempted formal characterization of this requirement). What this means is that the two instances of Kendall in (23)(a) would normally be interpreted as denoting two different individuals. However, it is clear from the context in which (23)(a) was uttered that there is no such noncoreferentiality constraint operating in the child's grammar, and that the two instances of *Kendall* are intended to be interpreted as coreferential. If this is so, then it suggests that nominals in early child English are free of *binding* (i.e. coreference) restrictions on their use. Now, it seems reasonable to suppose that the binding properties of nominals are determined by their D-system (given that e.g. adult pronominals like *he/she/they* have the syntactic status of determiners). If this is so, then the fact that *binding principles* do not appear to be operative in early child grammars of English is an automatic consequence of the absence of a D-system.

What we have suggested here is that one of the defining characteristics of children's speech at the lexical stage of their categorial development is the *nonacquisition of functional categories and their associated grammatical properties* (so that e.g. as a corollary of having no D-system, children have no mastery of the *case*, *person*, or *binding* properties encoded in the adult D-system). The converse of this is that a second characteristic of child grammars at this stage is the acquisition of *lexical categories and their associated grammatical properties*. For example, we have already produced extensive evidence that children have begun to acquire the morphological properties of lexical categories at this stage: e.g. they seem to 'know' that nouns form their plural in $+s$, and verbs form their progressive in $+ing$. Likewise, they seem to have acquired the thematic properties of lexical categories: as Goodluck and Behne (1988: 30, n.3) note, 'Children reliably assign the right thematic roles to subject position of a verb from a very early age' – and the same is true of children's theta-marking of complements; more generally still, children typically assign appropriate theta-roles to the arguments of items belonging to lexical categories from the very earliest clausal structures they produce. For example, child utterances such as:

(24)   Wayne hitting Danny

typically have an AGENT + ACTION + PATIENT interpretation. What this means is that children assign appropriate theta roles to appropriate arguments – e.g. the AGENT *Wayne* is correctly positioned in the specifier (not the complement) position, and conversely the PATIENT *Danny* is correctly positioned in the complement (not the specifier) position. This lends credence to our claim that when children acquire lexical categories, they also acquire the linguistic (i.e. morpho-syntactic and semantic-thematic) properties associated with those lexical categories (this is an issue which we shall return to discuss in more detail in chapter 9).

Given the arguments we have presented in this section, the natural conclusion to draw would seem to be that there are two main defining characteristics of early child grammars of English, namely:

(25)   (i)   the acquisition of lexical categories and their associated grammatical properties
      (ii)   the nonacquisition of functional categories and their associated grammatical properties

(*grammatical* here being used in the extended sense of 'morphosyntactic and semantic'). These might be taken to be the two principal criterial properties of the *lexical* stage in the child's categorial development.

Before we conclude our discussion in this chapter, we shall briefly turn to consider a number of potential counterexamples to the *lexical* analysis of early child grammars of English proposed here. It is important to clarify at the outset just what is (and is not) being claimed here. The specific claim we are making is that children acquiring English as their first language go through two stages of grammatical development: (i) an earlier *lexical* stage (typically between the ages of 20 and 23 months, ±20%), during which they are beginning to acquire the grammar of lexical categories but not yet of functional categories; and (ii) a later functional stage (which normal children typically enter at around 24 months, ±20%), during which they begin to acquire the grammar of functional categories. It is important to emphasize that the claim we are making is about *stages*, not about *ages*: thus, it would not be a counterexample to our claim here if we were to find a child who reached the functional stage markedly earlier or later than typical children, or if we found a child for whom the lexical stage was markedly longer or shorter than the three or four month norm which we have suggested here. What would constitute a genuine counterexample to our claim would be to find a child who showed no evidence of passing through a separate lexical stage, but rather went directly from the precategorial to the functional stage – e.g. a child who developed a D-system in parallel with an N-system. But do such children exist?

Before we try to answer this question, it may be useful to remind ourselves of the four key pieces of evidence which we adduced in support of our central claim in this chapter that children develop a lexical N-system earlier than the corresponding functional D-system. These relate to the fact that children at the lexical stage of development have not acquired the grammar of prenominal determiners such as *a/the/this/ that* etc, or of the genitive determiner *'s*, or of case-marked pronominal determiners such as *I/me/my*, and have likewise not acquired relevant aspects of the referential properties of nominals (viz. those aspects encoded by the D-system in adult grammars). Clearly, the overall claim being made is only as strong as the evidence on which it is based:

however, the evidence itself is not always entirely unequivocal, as we shall see.

Consider first the evidence we adduced from examples such as (1–3) above in support of the claim that children at this stage have not acquired the morphosyntax of referential determiners such as *a/the/this/that* etc. One potential source of counterexamples to this claim comes from the fact that some children at this stage use the demonstratives *this* and *that* as independent pronouns. The following examples (taken from a fine-grained longitudinal study of Daniel) are representative (his age is specified in months and weeks, so that 19.1 = 19 months and 1 week):

(26) (a) Want *that*. Like *that* (= 'I'd like that'). Allgone *that*. Want *this* (19.0)
      (b) *That* chair (= 'That is a chair') (19.1)
      (c) Open *that*. Want *this* (19.3)
      (d) Want *that* (20.0)
      (e) *That* daddy there (= 'That's daddy there'). *That* daddy (= 'That is daddy'). *That* doggy (= 'That's a doggy'). *That* car (= 'That's a car'). Take *that* (20.1)
      (f) Want *this*. *That* spoon (= 'That is a spoon'). *That*'s Teddy (20.2)
      (g) *That* ball (= 'That's a ball'). *This* tree (= 'This is a tree'). *That* daddy (= 'That's daddy'). What *this*? (= 'What's this?'). Want do *that* (20.3)
      (h) Want *this*. *This* Teddy (= 'This is Teddy') (21.0)
      (i) What *that*? (= 'What's that?'). What's *that*? *That*'s bee. Who's *that*? What *this*? (= 'What's this?') (21.2)
      (j) Danny open *this*. *This* doll (= 'This is a doll') (21.3)

At first sight, it might seem as if we should conclude that the demonstratives *this* and *that* should be analysed as functioning as pronominal DPs (e.g. DPs headed by a head pronominal D) in Daniel's system, so leading us to the conclusion that Daniel has indeed developed a D-system for noun phrases (contrary to our claim that early child nominals have no associated D-system). However, such a conclusion seems hasty. The main reason is that Daniel at this stage never combines demonstratives with nominals at all, so it is not clear in what sense we could say that *this/that* in his speech serve as determiners *for noun phrases*. After all, recall (from our discussion in chapter 3) that Abney (1987: 64–5) posits that it is a defining property of functional categories that they combine with a specific type of complement, so that C takes an IP complement, I takes a VP complement, and D takes an NP complement (cf. the list given in (11) in chapter 3). But far from combining with following NP complements, the demonstratives *this/that* seem to *stand in place of NPs* in Daniel's speech, and thus occur in typical NP positions (e.g. as the complement of verbs like *want, open, do*, etc.). The obvious conclusion to draw from this is that demonstratives are more plausibly analysed as having the status of pronominal NPs *within his system*. What makes such an analysis even more attractive is the fact that demonstratives do not overtly inflect for case in English (e.g. *this/that* have no genitive forms **this's*/**that's*): this makes it all the more plausible that a child should misanalyse demonstratives as uninflected caseless pronominal NPs, rather than as inflected case-marked pronominal DPs (cf. Bloom 1970: 68, and Guilfoyle and Noonan 1988: 15 for parallel suggestions). The methodological moral to draw from this discussion is that we can only categorize an item as a determiner in early child speech if we can show that it is being productively combined with nominal complements. Thus, from this point of view, a child's mastery of the articles *a/the* is probably a better indication of the acquisition of a D-system, since *a/the* cannot be used pronominally in adult English, but rather must be combined with a following nominal complement. More generally still, the point of principle being illustrated by our discussion is that we must draw a clear distinction between *item acquisition* and *category acquisition*: the fact that a child has acquired a specific *item* does not necessarily imply that he has acquired the *category* which that item belongs to in the corresponding adult grammar (for the obvious reason that a given word in the child's vocabulary may have a categorial status within the child's system which is different from that which its seeming adult counterpart has within the adult system).

We might extend the pronominal NP analysis from demonstratives to other types of pronoun occurring in early child speech, so that e.g. interrogative pronouns such as *what/who/where* might be analysed as pronominal NPs (meaning roughly 'what object/person/place?'). There are two pieces of evidence which lend credence to such an analysis. Firstly, the relevant forms are invariable in early child English (e.g. children use only the uninflected form *who*, never the inflected forms *whom* and *whose*), and thus are plausibly analysed as uninflected caseless pronominal NPs, rather than as inflected case-marked pronominal DPs. Secondly, although *what* in adult English can function as a determiner taking an NP complement (cf. 'What [*sensible alternative*] do we have?'), it is only used pronominally in early child English, and never combined with an NP complement (a fact which would be predicted under the analysis of *what* as a pronominal NP).

The net conclusion to be drawn from our discussion is that the observation by Bloom et al. (1978) that many young children have a *nominal* speech style characterized by the avoidance of pronouns has to be modified somewhat. It would seem that it is not pronouns as such that children avoid, but rather *pronouns overtly inflected for case*. Indeed, it is interesting to note that (in spite of the claim by Bloom et al. (1978) that Allison Bloom had a *nominal* speech style characterized by the complete absence of pronouns) we find the following example of a definite pronoun in Allison's transcript at age 22 months:

(27)   Spill *it*. Spill (*Allison 22)

However, since Allison has not acquired the genitive morpheme *'s* at this stage, it seems reasonable to suppose that *it* will lack the genitive form *its* in Allison's speech, and thus will be a form not overtly inflected for case (hence plausibly analyseable as a caseless pronominal NP, rather than as a case-marked pronominal DP); at any rate, there are no instances of *its* in the relevant transcript. Thus, instead of saying that children do not use *pronouns* at this stage, it would be more accurate to say that children do not use *pronominal DPs*: if we assume that case is an intrinsic property of the D-system, then this amounts to claiming that they do not use case-marked pronouns. This means that if they use pronouns at all, they will be (caseless) nominal pronouns (e.g. items like the N-bar proform *one* discussed in the previous chapter). Typical of the limited pronoun repertoire of many children at this stage are the examples in (28) below, which represent the only pronouns used productively by the children concerned in the transcripts specified:

(28)   (a)   Read *that*. *That* Luke, mum. *This*. Get *it*. Catch *it*. Open *it*. Put *that* in *there*. *What this*? (Lucy 20)
        (b)   Looka *that*. What *that*? Looka *this*. What *this*? Open *it*. Dump-*it* out. *Where* chicken? *Where* doggie? Daddy in-*there*. Mommy in-*there*. People right-*here*. Car right-*here*. (*Claire 24.0 from Hill 1983: 119–24)

Since pronouns such as *this/that/what/it* are uninflected forms not overtly marked for case, and since they occur in (what in terms of the child's grammar are) typical NP positions, they are probably best analysed as caseless pronominal NPs at this stage. It may well be that such proforms function as pro-NPs in early child English (i.e. as pronouns directly generated under NP): this would predict that they won't take adjectival or possessive premodifiers in child speech (i.e. that we won't find forms like *daddy big it*, corresponding to an adult DP such as 'daddy's big one'); and it is certainly true children don't generally produce structures of this kind. If we are correct in claiming that such items have the status of *nominal* proforms and not *determiner* proforms in early child grammars, then it follows that they are *impostors* – i.e. forms which have much the same phonological shape as their apparent adult counterparts, but which have a different (lexical rather than functional) categorial status.

For similar reasons, the pronominal locatives *here/there/where* are likewise probably best analysed in parallel terms: they too are arguably uninflected for case, and (*in terms of the child's system*) occur in the same range of positions as NPs specifying location (viz. as the complement of locative prepositions like *in/on*, or as the complement of verbs like *go* taking a locative complement), so that there would be an obvious parallelism between related pairs of typical child utterances such as 'Mummy go *there*', and 'Mummy go *school*', *there* being a pronominal NP, and *school* being a nominal NP. If our arguments here are along the right lines, prolocatives like *here/there/where* in early child English are likewise impostors, and would seem to be caseless NPs meaning something along the lines of 'this/that/which place'. However, given that *in* and *there* in the transcript from which (28)(b) was taken occur only as part of the sequence 'in there', it may be argued that the resulting sequence is better analysed as a monomorphemic preposition (which might be transcribed as *innere* to make its single-morpheme status clearer). Certainly, some children do seem to use *innere* in this way: for example, Bowerman's (1973: 242) transcript of Kendall's speech at age 23 months shows her producing the utterance 'Kendall innere bed', one interpretation of which would be that she has misanalysed *innere* as a monomorphemic preposition taking the NP *bed* as its complement. If this is so, then expressions such as *innere* clearly provide no evidence for postulating that such children have developed a pronominal locative *there*.

The conclusion to be drawn from the arguments outlined immediately above is that the sporadic occurrence of (caseless) pronouns in early child speech does not pose a serious threat to our lexical analysis of the earliest category systems developed by young children, since such pronouns are arguably *impostors* which have the status of nominal proforms (not determiner proforms) within the child's system. If this is so, then we should expect to find not only that children have not acquired the morphosyntax of pronouns (e.g. the case restrictions on their use), but also that they have not acquired the semantics of pronouns (viz. the referential properties which pronouns carry by virtue of their determiner status). Some evidence for this claim comes from the fact that children at this stage do not seem to be 'aware' of the 'variable reference' property of overt pronouns. We can illustrate this property of pronouns in adult English in terms of the following (soap-operesque) dialogue:

(29)   SCOTT: I love you
        CHARLENE (*feigning astonishment*): You love me?
        LUCY (*listening at the keyhole*): He loves her!

Thus, the individual named Scott is referred to by the first person pronoun *I* in the first utterance, by the second person pronoun *you* in the second, and by the third person pronoun *he* in the third; and likewise, the individual named Charlene is referred to by the second person pronoun *you* in the first utterance, by the first person pronoun *me* in the second, and by the third person pronoun *her* in the third. Conversely, the second person pronoun *you* is used to refer to Charlene in the first utterance, but to Scott in the second (and so forth). It has often been noted in the acquisition literature that young children not infrequently have problems in coping with the complexities of *person* in pronouns (cf. e.g. Gruber 1973, Clark 1974, Van der Geest 1977, Clark 1978, Tanz 1980, Chiat 1982, 1986). Illustrative of the person errors which young children make is the following dialogue (from Jespersen 1922: 58):

(30)   ADULT: Shall I carry *you?*
        CHILD: Carry *you* (*Frans 21)

The child refers to himself by the same pronoun *you* which the adult uses to refer to the child. Clark (1978) suggests that the nature of the person error is that pronouns are misanalysed by the child as a type of name, so that *I* = adult and *you* = child. Maratsos (1979: 235) characterizes the problem in similar terms, suggesting that 'The child hears himself addressed as *you* and the person talking to him is *I*. If the child believed these were names, his name would be *you* and the listener's *I*.' Given that names are nouns, these suggestions are obviously consistent with our hypothesis that pronouns are more noun-like than determiner-like in early child speech (e.g. a pronoun like *him* is a pronominal DP in adult English but may well be simply a pronominal NP in early child English). Moreover, the assumption that children are 'unaware' of the person properties of pronominals clearly ties up with our earlier suggestion (in relation to examples such as (20) and (21) above) that they are likewise 'unaware' of the person properties of nominals.

   If children do not 'know' what semantic properties are encoded in the adult D-system at this stage, then we should expect to find not only that they are not 'aware' of the *person* properties of pronominal DPs, but also that they are 'unaware' of their *binding* properties (since we suggested earlier in relation to examples like (23) above that children have no 'knowledge' of the binding properties of nominals at this stage). Some (admittedly flimsy) evidence that there are no binding constraints on the use of pronominals in early child grammars comes from sentences such as the following:

(31)   Want *me*...Want see *me* (Daniel 24, wanting to see himself in a mirror)

In adult English, the italicized pronominals would be interpreted as disjoint in reference from the 'understood' first person subject of the containing clause, and would have to be replaced by the anaphor *myself* if coreference with the subject were intended. However, the child clearly intends the first person pronominal object to be coreferential to its understood first person subject in both utterances, and this suggests that children are not 'aware' of the binding properties of pronominals at this stage. Of course, if the binding properties of pronominals are determined by their D-system, and there is no D-system operating in the child's grammar at this stage, then the absence of binding restrictions on the interpretation of pronominals (and indeed, nominals) is readily accounted for.

Overall, then, it seems that we have abundant evidence that the earliest pronouns used by young children are pronominal NP constituents which lack the full range of morphosyntactic and semantic properties carried by their adult pronominal DP counterparts. If this is so, then the use of 'pronouns' by some children at this stage poses no real threat to our lexical analysis of early child English. However, an alternative challenge to our overall hypothesis that early child grammars lack functional categories comes from the sporadic occurrence of possessive *'s* in early child English, as in example (32) below (from Bloom 1970: 48):

(32)   *Mommy's* milk (*Kathryn 21)

Given our assumption that possessive *'s* functions as a genitive determiner in adult English, the obvious suggestion is that examples such as (32) provide us with *prima facie* evidence that Kathryn has indeed developed a genitive determiner, and thus must be presumed to have developed a D-system. And yet, we must beware of taking isolated examples as being representative of the child's overall system. If we look at a wider range of data, we realize that Kathryn has little idea about how to use possessive *'s* at this stage. For example, the possessive *'s* inflection in (32) was elicited only after her mother had corrected a previous utterance by Kathryn in which she had omitted the *'s*: Kathryn had first of all said 'Mommy milk'; her mother then corrected this to 'Mommy's milk', and Kathryn responded by correctly repeating her mother's utterance. Clearly, however, we can't take isolated and sporadic 'blind repetitions' as reliable indicators of a child's linguistic competence. Much more significant is the fact that none of the other potential nominal possessives produced by Kathryn during the same period showed any use of the *'s* inflection: cf. the examples in (33) below:

(33)   *Mommy* slipper. *Mommy* sock. *Mommy* apple. *Mommy* cottage cheese. *Baby* milk. *Mommy* hangnail. *Mommy* vegetable. *Mommy* pigtail. *Kathryn* sock. *Mommy* shoe. *Kathryn* shoes (*Kathryn 21, from Bloom 1970: 46–49)

Clearly, the sporadic occurrence of the genitive *'s* inflection (elicited only as part of a correction exercise) cannot be taken as indicating acquisition of the morphosyntax of the genitive determiner in the child's sponta-neous speech.

A more interesting class of potential counterexamples to our claim that children have not acquired the morphosyntax of genitive *'s* at this stage comes from the observation in Cazden (1968) that some young children at this stage use genitive *'s* in *pronominal* possessives (i.e. possessives like *daddy's* where there is no overt nominal following the *'s*), but systema-tically omit *'s* in *prenominal* possessives (i.e. in structures like *daddy's new car* where the possessed nominal is overtly specified). She notes that between the ages of 18 and 24 months, Eve generally used possessive *'s* pronominally, but omitted it prenominally. An interesting illustration of this phenomenon is provided in Bloom (1970: 93): while holding up her mother's keys, Gia (at age 20 months) produces the following two possessive NPs in immediate succession:

(34)   *Mommy's. Mommy* key (*Gia 20, holding mother's keys)

A parallel illustration comes from the transcript of Kendall's speech at age 23 months in Bowerman (1973: 242), where we find the following sequence:

(35)   (a)   That *Daddy's* [= 'That is Daddy's']
        (b)   That *Kimmy* ball [= 'That is Kimmy's ball'] (*Kendall 23)

Likewise, Smith (1973: 68) reports that his son Amahl produced contrasts such as the following at a similar stage of development:

(36)   (a)   It *daddy's* (= 'It's daddy's')
        (b)   *Daddy* one (= 'Daddy's one')

The second member of each pair of examples clearly poses no problem for our hypothesis that early child possessive structures are NPs in which a possessor NP functions as the specifier of a following N-bar (so that *Mommy*, *Kimmy*, and *Daddy* in the second examples would be NPs functioning as the specifier of the following N-bar *key/ball/one*). But how are we to deal with the first example, *mommy's/daddy's*? After all, if genitive *'s* is a head determiner in adult English, won't it have the same status in early child English as well? The answer is, of course, that we have to bear in mind the possibility that *'s* may be an *impostor* – i.e. a morpheme which has a different status within the child's system than it has in adult grammars of English. But if *'s* is an impostor, what kind of morpheme could it be in child speech?

One possibility is that possessive *'s* in child speech might have the status of a pro-N-bar constituent: this would mean that in the 'elliptic' utterance *mommy's/daddy's*, the NP *mommy/daddy* would function as the specifier of the pronominal N-bar *'s*. If this were so, then the utterance *daddy one* in (36) would be assigned the structure (37)(a) below, while its 'elliptic' counterpart *daddy's* would be assigned the structure (37)(b):

(37)   (a)   [$_{NP}$ [$_{NP}$ daddy] [$_{N'}$ *one*]]
        (b)   [$_{NP}$ [$_{NP}$ daddy] [$_{N'}$ *'s*]]

Given that we have already presented evidence (in the previous chapter) that children have generally acquired the syntax of the pro-N-bar constituent *one* at this stage, it is conceivable that they might have (mis)analysed possessive *'s* as an N-bar proform, so that the italicized items *one* and *'s* would have the same categorial status in (37)(a) and (b). However, what would be problematic under such an analysis would be accounting for why we find structures like 'Want blue *one*' and 'Want *one*', but not (with the same intended interpretation) structures such as *'Want blue's'* or *'Want's'*. In order to account for this, we would have to posit (e.g.) that *'s* is an enclitic which can only attach to a preceding *nominal* host – and this clearly complicates the analysis somewhat.

A second possibility would be to analyse *'s* as a derivational suffix which has the function of converting a noun into a predicative possessive adjective: given that possessive forms like *mío/tuyo/suyo* etc. ('mine/

yours/his' etc.) are arguably predicative adjectives in adult Spanish, the analysis of child possessive *Noun* + *'s* structures as predicative adjectives is by no means intrinsically implausible. We shall not speculate here on whether the *'s* morpheme used by some young children at this stage in independent possessives is best analysed as a nominal proform or as an adjectivalizing suffix (both analyses have drawbacks which are not difficult to see): the main point we want to establish is the possibility that possessive *'s* might be a further example of an *impostor* (i.e. a morpheme with much the same phonological form as – but a different grammatical function from – its immediate adult counterpart). If this is so, then the fact that a restricted number of children make restricted pronominal use of possessive *'s* poses no threat to our overall claim that children have not acquired a genitive D-system at this (lexical) stage of development.

A third source of potential counterexamples to the claim that children at this stage have not developed a genitive D-system comes from the sporadic occurrence of possessive personal pronouns in early child speech: for example, Bloom (1970: 35) notes that Kathryn at age 22 months produced the following (italicized) example of a pronominal possessive:

(38)   *my* tiger book (*Kathryn 22)

Within the framework adopted here, we might suppose that (in adult speech) pronominal possessives like *my/your/her* etc. are pronominal DPs which function as the specifier for an empty allomorph of the genitive determiner *'s*, so that *my tiger book* would have the skeletal structure (39) below in adult English:

(39)   [$_{DP}$ my [$_D$ *e*] [$_{NP}$ tiger book]]

(where *e* is an empty allomorph of the possessive *'s* determiner which assigns genitive case to its specifier, the pronominal DP *my*). Might we not therefore posit that *my* has a similar function in the corresponding child utterance (38), and conclude that Kathryn has developed an abstract (phonologically null) genitive determiner at this stage?

There are two types of objection to any such claim – empirical and theoretical. The empirical objections stem from the fact that if we look at a wider range of the pronominal possessives which Kathryn produced during the period in question, we see that she is very far from having mastered the morphosyntax of genitive pronouns – as the examples in (40) below illustrate:

(40)   This *my*. This *mys*.This *mine*. These *my*. These *mines*. These *my*
       Kathryn's. That's *Kathryn my* book. That's *mine* toy. *My* have ə
       this. No, *I my* have ə this (*Kathryn 22)

It is clear that she is confused about the distinction between the forms
I/me/my/mine. Nor is this confusion on her part untypical of children at
this stage, as we see from the examples below:

(41)   (a)   ADULT: That one's Lisa's
             CHILD: *My...mine* (Hayley 20)
       (b)   ADULT: Whose truck is this?
             CHILD: *Me...my* (Bethan 20)
       (c)   ADULT: Bethan, whose chair is this?
             CHILD: *Me* (Bethan 21)
       (d)   ADULT: What's this?
             CHILD: *My* (Jenny 23)
       (e)   *Me* eye (Hayley 20)
       (f)   *My* egg...*mine* egg (Daniel 23)
       (g)   No, it *my...mine*. It *mine...my*. *My* sweet...*Mine* sweet
             (Daniel 24)

The general point of principle to be made here is that the sporadic
(faltering and hesitant) occurrence of isolated (pseudo-) genitive forms
(alternating apparently at random with other forms) can scarcely be taken
to indicate the development of a genitive D-system.

In addition to empirical objections to the suggestion that Kathryn may
have developed a genitive determiner system at this stage, there are also
theoretical objections. An essential point of principle which needs to be
underlined is that even if a child is making *systematic* use of a given item,
we cannot be sure that the item will have the same status in the child's
speech as it has in adult speech. For example, pronominal possessives
such as *my/your/her* etc. are arguably pronominal DPs which function as
specifiers of an empty allomorph of the genitive determiner *'s* in adult
English (as represented in (39) above): but the assumption that young
children who have not yet acquired any overt determiners (and in
particular have not yet acquired overt allomorphs of genitive *'s*) have
nonetheless developed a covert (i.e. phonologically null) allomorph of the
genitive *'s* determiner seems to strain credulity. It appears more likely
that pronominal possessives in early child speech are *impostors* – i.e.
forms which have much the same phonological shape and semantic
function as their adult genitive DP counterparts, but which have a

different morphosyntactic status. A natural suggestion to make would be that early child possessive pronouns may have the same status as the (uninflected) italicized possessive nominals in (8), (9), (17)(c), (18)(c), and (33) above, and hence would be analyseable as (pronominal) NPs which function as N-bar specifiers.

We can summarize the conclusions we have reached in this chapter in the following terms. In general, we find that early child nominals show no evidence of productive use of items which function as determiners in adult speech – hence we find no productive use of the articles *a* and *the*, or of genitive *'s*, or of case-marked pronouns like *I/me/my*. Where children do use items which are constituents of DP in adult English, they appear initially to miscategorize them as constituents of NP, so that (e.g.) the demonstrative pronouns *this/that* and possessive pronouns such as *my* appear to be initially misanalysed as pro-NP constituents. What this suggests is that the child's first attempt to incorporate into his grammar constituents which belong to functional categories and which are contained within functional projections in adult English is to miscategorize them as constituents belonging to lexical categories, and contained within lexical projections. For example, nominal and pronominal possessors are DPs which superficially function as specifiers of DP in adult English, but their child counterparts are NPs which function as specifiers of NP; demonstratives such as *this/that* are pronominal DPs in adult English, but seem to function as pronominal NPs in early child English; and genitive *'s* is a D constituent in adult English, but (if used at all) seems to function as a nominal proform (e.g as a pro-N-bar) in early child English.

What all of this suggests is that the child's initial *categorization strategy* at the lexical stage is to attempt to fit all constituents into the system of lexical heads and projections which he has developed. We might suppose that constituents which have a functional categorial status in adult English will be treated by the child in one of two ways. One possibility is that they may initially be *uncategorized*: i.e. if the child is unable to assimilate them into his existing system of lexical categories, he may simply fail to assign them to any category at all; the child's lexical entry for any uncategorised word in his vocabulary would have phonological and semantic properties, but no categorial properties, and uncategorized constituents could clearly not be used in the child's productive syntax (though they might play a pragmatically determined role in comprehension). The second possibility is that functional constituents may be *miscategorized* as having lexical categorial status: we might suppose that in such a case, a functional constituent is likely to be miscategorized as belonging to its immediate lexical counterpart (so that a pronominal D may be miscategorized as a pronominal N, whereas an I constituent might be miscategorized as a V constituent, for example). It seems reasonable to hypothesise that the child will only abandon his initial lexical (mis)categorization of such constituents when confronted with an overwhelming accumulation of positive evidence from the speech input he receives that such an analysis is clearly incompatible with the observed morphosyntactic properties of the relevant constituents in adult speech.

At the beginning of the previous chapter, we pointed out that there are three primary types of functional category system in adult English, namely the D-system, the C-system, and the I-system. In this chapter, we have argued that there is no D-system in early child grammars of English. In order to defend our more general thesis that there are no functional categories in early child grammars of English, we now need to go on to argue that there is likewise no C-system or I-system in early child grammars of English. We shall argue this in some detail in the next four chapters, beginning with a presentation of evidence that there is no C-system in chapter 5, and going on in chapters 6–8 to present parallel evidence that there is no I-system either.

5

Absence of a Complementizer System in Early Child English

In the previous chapter, we put forward the hypothesis that the earliest grammars developed by young children during the period of early multi-word speech (roughly between the ages of 20 and 23 months, ±20%) are purely lexical in nature, and thus are characterised by the absence of functional category systems. In support of this claim, we presented evidence that the earliest nominals and pronominals produced by young children are NPs which entirely lack a determiner system. However, in order to substantiate our *lexical* analysis of early child grammars of English, we need to establish not only that early child grammars lack a D-system, but also that they lack the other two primary functional category systems found in adult English, namely the complementizer system (C-system) and the inflection system (I-system). Since C and I are (head) constituents of clauses, then this means that in order to substantiate our more general claim, we need to show that early child clauses contain no C-system, and no I-system either. If this is indeed the case (as we shall argue in detail in the next four chapters), it follows that early child clauses would have a very different structure from '*Ordinary Clauses*' in adult speech, and would in fact closely resemble adult '*Small Clauses*' (these two italicized terms are used here in a technical sense made precise in Radford 1988a). We could then caricature clause structures in early child English by saying that 'Small children speak Small Clauses' (with an important proviso noted below) – a suggestion made in Radford 1985, 1986, 1988b, and echoed in Lebeaux 1987, 1988, Kazman 1988, Guilfoyle and Noonan 1988 and Platzack 1989.

We can illustrate the difference between Ordinary Clauses and Small Clauses in adult English by comparing the structure of the bracketed Ordinary Clause in (1)(a) below, with that of the bracketed Small Clause (= SC) in (1)(b):

(1)　(a)　I consider [*that* this candidate *would* be unsuitable for the post]

　　　(b)　I consider [this candidate unsuitable for the post]

The bracketed Ordinary Clause in (1)(a) clearly contains both a C-system (headed by the italicized C *that*), and an I-system (headed by the italicized I *would*). By contrast, the bracketed SC (= Small Clause) in (1)(b) appears to comprise simply a DP subject (= the determinate noun phrase *this candidate*) combined with an adjectival predicate (= the A-bar *unsuitable for the post*). Thus (superficially, at least) it would appear that Small Clauses in adult English have no C-system or I-system.

The range of adult English Small Clause constructions can be illustrated rather more fully by the bracketed SC structures in (2) below:

(2)　(a)　I've never found [*the rich* **kind to the poor**]

　　　(b)　I don't want [*your feet* **on my table**]

　　　(c)　We mustn't let [*the campaign* **come to nothing**]

　　　(d)　I can't imagine [*a film* **having so much influence**]

　　　(e)　You must have [*your injuries* **seen to by a doctor**]

In each of the examples in (2), the bracketed Small Clause comprises an italicized determinate noun phrase (= DP) subject and a (bold-printed) predicate phrase. Given the analysis of Small Clauses proposed in Stowell (1981), the bold-printed Predicate Phrase would be a single-bar constituent, and the italicized subject DP would be its specifier: under this analysis, the bracketed Small Clause in (2)(a) would have the simplified structure indicated in (3) below:

(3)　$[_{AP} [_{DP}$ the rich] $[_{A'} [_A$ kind] $[_{PP}$ to the poor]]]

The overall (adjectival) Small Clause would have the status of an AP (i.e. an adjectival phrase/clause), and its two immediate constituents would be the DP specifier (= subject) *the rich*, and the A-bar predicate *kind to the poor*, with the predicate phrase comprising the head adjective *kind* and its PP complement *to the poor*. More generally still, Small Clauses would be of the schematic form (4) below:

(4)　$[_{XP} [_{DP}$ subject] $[_{X'} [_X$ head] complement/s]]

where the head of the overall structure would be a nonfinite predicative lexical category (i.e. a category capable of functioning as the head of a predicate phrase).

If we now turn to look at the earliest clausal structures produced by young children, we see (from examples such as (5) below) that these bear a striking superficial similarity to adult Small Clauses:

(5)   (a)   *Sausage* **bit hot** (Jem 21)
      (b)   *Wayne* **in bedroom** (Daniel 21)
      (c)   *Teddy* **want bed** (Daniel 21)
      (d)   *Wayne* **taken bubble** (Daniel 21)
      (e)   *Mummy* **doing dinner** (Daniel 22)

Thus, early child clauses comprise an (italicized) NP subject which might be taken to function as the specifier of a (bold-printed) predicate phrase which appears to have the status of an A-bar in the (a) example, a P-bar in (b), and a nonfinite V-bar in (c), (d), and (e). Given these assumptions (carried over from our discussion in chapter 3), then a (prepositional) child clause such as *Wayne in bedroom* would have the simplified structure:

(6)   [$_{PP}$ [$_{NP}$ Wayne] [$_{P'}$ [$_P$ in] [$_{NP}$ bedroom]]]

The overall (prepositional) Small Clause would have the status of a PP (i.e. a prepositional phrase/clause), and its two immediate constituents would be the NP specifier (= subject) *Wayne,* and the P-bar predicate *in bedroom,* with the predicate phrase comprising the head preposition *in* and its NP complement *bedroom.* More generally still, clauses in early child English would be of the schematic form:

(7)   [$_{XP}$ [$_{NP}$ subject] [$_{X'}$ [$_X$ head] complement/s]]

where X would be a nonfinite predicative lexical category.

Now, if adult Small Clauses are of the schematic form [DP X'], and early child clauses are of the form [NP X'], then it seems reasonable to suggest that early child clauses have much the same internal constituent structure as adult Small Clauses - with the obvious difference that (because children have not yet acquired a D-system at this stage) the child's counterpart of an adult determinate DP subject is an indeterminate NP. If this is so, then the obvious conclusion to draw (following Radford 1985, 1986, 1988b) is that 'Small children speak Small Clauses' - i.e. early child clauses resemble adult Small Clauses in that they lack both a C-system and an I-system. In this chapter, we shall concentrate on presenting evidence in support of the claim that early child clauses lack a complementizer system, going on to argue that they likewise lack an inflection system in the following three chapters.

Before we turn to present evidence in support of our claim that early child clauses lack a C-system, we shall first provide a brief outline of the nature of the C-system in adult English. Given the assumption that functional categories have the same range of projections as lexical categories, then it follows that the adult English C-system will be of the (simplified) schematic form:

(8)   [$_{CP}$ specifier [$_{C'}$ [$_{C}$ head] complement/s]]

Furthermore, given the postulate made by Abney (1987: 65) that functional categories subcategorize unique complements, and that IP is universally the complement of C, then it follows that the complement of a head C will always be an IP, so that (8) can be made more specific along the lines of (9) below:

(9)   [$_{CP}$ specifier [$_{C'}$ [$_{C}$ head] [$_{IP}$ complement]]]

Thus, what remains to be determined is the range of constituents which can occupy the head and specifier positions within CP.

We assume here that Universal Grammar allows (in principle) for any given sentence position to be filled in one of two ways – viz. either by a *base-generated* constituent (which originates in the position concerned), or by a *moved* constituent (which originates elsewhere but is subsequently moved into the relevant position). We further assume that overt complementizers like *that/for/whether/if* are base-generated in C, as in the bracketed complement clauses in (10) below:

(10)   (a)   I feel sure [$_{CP}$ [$_{C}$ *that*] [$_{IP}$ you will win]]
       (b)   I am anxious [$_{CP}$ [$_{C}$ *for*] [$_{IP}$ you to succeed]]
       (c)   I wonder [$_{CP}$ [$_{C}$ *whether*] [$_{IP}$ he should apologise]]
       (d)   I doubt [$_{CP}$ [$_{C}$ *if*] [$_{IP}$ she can do it]]

However, there are no obvious candidates for constituents base-generated in the specifier position of CP: for example, argument expressions (e.g. DPs) could not be base-generated as specifiers within a functional category system, since they would not be assigned a theta-role (directly, at least), if we make the assumption that nominal arguments can only be theta-marked by lexical categories.

If the head and specifier positions within CP are underlyingly empty, then a second way in which they can be filled is *transformationally*, that is by movement of an appropriate constituent from some position within the complement IP to an appropriate position within CP. Since heads are word-level categories, it follows that the head C position of CP can only be filled by movement of another head word-level category. Thus, if we assume that finite auxiliary verbs in English are superficially positioned in I (when occupying post-subject position), then the phenomenon of 'subject–auxiliary inversion' in English can be described in terms of movement of a finite auxiliary from I into (an empty) C, in the manner schematized in (11) below:

(11)   [$_{CP}$ [$_C$ e] [$_{IP}$ John [$_I$ *can*] speak French]]

(Cf. '*Can* John speak French?'). It will then follow that in sentence pairs such as the following, the italicized auxiliary is positioned in the post-subject I position in the (a) example, but in the pre-subject C position in the (b) example:

(12)   (a)   The minister *should* resign
       (b)   *Should* the minister resign?

(13)   (a)   John *is* working hard
       (b)   *Is* John working hard?

(14)   (a)   The store *has* closed
       (b)   *Has* the store closed?

(See Radford 1988a: 411-20 for empirical arguments in support of the analysis of 'subject–auxiliary inversion' as involving movement of a finite auxiliary from I to C.)

Just as the head C position of CP can be transformationally filled, so too the specifier position of CP can likewise be filled by a moved constituent. If (following Stowell 1981: 70) we posit that all 'modifiers' of heads (viz. complements, specifiers, and adjuncts) must be maximal projections, then it follows that the specifier position is a maximal projection position, and thus is a position into which full phrases can be moved. We should therefore expect the C-specifier position to be filled by movement of a phrasal constituent (XP) out of IP into CP. In the light of the arguments presented in Radford (1988a: 462–508), we might posit that wh-phrases (i.e. phrases containing a wh-word like *which/what/who/ when/why/where/how* etc.) are constituents which originate within (a constituent of) IP, but are subsequently preposed into the specifier position in CP. If this is so, then it follows that preposed wh-phrases will be superficially positioned to the left of the head C of CP; and since – as we have just seen – the head C position can be filled by a preposed auxiliary (e.g. in direct questions), then it follows that preposed wh-phrases will be positioned in front of preposed auxiliaries, as represented schematically in (15) below:

(15) (a) [CP *Which one* [C did] [IP you choose ---]]?
      (b) [CP *How many cards* [C have] [IP you bought ---]]?
      (c) [CP *Where* [C are] [IP you going to ---]]?
      (d) [CP *How long* [C shall] [IP I wait for him ---]]?

In examples such as (15) above, it might be argued that the italicized wh-phrase originates in the position marked --- within the bracketed IP, and is subsequently preposed by the transformation of WH-MOVEMENT into the C-specifier position to the left of the head C position filled by the preposed auxiliary *did/have/are/shall*.

Our discussion so far has suggested that the head C position of CP can be filled either by a base-generated complementizer, or by a preposed auxiliary moved from I into C. However, a third possibility is that the head C position in CP can be *empty* (both underlyingly and superficially). Given our assumption that preposed wh-phrases are positioned to the left of C, then it seems likely that indirect question clauses such as that bracketed in (16) below should be analysed as CP constituents headed by an empty C:

(16) I wonder [CP *what kind of party* [C e] [IP he has in mind]]

Indeed, if we assume that Universal Grammar requires all constituents to be *endocentric* (i.e. properly headed), then it follows that we cannot say that the bracketed CP in (16) lacks a head C constituent; it therefore follows that CP in (16) must be headed by an empty C. Some support for this assumption comes from two sets of facts. The first is that the hypothesized C position in (16) can be filled (in so-called 'semi-indirect speech') by preposing the auxiliary *has*: cf.

(17) I wonder [CP what kind of party [C has] [IP he --- in mind]]

The second is that the C position in (16) can alternatively be filled by the indicative complementizer *that* in nonstandard varieties of English, so resulting in structures such as:

(18)   %I wonder [CP what kind of party [C *that*] [IP he has in mind]]

(where % indicates that this construction is only acceptable to a certain percentage of English speakers). Although we shall not attempt to deal with this here, there are numerous other constructions in which particular types of clause are analyseable as CPs containing an empty head C constituent (cf. Radford 1988a: 292–303 for relevant details). Indeed, we might go further (following Radford, ibid.) and argue that all *Ordinary Clauses* in adult English have an (overt or covert) C-system, and thus have the status of CP constituents.

Thus far, we have looked briefly at the C-system associated with Ordinary Clauses in adult English. But what of adult English *Small Clauses* (abbreviated to SC for convenience)? There are a number of reasons for supposing that Small Clauses have no C-system whatever. For one thing, they can never be introduced by overt complementizers like *that/for/whether/if*, as we see from the ungrammaticality of examples such as (19) below:

(19)   (a)   *I don't want *that* [your parents angry with me]
        (b)   *They won't let *for* [the students boycott exams]
        (c)   *I didn't consider *whether* [my remark in bad taste]
        (d)   *The jury will find *if* [the defendant guilty]

Such sentences are grammatical without the italicized complementizers, but ungrammatical if the complementizers are included. Why should this be? The ungrammaticality which results from introducing the bracketed SC complements by a complementizer can obviously be accounted for in a straightforward fashion if we posit that Small Clauses in English contain no C-system, since it will then follow that they have no head C constituent to contain the italicized complementizer.

Now, if Small Clauses contain no C-system and hence no C constituent, then it will also follow that we can never find Auxiliaries preposed into pre-subject C position in Small Clauses: this in turn would provide one reason why sentences such as (20) below are ungrammatical:

(20)   *Let *be* [there --- peace on earth]

It seems reasonable to attribute the ungrammaticality of (20) (at least in part) to the fact that the italicized auxiliary *be* has been preposed out of its underlying position marked --- into the italicized pre-subject C position outside the bracketed SC. But if Small Clauses have no C-system, then it will follow that auxiliaries in Small Clauses cannot in principle undergo preposing into C (since there is no C position for them to be preposed into).

Furthermore, if Small Clauses have no C-system, then not only will they lack a head C position, but also they will lack a C-specifier position to contain preposed wh-phrases. We should therefore expect that (in a language like English where preposed wh-phrases are superficially positioned in the C-specifier position), Small Clauses never allow preposing of wh-phrases outside their containing SC: and this prediction is borne out by the ungrammaticality of examples such as (21) below (where **e** denotes an empty complementizer):

(21)   (a)   *You wouldn't believe *how angry* **e** [your parents ---]
         (b)   *I can't imagine *what kind of party* **e** [there being ---]
         (c)   *Try and find *how comfortable* **e** [water beds ---]

In each of the examples in (21), the italicized wh-phrase would originate internally within the bracketed SC in the position marked ---, and would then be preposed outside the bracketed SC, into the C-specifier position to the left of the empty bold-printed C constituent (designated as **e**). Why should examples such as (21) be ungrammatical? The answer we are suggesting here is that Small Clauses lack a C-system, and hence contain no C-specifier position to act as the landing-site for preposed wh-phrases (it should be noted that if the bracketed SC complements in (21) are replaced by finite CP complements, the resultant sentences are grammatical, with the preposed wh-phrase occupying the specifier position within CP – cf. 'You wouldn't believe [*how angry* your parents were]', 'I can't imagine [*what kind of party* there was]', and 'Try and find [*how comfortable* water beds are]'). A fourth argument in support of our assumption that Small Clauses have no C-system comes from the fact that the subjects of SC complements can be passivized, as we see from examples such as (22) below:

(22)   (a)   *The Pope* is believed [--- infallible]
         (b)   *The defendants* were found [--- guilty of murder]
         (c)   *The cat* was let [--- out of the bag]
         (d)   *The situation* is considered [--- out of control]

We assume that the italicized nominals in (22) originate as the subjects of the bracketed Small Clauses in the --- position, and are subsequently moved into the italicized main clause subject position as a result of 'passivization'. By contrast, the subjects of complementizer clauses (i.e.

clauses containing a C-system) cannot be passivized, as we see from the ungrammaticality of examples such as the following:

(23)   (a)   *The ministers* were demanded [$_{CP}$ that [$_{IP}$ --- should resign]]
        (b)   *The passengers* were arranged [$_{CP}$ for [$_{IP}$ --- to catch a connecting flight]]

(though if the italicized nominals are not passivized and remain in the subject position within IP, the corresponding impersonal sentences are grammatical – cf. 'It was demanded that the ministers should resign', 'It was arranged for the passengers to catch a connecting flight'). The impossibility of passivizing the italicized nominals here is arguably a consequence of the fact that the passivized nominals in (22) have to cross only one clausal boundary (= the bracketed SC), whereas in (23) the passivized nominals have to cross two clausal boundaries (= IP and CP) – and we might suppose that (for theoretical reasons which need not concern us here) there is a constraint against moving constituents across more than one clause boundary in any single movement. At any rate, the fact that the subjects of complementizer clauses (= CP) cannot passivize, whereas the subjects of Small Clauses can, provides a strong empirical argument against claiming that Small Clauses have a C-system.

Overall, then, we see that there are at least four independent sets of facts which support our hypothesis that adult English Small Clauses entirely lack a C-system. Now if – as we suggested above – early child clauses resemble adult Small Clauses in their internal structure, then we should expect to find that early child clauses likewise lack a C-system. And in the remaining part of this chapter, we shall put forward a number of empirical arguments in support of this key claim. An equivalent suggestion (made within the earlier framework of Chomsky (1981)) to the effect that early child clauses lack COMP (= C) and S-bar (= CP) constituents is made in Phinney (1981), and Nishigauchi and Roeper (1987).

As we noted above, one of the main functions of the C constituent in adult English is to serve as the position occupied by overt complementizers like *that/for/whether/if* in complement clauses. Now, if we are correct in supposing that early child clauses are Small Clauses which lack a C-system, then we should expect to find that the earliest complement clauses produced by young children are likewise Small Clauses lacking a C-system. This prediction appears to be borne out, in so far as early child complement clauses show the same [NP X'] pattern as is found in independent clauses such as those illustrated in (5) above. For example, we find that prepositional Small Clause complements of the form [NP P'] are common, particularly after *want* – as illustrated by the following examples (where the Small Clause complement is bracketed):

(24) (a) Want [hat on] (Daniel 19)
      (b) Want [car out] (Daniel 21)
      (c) Want [hat on].Want [monkey on bed]. Want [coat on] (Daniel 23)
      (d) Want [telly on]. Want [top off] (Leigh 24)
      (e) Want [sweet out]. Want [sweetie in bag out]. Want [telly on]. Want [Roland on telly]. Want [shoes on]. Want [key in] (Daniel 24)

Also common at this stage are verbal Small Clause complements headed by a nonfinite verb generally (though not always) in the base form: the examples in (25) below illustrate Small Clauses headed by a nonfinite verb being used as the complement of *want* (though parallel examples with similar SC complements can be found after verbs like *let*, *make*, etc.); once again, the complement SC is bracketed:

(25) (a) Want [teddy drink] (Daniel 19)
      (b) Want [baby talking] (Hayley 20)
      (c) Want [mummy come] (Jem 21)
      (d) Want [lady open it] (Daniel 22)
      (e) Want[this go up] (Angharad 22)
      (f) Want [lady get chocolate] (Daniel 23)
      (g) Want [mummy do] (Anna 24)
      (h) Jem want [mummy take it out] (Jem 24)

What is particularly significant about the constructions in (24) and (25) from our point of view is that the bracketed complement clauses are never introduced by complementizers at this stage (though it is, of course, true that the adult counterparts of the bracketed complement clauses need not be introduced by a complementizer either). In fact, it is only several months later (at a much more advanced stage of development) that children start to use complement clauses introduced by complementizers. The fact that early child complement clauses are never introduced by complementizers lends obvious credence to our claim that early child clauses are Small Clauses. Moreover, imitative speech data yield much the same conclusion: Phinney (1981) argues that young children consistently omit complementizers like *that* on sentence repetition tasks.

Given that a second role of the C-constituent in adult speech is to act as the landing-site for preposed auxiliaries (e.g. in direct questions), we should expect that two-year-olds will not show any examples of 'subject–auxiliary inversion' in direct questions. In fact, early child interrogative clauses show no evidence whatever of auxiliaries preposed into C, and more generally lack auxiliaries altogether. Typical examples of auxiliariless interrogatives found in early child speech are given below (examples of yes–no questions from Klima and Bellugi 1966: 200):

(26)   Fraser water? Mommy eggnog? See hole? Have some? Sit chair? Ball go?

A similar pattern emerges from the transcripts of the speech of Claire at 24-25 months in Hill (1983), where we find questions such as the following:

(27)   Chair go? Kitty go? Car go? This go? That go? Jane go home? Mommy gone? (*Claire 24-5)

As Klima and Bellugi remark (1966: 201) it is characteristic of early child English at this stage that: 'There are no Auxiliaries, and there is no form of Subject–Verb Inversion'. Once again, the absence of preposed auxiliaries is consistent with our hypothesis that early child clauses lack a syntactic C-system (given that preposed auxiliaries are superficially positioned in C): cf. similar conclusions reached in Radford 1985, 1986, 1987, 1988b, and echoed in Guilfoyle and Noonan 1988.

On the assumption that children's clauses lack a C-system at this stage, it follows that they will also lack a specifier of C, and hence that young children will not show any evidence of having acquired the adult English rule of *wh-movement* which moves wh-phrases out of IP into the C-specifier position to the left of C. In this connection, it is interesting to note that Fukui (1986: 234) argues that the absence of syntactic *wh-movement* in Japanese is a direct consequence of the fact that Japanese is a language which has no C-system, since this will mean that Japanese has no C-specifier position to act as a landing-site for preposed wh-phrases (we shall explore further possible parallels between early child English and adult Japanese in chapter 8). Thus, if early child English resembles adult Japanese in respect of lacking a C-system, then we should expect that at this stage we will not find examples of interrogatives showing clear evidence of a wh-phrase having being moved into some pre-subject position within CP – i.e. we won't find children producing interrogatives such as:

(28) (a) **Who* (are) you watching?
      (b) **What* (are) you talking about?
      (c) **Where* (have) you been to?

(* is used here to indicate a non-occurring structure.) Studies of wh-questions in child speech over the past decade have generally agreed that children under two years of age do not show any evidence of having acquired a productive syntactic rule of *wh-movement* (cf. e.g. Klima and Bellugi 1966, Brown 1968, Bowerman 1973, Wells 1985). This finding is obviously consistent with our hypothesis that early child clauses have no C-system (given the assumption that preposed wh-phrases in adult English occupy the specifier position within CP).

In contexts where they attempt to imitate an adult question containing a preposed auxiliary and a preposed wh-word, children typically omit both the auxiliary and the wh-word, as examples such as the following illustrate (the last two examples being from Brown and Fraser 1963):

(29)   ADULT MODEL SENTENCE   CHILD'S IMITATION
       Where does Daddy go?   Daddy go? (Daniel 23)
       Where shall I go?   Go? (*Eve 25)
       Where does it go?   Go? (*Adam 28)

A similar pattern (no preposed wh-word or preposed auxiliary) is found in (what appear to be) child counterparts of adult wh-questions in spontaneous speech, as examples such as those in (30) below illustrate:

(30) (a) Bow-wow go? ('*Where did* the bow-wow go?', +Louise 15)
      (b) You got? ('*What have* you got?', +Harriet 18)
      (c) Mummy doing? ('*What is* mummy doing?', Daniel 21)
      (d) Car going? ('*Where is* the car going?', Jem 21)
      (e) Doing there? ('*What is* he doing there?', John 22)
      (f) My shoes gone? ('*Where have* my shoes gone?', Jenny 22)
      (g) Mouse doing? ('*What is* the mouse doing?', Paula 23)

The omission of the italicized preposed wh-phrases and preposed auxiliaries is obviously consistent with the assumption that children have not yet developed a syntactic C-system, and thus lack a landing-site for preposed auxiliaries and preposed wh-phrases. Omission of preposed wh-expressions is also reported in the early stages of the acquisition of French by Guillaume (1927: 241).

Further empirical evidence consistent with the assumption that children have no C-system in their syntax at this stage comes from the following attempt by Claire at age 23 months to imitate a wh-question involving a preposed wh-complement:

(31)   ADULT: *What are they doing there?*
        CHILD: Doing *what* there? (Claire 23)

The adult sentence contains a preposed auxiliary *are* in C, and a preposed wh-object *what* in the specifier position within CP. However, the child's imitation appears to be a simple VP which entirely lacks a C-system: in consequence, the auxiliary is simply omitted, and the wh-pronoun *what* is base-generated *in situ* (i.e. in the normal postverbal position associated with direct objects). It is interesting to note that the nominative pronominal determiner *they* is also omitted (in keeping with our overall hypothesis that child grammars of English at this stage lack functional category systems): cf. the parallel omission of the subject pronouns *I/it* by Eve and Adam in (29) above. The fact that Claire's behaviour is not untypical of children of her age is suggested by the remark made by Roeper and De Villiers (1989: 4, n. 8) that 'Mervis (pc) found "know what" to be frequent among the first wh-expressions, produced at 22 months. Roeper (pc) has found the same result.'

   Given our claim that children at the earliest (lexical) stage of their categorial development have no syntactic C-system (and thus use neither preposed auxiliaries nor preposed wh-phrases), then we might expect it to be the case that children produce no wh-questions containing initial wh-phrases at this stage. However, this is not in fact so. For we do indeed find examples of sentences containing initial wh-phrases in early child English. At the beginning of the Small Clause stage, we find that the child's repertoire of wh-questions is limited to 'a few routines' (Klima and Bellugi 1966: 201) – most notably *Whasat?* (= 'What's that' – an essential component of the child's repertoire in picture-book situations). Precisely because it is a formulaic utterance treated by the child as 'a rote-learned unanalysed whole' (Wells 1985: 198), *Whasat* tends to be extremely variable and unstable in its phonological form, and would typically have a number of variant pronunciations such as those in (32) below, many of which are so contracted that they show no trace whatever of the wh-word *what*:

(32)   /wɑsat/ /wɑsa/ /ɑsat/ /ɑsa/ /sat/ /sa/ /at/ /a/

Thus, we accept the traditional view that such formulaic utterances are not productive structures and hence cannot in principle be used to provide evidence about whether the child has developed a syntactic C-system.

However, we also find that other children at the Small Clause stage use a range of different wh-questions in what appears to be a productive fashion. The relevant questions typically comprise an initial wh-pronoun (*what*, *who*, or *where*), followed by (what in adult terms would be) an optional copula *'s* cliticized to the wh-pronoun, followed by a nominal or pronominal NP: examples of questions of this type are given in (33) and (34) below:

(33)   (a)   *What's* that? (Dewi 18)
         (b)   *What's* this? (Stefan 19)
         (c)   *Who's* that? (Hayley 20)
         (d)   *Where's* helicopter? (Stefan 17)

(34)   (a)   *What* that? (Dewi 19)
         (b)   *Who* that? (Dewi 19)
         (c)   *Where* helicopter? (Stefan 17)
         (d)   *Where* mummy? (Daniel 19, 23, 24)

These examples would appear to be of the general schematic form *[wh-pronoun('s) NP]*. Moreover, it seems likely that each of the wh-pronouns involved functions as a wh-NP: this seems reasonable enough in the case of *what* and *who*, but is clearly more questionable in the case of *where*. However, bearing in mind that children use its noninterrogative counterpart *there* in NP positions (so that 'Mummy go *there*' is the pronominal counterpart of 'Mummy go *school/shops*' in early child English), it is plausible to suppose that *where/there* are simply locative NPs in child speech, meaning 'which place/this place'. If this is so, then it follows that child wh-questions such as (33) and (34) comprise a wh-NP (*what*, *who*, or *where*) with an optionally suffixed *'s*, followed by another NP: they are thus of the schematic form:

(35)   [wh-NP(*'s*) NP]

– and (35) may well be a potentially productive structure for some children at this stage (though its productivity is clearly limited by the restricted range of wh-words which children have acquired).

However, the key point of interest to us here is whether or not there is any evidence that the initial wh-pronouns in questions such as (33) and (34) occupy the C-specifier position within CP, and thus provide us with evidence that such children have developed a C-system. There are several pieces of evidence which argue strongly against any such claim. For one thing, the relevant wh-questions have noninterrogative counterparts of the form [NP('s) NP], as we see from (36) and (37) below:

(36)   (a)   *That*'s teddy (Daniel 22)
         (b)   *Here*'s bubble/*There*'s mummy (Daniel 22)

(37)   (a)   *This* apple (Stephen 19)
         (b)   *That* ladybird (Bethan 20)
         (c)   *It* Wayne (Daniel 22)
         (d)   *Here* helicopter (Stefan 17)
         (e)   *There* mum (Daniel 19)

Given that there is no evidence that the italicized pronominal NPs in (36) or (37) have been 'preposed', there is likewise no evidence that their italicized wh-counterparts in (33) and (34) above have been preposed. Far from having been moved into some pre-subject position, it seems likely that the italicized wh-NPs in (33) and (34) occupy superficial subject position within their containing clause. If so, then such structures show no evidence of wh-preposing, and hence no evidence of the development of a C-system.

   The analysis we are proposing here receives further support from the fact that there is strong empirical evidence that children continue to (mis)analyse initial wh-expressions in copula constructions as subjects even after they have reached a later stage of development at which they have mastered the morphosyntax of functional categories like I and D. In this connection, it is interesting to examine agreement facts in sentences such as the following:

(38)   (a)   *What colour* is these? (Holly 24)
         (b)   *What*'s these? (Adam 26, Jonathan 28)
         (c)   *What*'s those? (Jonathan 28)
         (d)   *Where*'s my hankies? (Katy 28)
         (e)   *What*'s animals' names? (Kelly 36)

The relevant children who produced the utterances in (38) are all at a later (functional) stage of categorial development, and have all mastered the morphosyntax of subject–verb agreement, as we see from the examples in (39) below:

(39)   (a)   That'*s* nice coffee. *Is* it a bird? I'*m* pulling this. Those *are* pink and yellow. These *are* red flowers. That one *goes* here (Holly 24)

(b)   That one *does*. It *doesn't* work. That'*s* another one. This *is* a tractor (Adam 26)

(c)   That'*s* a owl. That'*s* not a dog. It *isn't* a dog. He'*s* doing that. He *hasn't* got it. The man'*s* done his hand. They'*re* lemons (Jonathan 28)

(d)   She'*s* gone. There it/he *is*. That'*s* a box. I'*m* walking (Katy 28)

(e)   Who'*s* that? It'*s* my toy now. He'*s* naughty. You'*re* holding it. We *were* watching the television in a cupboard. It *was* a shopping bag. I'*ve* got it (Kelly 36)

What is of particular interest to us in relation to (38) is the fact that the copula verb '*s* is third person singular in form, and thus is clearly agreeing with the preceding singular wh-expression *what colour/what/ where*, not with the following plural determinate noun phrase. Since this pattern of agreement holds between a finite verb and its superficial subject, the obvious conclusion to reach is that the children concerned have misanalysed the initial wh-constituent as the subject of the copula (whereas in adult English the wh-phrase is a preposed complement, the copula is a preposed auxiliary, and the following DP is a subject controlling agreement – cf. 'What *are* these?', 'Where *are* my hankies?'). This pattern of misagreement has also been observed in the acquisition literature: e.g. Menyuk (1969: 76) reports the utterance 'What's these things?'

Further evidence in support of the claim that even children at a later (functional) stage of development misanalyse initial wh-pronouns in copula constructions as subjects comes from case-marking facts, as in examples such as the following:

(40)   (a)   What's *them*? (Jonathan 28)
(b)   Where's *me*? (Michelle 29, trying to find a picture of herself in a photo album)

It seems clear from examples such as (41) below that the children concerned have mastered the morphosyntax of nominative and objective pronouns at this stage, since they use nominative forms as subjects of finite verbs, and objective forms as objects of transitive verbs or prepositions: cf.

(41)   (a)   *They*'re lemons. *They*'re apples. *They*'re not dogs. *I* can't
see that. *He* hasn't got it. *He*'s gotta catch *them*. *He*'s eating
them. *I* want other one. *I* can see a monster (Jonathan 28)
(b)   *I*'ll get this in. *I* can't open it. *I*'ll weigh this. What's for *me*?
Will you show *me*? Who bought *me* a present? (Michelle 29)

In the light of this, the obvious question to ask is why the italicized
postcopular pronoun in (40) should be assigned objective case, when its
adult counterpart would be nominative (cf. 'What are *they*?', 'Where am
I?'). The answer I suggest here is that although the adult counterpart of
(40) comprises a preposed complement of *be*, a preposed copula and a
following subject, the child misanalyses such copula structures as
comprising an initial wh-subject pronoun, a copula, and a following
complement. Accordingly, the italicized postcopular pronoun is misanalysed by the child as the complement of the verb *be*, and accordingly
assigned objective case (cf. adult forms such as 'It's *me*'). The fact that
the verb in (40) clearly agrees in person and number with the initial
wh-pronoun (assuming this pronoun to be third person singular in both
examples) provides further support for our wh-subject analysis.

Overall, then, we have clear empirical evidence that even at a much
later (functional) stage of development, children typically misanalyse
initial wh-pronouns in copula questions as subjects. If this is so at a later
stage of development, there is clearly every reason to assume that it is
equally true at the Small Clause stage, so that the initial wh-pronouns in
sentences such as (33) and (34) would be subject NPs. However, if they
are subjects, it seems reasonable to suppose that they occur in superficial
subject position in such sentences – and there is certainly no reason
whatever to assume that they have been preposed into (pre-subject,
pre-complementizer) C-specifier position. More generally still, if wh-
pronouns are base-generated in subject position in Small Clause
wh-questions, then there is no evidence that children at this stage have
developed a syntactic C-system. We therefore follow Brown (1968: 279)
in concluding that 'The first wh-questions seem to be unanalyzed
routines or constructions not involving transformations'.

Thus, the claim that we are making here is that the only nonformulaic
wh-questions which will be found in child speech at this stage are those
which involve wh-phrases which are base-generated *in situ* – e.g. in
object position in structures such as (31), and in subject position in
structures such as (35). It follows from this hypothesis that sentences
with initial wh-phrases in early child English involve wh-subjects, i.e.
wh-phrases which are clause-initial by virtue of their subjecthood, not by

virtue of having been preposed into pre-C specifier position. In connection with our claim that initial wh-expressions in early child English occupy superficial subject position and show no evidence of having been preposed into the specifier position within CP, it is interesting to note the following passage from Chomsky's (1986b) *Barriers* monograph: commenting on the (adult English) sentence-pair:

(42)   (a)   Who likes John?
       (b)   Who does John like?

he remarks (p. 42): 'Example (b) indicates that syntactic WH-MOVEMENT is permitted, but (a) is consistent with the assumption that it does not take place. A conclusion consistent with the evidence would be that WH-MOVEMENT takes place except for subjects.' Chomsky goes on to suggest that there is independent empirical evidence in support of the assumption that initial wh-subjects occupy superficial subject position in adult English (this provides an interesting account of certain extraction phenomena which are of no immediate concern to us here). Thus, our suggestion that initial wh-subjects in child speech occupy superficial subject position is far from being without precedent.

Although we have so far restricted ourselves to using speech *production* data, it should be noted that *comprehension* data reinforce our conclusion that children have not developed a C-system at this stage. The relevant data concern the fact that children at the lexical stage in their categorial development appear to have considerable difficulty in understanding wh-questions which show clear evidence of the preposing of a wh-phrase from some postverbal position within IP into the C-specifier position. This was noted by Klima and Bellugi (1966: 201–2), who observe that children at this stage frequently fail to understand questions involving a preposed wh-word (for example a preposed wh-object like *what* in '*What* are you doing?'). They remark (1966: 201) that 'If one looks at the set of *what*-object questions which the mother asks the child in the course of the samples of speech, one finds that at stage I the child generally does not respond or responds inappropriately.' Among the examples they provide (1966: 202) in support of this claim are the following, where the question is asked by the mother, and the italicized expression is the child's reply:

(43)   (a)   What did you do? – *Head*
       (b)   What do you want me to do with this shoe? – *Cromer shoe*
       (c)   What are you doing? – *No*

Klima and Bellugi conclude of children at this stage that 'They do not understand this construction when they hear it.'

The same incomprehension of questions involving preposed wh-expressions is found in my own data. The child's inability to understand questions containing preposed wh-phrases is reflected in the inability to provide an appropriate reply to such questions. In some cases, the child will reply simply with a *filler* of some kind, as in the examples in (44) below (where the question in each case is asked by an adult, and the italicized answer is provided by the child specified):

(44)　(a)　What have you got? – *Eh?* (Dewi 20)
　　　(b)　What are they doing with it? – *Uhm* (Jenny 24)
　　　(c)　What did you do it on? – *Erm* (Jenny 24)

In other cases, the child will simply repeat some word or phrase from the adult's question: e.g.

(45)　(a)　Where is it gone? – *Gone* (Elen 20)
　　　(b)　What did mummy say? – *Mummy* (Jenny 21)
　　　(c)　Who did you go for a walk with? – *Uhm...walk* (Jenny 24)
　　　(d)　What do you want money for? – *Money* (Jenny 25)
　　　(e)　What do you want them off for? – *Off* (Jenny 25)

Alternatively, the child may simply identify some entity referred to (e.g. by a pronoun) in the question: e.g.

(46)　(a)　What do they [= birds] want? – *Bird* (Dewi 20)
　　　(b)　What's he [= caterpillar] doing? – *Caterpillar* (Bethan 20)
　　　(c)　What are you doing with him [= snake]? – *Snake* (Jenny 23)
　　　(d)　What's he [= postman] doing here? – *Daddy* (Jenny 24)
　　　(e)　What's she [= nana] doing? – *Nana* (Jenny 24)

The nature of the answers provided by the children in (46) suggests that they tend to misinterpret such questions as copula questions of the form 'What's X?' (so that e.g. (46)(a) seems to have been interpreted in the same way as 'What are they?'). This would seem to indicate that the children are misanalysing the initial wh-pronoun as a base-generated *subject* rather than a preposed complement. Some additional support for this claim comes from responses such as those in (47) below:

(47)   (a)   Who did you play with? – *Me* (Hayley 20)
        (b)   What have you bumped your head on? – *Me* (Jenny 24)

Both children here seem to misinterpret the initial wh-NP as a subject, and hence respond as if they were answering questions such as 'Who played?', and 'Who bumped their head?'

The fact that children give inappropriate replies to wh-questions involving a moved wh-pronoun like *who* or *what* suggests that they simply don't understand this type of wh-question. But why should this be? The answer that we shall suggest here is that children at this stage have not yet acquired the syntax of the C-system, and thus not only are unable to *produce* structures involving preposed wh-phrases in the C-specifier position, but also are unable to *parse* adult utterances containing preposed wh-phrases correctly (to the extent that they are able to parse them at all, children seem to assume that wh-phrases are base-generated *in situ*, so that they tend to misanalyse preposed wh-complements as base-generated subjects). In consequence, where semantic/pragmatic knowledge does not suffice to enable the child to infer the intended meaning of the wh-question, the child is forced back onto syntactic competence: but since he has not acquired the syntax of the C-system at this stage, his syntax provides no basis for correctly parsing structures involving preposed wh-complements. The only possibility which the child's grammar allows for at this stage is to parse a sentence-initial wh-NP as a subject: hence the subject misinterpretation of structures such as (46) and (47) above.

All in all, it would seem that we have strong empirical evidence from several different quarters that early child clauses lack a C-system. However, before we conclude our discussion in this section, we shall briefly discuss a number of potential counterexamples to our claim. One apparent source of counterexamples comes from utterances such as the following:

(48)   *How are* you? (+Betty 18)

Given that (48) contains an italicized wh-pronoun *how* positioned in front of a preposed auxiliary *are*, it might at first sight seem as if examples such as (48) contradict our earlier claim that children at this stage have no syntactic C-system (since it might seem that *are* has been preposed into the C position, and *how* into the C-specifier position). However, it is clear that (48) is a purely *formulaic* utterance, since it was repeated (monotonously) several times in the same transcript, and since it was the only utterance involving a preposed wh-constituent or auxiliary in the whole transcript.

A more serious potential source of counterevidence concerns the fact that towards the end of the Small Clause stage we find that some young children start to make semi-productive use of a restricted range of structures with initial non-subject wh-pronouns. This phenomenon can be illustrated from the transcripts of Claire's speech at age 24 months provided in Hill (1983): at this stage, Claire produced two types of wh-question involving preposed wh-complements, as illustrated in (49) below:

(49)   (a)   Where *girl* go? Where *pencil* go? Where *cow* go? Where *daddy* go? Where *bathtub* go?
       (b)   What *kitty* doing? What *squirrel* doing? What *lizard* doing? (*Claire 24)

It is clear that the initial wh-pronoun *what/where* cannot be functioning as a subject in examples such as (49), since the clause in each case contains an (italicized) subject NP, and since the semantic role of the wh-pronoun is clearly that of complement of the verb. Hence, it is clear that the wh-pronoun must occupy some non-subject position. Now, given that initial nonsubject wh-constituents in adult English are superficially positioned in the C-specifier position, then an obvious interpretation of the relevant facts would be to suggest that sentences such as (49) provide us with evidence that Claire has developed a C-system; we might then suppose that a sentence such as *What kitty doing?* would have the skeletal superficial structure (50) below:

(50) $[_{CP}$ *What* $[_C$ **e** $]$ $[_{VP}$ kitty doing $---]]$

(where **e** is an empty C heading the bracketed CP, where --- marks the assumed position in which *what* originated before being moved into the italicized C-specifier position, and where VP designates a verbal Small Clause).

However, there are a number of reasons for rejecting the C-specifier analysis of initial wh-pronouns in sentences such as (49) above. For one thing, the structures in (49)(a) and (b) have an unmistakeably *semiformulaic* character about them, and are of the respective schematic forms:

(51)   (a)   Where NP go?
       (b)   What NP doing?

All of the questions containing initial wh-complements in the relevant transcripts conform to one of these two 'patterns'. Moreover, other studies have reported parallel semiformulaic wh-question types. For example, Klima and Bellugi (1966: 20) report examples such as (52) below in the speech of Adam, Eve and Sarah at this stage:

(52)   (a)   What (cowboy) doing?
      (b)   Where milk go? Where horse go? Where ball go?

and treat them as semiformulaic utterances. And the only wh-questions which Bowerman (1973: 242) lists in her transcript of the speech of Kendall at 23 months are the following:

(53)   Where doggie go? Where pillow go?

Examples such as (52) and (53) bear a remarkable resemblance to Claire's wh-questions in (49); all three seem to have the semiformulaic structure (51). Given that these 'formulae' appear to be partly lexical in character (i.e. two of the three positions in each formula in (51) are occupied by specific lexical items) and thus are not purely *categorial* in nature, then it might be argued that we cannot in principle use partly lexical structures as evidence for the development of categorial systems.

Moreover, it might also be argued that an analysis such as (50) violates principles of Universal Grammar. After all, if we follow Abney (1987: 65) in positing that functional elements subcategorize unique types of complement, and that IP is universally the complement of C, then an analysis such as (50) would be ruled out as genetically impossible. The reason is that the C-specifier analysis in (50) presupposes that the (empty) head C of CP takes a VP (i.e. verbal Small Clause) complement – in obvious violation of the requirement that C takes an IP complement. Furthermore, such an analysis would require us to reject our earlier postulate (made in relation to adult English) that Small Clauses have no associated C-system.

It is clear, therefore, that there are both methodological and theoretical objections to the C-specifier analysis sketched in (50). In addition, there are also strong empirical objections. These relate primarily to the fact that the relevant transcripts of Claire's speech at age 24 months provide no evidence whatsoever that she has developed a C constituent: in particular, she makes no use of complementizers, or of (preposed) auxiliaries. Thus, an analysis such as (50) would be unnecessarily abstract, in that it would require us to posit that Claire has developed an abstract category C which is always *obligatorily empty*, and which can never be filled by any item whatever. I take it as self-evident that any such purely abstract analysis is in principle undesirable, and should only be adopted as a last resort if no legitimate alternative is available.

Even if (counterfactually) structures such as (51) were purely categorial in nature and were analyseable as showing evidence of the acquisition of *wh-movement*, it is doubtful that the C-specifier analysis would be justified for children who otherwise show no sign of having developed a C-system. An obvious alternative would be to suggest that initial wh-complements in the speech of children at the Small Clause stage could be analysed as *clausal adjuncts* – i.e. as being adjoined to the left of the overall verbal Small Clause (= VP) structure. Under this alternative analysis, a sentence such as *What kitty doing?* would have the structure (54) below:

(54)   [$_{VP}$ *What* [$_{VP}$ kitty doing e]]

(where VP is a verbal Small Clause, and where e is an empty NP which might be the trace of the italicized wh-pronoun, or – if there is no evidence of movement rules in child grammars at this stage – might alternatively be a base-generated empty category which serves a 'reprise' function). A structure such as (54) would be reminiscent of the dislocation analysis which we proposed at the end of chapter 3 for potential *topic* + *comment* structures like 'Balloon throw', and thus might be argued to have independent motivation. Such an analysis would in effect amount to claiming that the child's wh-questions are *impostors*, in the sense that they superficially resemble adult wh-questions (e.g. in respect of the clause-initial position of the wh-word) but in fact have a different constituent structure: interestingly, Guilfoyle and Noonan (1988: 18) suggest a similar *adjunction* analysis of initial wh-phrases in early child speech.

I see no reason to suppose that such an adjunction analysis (under which initial complement wh-phrases are adjoined to VP in early child English) is excluded in principle by Universal Grammar. After all, Chomsky posits in *Barriers* (1986b: 21) that moved wh-phrases in adult English may be adjoined to VP in intermediate stages of derivation. Moreover, there is some evidence suggesting that moved wh-phrases in other languages may be adjoined to other clausal constituents. For example, if we make the standard assumption that preposed verbs in French are positioned in C, and that preposed subjects are in the C-specifier position, then it seems plausible to posit that preposed wh-constituents (which in turn can precede the preposed subject) can be adjoined to CP, in the manner illustrated in (55) below:

(55)   [CP *Pourquoi* [CP Jean [C est-] [IP il parti en Espagne]]]?
        Why   John   is   he left in   Spain?
        = 'Why has John gone off to Spain?'

In addition, Rudin (1988) has provided strong empirical evidence in
support of the claim that preposed wh-phrases may be adjoined to IP
(and thus be positioned after C) in languages such as Polish, so giving
rise to structures such as (56) below:

(56)   Maria myśli, [CP że [IP *co* [IP Janek kupił]]]
        Maria thinks   that what Janek bought
        'What does Maria think that Janek bought?'

Given that we have evidence that preposed wh-phrases can be adjoined
to two types of clausal structure (CP and IP), there is no reason to
suppose that UG excludes in principle the possibility of adjunction to the
third type, i.e. Small Clauses.

Indeed, it seems that we have independent evidence that moved
constituents can be adjoined to SCs: the relevant data come from pairs
such as:

(57)   (a)   I'd like [copies *of the chairman's report* available]
        (b)   I'd like [copies --- available] *of the chairman's report*

In (57), the PP *of the chairman's report* originates in the italicized position
in (57)(a) as the complement of *copies*, but is subsequently extraposed to
the end of the bracketed Small Clause: given the arguments in Radford
(1988a: 448–56) that extraposition involves adjunction, and given the
principle suggested there (ibid: 451) that 'an extraposed PP...is adjoined
to the first major (i.e. phrasal or clausal...) constituent containing the NP
out of which it is extraposed', then it follows that the italicized PP in (57)
is extraposed into a position where it is adjoined to the right of the overall
bracketed SC structure. If this is so, then it means that UG clearly allows
for the possibility of material being adjoined to SCs: and this in turn
means that we cannot rule out the possibility of child interrogative
structures such as (54), in which a preposed wh-expression is adjoined to
the left of the overall SC structure. (It should be noted that the
impossibility of adjoining wh-phrases to Small Clauses in adult
English – cf. (21) above – is attributable in part to the fact that only the
C-specifier position is licensed to serve as the ultimate landing-site for
preposed wh-phrases in adult English, and in part to the fact that
structures such as (21) violate case constraints which – as we shall argue

in chapter 7 – are not operative in early child grammars.) Of course, we should also bear in mind the alternative possibility that structures such as (54) might be base-generated structures which resemble the *dislocation* structures produced by young children at this stage (involving a null empty object serving a reprise function). We shall return to consider this construction briefly in chapter 9, so for the time being we shall say no more about it here.

There seems little purpose in pursuing speculation of this type any further here. There are two key points in our discussion which need to be underlined here. The first is that only structures which are both *productive* and purely *categorial* in nature can (in principle) provide us with evidence justifying the postulation of specific categorial systems in child speech. However, there is little convincing evidence that wh-questions involving initial wh-complements are *productive categorial structures* at this stage (rather, they seem to be semiformulaic utterances) – and correspondingly little evidence that children at the Small Clause stage productively prepose complement wh-phrases into the specifier position within CP. The second point to emphasize is that even if we do indeed maintain that children at this stage have developed a *wh-movement* rule, there is simply no evidence whatever that the landing-site for the rule in early child English is the specifier position within CP; on the contrary, it seems more likely that 'preposed' wh-complements are SC-adjuncts (i.e. they are adjoined to the overall Small Clause itself). Under either interpretation of the relevant facts, it follows that children at this stage have not developed a rule positioning initial wh-complements in the specifier position of CP. This in turn leads us to the more general conclusion that wh-question facts give us no reason to suppose that children at this stage have developed a C-system.

We can summarize the main arguments we have adduced in this chapter in the following terms: we have argued that four principal characteristics of early child clauses support the claim that they lack a C-system, viz.

(58)   (a)   Early child clauses lack complementizers
        (b)   Early child clauses do not contain preposed auxiliaries
        (c)   Early child clauses show no productive preposing of wh-constituents
        (d)   Children at this stage are unable to correctly parse clauses containing preposed wh-constituents.

As we have argued above, all four properties are directly consistent with our core assumption that children at this stage have not yet developed a

C-system. Thus, the absence of complementizers and preposed auxiliaries suggests nonacquisition of C (given that both types of constituent are superficially positioned in C in adult English). Likewise, the inability to produce or correctly parse structures containing preposed wh-phrases is consistent with our hypothesis that children have no C-specifier position in their syntax to act as a landing-site for preposed wh-constituents.

The hypothesis that there is no syntactic C-system in early child grammars of English (in conjunction with our earlier arguments that there is likewise no D-system either) clearly lends support to our more general postulate that early child grammars lack *functional* categorial systems. However, in order to substantiate this more general claim, we need to go on to show that there is likewise no I-system in early child clauses; and this we shall begin to do in the next chapter.

6

Absence of an Inflection System in Early Child English

Thus far, we have argued that the earliest grammars developed by young children acquiring English as their first language are intrinsically *lexical* in nature, and are characterized by the absence of functional category systems. In support of this claim, we have presented evidence that early child (pro)nominals are NPs which lack a D-system, and that early child clauses resemble adult Small Clauses in that they lack a C-system. However, if the analogy with adult Small Clauses is a sound one, then we should expect to find that early child clauses also lack an I-system, given that the absence of an I-system is arguably one of the defining characteristics of adult Small Clauses (as we saw at the beginning of the previous chapter). However, before we turn to look at the relevant child language data, let us briefly recapitulate the nature and function of the I-system in adult English.

Given the system of categories in Chomsky's (1986b) *Barriers* monograph, finite and *to*-infinitive clauses in English have the status of IPs, and thus are (double-bar) projections of a head functional I constituent. As we saw at the beginning of the previous chapter, the head I position of IP can be filled by either of two different types of base-generated constituent: if I is finite, it can be underlyingly filled by modal such as *should*, whereas if I is infinitival, it can be filled by infinitival *to*, so giving rise to IPs such as those bracketed in (1) below:

(1)   (a)   I'm anxious that [$_{IP}$ you [$_I$ *should*] [$_{VP}$ do it]]
          (b)   I'm anxious for [$_{IP}$ you [$_I$ *to*] [$_{VP}$ do it]]

If theta-roles can only be assigned by lexical categories to nominal arguments contained within their immediate maximal projection (so that nominal arguments cannot be theta-marked by functional categories), then it follows that in order to account for the AGENT theta-role assigned to the subject *you* in the bracketed IPs in examples such as (1), we shall have to posit that *you* originates as the underlying subject of the bracketed VP, and then subsequently gets 'raised' up to become the superficial subject of IP. If this is so, then it follows that the bracketed IPs in (1)(a) and (b) above would be derived in the manner indicated schematically in (2) below:

(2)   I'm anxious that/for [$_{IP}$ [$_I$ should/to] [$_{VP}$ *you* [$_V$ do] it]]

(where the assumed underlying structure is paraphraseable as 'I'm anxious that it should be the case/for it to be the case that you do it'). The derivation in (2) postulates that the (pronominal) DP *you* originates (in a theta-marked position) as the underlying specifier of VP, but is subsequently raised to become the superficial specifier of IP. Some evidence which suggests that the superficial (italicized) subject of IP originates as the underlying subject of VP comes from the fact that the moved subject can leave behind a floating quantifier in the VP-specifier position in which it originates, so resulting in structures such as (3) below:

(3)   I am anxious...
       (a)   that [$_{IP}$ *you* [$_I$ should] [$_{VP}$ *each* [$_V$ help] the other]]
       (b)   for [$_{IP}$ *you* [$_I$ to] [$_{VP}$ *each* [$_V$ help] the other]]

Sportiche (1988) argues that in such structures, *you* originates as the complement of *each* within the subject/specifier position of the VP, and that *you* is subsequently preposed on its own into the specifier position within IP, leaving *each* stranded in subject position within the VP. We might further suppose that movement of the subject DP (in this case, the pronominal DP *you*) out of the specifier position within VP into the specifier position within IP is motivated by *case* considerations – more specifically, by the requirement that DP be case-marked (or, equivalently, that DP is only licensed to occur in a case-marked position). Thus if the DP *you* remains in its underlying position as the subject of VP in (2), it will be in a position where it cannot be case-marked by *each* (since this is not a case-assigner, as we see from the ill-formedness of *each you*); if the DP *you* moves into the specifier position within IP, then it will be assigned nominative case by *should* in (1)(a), and objective case by *for* in (1)(b), so satisfying the case licensing requirement on DPs. Of course, the same case considerations will also 'force' movement of the underlying subject from the VP-specifier position into the IP-specifier position in sentences not involving floating quantifiers: thus, even if *each* were not present in the underlying structure in (3), the underlying subject of the VP *you* would not be able to receive case internally from within VP (since I in English does not assign case rightwards, and since an infinitival I is not in any event a case-assigner), and so would have to move into the specifier position of IP in order to receive case from *should/for*.

The overall thrust of our argumentation is that in the adult English target system, the superficial subject of IP must originate as the underlying subject of VP in order to be theta-marked, but must be 'raised' into the specifier position in IP in order to be case-marked. However, given our hypothesis that early child grammars of English lack functional categories and their associated grammatical (i.e. morphological, syntactic, and semantic) properties, we should expect to find that early child clauses lack (*inter alia*) both an I-system, and a case system. This in turn would lead us to expect that the child's counterpart of adult functional IPs would be simple lexical category systems, so that a verbal clause would have the status of IP in adult English, but VP in early child English. And, as we shall show, there is strong empirical evidence in support of the claim that there is no I-system in early child grammars of English (a claim echoed in earlier work by Radford 1985, 1986, Radford and Aldridge 1987, Radford 1988b, Kazman 1988, Guilfoyle and Noonan 1988, Aldridge 1988, 1989, and others).

Part of the relevant evidence comes from the fact that the child's counterpart of adult infinitival IPs headed by the I constituent *to* appear to be simple VPs lacking *to*. For example, we find that the child's counterpart of adult infinitive complements of verbs like *want* do not contain *to* at this stage; this is true not only where the [bracketed] complement clause has an overt subject, as in (4) below:

(4)   (a)   Want [teddy drink] (Daniel 19)
       (b)   Want [mummy come] (Jem 21)
       (c)   Want [dolly talk] (Daniel 21)
       (d)   Want [lady open it] (Daniel 22)
       (e)   Want [lady get chocolate] (Daniel 23)
       (f)   Want [mummy do] (Anna 24)
       (g)   Jem want [mummy take it out] (Jem 24)

but also where the bracketed complement clause lacks an overt subject, as in (5) below:

(5)   (a)   Want [do it]. Want [have money] (Daniel 19)
       (b)   Want [blow]. Want [put coat]. Want [open door] (Daniel 20)

(c) Want [read]. Want [put car]. Want [drink it] (Daniel 21)

(d) ə want [see] (*Kathryn 21)

(e) Want [open it]. Want [take it]. Want [kick him]. Want [go out]. Want [do it]. Want [sit]. Want [find bike] (Daniel 22)

(f) Want [get out her cot] (Angharad 22)

(g) Want [sit on knee] (Daniel 23)

(h) Want [see handbag]. Want [open it]. Want [get down]. Want [get dressed]. Want [go up]. Want [open door]. Want [smack Wayne]. Want [get up there]. Want [go there]. Want [get down]. Want [do it]. Want [dance in here]. Want [blow it] (Daniel 24)

(i) Want [do]. Want [do pon]. Want [drive car] (*Stephen 19–24)

The adult counterpart of all of the bracketed complements in (4) and (5) above would be an IP headed by an I constituent containing infinitival *to*: in place of the adult IP, the child uses (what would appear to be) a simple VP with an overt subject in (4), and with a null subject in (5). For example, the adult counterpart of (4)(g) would have the structure (6)(a) below, whereas the child's utterance arguably has the structure (6)(b):

(6)   (a)   Jem wants [$_{IP}$ *Mummy* [$_I$ to] [$_{VP}$ --- [$_V$ take] it out]]

      (b)   Jem want [$_{VP}$ *Mummy* [$_V$ take] it out]

(where --- marks the specifier position in VP in which the italicized subject is assumed to originate in (6)(a)). The fact that young children at this stage have not mastered the use of *to* (and so use *to*-less VPs in contexts where adults would require IPs headed by *to*) lends further empirical support to our overall claim that the initial categorial system developed by the child comprises a set of lexical categories and projections, and lacks functional categories and projections.

Now, given that I in adult speech serves not only as the position in which infinitival *to* is base-generated, but also as the position in which modals are base-generated, then we should expect to find that if early child clauses do indeed contain no I-system, then they will also lack modals. Since modals are followed by a VP complement headed by a V in the uninflected 'base' form, then our hypothesis that early child clauses lack I would lead us to expect to find that modals simply don't occur in clauses containing VPs of this kind. Numerous published studies have commented on the absence of modals as a salient characteristic of early child speech: cf. e.g. Brown 1973, Wells 1979, and Hyams 1986. And indeed, this pattern is reflected in my own data: we typically find no modals at all at this stage, as the following representative list of the relevant types of clausal structure occurring in the transcripts of a variety of children illustrates:

(7)   (a)   Mummy do it. Bethan do it. Me do it. Bethan sit down. Bethan want one. Me come in. Me want it. Me get it. Me help (Bethan 20)

       (b)   Hayley draw it. Hayley draw boat. Hayley read that. Hayley want that. Hayley talk. You get it out (Hayley 20)

       (c)   Pig go in. Man go up there. Baby Laura eat that. Mummy get bubbles (Claire 23)

       (d)   Jem get it out. Jem draw on box. Mummy cry. Mummy get it out. Mummy put it away. Lady put it away. Mummy sit down. Mummy smack Jem. Mummy get cross. Lady draw. Lady read (Jem 23)

Not only is it true that children's spontaneous speech shows no evidence of productive use of modals at this stage, but the same pattern is repeated in their imitative speech: thus, when repeating or replying to adult sentences containing modals, children systematically omit the modal in their responses, as examples such as the following (from the transcript of Claire at 24–5 months in Hill 1983) illustrate:

(8)   (a)   I'm getting my glasses so I **can** read the book – *Read book*
       (b)   You **can** put your finger through mummy's ring – *Finger*
       (c)   I wonder if Bear **could** do it – *Want Bear do it*
       (d)   **Shall** we read more books? – *Read book*
       (e)   **Shall** we go find her? – *Go find her*
       (f)   **Shall** I open the little one? – *Open little*
       (g)   **Shall** I open the big one? – *Big one*
       (h)   Do you think he'll wake up? – *Wake up*
       (i)   Mommy **won't** fit in the refrigerator – *Mommy fit refrigerator*
       (j)   **Would** you like some help? – *Help*
       (k)   That **must** be the dining-room – *Dining-room* (*Claire 24–25)

Moreover, the pattern in (8) is mirrored in published studies of imitative speech. For example (as we noted in chapter 3), Brown and Fraser (1963), Brown and Bellugi (1964) and Ervin-Tripp (1964) observed that children systematically omit modals when asked to repeat model sentences containing them, as illustrated by the following familiar examples:

(9) (a) ADULT: Mr Miller will try
         CHILD: *Miller try* (*Susan 24, from Ervin-Tripp 1964)
     (b) ADULT: I will read the book
         CHILD: *Read book* (*Eve 25, from Brown and Fraser 1963)
     (c) ADULT: I can see a cow
         CHILD: *See cow* (*Eve 25, from Brown and Fraser 1963)

It seems reasonable to suppose that whereas the adult model sentence in (9)(a) is an IP of the simplified form (10)(a) below, the child's imitation by contrast is a VP of the simplified form (10)(b):

(10) (a) [$_{IP}$ [$_{DP}$ Mr Miller] [$_I$ will] [$_{VP}$ --- [$_V$ try]]]
      (b) [$_{VP}$ [$_{NP}$ Miller] [$_V$ try]]

The systematic differences between the adult model sentence and its child counterpart are directly predictable from our hypothesis that early child grammars lack functional categories and their associated grammatical properties. Thus, the absence of an I-system means that the child uses the lexical counterpart of IP (= VP) in contexts where adults require IP. The absence of functional categories also means that the child uses the NP *Miller* in a context where an adult requires the DP *Mr Miller*. The absence of DP in early child grammars in turn will be directly correlated with the absence of a case system, if we posit that case is an inherent property of the D-system. This will mean that *Miller* in (10)(b) is a caseless NP (on the assumption that lexical categories do not case-mark their subject specifiers), whereas its adult counterpart *Mr Miller* in (10)(a) is a case-marked DP (assigned nominative case by the finite I constituent *will*): however, the fact that *Miller* in (10)(b) is in a caseless position will not lead to violation of the requirement that nominals have case, since this requirement is a functional one relating to DPs and therefore cannot come into operation until the child has acquired a functional D-system. Thus, numerous systematic differences between adult and child grammars of English can be accounted for in a principled way on the assumption that the key difference between the two systems is that child grammars lack the functional categories and properties found in adult grammars.

Having argued that the absence of modals and *to* in early child speech supports our hypothesis that early child clauses have no I-system, we shall now go on to argue that the nonmastery of finite verb inflections in early child speech provides additional evidence in support of this claim. However, since the relevant argumentation presupposes that the reader is familiar with the role played by I in determining the morphosyntax of finite verbs in adult English, we shall first present a brief summary of our assumptions about the relevant properties of I in the adult English target system, by way of background information. The framework which we shall be assuming here is essentially that of Radford (1988a), with some modifications (relating to points of detail rather than principle).

As we have already noted, I in adult English can either be finite (and hence contain a modal like *will/would*, *shall/should*, *may/might*, *can/could*, *must*, or the 'dummy' I constituent *do/does/did*), or infinitival (and hence contain *to*). A finite I carries tense and agreement properties, as we see from paradigms such as (11) below:

(11)　　(a)　[$_{DP}$ He/she/it] [$_I$ *does*] [$_{VP}$ put people off]
　　　　(b)　[$_{DP}$ I/you/we/they] [$_I$ *do*] [$_{VP}$ put people off]
　　　　(c)　[$_{DP}$ I/you/he/she/it/we/they] [$_I$ *did*] [$_{VP}$ put people off]

Thus, the form *does* is a present tense verb used in agreement with a third person singular subject, whereas the form *do* is a present tense verb used in agreement with other kinds of subjects. Similarly, the form *did* is a past tense form used in agreement with any kind of subject. By contrast, *to* is an invariable infinitival particle, not inflected for either tense or agreement (hence *to* has no third person singular present tense form **toes*, and no past tense form **toed*). We can formalize this in a conventional way by saying that I in English carries the features [αTNS, αAGR], where [α] is a variable over feature values which must either be positive in both occurrences, or negative in both occurrences. This means that I in adult English can either be [+TNS, +AGR] (i.e. carry both tense and agreement properties, and so be *finite* and thus able to contain a modal), or [−TNS, −AGR] (i.e. tenseless and agreementless, and so be *nonfinite* and thus contain infinitival *to*). The relevant tense properties carried by a finite I in English will specify whether I is present or past tense; and the relevant agreement properties will specify the grammatical number (singular/plural) and person (first/second/third) of the item contained in I (and the relevant number/person features of I must be compatible with those of the subject of I).

We shall assume a requirement that the tense/agreement features of I in adult English must actually be *discharged* – i.e. they must be realized on some appropriate lexical item: if *to* is the only item in English which can realize the negative tense/agreement features [−TNS −AGR] of an infinitival I, then it follows that it will in effect always be obligatory for an infinitival I constituent to contain *to*. This accounts for the fact that infinitival *to* cannot be omitted in typical infinitival IPs in English, as we see from examples such as (12) below:

(12)   (a)   It would be a good idea for you *to/*Ø0* stay at home
         (b)   I consider John *to/*Ø0* be a man of his word
         (c)   Why not ask *to/*Ø0* see his driving licence?

We further assume that the positive tense/agreement features of a finite I [+TNS +AGR] can only be discharged onto a *verbal* stem (either an auxiliary or a nonauxiliary verb). There are traditionally assumed to be four ways in which the positive tense/agreement features of a finite I can be discharged. The first possibility is that I can be underlyingly filled by a modal, in which case the tense/agreement features of I are realized on the modal in I (vacuously in the case of the relevant agreement features, since modals are not overtly inflected for agreement, and thus do not take the third person singular +*s* inflection). The second possibility is that I can be underlyingly empty, but superficially filled, as a result of the movement of a nonmodal auxiliary verb (*have* or *be*) out of the head V position in VP into an empty head I position in IP; if *have* or *be* are moved into I, they then acquire the tense/agreement features of I, and surface in the appropriate inflected form. The third possibility (in structures where the VP complement of I is headed by a nonauxiliary Verb) is that I can be underlyingly and superficially empty, in which case the relevant tense/agreement features of I are discharged onto the head (nonauxiliary) V of the VP complement of I; the head V then surfaces in an appropriate inflected form. The fourth possibility (giving rise to the phenomenon known as '*do*-support') is that I may be underlying empty, but superficially filled by the 'dummy' I-constituent *do*, inserted to act as a verbal stem onto which the tense/agreement properties of I can be discharged: this happens where I is underlyingly empty and has a VP complement headed by a nonauxiliary V, and where the I-features are prevented (by the presence of an intervening barrier of some kind) from being discharged onto the head V of VP. These four possibilities are illustrated in (13) below:

(13)   (a)   [$_{DP}$ He] [$_I$ *should*] [$_{VP}$ be writing it]
         (b)   [$_{DP}$ He] [$_I$ *should*] [$_{VP}$ have written it]
         (c)   [$_{DP}$ He] [$_I$ *was*] [$_{VP}$ --- writing it]
         (d)   [$_{DP}$ He] [$_I$ *had*] [$_{VP}$ --- written it]
         (e)   [$_{DP}$ He] [$_I$ *e*] [$_{VP}$ *wrote* it]
         (f)   [$_{DP}$ He] [$_I$ *did*] not [$_{VP}$ write it]

Thus, in (13)(a) and (b), the I position is underlyingly filled by the italicized modal, so that the relevant tense/agreement features (third person singular past tense) are realized on the inflected modal *should* (hence the fact that this carries the past tense suffix $+d$); by contrast, *have/be* occupy the head V position of the VP complement. In (13)(c) and (d), the nonmodal auxiliaries *have/be* again originate in the head V position of VP (in the position marked ---): but because I is underlyingly empty, *have/be* move into the empty I position (this is possible because a finite I position is an auxiliary position, and *have/be* can function as auxiliary verbs), and thereby acquire the relevant tense/agreement features, so surfacing in the appropriate inflected forms *was/had*. In (13)(e), I is both underlyingly and superficially empty ($= e$): the head V of the VP is the nonauxiliary verb *write*, and so cannot move into I (on the assumption that a finite I position can only be filled by an auxiliary verb); but because I-features must be discharged onto a verbal stem (and there is no such stem in I), the relevant tense/agreement features are discharged instead onto the head V of VP, which surfaces in the appropriate inflected form *wrote* (and remains positioned within VP). Finally, in (13)(f), it is traditionally supposed that I is underlyingly empty, but is superficially filled by the dummy auxiliary *do* in order to provide a verbal stem for the tense/agreement features of I to be discharged onto: we might suppose that the presence of an intervening negative particle *not* creates a barrier preventing the I-features from being discharged onto the head V of VP (hence the ungrammaticality of **John not wrote it*), and that *do* is inserted into I as a 'dummy' verbal stem, so enabling the I-features to be discharged (onto the 'dummy' verb *did* in I); subsequently, the negative particle *not* can cliticize onto *did* in the guise of its contracted allomorph *n't*, giving rise to forms like *don't/doesn't/didn't*. (It should be noted, however, that there are alternative accounts of *do*-support which presuppose that I is both underlyingly and superficially filled by *do* in cases where it appears: for our purposes here, it makes little difference which analysis of *do*-support we adopt.)

Thus, it is traditionally supposed that there are four different types of finite verb in English. Modal auxiliaries are both underlyingly and superficially positioned in I; finite nonmodal auxiliaries (*have/be*) are underlyingly positioned in V, and superficially positioned in I; nonauxiliary verbs are underlyingly and superficially positioned in V; and auxiliary *do* is a 'dummy' auxiliary Verb which is inserted in I in cases where the tense/agreement features of I would otherwise lack a verbal stem to be discharged onto. One essential assumption underlying this analysis is that all (uninverted) finite auxiliary verbs (viz. modals like *will/would*, etc., the nonmodal auxiliaries *have/be*, and the 'dummy' auxiliary *do*) are superficially positioned in I, whereas all nonauxiliary verbs are superficially positioned in V. Strong empirical support for this claim comes from the phenomenon of *verb preposing* in direct questions. It is well known that auxiliary verbs can be 'preposed' in front of their subject in direct questions, but nonauxiliary verbs cannot: cf.

(14)   (a)   *Should* John be writing it? [Modal Auxiliary]
        (b)   *Should* John have written it? [Modal Auxiliary]
        (c)   *Was* John writing it? [Nonmodal Auxiliary]
        (d)   *Had* John written it? [Nonmodal Auxiliary]
        (e)   *Didn't* John write it? [Dummy Auxiliary]
        (f)   * *Wrote* John it? [Nonauxiliary Verb]

This systematic contrast can be accounted for in a principled way if we posit that (post-subject) finite auxiliaries are superficially positioned in I, whereas (post-subject) nonauxiliary verbs are superficially positioned in V. Following the assumptions we made in the previous chapter, let us assume that 'preposed' verbs in direct questions move into an empty C (= complementizer) position to the left of IP. Given these two postulates, it follows that the preposing of auxiliary verbs involves movement from I to C in the manner represented in (15)(a) below, whereas the (illicit) preposing of nonauxiliary verbs would have to involve movement from V to C, as in (15)(b) below:

(15)   (a)   [$_{CP}$ [$_C$ e] [$_{IP}$ John [$_I$ *should*] [$_{VP}$ be writing it]]]

        (b)   [$_{CP}$ [$_C$ e] [$_{IP}$ John [$_I$ e] [$_{VP}$ *wrote* it]]]

We might further follow Chomsky (*Barriers*, 1986b: 12) in positing a principle of Universal Grammar to the effect that 'Two maximal projections constitute a *barrier*' to movement, where a *maximal projection* is a full phrasal (double-bar) constituent – i.e. an XP/X" constituent (it should be noted, however, that we are greatly simplifying the complex notion of *barrierhood* for the sake of simplicity of exposition). We might then maintain that this principle explains why a verb can be moved from I to C, but not from V to C: more precisely, in moving from I to C, an auxiliary verb will be moved out of only one containing maximal projection (= IP), as we can see in (15)(a) above. By contrast, in illicitly moving from V to C (as in (15)(b) above), a nonauxiliary verb would have to move out of two containing maximal projections (= VP, and IP), thereby violating Chomsky's *barrierhood* principle. However, this account of why auxiliary verbs can be preposed but nonauxiliary verbs cannot requires us to posit that finite auxiliary verbs are superficially positioned in I, but that nonauxiliary verbs are positioned in V. Numerous other facts support the same conclusion (as argued - within rather different frameworks – by Jackendoff 1972, Akmajian and Wasow 1975, and Pollock 1988, 1989), but it would lead us too far astray to pursue this issue any further here.

We can summarize our discussion of the morphosyntax of I in adult English by saying that I can either be positively or negatively marked for tense and agreement. If I is negatively marked, then I is filled by the tenseless, agreementless infinitive particle *to*. If I is positively marked for tense/agreement, then these features will be discharged on the auxiliary superficially positioned in I if there is one, but otherwise will be discharged on the head V of the VP complement of I.

Our discussion of the morphosyntax of I in adult English has obvious implications for our claim that early child clauses lack an I-system. For if – as we have argued here – I is the locus of the tense/agreement properties of finite verbs, then it follows (from our assumption that early child clauses are I-less) that we should expect to find that young children at this stage have no mastery of the tense/agreement inflections associated with finite verbs in English. In more concrete terms, this means that our Small Clause analysis of early child English clauses predicts that children will show no evidence of mastery of (any allomorphs of) the I-inflections $+s$ (indicating a third person singular present tense form) or $+d$ (indicating a past tense form): and we shall argue here that this is indeed the case.

As we noted in the previous chapter, the earliest verbal clauses produced by young children contain a head V which is either an uninflected base form, or a gerund form in $+ing$, or a participial form in $+n$. This observation is borne out by the larger data sample provided in (16) below:

(16)   (a)   Hayley draw it. Hayley draw boat. Hayley read that. Hayley talk. Me talk. You get it out. Baby talking. Him gone (Hayley 20)

        (b)   Helen ride. Helen do it. Mummy do it. Daddy do it. Daddy come. Daddy coming (*Helen 21)

        (c)   Geraint push me. Me want one. That go round. Me do it. Bethan do that. Lady do it. Joey eating. Doggy barking. Him swimming (Bethan 21)

        (d)   Lady do. Lady draw. Baby do it. Mummy come. Mummy coming. Jem draw mummy (Jem 21)

        (e)   Baby eat cookies. Mommy eat cookie. Mommy open. Baby doll ride truck. Horse tumble. Man drive truck. Baby open door. Baby drive truck. Baby ride truck. Pig ride (*Allison 22)

(f) Me have biscuit. Squash gone. Biscuit gone. Hammer gone. Car gone. Boots gone. Water gone. Her gone in there (Angharad 22)

(g) That go there. Pig go in. Baby Laura eat it. Man go up there. That take hat. That go in. Man taking, man take. That broken (Claire 23)

(h) Jem have it. Jem get it out. Jem put back. Jem do it with crayons. Jem draw on box. Mummy get it out. Mummy cry. Mummy sit down. Mummy go. Mummy take top off. Mummy get cross. Mummy smack Jem. Lady read. Lady put it away (Jem 23)

(i) Daddy want golf. Daddy want golf ball. Chicken want bread. Lady want bread. Wayne not eating it. Wayne got golf ball. Mummy fix it. Tractor broken (Daniel 23)

(j) Roland want sweet. Chicken want bread. Duck want bread. Pump go in. Wayne take stick. Roland coming as well. Roland going chicken (Daniel 24)

(k) Mommy sit. Daddy sit. Andrew walk. Daddy work. Daddy sleep. Daddy walk. Boy walk. Man walk. Elliot sleep. Andrew sleep (*Jonathan 24)

Since base forms, gerunds, and participles are not marked for tense or agreement, our observation that early child clauses do not contain finite verbs inflected for tense or agreement is thereby empirically substantiated. Indeed, further empirical support for this claim comes from the fact that children at this stage typically reply to questions containing a verb overtly marked for tense with a sentence containing a tenseless verb: cf. the following dialogue:

(17)   ADULT: What **did** you draw?
         CHILD: Hayley *draw* boat (Hayley 20)

Likewise, when asked a question containing a Verb overtly inflected for Agreement, children at this stage typically reply using an uninflected, agreementless verb: cf. e.g.

(18)   (a)   ADULT: What **does** Ashley do?
               CHILD: Ashley *do* pee...Ashley *do* poo (Jem 23)

 (b) ADULT: What **does** the pig say?
   CHILD: Pig *say* oink (*Claire 25)

Since tense and agreement are properties of I, the fact that children at this stage have not mastered the use of tense/agreement inflections provides further evidence in support of our claim that they have not yet acquired I.

 It is perhaps useful to pinpoint the exact nature of the differences between nonmodal finite clauses in adult English, and their child counterparts. Given the assumptions made here, the child's reply *Pig say oink* in (18)(b) would have the structure (19)(a) below, whereas its adult counterpart *The pig says oink* would have the superficial structure (19)(b) (where *e* denotes an empty category):

(19) (a) [$_{VP}$ [$_{NP}$ Pig] [$_V$ say] oink]
  (b) [$_{IP}$ [$_{DP}$ The pig] [$_I$ *e*] [$_{VP}$ --- [$_V$ says] oink]]

The differences between the two structures reflect the fact that adult grammars have functional category systems, whereas early child grammars have purely lexical category systems. Thus, the overall clause has the status of IP in adult English, but VP in early child English; the verb *says* carries the tense/agreement properties discharged by I in the adult structure (19)(b), but the child's verb *say* in (19)(a) carries no I-inflections for the obvious reason that the child's grammar has no I-system; the subject *the pig* is a DP in the adult sentence (19)(b), and hence has to move into the specifier position of IP in order to receive case from the empty finite I; but the subject in the child's clause is an NP, and can remain *in situ* in the specifier position in VP since there are no case constraints on nominals in child speech at this stage (the relevant case constraints only come into operation when the child acquires a D-system, since case is a property of the D-system). Thus, the hypothesis that early child grammars lack functional categories and their associated properties provides a natural account of the absence of tense/agreement inflections on verbs in early child English, as well as correlating the absence of these inflections with the systematic absence of numerous other *functional* properties.

 If we are correct in positing that children have not yet acquired an I-system at this stage (and therefore have not mastered the morphosyntax of I), then we should likewise expect to find that children have not mastered the use of so-called *dummy* auxiliaries – i.e. auxiliaries which seem to have no intrinsic semantic content, and whose essential function is to enable the tense/agreement features of a finite I to be discharged onto a verbal stem. As we have already noted in relation to sentences such as (13)(f) above, the auxiliary *do* functions as one such dummy constituent in adult sentences, so giving rise to the phenomenon traditionally referred to as *do*-support. In this connection, it is interesting to note that a negated finite clause in English cannot contain an empty I, as we see from the ungrammaticality of structures such as (20) below:

(20)　　*$[_{IP}$ They $[_I\ e]$ not $[_{VP}$ cut the grass]]

The ill-formedness of structures like (20) is arguably attributable to the fact that the presence of *not* creates a barrier which prevents the tense/agreement features of the empty I from being discharged onto the head V of VP, so leaving these features *undischarged* (in violation of the condition that I-features must always be discharged onto an appropriate verbal stem): cf. suggestions to this effect made by Akmajian and Heny 1975: 187, Jacobsen 1977: 276, Beukema and Coopmans 1988: 16, and Pollock 1988, 1989. If this is so, then it follows that the only way in which the relevant I-features can be discharged is if I is filled (at some stage of derivation) by an appropriate verbal stem onto which the tense/agreement features of I can be discharged. One way in which I can be filled is by a base-generated modal like *would*, so giving rise to structures such as:

(21)　　$[_{IP}$ They $[_I\ would]$ not $[_{VP}$ cut the grass]]

where the tense/agreement features of I are discharged onto *would* (hence the fact that *would* carries the inflection +*d*, marking tense overtly and agreement covertly; note also that *not* can optionally cliticize onto the auxiliary in I, so giving rise to *wouldn't*). A second way in which I can be filled is by movement of a nonmodal auxiliary (*have* or *be*) from V to I, so resulting in structures such as:

(22)　　$[_{IP}$ They $[_I\ had]$ not $[_{VP}$ --- cut the grass]]

(*not* can once again optionally cliticize onto the auxiliary in I, yielding *hadn't*). However, where a finite I is not filled by a base-generated or moved auxiliary and would otherwise be empty, the dummy verb *do* has to be used in order to 'support' I (i.e. in order to serve as a verbal stem on which the tense/agreement features of I can be discharged), so that the grammatical counterpart of (20) is (23) below:

(23)　　$[_{IP}$ They $[_I\ did]$ not $[_{VP}$ cut the grass]] (cliticization of *not* to the auxiliary in I will result in *didn't*). The 'dummy' auxiliary in I provides a verbal stem onto which the tense/agreement features of I can be discharged (so satisfying the *feature discharge requirement*). Thus, the function of the dummy auxiliary *do* in negative finite clauses is to serve as a 'carrier' for the abstract tense/agreement features of I in contexts where the relevant I-features would otherwise be undischarged.

Now, if we are correct in supposing that early child clauses contain no I-system (and thus have no I-features to be discharged), then we should expect that young children at this stage would show no evidence of 'knowing' that there is a requirement that a finite I in a negative clause must (at some stage of derivation) contain an auxiliary onto which the relevant tense/agreement features can be discharged. Significantly, we find that the child's counterpart of adult finite negative clauses at this stage is a structure which entirely lacks auxiliaries: thus, early child clauses are typically negated by positioning an invariable negative particle (*not* or *no*) before the predicate phrase; the examples in (24) below illustrate this pattern of *prepredicate negation*:

(24) (a) Man *no* go in there. Kathryn *no* fix this. Kathryn *no* like celery (*Kathryn 22)
      (b) Wayne *not* eating it. Wayne *not* eat it (Daniel 23)
      (c) Tina *not* have it (Domenico 24)
      (d) Kathryn *not* go over here (*Kathryn 24)
      (e) You *no* bring choochoo train (*Eric 25)

The adult counterpart of the child's independent sentences in (24) would be a finite clause headed by a finite I constituent containing an auxiliary carrying an inflectional suffix which discharges the tense/agreement properties of I. For example, the likely adult counterparts of child negatives such as *Tina not have it*, *Wayne not eating it* and *Kathryn no like celery* would be as in (25) below (ignoring the possibility of *not* cliticizing to the italicized auxiliary in I):

(25) (a) [$_{IP}$ Tina [$_I$ *can*] not [$_{VP}$ have it]]
      (b) [$_{IP}$ Wayne [$_I$ *is*] not [$_{VP}$ --- eating it]]
      (c) [$_{IP}$ Kathryn [$_I$ *does*] not [$_{VP}$ like celery]]

Thus, I would be filled by a base-generated auxiliary in (25)(a), by a moved auxiliary in (25)(b), and by a dummy auxiliary in (25)(c) – so that in each of the relevant examples, I would contain a verbal stem onto which the relevant I-features could be discharged. By contrast, the child's prepredicate negative sentences illustrated in (24) above contain no auxiliaries at all, a fact consistent with our assumption that verbal clauses have the status of *lexical* VPs rather than *functional* IPs in early child speech. Under the VP analysis, a child negative sentence such as *Man no go in there* might be analysed as a VP of the schematic form (26) below, if we assume that the negative particle *no(t)* functions as a predicative adjunct in early child speech (i.e. as an adjunct to the single-bar constituent which forms the predicate of the sentence):

(26)   [$_{VP}$ [$_{NP}$ Man] [$_{V'}$ *no* [$_{V'}$ [$_V$ go] in there]]]

A structure such as (26) has precisely the characteristics which our *lexical* analysis of early child category systems predicts. Thus, the overall clause has the status of a *lexical* VP rather than a *functional* IP; in consequence of this, it contains no I-system, and so lacks the requirement for the dummy auxiliary *does* to be used to discharge the relevant I-features onto. In addition, the child uses a caseless NP subject *man* where an adult would have required a (nominative) case-marked DP subject *the man*.

   Given the analogy we have drawn between early child clauses and adult Small Clauses, it is interesting to note that adult Small Clauses seem to show the same pattern of *prepredicate negation*, in that they are likewise negated simply by the use of an invariable negative particle (= *not*) positioned immediately before the predicate phrase, as the examples in (27) below illustrate (where the Small Clauses are bracketed):

(27)   (a)   I found [$_{SC}$ the chair *not* comfortable enough]
        (b)   I consider [$_{SC}$ that joke *not* in very good taste]
        (c)   He might let [$_{SC}$ you *not* attend the seminar]
        (d)   I can imagine [$_{SC}$ the students *not* paying attention]
        (e)   I found [$_{SC}$ my proposals *not* taken seriously]

It seems likely that the negative particle *not* here functions as a predicative adjunct, expanding the X-bar predicate into another X-bar of the same type: part of the evidence for claiming this comes from data such as (28) below:

(28)   (a)   I find [$_{SC}$ your behaviour *not compatible with your position* and *not consistent with our requirements*]
        (b)   They may [$_{SC}$ *each* not understand the other]

Given the traditional assumption that only identical constituents can be conjoined, sentences such as (28)(a) would seem to suggest that the negative particle *not* is an adjunct to each of the following single-bar predicates (= A-bar constituents) [*compatible with your position*] and [*consistent with our requirements*]. Likewise, if we assume that the floating quantifier *each* in (28)(b) occupies the subject/specifier position in the bracketed verbal Small Clause (= VP), then it seems likely that the negative particle *not* is an adjunct to the V-bar predicate [*understand the other*]. If our conclusions about sentences like (28) are along the right lines, then negation facts heighten the obvious similarities between early child clauses and adult Small Clauses, since in both instances we find a pattern of *prepredicate* negation. However, before we leave our discussion of negation, we shall comment briefly on an alternative pattern of *preclausal negation* reported in Klima and Bellugi (1966) – though not attested in my own corpus. This pattern involves the use of a *preclausal* negative particle, and can be illustrated by examples such as the following:

(29) (a) *No* Mom sharpen it (Bellugi and Klima 1966)
      (b) *No* Daddy hungry (*Kathryn 22)
      (c) *No* me go Mommy (Lebeaux 1988)

Although the pattern of *preclausal* negation illustrated in (29) is different from the pattern of *prepredicate* negation illustrated in (24) above, the two types of negative structure share in common the fact that they show no evidence whatsoever of an I-system, and thus appear to be (verbal) Small Clause structures. However, the obvious question to ask is how we can accommodate *preclausal* negation within the Small Clause analysis. Given our assumption that negatives like *no(t)* are adjuncts, the obvious solution to propose is that the negative particle in structures like (29) functions as an adjunct to the overall Small Clause structure itself. If this is so, then a sentence such as (29)(a) *No Mom sharpen it* would have the simplified structure (30) below:

(30)   [$_{VP}$ no [$_{VP}$ Mom sharpen it]]

– i.e. a structure in which the negative is an adjunct to the overall VP *Mom sharpen it* (where VP designates a verbal Small Clause) – cf. Lebeaux 1988: 39 for a parallel suggestion. Given the arguments in Radford (1988a: 255–6) that Universal Grammar must allow for constituents to serve as *phrasal adjuncts* (i.e. as base-generated adjuncts to maximal projections), it is clear that an analysis such as (30) would not violate principles of UG: indeed, we might even argue that adult English *not* has precisely the function of a phrasal adjunct in sentences such as:

(31)   (a)   I want you specifically to *not* [say anything]
        (b)   You can't simply *not* [turn up]
        (c)   What I'd like to see them do is *not* [each contradict the other all the time]

Indeed, in each of these examples, *not* arguably has the precise function of being an adjunct to the following bracketed VP. Thus, the VP-adjunct analysis in (30) would appear to have independent support (in the sense that *not* is licensed to function as a VP-adjunct in adult English); and we might therefore suggest that early child preclausal negative structures like (30) are simply an extension of an existing structure in adult English.

It is interesting in the context of our discussion here to note that Platzack (1989: 3–4) reports that a young child called Embla acquiring Swedish as her native language alternated between prepredicate and preclausal negatives when she was between 22 and 24 months of age – i.e. she alternated between structures such as (32)(a) and (b):

(32)   (a)   Mamma *inte* hjälpa Embla (prepredicate negative)
              Mummy not help Embla

        (b)   *Inte* mamma hjälpa Embla (preclausal negative)
              Not mummy help Embla

Under the *adjunct* analysis of negatives, we might posit that *inte* ('not') functions as a *predicate adjunct* (= V-bar adjunct) in structures like (32)(a), but as a *clausal adjunct* (= VP adjunct) in structures like (32)(b).

Returning once more to English, the upshot of our discussion is that early child negative sentences provide us with ample evidence that young children have not yet developed an I-system, and so have no 'knowledge' of the requirement for *do*-support in appropriate negative sentences. Given that children have not acquired the use of *do* as a dummy auxiliary, we might expect to find that they will likewise not have acquired the use of *be* as a dummy auxiliary in adult English (in constructions which involve a phenomenon sometimes referred to as *be*-support). If this is so, then we should expect to find that young children show no 'awareness' of the requirement in adult English for the so-called 'copula' *be* to be used in finite clauses which would otherwise be verbless, in order to 'support' I (that is, in order to serve as a verbal stem onto which the tense/agreement features of I can be discharged). We can illustrate this requirement for *be*-support in appropriate contexts in adult English in terms of the following pair of examples:

(33)   (a)   The president *is* very angry
       (b)   *The president very angry

Since only finite clauses can function as independent sentences in adult English, both of the independent sentences in (33) must be finite clauses containing a head finite I. But whereas the head I position in (33)(a) is filled by a finite form of the copula *be* (so enabling the relevant I-features to be discharged onto the resulting form *is*), in (33)(b) by contrast there is no copula in I onto which the I-features can be discharged, with the consequence that the resulting structure is ill-formed by virtue of violating the requirement that finite I-features must be *discharged* in adult English. It seems reasonable to suppose that *be* in its function as a copula is a 'dummy' verb in the sense that it has no apparent semantic content, and hence can be omitted with no obvious loss of meaning in contexts where there is no syntactic requirement for it to be used, as in the bracketed clauses below:

(34)   (a)   I have never known [the president (*be*) so angry]
       (b)   Try and make [the president (*be*) more conciliatory]

If this is so, then it follows that *be* can indeed be regarded as a 'dummy' auxiliary in English: its function in finite forms would then be to 'support' the tense/agreement features carried by I.

However, if we are right in supposing that early child grammars have a purely lexical categorial system and thus lack an I-system, then we should expect to find that young children will not have mastered the feature-discharge function of copula *be*, and so will omit the copula in contexts where adults require it (e.g. in a finite clause which would otherwise be verbless). And indeed, we find that in contexts where adults would use a copula sentence, children typically use a *verbless* sentence, as the examples in (35) and (36) below (familiar from our disussion in chapter 3) illustrate:

(35)   (a)   Geraint naughty (Bethan 20)
       (b)   Lisa naughty (Hayley 20)
       (c)   Hand cold. Fire hot (Elen 20)
       (d)   Bow-wow asleep (Stephen 20)
       (e)   Wayne naughty (Daniel 21)
       (f)   Man empty (*Allison 21)
       (g)   Mommy busy. Baby busy (*Kathryn 21)
       (h)   Cup tea ready. Potty dirty. It heavy (John 22)
       (i)   It hot (Angharad 22)

(j) Girl hungry. Daddy hungry. Mommy hungry. Boy hungry (*Kathryn 22)

(k) Doggie sleepy. Hair wet (*Kendall 22–23)

(l) Apple cold. Light hot (*Eric 22)

(m) Sausage bit hot (Jem 23)

(n) Joelle silly (Leila 23)

(o) That bushy (Leigh 24)

(p) Claire full (*Claire 24)

(q) Shirt wet. Shoe wet (*Jonathan 24)

(36) (a) Mouse in window. It in bag (Hayley 20)

(b) Daddy away. Mummy away (Jem 21)

(c) Wayne in bedroom. Bubble on dungaree (Daniel 21)

(d) Truck outside (*Allison 22)

(e) 'Frigerator on. Kendall innere (*Kendall 22)

(f) Stephen in school (Jem 23)

(g) Dolly on horsey. Mess on legs (Daniel 23–24)

(h) Shoes on. Hat on. Socks on (*Jonathan 23–24)

(i) Pixie outside. Daddy in there. Mummy in there (*Claire 24)

(j) Clock on there. Light up there. Kitty down there. Cover down there (*Andrew 18–23)

We can highlight the differences between the child's verbless clauses and their adult copula counterparts by comparing the structure of Jem's utterance (35)(m) *Sausage bit hot* with its adult counterpart *The sausage is a bit hot*. As we have already suggested in chapter 3, it seems likely that Jem's sentence is an adjectival Small Clause with a structure along the lines indicated in (37) below:

(37) $[_{AP} [_{NP}$ Sausage$] [_{A'} [_{NP}$ bit$] [_{A'} [_A$ hot$]]]]$

Since the child's sentences have a purely *lexical* categorial structure at this stage, there is no I-system, and hence no need for the use of a 'dummy' copula verb to 'support' the tense and agreement features of I. The *lexical* analysis also provides a natural account of why the child uses an NP *sausage* as the subject (whereas the adult would require the DP *the sausage*), and likewise uses an NP *bit* as an adjunct (whereas the adult would require the DP *a bit*). In contrast, the corresponding adult sentence might be argued to be derived in the manner represented schematically in (38) below (where we follow Stowell 1981 and Burzio 1986 in assuming that *be* is a 'raising' predicate):

(38)   [IP [I e] [VP [V *be*] [AP **the sausage** [A′ a bit hot]]]]

Under this analysis, the bold-printed DP *the sausage* would originate as the specifier of (and hence be theta-marked by) the A-bar predicate *a bit hot*: in order to receive case, it would have to be raised from being the specifier of AP to becoming the specifier of VP, and then ultimately the specifier of IP (in which position it could receive nominative case from the empty finite I heading the overall IP). In addition, the verb *be* would have to move from V to I, in order to 'support' the tense/agreement features of I, and would accordingly surface in the inflected form *is*. However, the absence of functional systems in grammars of early child English (e.g. the absence of an I-system, a D-system, and a case system) means that the child's grammar lacks the requirement for a 'dummy' copula to support I, lacks the requirement for the articles *a/the*, and lacks the requirement for the subject NP *sausage* to move out of its underlying position as the specifier of AP into a case-marked position as the specifier of IP. If we assume (following Chomsky 1988b) that Universal Grammar incorporates a principle of *economy of derivation* (requiring that 'Shorter derivations are chosen over longer ones', Chomsky 1988b: 8), then the child's non-use of copula *be* would follow from the fact that (since they lack functional systems in their early grammars) young children have no functional need for a copula in structures such as (35) and (36), and hence use the (derivationally less complex) *incopulate* (i.e. copula-less, hence verbless) structures.

In addition to its copula use, *be* in English is traditionally said to have a second use, viz. as a *progressive auxiliary*: this use can be illustrated by structures such as:

(39)   John is working too hard

In conjunction with the +*ing* inflection on the head V of the complement VP, the auxiliary *is* here marks progressive aspect (i.e. indicates an action in progress). It seems reasonable to suppose that progressive *be* (like its copula counterpart) has no real intrinsic semantic content, since it can be omitted from a clause such as that bracketed in (40) below without any apparent loss of meaning:

(40)   I wouldn't have wanted [you (to *be*) working too hard]

On the other hand, progressive *be* cannot be omitted in independent sentences such as:

(41)   (a)   [$_{IP}$ He [$_I$ *is*] [$_{VP}$ working too hard]]
        (b)   *[$_{IP}$ He [$_I$ *e*] [$_{VP}$ working too hard]]

We might suppose that (41)(b) is ungrammatical because the tense/ agreement properties carried by I (= third person singular present tense) cannot be discharged: more precisely, the relevant I-features cannot be discharged onto I, since I is empty; but likewise they cannot be discharged onto the head V of VP, since this already carries the progressive aspect inflection +*ing* (and morphological constraints determine that verbs cannot be doubly inflected, e.g. both with a finite and with a nonfinite inflection). Thus, the function of the use of *be* in (41) is to provide a stem onto which the relevant I-features can be discharged.

However, if we are correct in supposing that early child clauses have no I constituent, then it follows that progressive *be* will have no grammatical function within the child's grammar (it cannot serve as a stem onto which tense/agreement properties of I can be discharged, since there is no I-system in the child's grammar and hence there are no I-features to be discharged). In addition, we might argue that progressive *be* has no essential *semantic* function either: it is nonthematic (in the technical sense defined at the end of chapter 2), and although it marks progressive aspect, this is already indicated by the +*ing* inflection on the head V of its VP complement. Because (to the child) progressive *be* has no obvious syntactic or semantic function, we might therefore expect (in the light of the principle of *economy of derivation*) to find that children omit it in contexts where it is obligatory in adult speech. And sure enough, this is indeed the case, as examples such as the following illustrate:

(42)   (a)   Baby talking (Hayley 20)
        (b)   Bee going window. Wayne sitting gate (Daniel 21)
        (c)   Birdie flying. Dog barking. Him swimming. Joey eating (Bethan 21)
        (d)   Daddy coming (*Helen 21)
        (e)   Mummy doing dinner. Teddy crying (Daniel 22)
        (f)   Kimmy running. Phil running. Pam running (*Kendall 23)
        (g)   Her going on walk. Lady eating fingers (Angharad 23)
        (h)   Her bringing me more (Jem 23)
        (i)   Roland coming as well (Daniel 24)
        (j)   Daddy sleeping. Daddy sleeping bed. Mamma rocking. Bunny standing up (*Claire 24-25)

Since the examples in (42) are independent sentences, they would have the status of IPs headed by a finite I in adult English, and I would have to be filled by progressive *be*, as we see from (41) above. Why should children at this stage make no use of progressive *be*? One plausible hypothesis is that children do not make productive use of items which cannot be assigned any clear grammatical and semantic function within their own (child) grammars (this would provide an obvious account of why they make no use of the dummy auxiliary *do*, or of the copula *be*, or of infinitival *to*, all of which lack intrinsic semantic content and serve only as carriers for the tense/agreement properties of I). Given that progressive *be* has no grammatical function within the child's grammar (since there are no tense/agreement features in early child clauses for it to support) and no apparent semantic function (e.g. is nonthematic, and its function of marking progressive aspect is already fulfilled by the progressive +*ing* inflection on the head V of VP), the child's avoidance of progressive *be* finds a natural explanation. Since progressive *be* has no essential function in the child's system, the principle of *economy of derivation* would lead us to expect that children avoid using what (from the perspective of their own grammars) is a purely redundant item. Thus, instead of being *functional* IPs with the surface schematic form (41), progressive clauses in early child English are simply *lexical* VPs, so that a child sentence such as (42)(c) *Birdie flying* would have the schematic structure (43) below:

(43) $[_{VP} [_{NP}$ Birdie$] [_{V'} [_V$ flying$]]]$

Precisely as our *lexical* analysis of early child grammars would lead us to predict, the child's structure has no I-system (hence the absence of the auxiliary *is*), and no D-system (hence the absence of the determiner *the* to premodify *birdie*): thus, in place of functional IP and DP constituents, the child uses their immediate lexical counterparts VP and NP. The absence of the I-system and D-system in (43) are arguably interconnected facts, if we assume that a finite I must discharge nominative case onto its specifier in adult English, and that only DP can receive case; it then follows that children cannot in principle develop a finite (case-assigning) I-system until they have developed a (case-receiving) D-system.

Since children at this stage have not acquired the progressive auxiliary *be*, we might expect to find that they have likewise not acquired the perfective auxiliary *have*. One of the reasons why we might expect this to be so is that perfective *have* has little intrinsic semantic content – hence the fact that it can freely be omitted (without any apparent loss of meaning) in colloquial 'clipped speech' style in clauses such as:

(44)   (a)   You been anywhere interesting for your holidays?
         (b)   Whatcha (= What you) been up to?

The prediction that children will not have acquired perfective *have* at this stage is borne out by examples such as (45) below:

(45)   (a)   Daddy gone. It gone in (Paula 18)
         (b)   Baby gone out (+Betty 18)
         (c)   Dewi gone. Wayne gone (Daniel 19)
         (d)   Him gone (Elen 20, Hayley 20)
         (e)   Ashley gone (Stephen 20)
         (f)   Blanket gone. Geraint gone. Stick gone. Shapes gone (Bethan 20-21)
         (g)   Wayne taken bubble. Stick gone. Wayne gone (Daniel 21)
         (h)   Baby gone. Nana gone. Miaow gone. Postman Pat gone (Jenny 21)
         (i)   Hammer gone. Car gone. Boots gone. Water gone. Mummy gone. Man gone (Angharad 22)
         (j)   Chocolate gone. Daddy gone. Teddy gone to sleep. Teddy fallen over. Tractor broken. Drink gone (Daniel 22-24)
         (k)   Daddy drawn. Mummy thrown it. Her gone school (Jem 23)
         (l)   Bunny broken foot (*Claire 24)
         (m)   Car gone (Dewi 25)

The differences between perfective clauses in adult and child speech can be illustrated in terms of the superficial syntactic structures in (46) below:

(46)   (a)   [$_{VP}$ [$_{NP}$ Man] [$_{V'}$ [$_{V}$ broken] [$_{NP}$ stick]]]
         (b)   [$_{IP}$ [$_{DP}$ The man] [$_{I'}$ [$_{I}$ has] [$_{VP}$ [$_{V'}$ [$_{V}$ broken] [$_{DP}$ the stick]]]]]

Thus, whereas perfective clauses have the functional status of IP constituents in adult English, their child counterparts have the status of VP constituents; and whereas the adult nominals *the man/the stick* have the functional status of DP constituents, their child counterparts *man/stick* have the lexical status of NP constituents. The non-use of *has* in the child's clause follows from the fact that it has no obvious syntactic or semantic function in the child's grammar: *has* is not needed as a bearer of I-inflections, since the child has no I-system at this stage; but neither is it needed as a marker of perfective aspect, since this is marked by the +*n* inflection on the head V *broken* of the VP. Moreover, the perfective auxiliary is nonthematic since it can have a non-thematic pleonastic pronoun as its subject in adult English, as in '*There* has been very little progress'), and we have already seen that children at this stage use only *thematic* items (i.e. items which assign or receive theta-roles). Thus, from the child's perspective, perfective *have* is a redundant item, and the principle of *economy of derivation* would therefore determine that it is not used. Indeed, it may even be that (because of its intrinsically *functional* nature) perfective *have* remains an uncategorized item in the child's grammar at this stage (recall our earlier suggestion in chapter 4 that functional items which the child cannot incorporate into his lexical category system may simply remain *uncategorized*, and hence unused in productive speech).

What is striking is that even though children at this stage make no productive use of perfective *have*, they nonetheless make use of *have* in its *acquisitive* (or possessive) sense (e.g. they say 'Want have one' in the sense of 'I want to acquire one'): cf. examples such as the following:

(47)   (a)   Have one (Paula 18)
        (b)   Have money (Daniel 19)
        (c)   Want have drink (Daniel 22)
        (d)   Me have biscuit. Want have squash (Angharad 22)
        (e)   No, my have ə this. No, I my have ə this. No have ə this
              (*Kathryn 22)
        (f)   Jem have it (Jem 23)
        (g)   That go have lunch (Claire 23)
        (h)   Have that (Leigh 24)
        (i)   Tina not have it (Domenico 24)

Why should it be that children at the lexical stage in their categorial development have mastered the acquisitive (or possessive) use of *have*, but not the perfective use of *have*? We might suppose that whereas perfective *have* is a purely *functional* (and nonthematic) item, acquisitive *have* by contrast is a *lexical* (and thematic) item, since it can have the categorial status of a nonauxiliary verb in adult English (taking *do*-support, e.g. in structures such as '*Do* you have a villa in Spain?'), since it has the same sense as many adult English lexical verbs (e.g. 'get', 'obtain', 'possess'), and since it seems to theta-mark its subject (= AGENT) and object (= PATIENT). Thus, we might suppose that acquisitive *have* is an item which is early acquired because its characteristically lexical/thematic syntactic/semantic properties mean that it can readily be incorporated into the early lexical-thematic grammars developed by children, whereas perfective *have* is late acquired because its essentially functional/nonthematic syntactic/semantic properties mean that it cannot readily be assimilated into the child's system.

We can summarize the arguments which we have put forward in this chapter in the following terms. The overall thrust of our argumentation has been that there is no I-system in early child grammars of English. The empirical evidence in support of this claim is summarized in (48) below:

(48)   Early child English shows no evidence of acquisition of the morphosyntax of:
         (i)   infinitival *to*
         (ii)   modals
         (iii) finite verb inflections $(+s/+d)$
         (iv)   *do*-support
         (v)   copula *be*
         (vi)   progressive *be*
         (vii) perfective *have*

We have argued that each of these characteristics can be accounted for in a principled fashion if we posit that early child clauses are purely *lexical* structures which consequently contain no functional categories, and hence no I-system.

However, before we close this chapter, it is important to underline an essential point of principle, which we can illustrate in relation to our discussion of finite verb inflections. What we are claiming in (48)(iii) is that young children have not *acquired* the morphosyntax of finite I-inflections at this stage, not that *apparent* finite verb forms never occur in early child English. On the contrary, we find sporadic examples of verb forms which (superficially, at least) might appear to be inflected for tense/agreement. For example, the italicized verb forms in the examples in (49) below might at first sight seem to be past tense forms, so suggesting that some children have begun to master past tense formation at this stage:

(49)   (a)   *Lost* it (Bethan 20)
         (b)   *Found* it (Bethan 21)
         (c)   That *broke* (Claire 23)
         (d)   You *got* bear (Anna 24)

However, there are a number of reasons for supposing that the italicized forms don't correspond to adult past forms at all, but rather to adult *perfective/passive participles*. This is clear in part from the context in which the utterances occurred. For example, (49)(a) occurred immediately after Bethan had spilled some liquid, and so corresponds to the adult form 'I've lost it' (where *lost* is a perfective participle); likewise, (49)(b) occurred immediately after Bethan had found her toy screwdriver, and thus would have the adult counterpart 'I've found it' (where *found* is a perfective participle); (49)(c) occurred in response to an adult saying 'That one's broken' (where *broken* is an adjectival passive participle), so that *broke* here is likely to be a misarticulated form of *broken* (it is well known that children have problems with articulating word-final consonants, especially when syllabic) – and on other occasions in the same transcript, Claire does indeed say 'That broken'; and (49)(d) occurred in response to an adult saying 'I've got a bear', where *got* in the adult model is again a perfective participle.

The specific point being illustrated by examples like those in (49) is that in many verbs, the past tense form is homophonous with the perfect passive participle form, so that what may appear at first sight to correspond to adult past tense forms may in fact correspond more directly to adult perfective/passive participle forms. This is not, of course, to say that such items necessarily have the status of participles in the child's speech. On the contrary, since the items in question typically occur as isolated forms in the child's speech at this stage (so that e.g. we may find *lost*, but not the infinitive form *lose*), it may be more plausible to analyse them as uninflected stem forms, rather than as forms carrying (an irregular allomorph of) the perfective/passive +*n* inflection. In this connection, it is interesting to note the observation by Smith (1973: 175) that his son Amahl used *caught* and *catch* as free variants, and that (in my own corpus) Jem alternates freely between the forms *get* and *got* (seemingly using both as uninflected stem forms).

In much the same way, we can find sporadic apparent counter-examples to the claim that children have not mastered the morphosyntax of present tense/agreement inflections at this stage. For example, it is not uncommon to find utterances such as the following in early child English:

(50)   (a)   Here it *is*! (+Neville 18, +Gary 21, *Claire 24)
        (b)   There it *is*! (*Claire 24, +Darren 24)
        (c)   Here you *are*! (+Frances 18, +Gary 21, +Jack 24)
        (d)   There you *are*! (+Gary 21)

At first sight, it might seem plausible to suppose that the italicized items are finite verbs inflected for tense and agreement: e.g. we might suggest that *is* could be analysed as carrying the third person singular present tense inflection +*s* (attached to an irregular stem allomorph of *be*). However, utterances such as (50) have all the hallmarks of *formulaic* utterances (i.e. nonproductive set expressions). There are four reasons for thinking this. Firstly, the utterances show a highly marked [locative + subject + verb] word-order not found in other declarative utterances produced by the children concerned at this stage. Secondly, the subject is invariable (*it* in '(T)here *it* is', and *you* in '(T)here *you* are'), and is never replaced by other constituents: for example, in '(T)here *it* is', the subject *it* is never replaced by a nominal (e.g. we don't find 'There (*the*) car is') or by another pronominal (e.g. we don't find 'There *she* is'). Thirdly, the verb form is likewise invariable, and is always *is* in '(T)here it is', and always *are* in '(T)here you *are*': we find no alternative form of *be*, nor any other verb. Finally, there is simply no independent evidence whatever that the children concerned have mastered tense/agreement inflections at this stage: on the contrary, they systematically omit inflected auxiliaries in contexts where they are obligatory in adult English, and systematically omit tense/agreement inflections on nonauxiliary verbs (as we have already seen). There is thus good reason to think that examples like (50) are purely *formulaic* utterances, in no way representative of the range of productive structures which fall within the child's competence at this stage.

A potentially more serious challenge to our claim that there is no evidence of productive mastery of tense/agreement inflections in early child English comes from the occurrence of utterances which (superficially, at least) seem to contain the third person singular present tense copula form *'s* (which functions as a contracted allomorph of *is* in adult English): cf. e.g.

(51) (a) Where*'s* helicopter? Where*'s* bee? Where*'s* green car? (Stefan 17)
      (b) Here*'s* Teddy. Here*'s* one. Here*'s* baby (Paula 18)
      (c) Where*'s* hand? Where*'s* chocolate? Where*'s* bike? Where*'s* Mummy? What*'s* that? What*'s* this? There*'s* Mummy in kitchen. Here*'s* bubble. Here*'s* apple. That*'s* bee (Daniel 19–22)
      (d) What*'s* this? (Stephen 20)
      (e) It*'s* Alice (Lucy 20)
      (f) What*'s* that? (Bethan 21, Alison 21, Helen 21, Leigh 24)
      (g) That*'s* alright. That*'s* on there (Claire 23)
      (h) What*'s* that? What*'s* this? It*'s* nappy. It*'s* Peter book. That*'s* Veronica. There*'s* boots. There*'s* Tina (Domenico 24)

At first sight, it would seem tempting to suppose that *'s* here functions as a third person singular present tense inflection attached to a null allomorph of the stem of *be*. If this were so, then the copula sentences in (51) would be IPs headed by an I carrying tense and agreement features which are discharged onto the (null) copula stem in the form of the *'s* inflection. This would mean that (contrary to what we have claimed hitherto) such children have indeed developed an I-system, at least in copula sentences. If this were so, we might argue (on grounds of maximizing structural symmetry) that the IP analysis should be extended from copula clauses to all other types of clause, so that the latter would be analysed as IPs which contain an 'abstract' I-system, i.e. one in which the tense/agreement features of the head I are *covert* (in the sense that they surface as a phonologically null inflection).

However, what has to be said about examples such as (51) is that (as far as I am aware) there is universal agreement among child language researchers that (whatever its precise function), the clitic copula *'s* definitely does not function as a finite tense/agreement inflection in early child English sentences such as (51). The evidence for saying this is fivefold. Firstly, children are not productively attaching the third person singular +*s* inflection to overt verb stems at this stage (i.e. they are not producing forms such as *wants*, *goes*, *sees* etc. or overgeneralized forms such as *bes* and *haves*), as we saw earlier in relation to examples such as (16) and (18) above: and it seems to strain credulity to posit that children can attach a third person singular present tense inflection to a phonologically null verb stem, but not to an overt verb stem. Secondly, the *s*-forms are used only sporadically, alongside *s*-less forms, as the cross-sectional data in (52) below illustrate:

(52)   (a)   *Where's* helicopter?/*Where* helicopter? (Stefan 17)
        (b)   *What's* that?/*What* that? (Dewi 18)
        (c)   *What's* this?/*What* this? (Stephen 20)
        (d)   *What's* that?/*What* that? (Hayley 20)
        (e)   *That's* car/*That* bear book (*Kathryn 22)
        (f)   *Here's* bubble/*Here* bubble. *Where's* Dewi?/*Where* Dewi? (Daniel 22)
        (g)   *That's* on/*That* on (Claire 23)
        (h)   *It's* basket/*It* lion (Anna 24)
        (i)   *It's* bum/*It* bike. *What's* that/*What* that? (Leigh 24)
        (j)   *That's* Veronica/*That* Domenico (Domenico 24)
        (k)   *Where's* Daddy/*Where* Mommy? *What's* that/*What* that? *What's* this/*What* this? (*Claire 24)

The same pattern (of *s*-forms alternating with *s*-less forms) is revealed in our fine-grained longitudinal study of Daniel: cf.

(53)　　(a)　*Where's* hand? *Where's* chocolate? *Where's* bike? *Where's* Mummy? *Where's* kangaroo? *Where's* hat? *What's* that? *What's* this? *There's* Mummy in kitchen. *Here's* bubble. *Here's* apple. *Here's* bike. *Here's* key. *Here's* cat. *That's* bee. *That's* Teddy. *It's* Roland

　　　　(b)　*Where* Carol? *Where* Teddy? *Where* Daddy? *Where* money? *Where* shoe? *Where* van? *Where* bike? *Where* tractor? *What* this? *There* Mum. *There* coat. *There* Daddy. *Here* bubble. *Here* coat. *Here* Teddy. *Here* cow. *Here* book. *Here* tractor. *That* chair. *That* Wayne. *That* car. *That* spoon. *It* Wayne (Daniel 19–23)

The fact that children are clearly not 'aware' of the obligatory requirement for the *'s* inflection to be used in such structures in adult English (in order to satisfy the requirement that the relevant I-features must be discharged) provides a strong indication that they have no real 'understanding' of the function of *'s* (and certainly no 'awareness' that *'s* is a finite inflection which realizes abstract tense/agreement properties carried by I).

A third reason for discounting any suggestion that *'s* is a tense/agreement-marked copula is that *'s* is the only (apparent) copula form being used at this point: we find no productive use of other forms of the copula at all, either full forms like *is/am/are/was/were*, or contracted forms like *'m/'re*. Fourthly, forms such as *there's/where's* are used not only with singular complements, but also (inappropriately) with plural complements, as illustrated by (54) below:

(54)　　(a)　There's *birds* (+Sean 21)
　　　　(b)　There's *boots* (Domenico 24)

(In this context, an adult would require a plural copula – cf. 'There *are* the birds', 'There *are* my boots'.) Fifthly, the *'s* is restricted to being suffixed to a specific restricted range of lexical items, viz. to (a subset of) the inanimate pronouns *it/that/what* and the locative pronouns *there/where*: this fact has led many researchers to suggest that the attached *'s* is mis-segmented by the child as part of the stem of the pronoun - cf. e.g. Bloom (1970: 40–45), Brown (1973: 65), and Hill (1983). For reasons such as these, it seems likely that utterances such as those in (51–54) are semiformulaic utterances of the schematic form:

(55)   *What/that/it/where/there('s)* + NP

Clearly, the sporadic use of *s*-forms in semiformulaic utterances of the schematic form (55) cannot be taken as evidence of acquisition of tense/agreement inflections – far from it.

The overall conclusion to be drawn from our discussion in this chapter is that there is simply no evidence whatever that children at this stage have begun to unravel the intricacies of the morphosyntax of tense/agreement inflections in English. And indeed our conclusion is borne out by published studies in the relevant acquisition literature (cf. e.g. Cazden (1968), Brown (1973), De Villiers and De Villiers (1973a), Kuczaj (1977)). Within the framework adopted here, the significance of the child's nonacquisition of finite tense/agreement inflections is that (since such inflections are properties of I) it suggests that children's grammars at this stage lack an I constituent: and this conclusion in turn is consistent with our more general hypothesis that early child grammars lack functional categories.

We can summarise the contents of this chapter in the following terms. We have argued that early child clauses are very different in nature from adult inflection clauses, the latter being of the schematic form [DP I VP]: more specifically, we have claimed that early child clauses are Small Clauses which show no evidence that children at the relevant stage have developed an I-system. Among the key properties of early child clauses which led us to this conclusion were the following (repeated from (48) above):

(56)   Early child English shows no evidence of acquisition of the morphosyntax of:
   (i)   infinitival *to*
   (ii)   modals
   (iii)   finite verb inflections (+*s*/+*d*)
   (iv)   *do*-support
   (v)   copula *be*
   (vi)   progressive *be*
   (vii)   perfective *have*

Since (in adult English) finite auxiliaries are all positioned in I at some stage of derivation, since *to* is base-generated in I, and since the tense/agreement properties of finite verbs originate in I, then an obvious conclusion to be drawn from our discussion here is that children at this stage have simply not acquired the morphosyntax of I at all – and indeed show no evidence whatever of having developed an I-system. In consequence, early child clauses are purely lexical structures of the schematic form [NP X']. Early child clauses thus bear a close resemblance to adult Small Clauses of the form [DP X']: the most obvious difference between the two is that early child clauses have NP subjects, whereas adult Small Clauses require DP subjects; this difference is a consequence of the absence of functional categories in early child grammars of English.

We conclude this chapter with a brief technical postscript. Throughout our discussion of the morphosyntax of finite verbs in adult English, we have assumed the system of categories in Chomsky's (1986b) *Barriers* monograph, under which tense and agreement are both morphosyntactic properties of the same single category I (so that I carries both tense and agreement properties). It should be noted, however, that some recent work since *Barriers* has argued that tense and agreement are not different reflexes of the same category I, but rather are themselves different categories, each heading a separate projection (so that T(ense) projects into TP, and (a)G(reement) likewise projects into GP – see e.g. Pollock 1988, 1989, and Chomsky 1988b). However, the conclusions which we have reached about early child English in this chapter here can be carried over into this alternative framework with only trivial modifications: i.e. rather than saying (as in the *Barriers* framework) that early child clauses are Small Clauses which lack an I-system, we would instead conclude that early child clauses are Small Clauses which lack a T-system and a G-system. Since it makes no difference for our discussion of early child English which of the two analyses of adult English we adopt, we shall continue to assume the *Barriers* analysis of adult English categories, because this is the one familiar to most readers (e.g. from textbooks such as Radford 1988a). It should be noted, however, that the two different analyses make potentially distinct predictions about how tense and agreement will be acquired once the child reaches the (later) *functional* stage of development. Thus, under the *Barriers* analysis in which tense and agreement are different reflexes of the same category I, we might expect the two to be acquired simultaneously. But under Pollock's revised analysis in which tense and agreement head different category systems, we might expect to find that one is acquired before the other (e.g. tense before agreement). In this connection, it is interesting to note the claim made by Radford and Aldridge (1987) that for many children, the earliest manifestation of an I-system is the emergence of a restricted class of modals (especially *can* and *will*): since modals are base-generated T constituents under Pollock's system, this might suggest that (for such children) the T-system is acquired before the G-system; and indeed, some studies of the acquisition of inflectional morphemes have suggested that tense inflections are mastered earlier than agreement inflections (cf. e.g. the classic study of Brown 1973). However, since such claims raise numerous complex problems (not least the familiar problem of the distinction between *acquisition* and *mastery*), and since we are concerned with the earlier *lexical* stage of the child's development here, we shall leave this as a topic for future research.

7

Absence of a Case System in Early Child English

In the previous chapter, we argued that early child clauses are Small Clauses with no I-system, and thus lack the tense/agreement properties of their adult finite clause counterparts. The absence of I-agreement features in early child clauses might be expected to be of enormous significance, given that recent work has argued that I-agreement features play an important role in determining the grammar of a variety of other phenomena, including the use of null subjects (discussed in chapter 8) and nominative case assignment. Thus, we might expect (e.g.) that if early child clauses are Small Clauses which have no I-system (and hence no I-agreement features), young children at this stage cannot in principle 'know' how nominative case forms are used in the adult English target system. There are also additional theoretical considerations which would lead us to the same conclusion. If case is a property of the D-system in adult English, and if early child grammars of English lack a D-system (as we argued in chapter 4), then this would again lead us to expect that young children have not acquired the morphosyntax of case-marking. After all, if nominative case is a functional property assigned to a functional category (= DP) by a functional category (= an agreement-marked I), then the absence of functional categories and functional properties in the purely *lexical* grammars developed by young children would lead us to predict that such children have no 'knowledge' of the morphosyntax of nominative forms. In this chapter, we argue that this is indeed so; we shall then go on to argue in more general terms that there is no case system at all operating in early child English (a claim also made e.g. in Radford 1985, 1986, 1988b, Kazman 1988, and Guilfoyle and Noonan 1988).

The interdependence between nominative case-marking and I-agreement marking in adult English can be illustrated in terms of an example such as the following:

(1)   [IP [DP *He*] seldom [I **does**] [VP say anything]]

In (1), the bold-printed finite I constituent carries agreement features (third person singular, realized as the +*s* inflection on **does**) which are determined by the person and number of the italicized nominative pronoun; thus, we might say that the agreement inflection on the verb **does** is in effect a *nominative* agreement inflection, since the person and number properties of the inflection are determined by properties of the italicized nominative pronoun. Conversely, the pronoun *he* carries a case feature (nominative) which is determined by the italicized I constituent, given that only the subject of a finite IP (= an IP headed by an agreement-marked I) is assigned nominative case. So, the agreement-marking of I by a nominative subject, and the case-marking of the subject by an agreement-marked I appear to be two different reflexes of a common structural relationship between a finite I and its subject.

There is abundant evidence that the interdependence between nominative case and subject-verb agreement is not just an accidental property of English, but rather reflects a deep-seated (hence potentially universal) link between the two. The 'inflected infinitive' construction in Portuguese provides some evidence in support of this claim. Portuguese has a set of infinitives which are inflected for agreement (but not for tense), and which assign nominative case to their subjects. For instance, in a sentence such as the following (from Rouveret 1980: 76):

(2)   O Joao lamenta [*eles* ter**em** gastado esse dinheiro para nada]
        The Joao deplores [they have+3PL spent this money for nothing]
        'Joao deplores the fact that they have spent this money for nothing'

the infinitive form *terem* comprises the infinitive stem *ter* plus the third person plural inflection -*em* (here glossed as '3PL'), and the subject *eles* 'they' is assigned nominative case. The fact that the head I of the bracketed infinitival IP carries agreement but not tense features suggests that it is the agreement properties of I (not its tense properties) which condition nominative case assignment. Further evidence of a potentially universal link between nominative case assignment and I-agreement features comes from McCloskey 1986.

Of course, if there is indeed a universal link between I-agreement features and nominative case-marking, then we should expect to find that languages with no I-agreement properties will likewise have no nominative case-forms. Kikongo (= Congolese) is arguably one such language (the relevant examples have kindly been provided by Malele Ma Ludani). Finite verbs in Kikongo are inflected for tense, but are never overtly inflected for agreement – the following paradigm:

(3) (a) **Munu/nge/yandi/beto/beno/bau** *kekudiaka* loso
          I/you-SG/(s)he/we/you-PL/they eat rice

     (b) **Munu/nge/yandi/beto/beno/bau** *kekudia* loso
          I/you-SG/(s)he/we/you-PL/they will-eat rice

     (c) **Munu/nge/yandi/beto/beno/bau** *kudiaka* loso
          I/you-SG/(s)he/we/you-PL/they ate rice

(where SG = singular, and PL = plural). Note that the italicized verbs in (3) inflect for present/future/past tense, but carry no agreement inflection whatever (and thus can freely occur with any of the bold-printed subjects). From such examples it would seem reasonable to conclude that I in Kikongo carries tense properties but lacks agreement properties. Now, in a language with I-agreement properties (e.g. adult English), the subject of a finite I is typically assigned a different case (= nominative) from the object of a transitive verb or preposition (= objective), as we see from contrasts such as the following:

(4) *I/*me* will introduce *him/*he* to *them/*they*

(where *I/he/they* are nominative forms, and *me/him/them* objective forms). This creates an obvious *subject/object asymmetry* with respect to case-marking in finite clauses, since subjects are assigned nominative case by I whereas objects are assigned objective case by V or P. But if it is the existence of I-agreement properties in a language like (adult) English which determines that the subject of a finite verb is assigned a morphologically distinct case (= nominative) from the object of a verb or preposition (= objective), then we might expect to find that in a language like Kikongo which has no I-agreement features, there will be no subject/object case-marking asymmetry in finite clauses, so that the subjects of finite verbs will not be case-marked differently from their objects. And sure enough, it turns out that Kikongo has no correlate of English nominative case: on the contrary, subjects of finite verbs have precisely the same morphological form as objects of verbs (or indeed objects of prepositions), as the following examples illustrate:

(5) (a) *Yandi* bulaka **munu**
          (S)he hit me

(b)   **Munu** bulaka *yandi*
      I hit him/her

(c)   *Yandi* tubaka na **munu**
      (S)he spoke to me

(d)   **Munu** tubaka na *yandi*
      I spoke to him/her

So, it would seem that languages with I-agreement are characterized by a subject/object asymmetry with respect to case-marking in finite clauses, in that they assign the subject of an agreement-marked I a different case (= nominative) from that assigned to the object of V (= objective). By contrast, languages which lack I-agreement show no such subject/object case-marking asymmetry (so that in agreementless languages like Kikongo, the subject and object of a finite verb are not morphologically distinct).

The link between I-agreement and nominative case-marking has obvious implications for our claim that early child clauses are Small Clauses which lack an I-system. For if there is no I-system in early child clauses, then it follows that such clauses are tenseless and (more importantly) *agreementless*. Now, if it is a characteristic property of agreementless languages (like Kikongo) that they show no subject/object case-marking asymmetry, then we should expect to find that subjects and objects are not morphologically distinct in early child English. Given that only (a subset of) pronouns in adult English are overtly inflected for the nominative/objective contrast (viz. pairs such as *I/me*, *we/us*, *he/him*, *she/her*, and *they/them*), then the obvious place to look for relevant evidence of the presence (or absence) of a nominative/objective contrast in early child speech is in children's use of pronouns. One complication which this poses is that – as we noted in chapter 4 – many children at this stage have an essentially *nominal* speech style, and thus avoid the use of pronouns altogether (more precisely, they avoid pronouns overtly inflected for case). However, there are some children at this stage with a *pronominal* speech style (i.e. children who use both nominals and pronominals): thus, the obvious question which arises is whether the speech of such children shows evidence of a systematic nominative/ objective contrast in their grammars.

When we examine the speech production of children with a *pronominal* style, we find that they unerringly use objective pronouns in objective contexts (i.e. in contexts where adults would require an objective pronoun, e.g. when governed by a transitive verb) – as examples such as the following illustrate:

(6) (a) Paula put *them*. Throw *them* in (Paula 18)
     (b) Help *me* out. (Hayley 20)
     (c) Geraint hit *me*. Put *them* on (Bethan 20)
     (d) Pinch *him*. Hit *him*. Pick *him* up. Put *them*. Get *them* out. Geraint push *me* (Bethan 21)
     (e) Cuddle *me* (Jem 21)
     (f) Mum, Wayne hit *me*. Want kick *him*. Put *him* bed (Daniel 22)
     (g) Cuddle *him*. Her bringing *me* more (Jem 23)
     (h) Want *them* off (Angharad 22)
     (i) Want *them* (Anne 24)

Significantly, however, such children do not use nominative pronouns but rather *objective* pronouns in contexts where adults would require a nominative pronoun. For example, independent sentences in adult English are finite clauses headed by an agreement-marked finite I, and thus require nominative subjects (since an agreement-marked I assigns nominative case to the subject which it agrees with): but independent sentences in early child English have *objective* subjects, as we see from examples such as the following:

(7) (a) *Me* got bean (Stefan 17)
     (b) *Me* do (Helen 18)
     (c) *Me* talk. *Me* look (Stephen 19)
     (d) *Me* do it. *Me* do. *Me* come in. *Me* want it. *Me* help. *Me* get it (Bethan 20)
     (e) *Me* want one. *Me* do it (Bethan 21)
     (f) *Me* ask him. *Me* soap floor (Daniel 21)
     (g) *Me* going out back (+Gavin 21)
     (h) *Me* up (+Gerald 21)
     (i) *Me* begin (+Olivia 21)
     (j) *Me* sit there (+Betty 21)
     (k) *Me* show mommy. *Me* like coffee (*Kathryn 21–22)
     (l) *Me* have biscuit (Angharad 22)
     (m) *Me* want biscuit (Daniel 22)
     (n) *Me* have. *Me* hello [wanting to say 'Hello' on phone] (Anna 24)
     (o) *Me* do it (Leigh 24)

(p)   *Me* play (+Frances 24)

(q)   *Me* buy birdie. *Me* out. *Me* get baby. *Me* do that. *Me* nice (+Ellen 24)

(8)   (a)   *Him* on there (+Neil 18)

(b)   *Him* gone (Hayley 20)

(c)   *Him* swimming (Bethan 21)

(d)   *Him* naughty. *Him* bad (Daniel 24)

(e)   *Him* asleep (Jem 24)

(9)   (a)   *Her* do that (Hayley 20)

(b)   *Her* gone in there (Angharad 22)

(c)   *Her* go back in. *Her* bringing me more (Jem 23)

(d)   *Her* read that (Paula 23)

(e)   *Her* climbing ladder (Jem 24)

(f)   *Her* gone school (Domenico 24)

Thus, the obvious conclusion is that there is no nominative/objective contrast in pronouns in early child grammars, and that children with a *pronominal* speech style generalize the use of (what in adult terms are) objective pronouns from object position to subject position. Given that there is likewise no subject/object asymmetry in nonpronominal NPs (so that a nominal like *Daddy* can function equally as subject or object), the overall conclusion we reach is that there is no subject/object asymmetry in any kind of NPs in early child English (either in pronominal NPs, or nominal NPs). The situation in early child English thus seems to be analogous to that in Kikongo, in that there is no subject/object asymmetry, and hence subject NPs and object NPs are morphologically nondistinct.

The significance of children's nonacquisition of nominative pronouns should be obvious at this point. If nominative case is a functional property (in the sense that it is assigned to a functional DP by a functional agreement-marked I) then children's nonacquisition of nominative case-marking is entirely consistent with our overall hypothesis that early child grammars of English are purely lexical in nature, and show no evidence of the acquisition of functional categories and their associated functional properties. The absence of a D-system and I-system in early child grammars of English means that there is no possibility of nominative case-forms being used correctly.

At this point, however, it is important to emphasize a key point of principle. Our central claim here is that children at the lexical stage in their categorial development have not *acquired* the morphosyntax of nominative case forms (i.e. they do not 'know' that nominative case is assigned by an agreement-marked I to its DP subject/specifier). However, the hypothesis that children are not 'aware' of the conditions under which nominative case-forms are used in adult English should not be taken as implying that we never find any examples of (what might appear to be) nominative forms in the speech of children at this stage. Thus, it is simply not true to say (as Fletcher 1987: 6 does) that the Small Clause analysis of early child clauses predicts 'complete absence of nominative case marking'. On the contrary, the central claim made here is that children at this stage *have not acquired the morphosyntax of nominatives* (i.e. they do not 'know' that nominative case is assigned to a DP which functions as the specifier of an agreement-marked I) – not that they never use forms which (if analysed in adult terms) might seem to have the status of nominatives. It is certainly true to say that we find the sporadic occurrence of nominative pronouns in the transcripts of some children who otherwise appear to be at the lexical stage in their categorial development. For example, we find Jem at age 21 months repeating on three separate occasions in the same 45-minute recording:

(10)   Off *he* goes! (Jem 21)

However, an utterance such as (10) has all the hallmarks of a stereotyped 'set phrase' – as indicated by the exceptional word order, the exceptional agreement-marking on *goes*, and the exceptional nominative case-marking of *he* (all of which are totally uncharacteristic of Jem's sponta-neous speech at this stage). To be interpreted in the same light is the following utterance produced by Kathryn at age 21 months (discussed in Bloom 1970: 76):

(11)   *I*'m busy now (*Kathryn 21)

Should we take sentence (11) as indicating that Kathryn has acquired nominative case marking in English (and indeed that she has acquired the tense/agreement inflections used on finite forms of *be*)? This is certainly not the stance taken by Bloom: on the contrary, she dismisses examples such as (11) as one of a class of 'structures that were not productive in that they occurred only once and appeared to be unana-lysed "stereotype" sentences' (1970: 75). If Bloom is right, isolated sentences like (11) cannot in principle demonstrate acquisition of nominative case assignment.

Support for Bloom's position comes from the fact that Kathryn's transcripts at 21 and 22 months show her using not only nominative pronouns like *I* as the subject of an independent sentence, but also the corresponding objective form *me*, and even the genitive form *my*: cf. the following examples (from Bloom 1970: 49, 153, and 159)

(12)   (a)   *Me* show mummy
        (b)   *Me* like coffee
        (c)   No, *my* have ə this
        (d)   No, *I my* have ə this

Thus, while Kathryn may 'know' that the first person singular pronoun has three distinct allomorphs (*I/me/my*), it is equally clear that she does not 'know' the conditions under which each of these three variants is used. Kathryn is apparently unable to identify the precise structural context appropriate to each of the three allomorphs, and so seems to use them interchangeably. Clearly, data such as (12) are very far from demonstrating acquisition of nominative case-marking – quite the opposite, in fact.

  Similarly, the sporadic occurence of nominative pronouns in imitative utterances such as:

(13)   ADULT: I can see you
        CHILD: *I* see (+Neville 18)

can scarcely be taken as reliable evidence of the acquisition of the morphosyntax of nominative pronouns, for reasons which I take to be self-evident. The same might be said of semiformulaic utterances of the form '*I want* + NP', found in the speech of a few children at this stage. For example, Greenfield and Smith (1976: 174) note that Nicky at age 18 months produced both *awa* and *awada* with NP complements (e.g. *Awada cacoo* = 'Want record'). However, they reject any suggestion that *aw(ad)a* should be analysed as a multimorphemic sequence (e.g. a contracted counterpart of the adult sequence 'I want a/the'), and instead adopt the common-sense position that '*awa* and *awada* are treated as a single word rather than as *I want the* because none of the words *I*, *want*, or *the* had appeared up to that time either alone or in any other combination' (ibid.).

  The overall conclusion to be drawn from our discussion of nominative case-marking here is that there is no evidence whatever that children at the lexical stage of their categorial development have acquired the the morphosyntax of nominative case in adult English (i.e. they do not 'know' that nominative case is assigned by a head agreement-marked I constituent to its DP subject). On the contrary, children show no evidence at all of 'knowing' the morphosyntax of nominative pronouns at this stage. This fact in itself suggests that they have not yet developed an I-system or D-system – and this in turn is exactly what our *lexical* analysis of early child grammars of English would lead us to expect.

Our conclusion thus far in this chapter that young children at the *lexical* stage of their grammatical development have no 'knowledge' of nominative case assignment clearly ties up with our earlier conclusion in chapter 4 that they have likewise no 'knowledge' of genitive case assignment. The obvious generalization to extract from these two observations is that children have no 'knowledge' of the morphosyntax of case at all at this stage. Indeed, if we follow Abney (1987) in positing that case is a morphosyntactic characteristic of the (functional) D-system, then our lexical analysis of early child grammars of English would provide a principled account of the nonacquisition of case-marking, given the (not unreasonable) assumption that a specific category system will not be used productively by children until they have begun to master the morphosyntactic characteristics of the system.

There are several pieces of evidence which appear to support the more general claim that there is no evidence of the acquisition of a case system in early child grammars of English. We noted in chapter 4 that children have not acquired the genitive determiner *'s* at this stage; and we have noted in this chapter that they have not acquired the morphosyntax of nominative forms. We also noted (in chapter 4) that many children avoid using case-marked pronouns such as *I/me/my* at this stage: in place of case-marked pronouns, they either have a nominal, or a 'gap' (i.e. a 'missing argument', here symbolized as Ø): cf. the following examples from the transcripts of Claire at 24 months:

(14)   (a)   *Claire* do it [= '*I*'ll do it']
       (b)   *Jane* do it [= '*You* do it']
       (c)   What Ø doing? [imitation of 'What's *he* doing?']
       (d)   Where Ø go? [= 'Where do *they* go?'] (*Claire 24)

(We shall discuss the grammar of 'missing arguments' in early child English in the next chapter, so for the time being we shall have no more to say about them here.) Moreover, some children appear to use the neutral vowel schwa /ə/ as a 'filler' in contexts where adults would use case-marked pronouns: this strategy seems to have been used by all three of the children studied in Bloom 1970: e.g.

(15)   (a)   ə write [scribbling on paper]. ə ride [pointing to picture of a bus] (*Gia 19)

(b) ə pull hat [in reply to 'You pull']. ə want see [looking for marshmallow in her pudding] (*Kathryn 21)

(c) ə sit [about to sit down]. ə play it [playing a toy drum]. ə find it [picking up his pail]. ə need shoes [pointing to top of cabinet]. ə eat juice [going after his juice and drinking it] (*Eric 19–22)

In each of the examples in (15), schwa would seem to correspond to the adult nominative pronoun *I* (though schwa is used in place of other case-marked pronouns as well). The fact that in place of (overtly) case-marked pronouns many children have (apparently caseless) nominals, 'gaps', or 'dummies' suggests that they have not acquired the complex morphology of case forms, since *avoidance* is a strategy often used by young children to mask incompetence. The use of a neutral vowel as a 'dummy' is a strategy reported elsewhere in the acquisition literature: cf. Dore et al. (1976), and Ramer (1976).

However, an obvious challenge to our claim that there is no evidence of the acquisition of the morphology of case-marked pronouns in early child English comes from the fact that (as we saw above), some children at this stage seem to show relatively productive use of (what in adult terms would be) objective pronouns: typical of this type of child are the following utterances produced by Bethan at ages 20–21 months (cf. the examples in (6–7) above for a fuller set of examples from a range of different children):

(16)   Pinch *him*. Hit *him*. Pick *him* up. Put *them*. Get *them* out. Geraint push *me*. Geraint hit *me*. Put *them* on. *Me* do it. *Me* do. *Me* come in. *Me* want it. *Me* help. *Me* get it. *Me* want one. *Him* swimming (Bethan 20–21)

The fact that a child like Bethan appears to make productive use of objective pronouns might seem to point to the conclusion that she has acquired a set of case-marked (= objective) pronouns, and thus lead us to reject our earlier hypothesis that children at her stage of development have no 'knowledge' of the case-inflections associated with the D-system.

However, there are good reasons for supposing that this would be a hasty and erroneous conclusion. The crucial observation to make here is that there is no systematic (i.e. rule-governed) *case contrast* operating in early child English: by this, we mean that such children make limited productive use of (what appear to be) objective pronouns, but have no productive use of the corresponding nominative or genitive pronouns. It would seem reasonable to suppose that the absence of any systematic contrast between objective forms and nominative/genitive forms implies the absence of *case* as a formal property in early child English. Indeed, we might well argue that such a conclusion is forced upon us by universal linguistic principles. After all, it is a generally accepted analytic postulate that we are only justified in positing the existence of an abstract grammatical property (e.g. case, gender etc.) in the grammar of a given language if there is some formally marked *contrast* in the language between forms which have that property and those that do not. Given this *contrast principle*, it would follow that we could not argue (e.g.) that adult English verbs are inflected for gender, since verbs in English never carry any overt gender-marking, and there is thus no formal contrast between (e.g.) masculine and feminine verb forms in English (unlike Arabic, where formal gender contrasts are found in some verb forms).

This very same *contrast principle* which leads us to conclude that English verbs are not inflected for gender (because of the lack of any formally signalled gender contrast in English verb forms) would also seem to lead us to conclude that forms which show no overt case contrasts have no morphological case. Indeed, it is precisely the lack of any case contrast in nonclitic NPs in French which leads Kayne (1983: 125) to conclude that 'Nonclitic NPs in French never bear morphological case' – i.e. because they are invariable in form, and thus exhibit no case-contrast. Given the logic of this kind of argumentation, the natural conclusion to draw would be that early child pronouns such as *me/him/ her* etc. are not case-marked objective forms, but rather are *impostors* which in reality have the status of caseless pronominal NPs (in contrast to their adult counterparts which function as case-marked pronominal DPs). The very same logic would also lead us to conclude that early child nominals are likewise caseless NPs, since they too are uninflected for case (e.g. a nominal such as *baby* has no genitive counterpart *baby's* in early child English). The obvious generalization to draw would then be that early child nominals and pronominals have the status of caseless NPs (whereas their adult counterparts have the status of case-marked DPs). More specifically, we might suggest that pronouns such as *me/him/them* etc. are case-marked pro-determiner constituents in adult English (as Abney (1987) suggests), whereas their child counterparts are caseless pro-noun constituents. The pro-N analysis would provide a natural account of the following 'replacement sequence' produced by Bethan at 21 months:

(17)   Big Geraint...Big *him* (Bethan 21)

where Bethan appears to have replaced the noun *Geraint* in her first utterance by pronoun *him* in her second, so suggesting that (for her) nouns and pronouns like *him* are interchangeable. If *him* is being used as a nominal pronoun in early child English, then it reinforces our earlier suggestion in chapter 4 that children may initially miscategorize items which have a functional categorial status in adult English, and analyse them as items belonging to the corresponding *lexical* category.

Although we have limited the scope of our study here to English, data from published studies on the acquisition of other languages suggest that the earliest (pro)nominals developed by all children at the lexical stage in their categorial development (viz. roughly under two years of age) are typically *caseless*. For example, Rom and Dgani (1985) report that children under 24 months of age acquiring Hebrew as their first language have no productive case-system. Likewise, Schieffelin (1981) argues that children acquiring Kaluli as their first language do not begin to make productive use of case-marking particles until after two years of age. Various studies of the acquisition of German (e.g. Park 1981, Clahsen 1984, Tracy 1986) have concluded that at the earliest stage of development there are 'No case markers present' (Tracy 1986: 54). In much the same vein, Slobin (1966: 134) reports on a study of the acquisition of Russian suggesting that the first stage in the development of (pro)nominals is characterized by a lack of case contrasts, and by the exclusive use of 'unmarked forms – generally the noun in what corresponds to the nominative singular' (given the absence of case contrasts, these supposed 'nominatives' would of course have the status of *caseless* forms in child speech). A similar situation is reported for two children acquiring Finnish by Bowerman (1973), who remarks that 'The children both used the nominative singular form of Nouns for all syntactic roles' (because of the lack of case contrast, it would be reasonable to regard such pseudo-nominatives as *impostors* whose real status is that of *caseless* forms). Thus, the claim that children in the earliest stage of their categorial development use caseless (nominal and pronominal) lexical NPs in contexts where adults require case-marked functional DPs would thus seem to be applicable not only to the first stages in the acquisition of English, but also more generally.

The evidence which we have produced so far suggests that children have not begun to acquire the morphology of case at the lexical stage in their categorial development. This in turn might lead us to expect that they have similarly not acquired the *syntax* of case either. We can elaborate on the syntactic function of case in adult grammars in the following terms (adapting ideas put forward by Rouveret and Vergnaud (1980), Emonds (1985), Chomsky (1986b), Abney (1987) and Brody and

Manzini (1988)). We shall assume that DPs are licensed (in part) by principles of Case Theory: for example, an overt DP must carry a specific morphological case (nominative, objective, or genitive in English), and is restricted to occurring in a correspondingly case-marked position; thus, a nominative DP is restricted to occurring in a nominative position (i.e. as the specifier of an agreement-marked I), a genitive DP is restricted to occurring in a genitive position (i.e. as the specifier of an appropriate allomorph of the determiner *'s*), and an objective DP is restricted to occurring in an objective position (i.e. in the case domain of a transitive V, P, or C). It follows from this that there are *case constraints* on the distribution (i.e. syntax) of DPs in adult grammars: for example, a nominative DP cannot occur in an objective position (hence the ungrammaticality of *'John loves *she*'); and (more generally), no overt DP (whether nominative, objective, or genitive) can occur in a *caseless* position – i.e. a position in which it does not fall within the domain of any case assigner at all (hence the ungrammaticality of *'I am keen *you* to go there').

It follows from the case principles which operate in adult grammars that Small Clauses can occur as the complements of transitive verbs in adult English, but not as independent sentences: cf. the contrasts in (18–19) below:

(18)   (a)   I consider [*him* unsuitable for the post]
        (b)   She won't have [*me* in the kitchen]
        (c)   I don't want [*them* upsetting you]

(19)   (a)   *Him* unsuitable for the post
        (b)   *Me* in the kitchen
        (c)   *Them* upsetting you

In (18), the italicized objective pronouns (i.e. pronominal DPs) are licensed to occur as subjects of the bracketed Small Clauses because they fall within the case domain of the immediately preceding transitive verbs *consider/have/want* (and thus occupy objective positions). By contrast, the italicized objective pronouns in (19) are unlicensed, for the simple reason that they do not fall within the domain of an objective case assigner (and indeed, nominative and genitive pronouns are likewise unlicensed in the italicized subject positions in (19), for analogous reasons). This means in effect that it follows from principles of Case Theory that a Small Clause with an overt subject DP cannot function as an independent sentence in adult English.

However, the situation is very different in early child English. As we have already noted (and exemplified extensively) in earlier chapters, children at this stage produce numerous examples of lexical Small Clauses used as the complements of transitive verbs, for example:

(20)   (a)   Want [baby talking] (Hayley 20)
       (b)   Want [mummy come] (Jem 21)
       (c)   Want [lady open it] (Daniel 22)
       (d)   Want [car out] (Daniel 21)
       (e)   Want [them off] (Angharad 22)
       (f)   Jem want [mummy take it out] (Jem 24)
       (g)   Let [it go] (Jem 23)
       (h)   Let [me have a look] (Chrissie 23)
       (i)   Let [dolly sit down] (*Helen 24)
       (j)   Make [him sit down] (*Kathryn 21)

However, what is far more significant from our point of view is that we also find young children using Small Clauses as independent sentences: cf. the extensive examples already given in earlier chapters, a brief selection of which is presented below:

(21)   (a)   *Sausage* bit hot (Jem 21)
       (b)   *Girl* hungry (*Kathryn 22)
       (c)   *Mouse* in window (Hayley 20)
       (d)   *Wayne* in bedroom (Daniel 21)
       (e)   *Birdie* flying (Bethan 21)
       (f)   *Car* gone (Angharad 22)
       (g)   *Man* no go in there (*Kathryn 22)
       (h)   *Man* drive truck (*Allison 22)
       (i)   *Pig* say oink (*Claire 25, in reply to 'What does the pig say?')

The corresponding Small Clause structures in adult English would be ungrammatical as independent sentences, since the italicized subject would be a DP occurring in a caseless position (i.e. in a position where it is not within the domain of any case assigner), and thus would be unlicensed. Why, then, should it be that there is apparently no violation of the principles of Case Theory in child sentences such as (21)? A clue to solving this problem may lie in our earlier suggestion (in chapter 4) that children use caseless NPs in contexts where adults require case-marked DPs: for example, the child NP *sausage* in (21)(a) corresponds to the adult DP *the sausage*; the child NP *girl* in (21)(b) corresponds to the adult DP *the girl*; the child NP *mouse* in (21)(c) corresponds to the adult DP *the mouse*...and so on and so forth. If case is a functional property which is carried by the D-system, then we might suppose that the principles of Case Theory can only become (nonvacuously) operative in child grammars at the point when the child has developed a D-system, and acquired the morphosyntactic (e.g. case) properties of that system. If this is so, then it follows that because case is a functional property of the D-system and there is no D-system in early child grammars, there can be no case constraints operating (nonvacuously) on the distribution of nominals in early child English. Thus, whereas adult nominals are case-marked DPs which have to be licensed by principles of Case Theory, child nominals by contrast are caseless NPs, and thus are not subject to case licensing requirements – or alternatively, are *vacuously* subject to them (by this we mean that if case licensing requirements apply to DPs, and there are no DPs in early child English, then the set of constituents subject to the requirement would be a vacuous one). In consequence, nominals in early child English can occur in caseless positions: one of the consequences of this is that Small Clauses such as those in (21) above can occur as independent sentences in early child English, since there is no requirement for their italicized subject NPs to be in a case-marked position. However, the obvious question to ask at this juncture is whether there is any independent empirical evidence in support of our key assumption that there are no case constraints on the distribution of (pro)nominals (nonvacuously) operative in early child grammars of English. The answer is that there is quite a considerable body of evidence in support of this claim. Part of the relevant evidence comes from the twin observations which we made in chapter 4 that children use NPs both as specifiers and as complements of nouns: cf. the detailed examples given there, a brief selection of which are repeated in (22) and (23) below:

(22) (a) *Mummy* car. *Mummy* tea. *Daddy* hat (Stefan 17)
      (b) *Mummy* coat. *Daddy* shoe (Daniel 19)
      (c) *Dolly* hat. *Mommy* key. *Lamb* ear. *Gia* eyes (*Gia 19–20)
      (d) *Tiger* tail. *Sheep* ear (*Kathryn 21)
      (e) *Big teddy bear* supper. *Baby* supper. *Baby* feet. *Jem* chair. *Mummy* box (Jem 21)
      (f) *Dewi* party. *Mummy* bag. *Mummy* key (Daniel 23)

(23) (a) Cup *tea* (Stefan 17)
      (b) Bottle *juice* (Lucy 20)
      (c) Picture *Gia* (*Gia 20)

    (d)   Want piece *bar* (Daniel 20)
    (e)   Have drink *orange* (Jem 21)
    (f)   Picture *Kendall* (*Kendall 23)

Given the assumption that nouns are not (direct) case assigners, it follows that both the italicized specifier position in (22) and the italicized complement position in (23) are *caseless* positions: in consequence, the adult counterparts of structures like (22) and (23) would be ungrammatical, by virtue of the fact that the italicized nominals would be DPs, and would thus be required to occur in a case-marked position (in adult English, the case-assigning determiner *'s* would be required in (22), and the case-assigning 'dummy' preposition *of* in (23)). The fact that structures such as (22) and (23) are grammatical in early child English even though the italicized NPs are not within the domain of a case assigner provides us with further evidence that early child nominals are caseless NPs, not subject to case constraints on their distribution.

Additional evidence in support of this conclusion comes from the fact that young children at this stage use nominals as direct complements of intransitive verbs: we can illustrate this phenomenon in terms of the way that children use the verb *go*:

(24)   (a)   Wayne go *river*. Daddy gone *van*. Want go *mummy* [wanting to go to his mummy] (Daniel 22)
        (b)   That go *shop* [glossed by mother as 'She's going to the shops'] (Claire 23)
        (c)   Go *work* (Jenny 23)
        (d)   Go *school*. Gone *school* (Daniel 23)
        (e)   Go *daddy* [wanting to go to her daddy] (Anne 24)
        (f)   Her gone *school* (Domenico 24)
        (g)   Going *village*. Roland going *children* (Daniel 24)

Such examples are a mere handful of the dozens of examples of structures of this type in my corpus (involving not only *go* but also other intransitive verbs). Given that *go* is an intransitive verb, it does not directly case-mark its complement: one immediate consequence of this is that structures such as those in (24) would be ungrammatical in adult English, since the italicized nominals would be DPs (hence required to occur in a case-marked position) occupying caseless positions. Their grammatical counterparts in adult English require the use of a transitive preposition such as *to* in order to case-mark (or license) the italicized complement. For example, the adult counterpart of 'Wayne go river' would be a structure such as (25) below:

(25)   [$_{IP}$ [$_{DP}$ Wayne] [$_{I}$ e] [$_{VP}$ [$_{V}$ went] [$_{PP}$ [$_{P}$ to] [$_{DP}$ the river]]]]

where the DP [*the river*] would be case-marked (or, equivalently, licensed to occur) not by the intransitive verb *went*, but rather by the transitive preposition *to*. However, the child's counterpart *Wayne go river* differs from (25) in three (inter-related) respects: (i) absence of any tense/ agreement marking on the verb (*go* rather than *went*); (ii) absence of the preposition *to*; and (iii) absence of the determiner *the*. It is thus the morphemes which have the function of carrying or assigning case that are missing from the child's utterance, in keeping with our generalization that early child grammars are inherently lexical in character. Of more specific concern to us here, however, is the fact that whereas the adult's complement is a DP [*the river*] occupying a (prepositionally) case-marked position, the child's complement is a simple NP *river*, occupying a caseless position. The absence of *to* in structures such as (24), taken together with the absence of *of* in structures such as (23) provides us with strong evidence that children have not yet mastered the case-marking function of prepositions. This is turn is consistent with our overall hypothesis that there is no case system operating (nonvacuously) in early child grammars of English.

Further evidence that young children are not (tacitly) aware of the case-marking function of prepositions comes from children's answers to nonprepositional *where*-questions (i.e. questions in which *where* does not function as the object of a preposition). In adult English, a locative DP used as a phrasal response to a prepositionless *where*-question must be case-marked by an appropriate preposition (*in/under/on/at* etc.) – as we illustrated in chapter 2. But children at this stage frequently use 'bare' (prepositionless) NPs to reply to such questions: e.g.

(26)   (a)   Where's Pip? *Garden* (Bethan 21)
         (b)   Where's it gone? *Chair* (*Helen 21)
         (c)   Where are you going? *School* (*Allison 22)
         (d)   Where are you tickling her? *Foot* (Jenny 22)
         (e)   Where's daddy? *Work* (Jenny 23)
         (f)   Where did you take James? *School* (Jenny 23)
         (g)   Where are these children? *Slide* (Jenny 23)
         (h)   Where's she sitting? *Horsey* (Jenny 25)
         (i)   Where are you going? *Park* (Jenny 25)

In adult speech, to reply to the relevant question with a 'bare' prepositionless DP would result in a violation of case constraints to the effect

that overt DPs must carry morphological case, and must occur in a
case-marked position. For example, in reply to the question 'Where's
Pip?' in (26)(a), an adult would have to use a structure such as (27)
below:

(27)   [PP [P in] [DP the garden]]

where the DP *the garden* would fall within the case domain of the
transitive preposition *in*. However, the child's response *garden* is a simple
NP occurring in a caseless position (i.e. not falling within the domain of a
case assigner). Thus, data such as (26) provide further support for our
claim that children have not mastered the case-marking function of
prepositions. More generally, such data are consistent with our view that
there is no case system operating in early child grammars of English, so
that early child nominals are caseless NPs free of case constraints on
their distribution.

Our overall conclusion is thus that children at this stage are unaware
of the case-marking function of (both 'real' and 'dummy') transitive
prepositions, and so use caseless NPs in contexts where adults require
case-marked DPs. Nonacquisition of the case-marking function of
prepositions is a well-known characteristic of early child English which
has frequently been commented upon in the acquisition literature. For
example, Brown (1973: 262–3) reported that at a similar stage of
development:

> Eve omitted prepositions more often than she supplied them. I found
> that it was almost always possible to judge which preposition ought to
> have been supplied when none was. *Sitting chair* called for *in*; *Fall
> down floor* for *on*; *Piece celery* for *of*; *One mummy* for *for*; *Play toys* for
> *with*.

The interpretation which we put on the relevant facts here is that the
child's failure to use prepositions in contexts where they are required in
adult speech betokens (*inter alia*) nonacquisition of the case-marking
function of prepositions, and that this in turn signifies the absence of a
case system (and the consequent absence of a D-system) in early child
grammars of English.

It is important, however, to be clear about precisely what is (and is not)
being claimed here. The essential point we are making is that children
use caseless NPs in *prepositional* contexts (i.e. in contexts where adults
require DPs case-marked by a transitive preposition). This emphatically
does *not* mean that we are claiming that children never use transitive

Prepositions at this stage – any such claim would be immediately falsified by the numerous examples of transitive prepositional phrases used by young children which we have already provided: see, for example, transitive prepositional Small Clauses such as those in (28) below:

(28)   (a)   Mouse in window. It in bag (Hayley 20)
       (b)   Wayne in bedroom. Bubble on dungaree (Daniel 21)
       (c)   Stephen in school (Jem 23)
       (d)   Dolly on horsey. Mess on legs (Daniel 23–24)
       (e)   Daddy in there. Mummy in there (*Claire 24)
       (f)   Clock on there. Light up there. Kitty down there. Cover down there (*Andrew 18–23)

What we are actually claiming is that (because there is no case system operative in early child grammars) children are not 'aware' at this stage of the *requirement* (imposed by Case Theory) for a case-marking preposition to be used in prepositional contexts (e.g. in structures such as (24) and (26) above). This means that if they use prepositions in such contexts, they will only do so *sporadically*, because (in terms of the overall organization of their own grammars) there is no case *requirement* for the use of the preposition. The sporadic use of prepositions in prepositional contexts can be illustrated by the following dialogue typical of children at this stage:

(29)   ADULT: Where's your daddy?
       CHILD: Bed. In bed. Bed. Bed (*Helen 21)

Clearly, the fact that Helen uses *in* only once in four utterances indicates that she has no 'awareness' of the case requirement for the use of a preposition to case-mark the nominal *bed* in adult English.

Thus, the fact that children seem to be 'unaware' of the case-marking function of transitive prepositions at this stage lends further support to our hypothesis that there are no case constraints on the distribution of nominals in early child English. Not surprisingly, the same is also true of the distribution of *pronominals* in early child English. Although (as we have already seen from examples such as (6–9) above) some children make limited use of (what in adult terms would be) objective pronouns at this stage, these do not appear to have their adult function of case-marked pronominal DPs, but rather seem to be *impostors* which function as caseless NPs. In consequence, they occur in early child English not just in *objective* positions (i.e. in positions where they are governed by a transitive V or P, as in (6) above), but also in caseless positions. For instance, examples such as (7–9) above show that young children at this stage use objective pronouns as the subjects of independent sentences (i.e. where adults would require nominative pronouns): an illustrative subset of the relevant examples is repeated in (30) below:

(30)   (a)   *Him* gone. *Her* do that (Hayley 20)
         (b)   *Me* do it. *Me* do. *Me* come in. *Me* want it. *Me* want one. *Me* help. *Me* get it. *Him* swimming (Bethan 20–21)
         (c)   *Me* have biscuit. *Her* gone in there (Angharad 22)
         (d)   *Me* sit in pram. *Her* read that (Paula 23)
         (e)   *Me* nice (+Ellen 24)
         (f)   *Him* naughty. *Him* bad (Daniel 24)
         (g)   *Him* asleep. *Her* climbing ladder (Jem 24)

We also find children using objective pronouns in (what would be in adult terms) genitive contexts, as we can illustrate for the objective pronoun *me* by the data in (31) below:

(31)   (a)   *Me* bot (= 'my bottle', +Gavin 18)
         (b)   *Me* eye (Hayley 20)
         (c)   *Me* (Bethan 21, in reply to 'Whose chair is this?')
         (d)   *Me* dad (+Ellen 24)
         (e)   *Me* hand (+Nancy 24)

Examples such as those in (30) and (31) would seem to suggest that the relevant pronouns are not restricted to occurring within the domain of an objective case assigner: on the contrary, the pronouns seem to be free of specific case constraints on their distribution in early child grammars, and thus can occur in any argument position. But if this is so, then the obvious conclusion to draw is that what appear to be objective pronouns in early child English are actually *impostors* whose true status is that of *caseless* pronominal NPs free of case restrictions on their distribution.

Further support for the claim that NPs are free of case constraints on their distribution in early child English comes from the fact that children appear to use NPs freely as complements or specifiers of empty heads. There are complex restrictions which determine the conditions under which empty head categories can be case assigners in adult grammars. It seems clear that the *trace* of a moved head is able to assign case, as is suggested by examples such as (32) below:

(32)   [$_C$ *Has*] he [$_I$ *t*] [$_{VP}$ [$_V$ *t*] any money]?

In (32), the transitive verb *has* originates in the head V position of VP, and then moves first into I and then into C: clearly, the rightmost trace of *has* in the head V position of the bracketed VP must be able to assign objective case to its DP complement *any money*, if we are to avoid violation of the requirement for a DP like *any money* to occur in an appropriately case-marked position. Now, we might suppose that the moved verb *has* is the *antecedent* of its traces, and that an empty category inherits the grammatical properties of its antecedent. If this is so, then the rightmost trace in the head V position of VP will inherit the case-marking properties of its transitive antecedent *has*, and so will assign objective case to its DP complement *any money*.

A second condition under which an empty category can assign case in adult English is in certain types of 'elliptical' construction: for example, an empty V can function as a case-assigner in elliptical comparative structures such as (33) below:

(33)   She will help him more than [IP he [I will] [VP [V *e*] her]]

Although the italicized head V of the VP in the second conjunct is empty, it must clearly be able to assign objective case to its (pronominal) DP complement *her*. How is this possible? The obvious suggestion to make is that the overt verb *help* in the first conjunct serves as the *antecedent* of the empty V *e* in the second conjunct, with the result that the empty verb *e* 'inherits' all the grammatical properties of its antecedent. Since its antecedent *help* is a transitive verb, this means that the empty V in the right-hand conjunct will also be transitive, and so will assign objective case to its pronominal DP complement *her*.

What our discussion so far suggests is that in adult English, an empty category can function as a case assigner if it has an antecedent which is itself a case assigner. By contrast, it would seem that an empty category which has no identifiable antecedent cannot function as a case-assigner. This is suggested by the ungrammaticality of structures such as (34) below in an 'out of the blue' context:

(34)   *[IP He [I will] [VP [V *e*] her]]

What's wrong with (34)? Part of the answer is that the DP complement *her* cannot be case-marked by the empty verb *e*, for the simple reason that an empty V can only assign objective case to its complement if V has a transitive antecedent: since *e* in (34) lacks a transitive antecedent (and indeed has no linguistic antecedent at all), it lacks the ability to case-mark its complement DP *her*, so leading to a violation of the requirement that DP must carry case, and must occur within the domain of an appropriate case assigner. Thus, it would seem that an empty head can only function as a case assigner if it has a proper antecedent (i.e. if it has a linguistic antecedent which has the same categorial status as the empty category, and which assigns case in the appropriate way): we might refer to this for convenience as the *Proper Antecedent Condition* on the case-marking properties of empty categories. Given the abstractness of this condition, it seems plausible to suppose that the condition is a fundamental principle of UG, and thus part of the child's genetic endowment.

In the light of the hypothesis that empty heads which lack a proper linguistic antecedent cannot function as case-assigners, it is interesting to note that children frequently produce what we shall call *binominal structures* – i.e. structures which arguably comprise an antecedentless empty head of some kind with an NP subject and an NP complement. Such binominal structures have frequently been reported in the acquisition literature: for example, Bloom (1970: 70) observes that in her corpus of Kathryn's speech at age 21 months there were '31 subject–object strings' – i.e. [NP *NP*] structures in which the first NP appeared to function as the subject and the second (italicized) NP as the object of a missing 'understood' head predicate. Some of the relevant examples are given in (35) below:

(35)   (a)   Mommy *sock* (*Kathryn 21, while M is putting K's sock on K)

      (b)   Mommy *diaper* (*Kathryn 21, as M is folding up diaper preparing to put it on K)

      (c)   Mommy *shoe* (*Kathryn 21, as M is putting K's shoe on K)

      (d)   Mommy *vegetable* (*Kathryn 21, as M is preparing lunch and takes vegetables from the refrigerator)

      (e)   Wendy *cottage cheese*. Baby *cottage cheese*. Cat *cottage cheese* (*Kathryn 21, while eating cottage cheese)

      (f)   Lois no *hat* (*Kathryn 22, remarking on the fact that Lois was not wearing a hat)

      (g)   Kathryn no *shoe* (*Kathryn 22, pointing to her bare feet)

Brown (1973: 262) reports a similar phenomenon in early child English, commenting that 'When Eve said *Fraser pencil*, the expansion was *Fraser needs his pencil*'. Likewise, Bowerman (1973: 241) reports the following examples of what she classifies as *Subject–Object* structures in the speech of Kendall at 23 months (the glosses given are the ones Bowerman herself provides):

(36)   (a)   Kendall *bath* ['Kendall takes a bath']
          (b)   Kendall *shower* ['Kendall takes a shower']
          (c)   Kendall *book* ['Kendall reads/looks at a book']
          (d)   Kendall *spider* ['Kendall looked at a spider']

Anisfeld (1984: 137) comments in more general terms that in transitive structures 'Occasionally the action term may be missing, the action being implicit'. Given the widely reported occurrence of such [NP *NP*] structures in the acquisition literature, it is not surprising that there are also examples of similar binominal structures in my own corpus, as the examples in (37) below illustrate:

(37)   (a)   Wayne *coat* (Daniel 19, wanting Wayne to put his coat on and go out)
          (b)   Ashley *door* (Stephen 20, reporting that Ashley has opened the door)
          (c)   Gerry *beans* (+Gerald 21, indicating that he wants beans for tea)
          (d)   Roland *sweet* (Daniel 24, indicating that Roland Rat wants a sweet)
          (e)   Nana *pocket*. Nana *buttons* (Jenny 24, indicating that Nana has got a pocket and buttons on her dress)

Parallel binominal structures are reported in the speech of a German-speaking child in Park (1981: 90). Thus, binominal clauses of the form [NP NP] appear to be a characteristic phenomenon in early child speech.

How are we to analyse binominal structures in early child speech? Clearly, the second (italicized) nominal is not in any sense a *predicate*: for example, an utterance such as (37)(d) 'Roland sweet' is not predicating the property of sweetiehood of Roland. Rather, it seems (from contextual and interpretive clues) that the second nominal is best analysed as the complement of an empty verb which is 'understood' from the context. If this is so, then an utterance such as (37)(d) *Roland sweet* would be a verbal Small Clause (i.e. a VP) headed by an empty V, with the simplified structure indicated in (38) below:

(38) $[_{VP}\ [_{NP}\ Roland]\ [_{V}\ e]\ [_{NP}\ sweet]]$

By contrast, the adult counterpart of (38) would be a finite IP with a structure along the lines of (39) below:

(39)   [$_{IP}$ [$_{DP}$ Roland] [$_I$ e] [$_{VP}$ [$_V$ *wants*] [$_{DP}$ a sweet]]]

In adult English, it would not be possible for the italicized head V of the VP in (39) to be empty (in an *out-of-the-blue* context), since the V would lack a proper case-assigning antecedent, and thus be unable to case-mark its complement DP [*a sweet*]. However, the head V of VP is empty in structures such as (38), in spite of the fact that it lacks a proper linguistic antecedent. Given the (putatively universal) *Proper Antecedent Condition*, it follows that the empty V in (38) cannot inherit case-marking properties from an antecedent (since it has no linguistic antecedent), and hence cannot case-mark its complement *sweet*. The result is that *sweet* is in a caseless position, so lending further support to our claim that early child nominals are caseless NPs, and hence occur in caseless positions (of course, *Roland* would also be a caseless NP in (38), since lexical categories do not case-mark their specifiers, and since there is no finite I to assign nominative case to *Roland*).

The suggestion that binominal structures may be VPs headed by an empty V offers an interesting alternative way of handling alternations such as the following in early child English:

(40)   (a)   *That's* car/*That* bear book (*Kathryn 22)
         (b)   *It's* basket/*It* lion (Anna 24)
         (c)   *It's* bum/*It* bike (Leigh 24)
         (d)   *That's* Veronica/*That* Domenico (Domenico 24)

If we are right in assuming that children's binominal structures have an empty head, we might suppose that the *s*-less structures here are VPs headed by an empty copula V. Binominal structures which would seem to involve an empty 'understood' copula V are quite frequent in early child English: thus, the binominal structures illustrated in (41) below appear to have adult counterparts involving use of the copula *is*, so that the children's utterances might be analyseable as VPs headed by a null copula:

(41)   (a)   Paula good girl (Paula 18)
         (b)   That Ashley (Stephen 19)
         (c)   This hand (Daniel 19)
         (d)   That Luke (Lucy 20)
         (e)   Chicken Mog (Daniel 21)

(f) It Wayne (Daniel 22)

(g) That Kathryn hair (*Kathryn 22)

(h) That dick-dick [= 'dicky-bird'] (Claire 23)

(i) That Kimmy. That Scott. That lady. That hole. That...candy. That Kimmy ball. Mommy lady. Daddy Shawn. Kendall monkey. Kimmy monkey. Kurt boy (*Kendall 23)

(j) Mommy girl. Daddy boy (*Jonathan 24)

Now, if the *s*-less structures in (40) are analysed as VPs headed by a null copula V, then a natural suggestion would seem to be that the *s*-structures in (40) might be analysed in a parallel fashion, save that the head V position is occupied not by a null copula, but rather by the overt copula *'s*. Given that (as we argued in the previous chapter) *'s* in early child English is invariable (in that it is not inflected for tense or agreement), we might suppose (contrary to the analysis proposed in the previous chapter) that *'s* is in fact a tenseless and agreementless copula verb, i.e. in effect an uninflected clitic stem form of the verb *be*. If this were so, then it would mean that a hypothetical child binominal equative structure such as 'That('s) daddy car' would be a VP with the simplified structure indicated in (42):

(42) $[_{VP}\ [_{NP}\ \text{That}]\ [_V\ \text{'s/e}]\ [_{NP}\ \text{daddy car}]]$

where the head copula V would surface either in the shape of the invariable (hence tenseless and agreementless) overt allomorph *'s*, or in the shape of a null allomorph (here designated as *e*).

Although we have analysed binominal structures such as those in (35–38) above as verbal Small Clauses headed by an empty V, it should be noted that it is often implicitly suggested in the acquisition literature that some binominal clauses are headed by an empty preposition (and thus – in our terms – are prepositional Small Clauses). For example, Bowerman (1973: 241) classifies the following binominal structures produced by Kendall at age 23 months as *Noun + Locative* structures (the gloss on (43)(a) is hers):

(43)   (a) Kendall *bed* ['Kendall is in bed']

(b) Kendall *water*

(c) Kendall *pool*

(d) Lotion *tummy*

(e) Towel *bed*

The gloss on (43)(a) would appear to suggest that Bowerman thinks that the 'missing' prepositional predicate is a null allomorph of *in*. Braine (1976: 34) is rather more explicit: in cases where binominal structures appear to involve a 'missing' preposition, he supplies the 'missing' preposition in the format illustrated in (44) below:

(44)   (a)   Sand ball "ON"
       (b)   Hand hair "IN"
       (c)   Ball house "IN/TO"
       (d)   Man car "IN"
       (e)   Fly light "ON"
       (f)   Sand toe "ON"
       (g)   Sand eye "IN"
       (h)   Key door "TO" (*Jonathan 24)

Examples of binominal structures which might be analyseable in similar terms appear in my own corpus, and in data from other sources: for example,

(45)   (a)   Bubble *kitchen* (Daniel 21, indicating the bubble container is in the kitchen)
       (b)   Bee *window* (Daniel 21, indicating there is a fly on the window)
       (c)   Sweater *chair* (*Kathryn 21, carrying her sweater into the living room to put it on the chair)
       (d)   Wendy *elevator* (*Kathryn 21, after Wendy had visited a few days previously)
       (e)   Hanky *pocket* (+Jonathan 21, indicating that his hanky is in his pocket)
       (f)   Mummy *kitchen* (Daniel 22, indicating that his mother is in the kitchen)

Clearly, the italicized nominal in such structures is not interpreted as a predicate: for example, (45)(f) 'Mummy kitchen' is not interpreted as predicating the property of kitchenhood of Mummy. On the contrary, the italicized nominal would seem to have a locative interpretation. Now, the very same type of argumentation which led us to posit that in a structure such as (37)(d) 'Roland sweet', the NP *sweet* should be analysed as the object of an 'understood' empty verb might lead us to posit that in structures such as 'Mummy kitchen', the NP *kitchen* is to be analysed as the object of an 'understood' empty preposition. Braine (1973: 422) argues that such an analysis is given added plausibility by the fact that children often produce 'replacement sequences' in which they 'expand' an original binominal structure into one with a prepositional predicate, so resulting in sequences such as the following:

(46)   Man car. Man in car (Braine 1973: 422)

If we espouse the 'empty preposition' analysis, then binominal structures such as (45) would have essentially the same structure as prepositional Small Clauses such as (28), save for the fact that the head preposition would be covert rather than overt: in other words, an utterance such as *Mummy kitchen* would have the simplified structure (47) below:

(47)   [$_{PP}$ [$_{NP}$ Mummy] [$_{P'}$ [$_P$ *e*] [$_{NP}$ kitchen]]]

However, the key point about empty-headed structures like (47) from our point of view is that neither the 'subject' nor the 'object' would be assigned case, so that both must be presumed to be caseless NPs occupying caseless positions. More specifically, given that P lacks a proper linguistic antecedent, it cannot case-mark its complement *kitchen*; and given that there is no finite I constituent in (47), it follows that the 'subject' *Mummy* is likewise in a caseless position. Thus, children's binominal structures (whether analysed as having empty V or P heads) provide us with further evidence that nominals in early child English are caseless NPs occupying caseless positions (for the obvious reason that both 'subject' and 'object' positions are caseless positions in binominal structures where the head empty predicate lacks a proper linguistic antecedent).

At this point, let us briefly summarize the conclusions which we have reached in this chapter. We have presented a considerable body of evidence in support of our hypothesis that there is no case system (nonvacuously) operative in early child grammars of English. This implies (*inter alia*) that there is no morphological case in early child English – hence there is no systematic formal *case contrast*. It also implies that Case plays no role in the syntax of early child English: we supported this claim by arguing that there are no case constraints on the distribution of (overt) nominal or pronominal NPs in early child English. However, our discussion thus far has been limited to *overt* (i.e. phonologically non-null) NPs. The obvious question to ask at this point is whether or not the same is true of *null NPs* in early child English, that is, whether they too are free of case constraints on their use. This is a question which we turn to consider in the next chapter.

8

The Grammar of Missing Arguments in Early Child English

Thus far, our discussion has largely been concerned with the syntax of overt (i.e. phonologically non-null) constituents in early child English. However, one of the best known characteristics of early child speech (looked at from an adult perspective) is that certain obligatory constituents of the adult sentence are sometimes 'missing' from the child's counterpart, so that early child speech may seem to have a peculiarly *elliptical* character. One particularly noticeable trait of early child English which has frequently been commented upon in the acquisition literature is the tendency for children to omit arguments of predicates (particularly subjects) in contexts where adults would use pronouns. Thus, the child's counterpart of an adult utterance such as (1)(a) below might be an apparently subjectless structure such as (1)(b):

(1)   (a)   *I* want Daddy (adult)
        (b)   Want Daddy (child)

Compared to its adult counterpart (1)(a), the child's utterance (1)(b) would appear to have a 'missing argument' in subject position, in that the child's sentence seemingly contains no subject argument for the predicate *want* (whereas in the adult utterance, the pronoun *I* is the subject argument of *want*). There has been a burgeoning literature in the past few years on the syntax of 'missing arguments' in early child speech. A number of linguists have argued that children's 'missing arguments' should be analysed as empty categories: for example, Hyams (1986, 1987a, 1987b, 1988, 1989) argues that just as adult utterances such as (1)(a) contain an overt pronominal subject (= *I*), so too apparently subjectless child utterances such as (1)(b) should be analysed as containing an empty (i.e. phonologically null) pronominal subject designated as *pro* (affectionately known as 'little *pro*') – a covert pronoun with much the same syntactic and semantic properties as overt adult subject pronouns such as *I/me/he/she*, etc. Under Hyams' analysis, a child utterance such as (1)(b) 'Want Daddy' would not be subjectless, but rather would have an abstract *pro* subject, and thus would be assigned a structure which (details aside) we can represent informally as:

(2)   *pro* want Daddy

The potential interest of empty category analyses of 'missing arguments' lies in the fact that the syntax of empty categories (e.g. empty pronouns) in child grammars might be argued to provide a 'direct window' (to borrow a metaphor from Jaeggli 1982: 1) onto the contribution which UG makes to the nature of the earliest grammars developed by young children. As Chomsky (1982: 63) notes, 'The properties of empty pronouns can hardly be determined inductively from observed phenomena, and therefore presumably reflect inner resources of the mind.' This assumption has provided the inspiration for a considerable body of research into the syntax of 'missing arguments' in early child speech. The significance (from our point of view) of this research is that a recurrent theme of much of the relevant work has been to argue that there are *functional* constraints on the use of 'missing arguments' in early child speech, and that the existence of such constraints requires us to posit that functional category systems must already be 'in place' in some abstract form in the initial grammars developed by young children (and if so might be assumed to be a legacy of UG). Since this is a conclusion which is clearly at variance with the central thesis put forward in this book (namely that the earliest grammars developed by young children are purely *lexical* in nature), we shall devote the whole of this chapter to a detailed discussion of the syntax of 'missing arguments' in early child English – ultimately concluding that the proposed functional analyses are inadequate, and that the syntax of 'missing arguments' can be given a more satisfactory characterization within the *lexical* model of early child grammars proposed here.

The earliest *functional* account of the syntax of 'missing arguments' in early child speech is found in a number of papers by Nina Hyams (1986, 1987a, 1989), where she argues that the subjectless sentences produced by young children acquiring English resemble the subjectless sentences produced by adult speakers of Italian. She analyses 'missing subjects' in both early child English and adult Italian as instances of the null pronominal *pro*, and argues that *pro* is subject to much the same functional constraints on its use in early child English as its counterpart is in adult Italian. For those not familiar with the relevant work on Italian, we shall begin by presenting a brief outline of the grammar of *pro* in (adult) Italian, basing our account on the seminal paper on this topic by Rizzi (1986) (it should be noted, however, that Hyams' analysis of both adult Italian and early child English is based on an earlier account of null pronominals in Rizzi 1982: what we shall do here is recast her conclusions in the light of the revised account of null pronominals in Rizzi 1986; this preserves the essential spirit of Hyams' analysis, while eliminating some technical problems).

We can illustrate the nature and function of *pro* in adult Italian in terms of the following contrast between English and Italian:

(3)   (a)   *She* has injured herself
      (b)   *pro* si è ferita
            pro self is injured-FSG (FSG = feminine singular)
            'She has injured herself'

The English sentence (3)(a) has an overt pronominal *she* in the italicized subject position; its Italian counterpart (3)(b), however, has a phonologically null pronoun (designated as *pro*) in subject position – and this null pronoun seems to fulfil the same syntactic and semantic role as the overt pronoun *she* (hence the fact that it is translated by 'she' in English). The obvious question to ask is why we posit that the Italian sentence (3)(b) has a null pronominal subject, rather than saying that it is subjectless. There are both theoretical and empirical reasons for positing that such apparently subjectless sentences have an 'understood' null subject rather than no subject. One traditional theoretical argument relates to what we might call the *Subject Principle*. Chomsky (1982) argues that it is an inherent syntactic property of clauses that they require subjects, and posits a 'requirement that a clause have a subject position' (1982: 10). Rothstein (1983: 130) argues that the syntactic requirement for clauses to have subjects follows from a more general principle of predication to the effect that all predicates require syntactic subjects. However it is formulated, the *subject requirement* (viz. that clauses/predicates have syntactic subjects) would necessitate the postulation of a *pro* subject in sentences such as (3)(b).

A second theoretical argument in support of the postulation of a *pro* subject in such cases can be formulated in terms of the *projection principle*. In the version outlined in Chomsky (1988a: 75), this principle 'requires that the lexical properties of each lexical item must be preserved at every level of representation'. The relevance of the principle in relation to (3)(b) is that it is a lexical property of the Italian verb *ferire* 'injure' that (in active forms) it requires an AGENT subject and a PATIENT object:

thus, unless we say that (3)(b) has an understood (albeit null) subject, there will apparently be no possibility of the relevant structure satisfying the requirement that *ferire* must have an AGENT subject. More specifically, unless we posit a *pro* subject for (3)(b), we will wrongly predict that the sentence is ill-formed (because if it is subjectless, it will violate the *projection principle*).

In addition to theoretical arguments, we can also adduce a number of empirical arguments in support of positing a null pronominal subject in (3)(b). One such argument can be formulated in relation to the fact that (3)(b) contains the third person (singular/plural) reflexive anaphor *si* 'himself/herself/themselves': given that reflexives cannot have independent reference but must have an appropriate antecedent to bind them (i.e. to assign them reference), it follows that unless we posit the existence of a *pro* subject to serve as the antecedent for the reflexive, there will be a violation of Binding Theory – and the sentence will then (wrongly) be predicted to be ill-formed by virtue of the fact that the reflexive cannot be assigned an antecedent and so lacks referential properties. Moreover, morphological considerations also lead us to conclude that (3)(b) has a null third person feminine singular subject (designated as *pro*): in structures containing a finite form of the perfective auxiliary *essere* 'be', the auxiliary itself agrees in person and number with its superficial subject, while the perfective participle agrees in number and gender with its subject. Clearly, it would be difficult to account for why the auxiliary *è* 'is' is third person singular and why the participle *ferita* 'injured' is feminine singular unless we posit that (3)(b) has a null subject which has the grammatical properties of being third person feminine singular. Since the 'understood' null subject has the same kind of grammatical and referential properties as overt pronominals like English *she*, it seems reasonable to hypothesize that it is a null pronominal – hence the use of *pro* to designate it.

Recent research on the use of *pro* in a wide range of (adult) languages (inspired by the seminal work of Rizzi 1986) has suggested that there is parametric variation between languages in respect of the way in which *pro* is used (if at all). Rizzi suggests that the use of *pro* in different languages varies along two main parameters, relating to (i) the *licensing* conditions for *pro* (= conditions which determine which sentence positions *pro* is licensed to occur in, and hence determine the distribution of *pro*), and (ii) the *identification* conditions for *pro* (= conditions which determine whether *pro* is referential or not, and if so what *pro* can refer to – i.e. conditions which determine the *interpretation* of *pro*). In languages like Italian with relatively rich case and agreement systems, *pro* is typically subject to *case* licensing conditions on its distribution, and *agreement* identification conditions on its interpretation. We shall illustrate each of these in turn, looking first at case constraints on the distribution of *pro*.

Rizzi argues that in Italian-type languages, *pro* is licensed to occur only in positions where it is case-marked by an appropriate kind of licenser (cf. his 1986: 546 remark that '*pro* is formally licensed through case assignment by a designated head'): there is parametric variation between languages in respect of the range of categories which can function as licensers for *pro*. For example, in Italian *pro* can occur where it is case-marked by a finite I or by a transitive V, but not where case-marked by a transitive P: this restriction can be illustrated by the paradigm in (4) below:

(4)   (a)   Gianni crede che [$_{IP}$ *pro* potrebbero vincere]
           Gianni thinks that *pro* might win
           'Gianni thinks that *they* might win'

     (b)   La buona musica riconcilia *pro* con se stessi
           The good music reconciles *pro* with self same
           'Good music reconciles *people* with themselves'

     (c)   Gianni ritiene [$_{SC}$ *pro* probabile che [$_{IP}$ *pro* piova]]
           Gianni thinks *pro* likely that *pro* rain
           'Gianni thinks *it* likely that *it* will rain'

     (d)   *Gli insegnanti sono severi con *pro*
           The teachers are severe with *pro*
           (intended as 'Teachers are hard on *people*')

Thus, *pro* is grammatical in (4)(a) because it is case-marked by a finite I, and in (4)(b) because it is case-marked by a transitive V: likewise, (4)(c) is also grammatical, because the first *pro* is case-marked by the immediately preceding transitive V, and the second by a finite (subjunctive) I; by contrast, in (4)(d), *pro* is ungrammatical because it is case-marked by a transitive P. Examples such as (4) illustrate typical case restrictions on the distribution of *pro* in a language with a relatively rich case system.

In addition to case constraints on the distribution of *pro* in languages like Italian, there are also agreement constraints on the identification (= interpretation) of *pro*. In principle, *pro* can have three different types of interpretation, as illustrated by the examples in (4) above. For example, *pro* in (4)(a) has much the same range of interpretations as the English definite pronoun *they*, and so might be said to be *definite* in interpretation: by contrast, in (4)(b), *pro* denotes much the same set of arbitrary individuals as the English expression 'people', and so might be said to be *arbitrary* in interpretation; however, in (4)(c), *pro* has essentially the same function as the English pleonastic pronoun *it*, and so might be said to be *pleonastic* in nature. The kind of constraints which determine the interpretation of *pro* can be illustrated by the fact that although *pro* in (4)(b) can be interpreted as *arbitrary* in reference, it cannot be interpreted as *definite* in reference (hence *pro* there can have the sense of the English word 'people', but cannot be interpreted as equivalent to the English definite pronoun *them*). Rizzi (1986: 520) argues that *pro* can be interpreted as having definite reference only where its licenser carries sufficiently rich agreement properties to identify the grammatical (and hence referential) properties of *pro* (so that Italian *pro* can only be interpreted as having the same definite reference as English *they* if it is the subject of a finite I which carries a third person plural agreement inflection). It follows from this that only in the (a) example in (4) (where *pro* is the licensee and subject of a finite agreement-inflected I whose agreement properties surface in the form of the third person plural inflection +*ero*) can *pro* be interpreted as a definite (third person plural) pronoun. So, it would seem that definite *pro* is only licensed to occur where the licenser of *pro* carries sufficiently rich agreement morphology to identify the grammatical properties (and hence the referential properties) of *pro*. Additional evidence of agreement restrictions on the use of definite *pro* is found in Borsley (1984), Georgopoulos (1984), McCloskey and Hale (1984), and Borer (1986).

At first sight, it might seem far from obvious what our brief discussion of the use (i.e. licensing/distribution and identification/interpretation) of *pro* in languages like Italian has got to do with the nature of early child grammars of English. The answer is this. Given the wide range of genetically unrelated languages which make use of *pro*, we might suppose that *pro* is a substantive universal (in the sense of Chomsky 1965: 28), and hence part of the child's genetic endowment. What this means in more informal terms is that the child is born knowing that one of the devices available to him (in principle) to use in argument positions in sentences is *pro*. This in turn might lead us to expect that young children may make use of *pro*, and that the way in which they use *pro* will give us an insight into the nature of early child grammars. More specifically, if we find evidence that there are functional constraints on the use of *pro* in early child speech, then this will suggest the existence of functional category systems in early child grammars.

The significance of the child's use of *pro* has by no means gone unnoticed. Indeed, Hyams' (1986, 1987a, 1989) 'Italian' analysis of early child English takes as its primary source of evidence the use of *pro* by young children. What Hyams argues in essence (translating the claims she makes from the earlier framework of Rizzi 1982 to the more recent framework of Rizzi 1986) is that there are functional licensing conditions on the use of *pro* in early child English, in that *pro* is licensed to occur in nominative positions only (so resulting in an obvious *subject/object* asymmetry, in that *pro* is used in subject position in finite clauses, but never in object position in any kind of clause). If this is so, then since a nominative position is one which is case-marked by a finite I, the natural conclusion (within the theory of null pronominals outlined in Rizzi 1986) would be that *pro* is licensed in early child English only when case-marked (= when assigned nominative case) by a finite I. But if this were so, then it would lead us to the conclusion that young children must indeed have developed an I-system – contrary to the claims we have made in the previous two chapters. Given the obvious importance of this issue, we shall look in some detail at the evidence which Hyams presents in support of her claim that grammars of early child English contain a nominative *pro*.

The main pillar of her evidence is the claim that young children acquiring English use null subjects (= *pro*) in contexts where adult English speakers would require an overt nominative subject. For example, independent sentences in adult English are finite IPs whose subjects are assigned nominative case by the head I of IP – hence, subject position in an independent sentence is a nominative position. However, Hyams argues, independent sentences in early child English frequently have 'missing' subjects: in support of this claim she adduces (1986: 63) examples such as the following (taken from the samples of the speech of Eric at 20 and 22 months provided in Bloom 1970):

(5)   (a)   Play it
       (b)   Eating cereal
       (c)   Shake hands
       (d)   See window
       (e)   No go in (*Eric 20, 22)

Hyams posits that such sentences have null pronominal (= *pro*) subjects; and since the null subject is occurring in a nominative position (viz. as the subject of an independent sentence), she concludes that examples like (5) provide us with empirical evidence that children have developed a nominative *pro*. She notes that the evidence provided by Bloom's (1970) study of three children shows that Kathryn used sentences with null subjects from 21 to 24 months, and Eric and Gia from 20 to 25 months. Thus, it would seem as if the use of null subjects is an inherent characteristic of precisely the stage of 'early child English' which we are concerned with in this book.

Of course, one of the key issues raised by data such as (5) relates to the question of what evidence there is that the relevant utterances do indeed have syntactically present null subjects (rather than having *implicit* subjects which are 'understood' though not syntactically represented). Hyams adduces four arguments in support of this claim. The first (1986: 64) relates to 'the definite reference associated with the null subject' – i.e. to the fact that the 'missing' subject has the same definite interpretation as adult pronominals like *I/you/he* etc. The tacit assumption she is making here would seem to be that the definite reference of the understood subject makes it unlikely that it could be an *implicit* argument (in the sense of Chomsky 1986a, Rizzi 1986, or Brody and Manzini 1988 – i.e. one which is not syntactically present), since implicit arguments are generally interpreted as *arbitrary* in reference: thus, in a sentence such as 'I haven't eaten yet', the implicit object of *eat* is understood as having the arbitrary (indefinite) sense of 'anything', not the definite sense of 'it'. However, since we know that *pro* in languages in which it occurs can typically have definite reference, then this increases the plausibility of positing that sentences like (5) have *pro* subjects (since the understood subjects of the sentences in (5) seem to have definite reference).

The obvious question to ask at this point, however, is what evidence there is that the subjectless sentences produced by young children do indeed have definite null subjects. Hyams argues that by making use of suitable elicitation techniques, the linguist can induce the child to make explicit the reference of the hypothesized null subject; commenting on work by Braine (1973), Hyams remarks (1986: 68):

> Braine was also able to elicit 'missing subjects' by pretending to misunderstand what the child was referring to when he used the predicate alone. For example, if the child said 'In kitchen' in a context in which it was clear that he intended to convey that his mother was in the kitchen, Braine would respond by saying 'Your car's in the kitchen? No, the car's over there, see?' The child would then correct him with 'Mommy in kitchen'.

The tacit inference drawn by Hyams is that the fact that the child's ability to supply an overt subject when suitable elicitation procedures are employed suggests that apparently subjectless sentences have a (syntactically present) null *pro* subject.

A second argument which Hyams puts forward to reinforce this conclusion is a pragmatic one, to the effect that contextual clues enable us to infer that the subjectless sentences produced by young children are interpretable as having definite subjects whose 'reference can clearly be inferred from the context' (Hyams 1986: 69). In support of this claim, Hyams cites the following dialogue between Eric at 23 months and his mother (from Bloom 1970: 122):

(6)   (*Eric has just eaten an apple*)
       ADULT: You ate all the apple up. There's no more apple
       (*Eric starts to cry and hits the toys*)
       ADULT: What's the matter?
       CHILD: Want more apple

The conclusion drawn from dialogues like (6) by Bloom and tacitly endorsed by Hyams is that 'The inclusion of the lexically unspecified subject position is necessary to account for the semantic interpretation associated with subjectless sentences' (Hyams 1986: 69).

A third piece of evidence which Hyams presents in favour of positing that apparently subjectless sentences have *pro* subjects is that 'These subjectless sentences...co-exist with sentences containing overt subjects' (1986: 65): what she apparently means by this is that verbs which occur in subjectless sentences are also used by the same children in sentences with overt subjects. In support of this claim, Hyams adduces a wide range of child speech data (from Bloom 1970, and Bloom et al. 1975), a representative sample of which is given in (7) below:

(7)   (a)   Throw away. *Mommy* throw it away (*Kathryn 21)
       (b)   Read bear book. *Kathryn* read this (*Kathryn 22)
       (c)   Sit on piano. *Man* sit down (*Kathryn 22)
       (d)   No like celery, mommy. *Kathryn* no like celery (*Kathryn 22)
       (e)   Ride truck. *Gia* ride bike (*Gia 22)

The implication is that since the second sentence of each pair shows clearly that the child is 'aware' that the verb concerned requires an (italicized) NP subject which is assigned a specific thematic role (AGENT, EXPERIENCER, etc.), it is plausible to posit that the first sentence of each pair should be analysed as having a syntactic *pro* subject which is assigned the same thematic role.

A final piece of evidence adduced by Hyams in support of the *pro* analysis comes from the occurrence of what Braine (1973) terms 'replacement sequences' in early child speech. Thus, children who produce a subjectless sentence will sometimes follow it by an expanded version containing an overt lexical subject; examples of this kind of 'replacement sequence' (taken from Braine's 1973 corpus of Stevie at 25–26 months) are given below:

(8) (a) Fall...*Stick* fall
     (b) Go nursery...*Lucy* go nursery
     (c) Push Stevie...*Betty* push Stevie
     (d) Get...*Lucy* get
     (e) Crawl downstairs...*Tommy* crawl downstairs
     (f) Build house...*Cathy* build house (*Stevie 25–26)

The tacit assumption made by Hyams is that the fact that the 'expanded' utterance contains an overt (italicized) subject makes it plausible to claim that the 'unexpanded' form contains a syntactically represented *pro* subject.

On the basis of arguments such as those presented above, Hyams concludes that the use of *pro* subjects is an intrinsic characteristic of early child English. However, in order to demonstrate that children restrict the use of *pro* to nominative positions (and hence to demonstrate the existence of an I-system in early child grammars), it is crucial for Hyams to demonstrate a clear *subject/object asymmetry* in children's use of *pro*: more specifically, she has to show that they never use *pro* in non-nominative positions (e.g. as the object of a verb or preposition). In this connection, it is interesting to note her remark that there is 'no provision in the early grammar for null objects. Hence, while subjectless sentences are frequent, we do not find regular production of objectless sentences' (Hyams 1986: 97). Thus, the fact that children's sentences may have 'missing subjects' but not 'missing objects' is consistent with her view that early child English is a null subject language (more precisely, a language which licenses a null *pro* in nominative positions only).

Although her original (1986, 1987a, 1989) *Italian* analysis of 'missing subjects' in early child English received a considerable accolade from the linguistic community (deservedly so, since it represented one of the first and best attempts to provide a detailed account of aspects of the syntax of early child speech within a *Government and Binding* framework), Hyams herself has acknowledged a number of shortcomings in more recent work (Hyams 1987b). We shall highlight just two of the problems posed by her 'Italian' analysis here. The first of these is that although the analysis provided an account of the *licensing* conditions for *pro* (viz. to the effect that *pro* is licensed to occur only where assigned nominative case by a finite I), it failed to provide any account of the *identification* conditions for *pro* (viz. of the mechanism by which *pro* is identified as having definite reference in early child English). As we saw earlier, Rizzi (1986: 520) argues that in the grammar of an adult language like Italian, *pro* can be interpreted as having definite reference only where its licenser carries sufficiently rich agreement properties to identify the grammatical (and hence referential) properties of *pro*. However, the obvious problem with analysing early child English in the same terms as adult Italian (as Hyams 1986, 1987a, 1989 does) is that although Italian has a rich system of agreement inflections on finite verbs which can serve to identify *pro*, early child English by contrast has no verbal agreement inflections at all (as we argued in detail in chapter 6), so that we cannot in principle argue that the English-acquiring child's *pro* is identified in terms of agreement inflections. This means that (as Hyams herself admits, 1987b: 4) *pro* is 'unidentified' in her earlier account – that is, the account provides no satisfactory *identification* mechanism for *pro*.

The second major problem identified by Hyams (1987b: 5) in respect of her 'Italian' analysis relates to the inadequacy of the proposed *licensing* conditions for *pro* (i.e. the conditions which determine the distribution of *pro*, limiting *pro* to occurring in nominative positions). The assumption underlying her account is that *pro* is licensed by principles of Universal Grammar to occur only in positions where it can be case-marked by an agreement-marked I. However (as Hyams herself points out, 1987b: 5), the validity of this assumption is called into question by the fact that there are languages like (adult) Chinese which have no agreement inflections whatever and yet permit null definite subjects – as can be illustrated by the Chinese example in (9) below (kindly provided for me by Martin Atkinson):

(9)   Kanjian Beijing
        =*pro* kanjian Beijing
        'I/you/they etc. see/saw Peking'

The fact that agreementless languages permit null subjects clearly calls into question the assumption of a universal link between rich I-agreement inflections and *pro*. Thus (Hyams concludes) her earlier 'Italian' account proves inadequate both in respect of its account of the licensing conditions for *pro*, and in respect of its failure to provide any account of the *identification* conditions for *pro*. Given that both Chinese and early child English are agreementless languages which allow subject-less sentences, Hyams suggests that early child English resembles

Chinese more closely than Italian: hence, we shall refer to the revised analysis which she proposes as her *Chinese* analysis of early child English. (It is interesting to note *en passant* that a similar analogy had been suggested some 65 years earlier by Karl Bühler: cf. his (1922: 53) remark that 'The constructions of the child are – one is tempted to say – Chinese'.)

Hyams attempts to overcome the apparent shortcomings of her original ('Italian') analysis by offering a complete reanalysis of the 'missing subject' phenomenon (Hyams 1987b, 1988, Jaeggli and Hyams 1988). She (implicitly) rejects Rizzi's case-marking account of the licensing of *pro* in favour of an alternative account based on the *morphological uniformity principle* proposed by Jaeggli and Safir (1987): this principle can be paraphrased informally as in (10) below:

(10)   MORPHOLOGICAL UNIFORMITY PRINCIPLE (MUP)
         Null subjects are licensed in languages which have morphologically uniform inflectional paradigms

The notion of morphological uniformity can be illustrated in terms of the paradigm for the verb *speak* and its Italian and Chinese counterparts given in the table (the forms are those which could be used in a *present* context) below:

	ITALIAN	CHINESE	ENGLISH
1 SG	parl*o*	shuo	speak
2 SG	parl*i*	shuo	speak
3 SG	parl*a*	shuo	speak*s*
1 PL	parl*iamo*	shuo	speak
2 PL	parl*ate*	shuo	speak
3 PL	parl*ano*	shuo	speak

(1/2/3 indicate first/second/third person, and SG/PL indicate singular/plural number.) In a fairly obvious sense, both Italian and Chinese verbs are morphologically *uniform* – i.e. Italian verbs are uniformly inflected for tense/agreement, and Chinese verbs uniformly uninflected. By contrast, English is morphologically *non–uniform* in the relevant sense, since (e.g.) in the present tense, only the third person singular form *speaks* carries a tense/agreement inflection.

Given the assumption that Chinese and Italian are morphologically uniform whereas English is not, and given Jaeggli and Safir's postulate in

(10) that null subjects are licensed only in morphologically uniform languages, then it follows that we should expect to find that Italian and Chinese permit null subjects, but English does not: and indeed, this is precisely correct, as data such as (11) below illustrate:

(11)　　(a)　Parla italiano
　　　　　　　　=*pro* parla italiano
　　　　　　　　'He/she speaks Italian'

　　　　(b)　Shuo zhongguo hua
　　　　　　　　=*pro* shuo zhongguo hua
　　　　　　　　'I/you/they etc. speak China talk (= Chinese)'

　　　　(c)　*Speaks English
　　　　　　　　=*pro* speaks English
　　　　　　　　(intended in the sense of 'He/she speaks English')

Hyams would argue that such sentences in all three languages have the categorial status of IPs headed by an abstract I constituent. However, the set of I-inflections (i.e. inflections which realize the abstract features carried by I) is morphologically uniform in Italian (since I-inflections are uniformly overt) and in Chinese (where I-inflections are uniformly null), but not in English (where e.g. in present tense forms, I-features are realized in the form of an overt inflection in third person singular forms, but not in other person/number forms). The fact that Italian verbs are uniformly inflected and Chinese verbs uniformly uninflected means that both are morphologically uniform languages, and so allow null subjects; however, the fact that *some* verb forms are overtly inflected for tense/ agreement in English and *others* are not means that English is morphologically non-uniform, and so does not permit null subjects.

　　The obvious question to ask at this point is how early child English can be handled within the *morphological uniformity* account of null subjects. Hyams assumes that clauses in early child English have the status of IPs headed by an abstract (phonologically null) I constituent. She notes that in early child English, there are no overt I-inflections (i.e. children make no productive use of the tense/agreement inflections +s/+d, as we argued in detail in chapter 6), and sentences can freely have null subjects. However, she also notes the claim by Guilfoyle (1984) that once children master the use of the I-inflections +s/+d, they cease to use null subjects (other than in contexts where adults permit them, e.g. in imperatives): cf. her (1987b: 9) remark that 'The acquisition of the present and past tense morphemes coincides with the end of the null subject stage in English'. The relevant facts – she argues – can be accounted for in a straightforward fashion in terms of the *Morphological Uniformity Principle*. Thus, at the earlier stage, the child's I-inflections are uniformly null, and hence morphologically uniform, so that null subjects are licensed by the MUP (10). However, at the later stage, the child's I-inflections are non-uniform (since e.g. present tense verbs carry the I-inflection +*s* in the third person singular, but no overt inflection in other person/number forms), with the result that null subjects are no longer licensed. What is of particular interest to us about Hyams' *morphological uniformity* analysis is the claim that early child English resembles Chinese in that both languages have a morphologically uniform set of (null) I-inflections, and (consequently) both languages permit null subjects. This leads Hyams to the (informal) conclusion that English-acquiring children in effect 'start out speaking Chinese' (1987b: 14).

Although the *Morphological Uniformity Principle* provides an account of the *licensing* conditions for *pro*, it obviously does not deal with the question of the *identification* of *pro* (either in early child English, or more generally): hence some account needs to be offered of how *pro* is identified. Hyams follows Rizzi (1986) in positing that in languages (like Italian) with rich systems of agreement inflections, *pro* will be identified (as definite etc.) by the agreement inflections carried by I: however, since early child English is an agreementless language, some alternative mechanism will have to be found for identifying *pro* in this case. Hyams suggests a mechanism which is an adaptation of the analysis of 'missing arguments' (for agreementless languages like Chinese) proposed by Huang 1984. More specifically, she hypothesizes that the child's *pro* (licensed by the *Morphological Uniformity Principle* to occur only in subject position) is identified (= assigned its reference) by a phonologically null sentence-initial *topic* phrase, with the reference of the topic being determined pragmatically (i.e. by being linked to an appropriate discourse topic). Given these assumptions, an (apparently) subjectless early child utterance such as (7)(e) *Ride truck* would be analysed by Hyams as having a syntactic structure along the (simplified) lines of (12) below:

(12)   TOP$_i$ [$_{IP}$ *pro*$_i$ [$_I$ e] [$_{VP}$ [$_V$ ride] truck]]

where TOP is a null topic phrase (referring to an appropriate topic in the discourse, in this case the speaker Gia) which serves to identify the null subject *pro*. Since the head I constituent of the child's clauses is morphologically uniform (in the sense that the features of I are uniformly realized as a null inflection), *pro* is licensed to occur in subject position in early child English (by virtue of the *Morphological Uniformity Principle*, (10)), but not in other (e.g. object) positions – hence it follows that early child clauses can only contain 'missing' subjects, not 'missing' objects.

In an obvious sense, both Hyams' original *Italian* analysis of early child English and her later *Chinese* analysis are *functional* analyses – that is, analyses which assume that the child's clauses incorporate an I-system headed by an abstract I whose properties determine the *licensing* (i.e distribution) of null subjects. Under the (modified) version of her earlier 'Italian' analysis which we have presented here, it is the case-assigning properties of I which would license *pro* (since *pro* would be licensed to occur when case-marked by a finite I, i.e. in nominative positions). Under her later 'Chinese' analysis by contrast, *pro* would be licensed to occur as the subject of IP in early child English by virtue of the fact that this is a language with a morphologically uniform (i.e. not overtly inflected) I. Since both of her analyses posit that early child clauses are IPs and that (some morphosyntactic property of) the head I licenses *pro*, and since IP is a *functional* category system, it follows that both of her analyses are intrinsically *functional* analyses – and thus incompatible with the *lexical* analysis of early child grammars proposed here. In other words, if Hyams' functional account of the syntax of 'missing subjects' is empirically substantiated, then our lexical analysis of early child grammars is thereby falsified.

Since Hyams herself has explicitly repudiated her earlier 'Italian' analysis of early child English, we shall have little more to say about it here. An obvious point to make, however, is that the assumption that there are case conditions on the licensing of null subjects in early child grammars of English (e.g. to the effect that *pro* is licensed to occur only in nominative positions) is called into question by our conclusion in chapter 7 that there is no case system operating in early child grammars of English. Moreover, we shall see shortly that there is some reason to question the empirical adequacy of Hyams' claim that 'missing arguments' are found only in subject (more specifically, *nominative*) positions.

What of Hyams' alternative 'Chinese' analysis of early child English as a language which allows null pronominals as the subject of IP by virtue of the fact that I in early child English is morphologically uniform? One obvious point to make here is that the proposed *morphological uniformity analysis* can be adapted in a relatively trivial fashion so as to make it entirely compatible with the *lexical* analysis of early child grammars proposed here (and more specifically, with the Small Clause analysis of early child clauses). Although Hyams seems to assume that early child clauses are universally headed by an I constituent, and that early child English is morphologically uniform by virtue of the fact that whatever features I carries remain uniformly unrealized (or covertly realized), the morphological uniformity analysis seems equally compatible with the lexical analysis of early child English proposed here. Thus, under the alternative lexical analysis, early child English would be a language with morphologically uniform inflectional paradigms in consequence of the fact that there would be no I-constituent in early child grammars to 'carry' tense and agreement inflections – hence no possibility of morphologically non-uniform I-inflections (since all verbs would lack I-inflections, precisely because early child clauses are I-less). Thus, Hyams' *morphological uniformity* analysis can be adapted in minor ways to make it compatible with the *lexical* analysis proposed here.

However, although there seems no reason in principle why we should not 'graft' an appropriate variant of the morphological uniformity analysis of 'missing arguments' onto the lexical analysis of early child grammars proposed here, there is some reason to doubt whether such an analysis (in any variant) would attain observational adequacy. A key prediction made by the morphological uniformity analysis (and indeed by Hyams' earlier *Italian* analysis) is that there is 'a subject–object asymmetry in the child's use of null arguments', in that 'children systematically omit subjects, but rarely objects' (1987b: 16–17). However, the qualification *'rarely'* added to the last remark indicates that Hyams is aware that this is somewhat of an idealization of the relevant acquisition data. In this respect, it is interesting to note her qualifying remark (1986: 109, n. 41) that 'In the earliest utterances the object of a transitive verb is occasionally missing (Bloom 1970). The number of omissions, however, is far too low to be the product of a regular grammatical process. More likely, these errors are performance errors, though this is an empirical question.' Since it is indeed an empirical question, let's examine some of the relevant empirical data and see whether they support Hyams' conclusion.

Although Hyams' study is based on naturalistic data, she has no primary English data of her own, and so relies on 'second-hand' data gleaned from existing published studies of the acquisition of English (primarily work by Bloom). When we examine the data presented in the published literature, however, we find that they would seem to call into question Hyams' claim, in that we find abundant examples of (what might be analysed as) *pro* being used in non-nominative (or non-subject) positions – particularly as the object of a transitive verb. For example, if we examine Bloom's study of Allison, Eric, Gia and Kathryn (as reported in Bloom 1970, 1973, and Bloom et al. 1975), we find that the relevant studies show numerous examples of transitive verbs used without overt objects: e.g.

(13)   (a)   Spill (*Allison 20, in reply to 'What did mommy do?', after her mother has spilled some juice)

     (b)   Mommy, you wiping (*Allison 20, wanting her mother to wipe a doll)

     (c)   Mommy open (*Allison 22, wanting her mother to open a box)

     (d)   Shaking (*Allison 22, picking up a can and shaking it)

     (e)   Put away Allison bag (*Allison 22, wanting to put the cookies in her bag)

     (f)   Pull (*Allison 22, gesturing with her arm as though moving her truck back and forth)

     (g)   Squeeze (*Allison 22, as she squeezes a cup)

     (h)   Push. Mommy push (*Kathryn 21, wanting her mother to push a piece into a puzzle)

     (i)   Mommy bounce (*Kathryn 22, as her mother bounces her on her bed)

     (j)   Me show mommy (*Kathryn 22, taking car to mother in kitchen)

     (k)   Mommy pull (*Kathryn 21, wanting her mother to pull the ribbons on a hat)

     (l)   Mommy kiss. Lois kiss (*Kathryn 21, wanting her mother Lois to kiss her)

     (m)   Do again (*Gia 22, stacking blocks again after she made a tower and knocked it over)

     (n)   Gia push (*Gia 23, pushing cart)

The same kind of evidence which Hyams adduces in support of claiming that subjectless sentences have *pro* subjects can be adduced in support of the parallel claim that objectless transitive structures have syntactically represented *pro* objects. Thus, it is clear from the context in which the relevant utterances are used that the 'missing' objects have definite reference (a point also made by Kazman 1988: 14–15); for this reason, it cannot be that the objects are *implicit* (i.e. 'understood' but not syntactically represented), if we follow Hyams' assumption that implicit objects are arbitrary in reference. Moreover, we find in Bloom's data 'replacement sequences' such as the following, in which an objectless sentence is expanded into one with an overt object:

(14) (a) Throw away. Mommy throw *it* away (*Kathryn 21)
      (b) ə pull. ə pull *hat* (*Kathryn 22, pulling ribbons on hat)
      (c) No want. No want *this* (*Kathryn 22)
      (d) Open. Baby open *door* (*Allison 22, trying to open the door of a toy truck)
      (e) Baby eat. Cookie. Baby eat *cookie* (*Allison 22)
      (f) Mommy help. Baby doll. Help *baby* (*Allison 22, wanting her mother to help her doll)

Conversely, we may find that the expanded sequence occurs first, as in the following conversation between Allison at 22 months and her mother (from Bloom 1973: 239):

(15)   ADULT: Oh, what did I do?
       CHILD: Spill *it*
       ADULT: I spilled it
       CHILD: Spill (*Allison 22)

Alternatively, the 'understood' object of the transitive verb is sometimes mentioned either before or after the relevant objectless sentence: cf. e.g.

(16) (a) *Diaper.* Mommy *diaper.* Fold up (*Kathryn 22, as her mother is folding up a diaper, preparing to put it on Kathryn)
      (b) Mommy iron. Mommy. Hot. Hot. *Shirts. Shirts.* Daddy (*Kathryn 22: mother responds by saying 'Mommy iron daddy's shirts?')
      (c) Baby eat. *Cookies* (*Allison 22, wanting to eat some cookies)
      (d) Squeezing. *Cup* (*Allison 22, crushing a cup continuously)

Thus, it might be argued that the Bloom studies show not only the use of *pro* subjects, but also the use of *pro* objects (the arguments for positing the existence of syntactically present *pro* objects are neither more nor less convincing than those for positing the existence of syntactically present *pro* subjects).

Other published studies likewise show children using (what might be analysed as) *pro* in an objective position, as illustrated by the following brief selection of representative examples:

(17) (a) Bunny do. Daddy do. Momma do. Want do. Want get (*Steven 19–25)

    (b)   Fix on [= 'Fix it on']. Take off me [= 'Take it off me']
          (*Susan 22)

    (c)   Get...Lucy get (*Stevie 25)

    (d)   Kendall break. Daddy pick up (*Kendall 23)

    (e)   Put right-here. Put in. Open, Mommy. Close. Pick up
          (*Claire 24)

Thus, even if we restrict ourselves (as Hyams does) to the data provided by earlier published studies of children acquiring English, the obvious conclusion to reach is that children use *both* null subjects *and* null objects.

Moreover, this very same pattern is reflected in my own corpus. For example, there are numerous null-subject sentences, including:

(18)   (a)   Want that. Want Lisa. Want baby talking (Hayley 20)

          (b)   Want one. Gone out. Got it. Lost it. Coming to rubbish
              (Bethan 20)

          (c)   Want paint (Lucy 20)

          (d)   Want crayons. Want biscuit. Want mummy come. Pee in
              potty (Jem 21)

          (e)   Want press that (Angharad 22)

          (f)   Not go shops (Claire 23)

          (g)   Want tiger. Get tiger. Get that. Get daddy. Get trousers.
              Get Tina. Shoot Tina. Shoot plant (Domenico 24)

          (h)   Have top off (Leigh 24)

But there are also numerous null object sentences, such as:

(19)   (a)   You do (+Neville 18)

          (b)   Me do (Bethan 20)

          (c)   Lady do (Jem 21)

          (d)   Wayne do (Daniel 21)

          (e)   Wayne got (Daniel 22)

          (f)   Mummy get. Man taking. Man take (Claire 23)

          (g)   Jem put back [in reply to 'Please put that back']. Lady read
              [handing book to recordist for her to read to him]. ə throw
              [in reply to 'What are you going to do with the balls?'] (Jem
              23)

          (h)   Lady get (Daniel 23, wanting sound recordist to get him
              some sweets)

          (i)   Jem have (Jem 24, reaching for pot of yoghurt)

          (j)   Me have. Want mummy do (Anna 24)

(k)   You say (Domenico 24, wanting mother to say the word
       'Veronica')

And there are also sentences which show both null subjects and null
objects, for example:

(20)   (a)   Throw [wanting mother to throw ball]. Close [wanting
               mother to close door] (Dewi 18)
        (b)   Open [handing container to recordist for her to open]
               (Daniel 20)
        (c)   Get out [getting shapes out of box]. Getting out [wanting
               to get her toys out]. Spit out [spitting something out of her
               mouth]. Push [pushing toy bus]. Want [wanting a sweet]
               (Bethan 21)
        (d)   Cuddle [cuddling his mum]. Get [wanting his mum to get
               the xylophone]. Open, mummy [wanting his mum to open
               the door]. Have [in reply to 'You want a drink?'] (Jem 21)
        (e)   Push in there (Angharad 22, in reply to 'You push the
               pram to the other room')
        (f)   Want again (Daniel 22, wanting to be tickled again)
        (g)   Put on (Daniel 23, wanting his mother to put his shoes on)
        (h)   Want again (Daniel 24, wanting bubble container again)
        (i)   Not reach [= 'I can't reach it'] (Anna 24)
        (j)   Watch (Domenico 24, wanting to watch tv)
        (k)   Put on, put on [wanting recorder on]. Want put on there
               (Daniel 25)

Not only can the subject of an independent sentence be null, but so too
can the subject of a Small Clause used as the complement of a preceding
transitive verb – as in the following examples, where we indicate the
hypothesized null pronoun subject of the bracketed Small Clause by *pro*:

(21)   (a)   Want [*pro* in] (Daniel 19, wanting to get key in door)
        (b)   Want [*pro* out] (Daniel 19, wanting to get shapes out of
               box)
        (c)   Want [*pro* back] (= 'I want it back', Hayley 20)
        (d)   Want [*pro* in car] (Daniel 21, wanting doll to be put in car)
        (e)   Want [*pro* down] (Daniel 21, wanting his brother Wayne to
               come downstairs)

In fact, the use of null pronouns extends beyond that of being the subject
or primary complement of a verb. For example, it appears that *secondary*

complements of verbs can also be null (i.e. complements which represent the third argument of a three-place predicate like *bring* or *put*): cf. the following examples (where we use *pro* to indicate the missing third argument, but do not represent 'missing' subject arguments):

(22)   (a)   Bring mummy *pro* (Domenico 24, promising to bring his mother an orange)
        (b)   Paula put them *pro*. Paula put it *pro* (Paula 18)
        (c)   Put car *pro* (Daniel 21)
        (d)   Put them *pro* (Bethan 21)

In (22)(a), a secondary THEME complement (corresponding to adult 'one') is missing, while in (22)(b–d), a secondary LOCATIVE complement (corresponding to adult 'there') is missing. And indeed it seems that even the object of a transitive preposition like *on/under* can be null: e.g.

(23)   (a)   Me want stand on *pro* (Bethan 20)
        (b)   Crayon under *pro* (Bethan 21)

It would appear that children use *pro* at this stage not only as a subject, but also as the primary or secondary complement of a verb, and even as the complement of a preposition. There would seem to be no empirical evidence of any subject/object asymmetry in the child's use of *pro* at this stage. Thus, we have abundant evidence that Hyams' claim that young children use *pro* only in nominative (or subject) positions is empirically false. Clearly, this conclusion severely undermines both of Hyams' analyses of 'missing arguments' in early child English (i.e. both her *Italian* and her *Chinese* analyses).

    Moreover, we might also object to Hyams' analyses on theoretical grounds. If the arguments we have presented in chapters 3–7 are along the right lines, then it follows that early child grammars of English are purely *lexical* systems which lack functional categories and functional licensing conditions. But if this is so, then Hyams' *pro* analysis would seem to be excluded in principle. The assumption made in most recent work on the syntax of *pro* is that *pro* is a null counterpart of adult pronominals like *he/she/it*, etc. Since the latter are pronominal determiners, it seems reasonable to conclude that *pro* has the categorial status of a null pronominal DP in adult grammars. But if this is so, then *pro* has a *functional* categorial status. Moreover, under Hyams' analysis, *pro* is subject to *functional* licensing conditions, in that *pro* is only licensed to occur as the subject of an I which carries appropriate morphosyntactic properties (e.g. which is morphologically uniform, or which assigns nominative case to its subject). Thus, Hyams' *pro* analysis is doubly functional in that it would seem to involve positing the existence of a null functional (pronominal DP) category *pro* which is subject to functional licensing conditions on its distribution. Such an analysis could clearly not be extended to early child grammars of English if the purely *lexical* analysis of early child grammars proposed here proved to be essentially correct.

However, before we rush to the precipitate conclusion that functional analyses of early child English offer no satisfactory account of the syntax of 'missing arguments', we might explore an alternative functional analysis proposed by De Haan and Tuijnman (1988), which offers the advantage over Hyams' analyses that it accounts for the fact that children 'miss out' *both* subjects *and* objects: their analysis is a *functional* one in the sense that it involves positing that early child clauses are CPs headed by an abstract (functional) C constituent. The study in question is based on data from a single child called David (aged 26 months, less two days) acquiring Dutch as his native language – though De Haan and Tuijnman suggest that their analysis can be extended to the acquisition of English. They note that David systematically produces clauses with 'missing' (subject or object) arguments, and claim that such missing-argument sentences are always verb-initial. They propose to account for this fact (adapting work by Huang 1984) by positing that in such verb-initial missing-argument sentences, the verb superficially occupies the head C position of CP, and the missing argument is an empty category (a variable) bound by a null Topic phrase occupying the specifier position of CP, the reference of the Topic being pragmatically determined. If such an analysis were extended from Dutch to early child English (as they propose), it would predict that either subjects or objects can freely be null (i.e. can be variables bound by a null Topic). Under the proposed analysis, a child utterance such as (19)(i) *Jem have* might be assigned a skeletal structure along the lines of (24) below:

(24) $[_{CP} TOP_i [_{C'} [_C e] [_{IP} Jem have e_i]]]$

where the specifier of CP is a TOP(ic) phrase (with pragmatically determined reference) which binds the coindexed empty (variable) object *e* of *have*. The analysis proposed by De Haan and Tuijnman is essentially a *functional analysis*, in the sense that it presupposes that children at this stage have developed an abstract C-system containing a null topic specifier. However (as already noted), the obvious advantage offered by this alternative CP analysis over Hyams' IP analyses is that it correctly predicts that children produce not only sentences with 'missing subjects', but also sentences with 'missing objects' (like those in (13–17), (19), (20), (22), and (23) above). Clearly, if we adopt this analysis of 'missing arguments' as variables bound by a Topic in the specifier position of CP, we have to reject the conclusion which we arrived at in chapter 5 – namely that there is no C-system in early child grammars of English; more generally, we would also have to reject the central thesis of this book, namely that the categorial component of early child grammars is purely *lexical* in nature.

However, there are a number of reasons for thinking that the CP analysis cannot provide a principled account of the grammar of 'missing arguments' in early child English. It may well be perfectly plausible to claim that De Haan and Tuijnman's subject David has developed a C-system (recall that we are claiming that children typically begin to develop functional category systems from around 24 months onwards, so that David at age 26 months would be expected to have reached a later functional stage of development, much like the children whom we discuss briefly at the end of chapter 10). However, it is anything but plausible to claim that younger English children (typically aged 20–23 months) at an earlier *lexical* stage of development have developed a C-system: after all, we presented considerable empirical evidence in chapter 5 that there is no syntactic C-system in early child grammars of English, and it seems to stretch credulity to breaking-point to posit that children under two years of age have an abstract C-system in which both the head and the specifier position are always obligatorily empty.

Moreover, there is strong empirical evidence against extending De Haan and Tuijnman's CP analysis to early child English. Given their postulate that the null topic is positioned in the specifier position of CP, and given the standard assumption that each category permits only a single specifier, then (as De Haan and Tuijnman note), it follows that the null-topic analysis predicts that it is not possible to have a clause with more than one 'missing argument' – e.g. 'It is not possible to have a sentence with both an empty subject and an empty object' (De Haan and Tuijnman 1988: 114). However, this prediction is simply not borne out by the relevant data from the acquisition of English: as we have already seen, there are abundant examples of sentences with more than one 'missing argument' in early child English – see, for instance, the relevant examples in (13)(a), (13)(d–h), (13)(m), (14)(a), (14)(c), (14)(d), (15), (16)(a), (16)(d), (17)(a–c), (17)(e), (20)(a–k), (21)(a–e), (22)(a), (22)(c) and (22)(d) above. To take just one of the many sentences of this kind found in early child English, consider the problems posed for the topic analysis by the following utterance produced by Daniel at age 20 months, when trying to reach a chocolate bar:

(25)   Want (Daniel 20, trying to reach chocolate bar)

Since the verb *want* in (25) has both a missing subject and a missing object, the topic analysis requires us to posit *two* abstract topic phrases – i.e. it requires us to posit an analysis which we can represent informally as in (26) below:

(26) TOP_i TOP_j [e_i want e_j]

(where TOP designates an empty topic phrase, and *e* designates an empty category bound by the relevant topic phrase, so that (26) might be paraphrased as 'As for me and as for the chocolate bar, I want it'). However, De Haan and Tuijnman's assumption that null topics occupy the specifier position within CP means that a multiple-topic analysis is precluded by principles of Universal Grammar, given the assumption that heads universally permit no more than one specifier. In other words, the CP analysis wrongly predicts that sentences with multiple missing arguments will never occur in early child English; the analysis is therefore empirically falsified by the numerous examples of '*multiple missing argument* sentences' in early child English which we cited earlier. However, it should be emphasized that the problems posed by multiple-missing-argument sentences are posed not by the assumption that missing arguments are empty categories bound by null topics, but rather by the assumption that the relevant null topics function as *specifiers* within the C-system. There seems no reason to think that UG excludes in principle the possibility of sentences containing multiple topic phrases, with each such topic phrase binding a separate empty category, as Huang (1984: 555) notes. However, a multiple-topic analysis would require us to posit that topic position is not the specifier position within CP (since specifier position is a unique position, and hence the analysis is not compatible with multiple-topic structures) but rather 'a position adjoined to some clausal node' (Huang 1984: 555). Given our Small Clause analysis of clauses in early child English, we might propose that the relevant null topics are adjoined to the overall Small Clause itself (a suggestion which we made in a different context in chapter 3). Under this version of the null-topic analysis, a child utterance such as (25) above would have the structure indicated informally in (27) below (where we assume that verbal Small Clauses have the status of VP constituents, and where each TOP denotes a null topic NP, and each *e* denotes an empty NP functioning as a variable bound by the relevant topic NP):

(27)   [$_{VP}$ TOP_i [$_{VP}$ TOP_j [$_{VP}$ e_i want e_j]]]

Such an analysis would clearly allow us to account for sentences with multiple missing arguments. Crucially, however, this version of the null-topic analysis does not require us to posit the existence of a C-system (or indeed *any* functional category system) in early child grammars of English: on the contrary, the analysis proposed here is entirely compatible with our lexical analysis of early child grammars – for example, the only categories postulated in (27) are (projections of) N and V; topic phrases are NPs adjoined to the (purely lexical) Small Clause structures which the child has developed (in this case a Small Clause VP).

However, there are a number of problems which beset an analysis which allows both subject-linked and object-linked null topics. One of these relates to the seemingly excessive abstractness of the analysis: we can illustrate this by comparing (25) – repeated as (28)(b) below – with its overt-argument counterpart (28)(a):

(28)   (a)   Danny want bar
        (b)   Want (Daniel 20, trying to reach chocolate bar)

Intuitively, (28)(a) would seem to have a more complex syntactic structure than (28)(b); but under the *topic* analysis of missing arguments, the reverse is the case. Thus, (28)(a) is a simple verbal Small Clause (i.e. a VP) of the form [NP V NP]; by contrast, the topic analysis requires us to posit that (28)(b) involves a far more complex structure in which the VP has two null topic phrases adjoined to it, and that the resulting structure involves a complex network of binding relationships in which each topic phrase binds an appropriate variable (empty category), as represented schematically in (27) above.

There are two additional aspects of the topic analysis which seem questionable. Firstly (as Brown 1973 notes), children at this stage rarely produce sentences containing a single overt topic (i.e. sentences such as '*Bar* Danny want'), and (as far as I know) they never produce sentences with multiple overt topics; hence a 'multiple null topic' analysis again seems implausible. Secondly, children at this stage do not seem to have acquired the syntax of variables (a point made by Hyams 1987b: 15): for example, as we noted in chapter 5, they have not acquired the syntax of wh-movement at this point in their development (i.e. structures in which a preposed wh-phrase binds a variable, viz. the trace of the moved wh-phrase). Indeed, we might argue that there are good theoretical reasons for supposing that children cannot in principle have acquired the syntax of variables at the lexical stage in their development, since variables are (empty pronominal DPs) *bound* by an appropriate antecedent, and *binding* is a property of a D-system not yet acquired (recall that we argued in chapter 4 that children at this stage have not mastered the binding properties of nominals). Moreover, variables are *case-marked* empty categories; and yet children have no case system as yet. For these reasons, an analysis which equates 'missing arguments' in early child English with variables bound by an empty topic phrase seems implausible.

If children's 'missing arguments' are not *pro* (i.e. null pronominal DP) constituents, and are not *variables* (i.e. null DP constituents bound by a null topic phrase) either, then what are they? One suggestion which we might make (which would be consistent with our lexical analysis of early child grammars) would be to posit that they are *null NPs* – i.e. NPs which are phonologically null: for the sake of ease of identification, we'll use lower-case italic *np* to indicate a null NP. Such an *np* analysis would clearly be consistent with the analysis put forward in chapter 4, under which all nominals in early child English have the status of simple lexical NPs (unlike their adult English counterparts, which have the status of functional DPs). Moreover, the *np* analysis would provide a straightforward account of why there are no functional licensing conditions (e.g. I-conditions) determining the distribution of *np*: given the absence of functional categories and functional licensing conditions in early child grammars, it follows that both overt and null NPs would be free to occur in any argument position in any sentence. We have already presented extensive evidence (cf. the relevant data in (13–23) above) that there are no case constraints on the distribution of 'missing arguments' in early child English: hence an empty *np* can occur in any argument position, whether as the subject of a matrix or complement clause, as a primary or secondary verbal object, or as a prepositional object. Indeed, given the assumption that null nominals are free of functional constraints on their distribution in early child English, it follows that there are no constraints on the use of multiple null arguments in children's sentences. Hence, a sentence such as (25) above *Want* would (on these assumptions) be assigned a skeletal structure such as:

(29)   *np* want *np*

where the first *np* is interpreted as denoting the speaker Daniel, and the second as denoting the chocolate bar which he is relentlessly pursuing. Thus, 'multiple missing argument' sentences prove unproblematic under this analysis.

However, the obvious question raised by any such analysis is how the *contents* of the empty *np* would be determined (this relates to the *identification* problem for empty categories discussed earlier). A natural suggestion to make in this regard is that the contents of *np* are *pragmatically* determined. Numerous child language researchers have made remarks which can be reinterpreted (within the framework used here) in these terms. For example, Miller 1979: 75 writes that 'Certain pragmatic conditions determine what the child perceives as being redundant information and thus may remain implicit'. In a similar vein, Greenfield et al. (1985: 251) argue that 'Relatively constant features of the environment, constituting old or redundant information, are...taken for granted and go unspoken'. If we analyse the pretheoretical notion of an 'implicit' or 'unspoken' argument as a null nominal (i.e. as *np*), then we can reinterpret these observations as implying that children use null *np* to denote an entity whose reference is recoverable from the context, and hence that the reference of *np* is pragmatically determined. To illustrate how this might work, consider how the structure (29) '*np* want *np*' (produced by Daniel when reaching for the chocolate bar) would be interpreted. We can infer easily from our nonlinguistic knowledge (about the egocentricity of children, and their insatiable craving for chocolate!) that the first *np* denotes the speaker (i.e. Daniel himself), and the second *np* denotes the tantalizing chocolate bar (so that (29) can be paraphrased in adult English as 'I want the chocolate bar').

Our suggestion that the contents of empty categories in child speech may be pragmatically determined seems to be independently motivated by the frequent occurrence in early child English of (what have often been taken to be) 'verbless transitive' structures like the binominal structures discussed in the previous chapter – structures such as:

(30)   (a)   Wayne sweetie (Daniel 20, in reply to 'Who's got the sweeties?')
        (b)   Roland sweet (Daniel 24, indicating that Roland Rat wants a sweet)

As we argued in the previous chapter, *binominal* structures such as those in (30) are arguably best analysed as verbal Small Clauses (i.e. VPs) headed by an empty V, so that (30)(a) and (b) would have the respective (simplified) syntactic structures (31)(a) and (b) below:

(31)   (a)   [$_{VP}$ Wayne [$_V$ *e*] sweetie]
        (b)   [$_{VP}$ Roland [$_V$ *e*] sweetie]

If this is so, then it seems reasonable to suppose that the interpretation of the empty V is pragmatically determined (from the linguistic or nonlinguistic context of the utterance). Thus, the interpretation of the empty V in (31)(a) could be inferred from the *linguistic* context in which the utterance (30)(a) occurred, whereas the interpretation of the empty V in (31)(b) would be determined by the *nonlinguistic* context in which (30)(b) was uttered. If the contents of an empty V can be pragmatically determined in early child grammars of English, I see no reason not to suppose that the contents of an empty nominal can likewise be pragmatically determined.

However, one potential objection to the empty *np* analysis is that it might seem to violate principles of UG, in so far as it involves positing that early child English is a language which makes 'free' use of null nominals (i.e. posits a class of empty nominals which are free of syntactic licensing or identification conditions): we might object that since there is no precedent in adult grammars for the 'free' use of null nominals, the proposed analysis is an *unnatural* one (in the sense that it violates the principles of UG which determine the use of empty categories). However, the assumption that there are no adult languages which allow 'free' use of a null nominal in argument positions seems to be a questionable one. For example, Xu (1986) argues that Chinese is just such a language; and we shall suggest here that Japanese may also be a 'free null nominal argument' language. Japanese is of particular relevance to our discussion here, given that it arguably resembles early child English in being *determinerless*, and *caseless*. Thus, Fukui (1986) argues that Japanese has no D-system (hence no determiners); and in a similar vein, Dunn and Yanada (1973: 7) claim that nominals are uninflected for case in Japanese: given the assumption that case is a property of DPs, the absence of a case-system in Japanese would be a consequence of the absence of a D-system. Thus, if Japanese is a language which has null nominal arguments in its syntax, then it follows that the arguments concerned cannot be null DPs (since Japanese has no D-system), but rather must be null NPs (i.e. *np*). If this is so, then we should expect to find that the relevant null nominals are not subject to case licensing conditions on their distribution (if we are correct in hypothesizing that Japanese has no case system). Moreover, given that there are no agreement inflections in Japanese, we should expect to find no functional (e.g. I-agreement) constraints on the *identification* of null nominals in Japanese. In other words, we should expect to find that null nominal arguments are free of functional constraints on their licensing and identification in Japanese.

In this connection, it is interesting to note the claim made by Gunji (1987) that Japanese allows the occurrence of (what he calls) *free gaps* within sentences: by this, he means that 'Japanese allows one of the

constituents of a sentence not to be explicitly stated when it is understandable from the context' (p. 107; *one* here should be taken to mean
'one or more'). If we translate Gunji's rather different terminology
(drawn from a different theoretical framework) into its counterpart in the
theory used here and equate his term *gap* with our term 'null argument',
then what he is saying (in our terms) is that Japanese allows free use of
null arguments. More specifically, he claims that there are no syntactic
constraints (hence no case constraints) on the distribution of null
arguments (cf. his 1987: 108 remark that 'Gaps are freely generated'),
and likewise that there are no grammatical constraints (hence no
agreement constraints) on the interpretation of null arguments; on the
contrary, 'Free gaps are subject to pragmatic control' (ibid.) – that is,
null arguments can be used to refer to any entity which can readily be
identified on the basis of pragmatic clues provided by the (linguistic or
nonlinguistic) context in which the sentence was uttered. Hence, Gunji
claims that 'Gaps are freely generated as long as the context can
pragmatically supply the missing element' (1987: 108). We can illustrate
the 'free' use of null arguments in Japanese in terms of the following
example (adapted from Gunji 1987: 144), where we use *np* to designate a
null nominal argument:

(32)   Naomi-ga Ken-ni [*np* moo *np* aisitei-nai-to] itta
        Naomi-P Ken-to [*np* more *np* love-not-that] said
        'Naomi told Ken that *np* didn't love *np* any more'
        (= Naomi told Ken that *he/she* didn't love *him/her* any more)

(P here is used to gloss the postposition *ga* in Japanese which has no
immediate counterpart in English, and whose precise function need not
concern us.) The example (32) illustrates the fact that a null argument
(*np*) can freely occur in either subject or object position in the embedded
clause: moreover, in each case, the null argument *np* can refer either to
one of the constituents of the main clause (so that e.g. (32) might mean
that Naomi told Ken that Naomi didn't love Ken any more), or to
someone else previously mentioned in the discourse (e.g. if Ken and
Naomi had just been discussing an affair between Marie and Tomio,
then (32) could mean that Naomi told Ken that Marie didn't love Tomio
any more).

The fact that in a determinerless, caseless, and agreementless language like Japanese we find precisely the same 'free' use of null nominals as
in a determinerless, caseless, agreementless language like early child
English suggests that our analysis of early English as allowing 'free' use
of empty *np* arguments (with pragmatic determination of the contents of

the *np*) is not in any sense 'unnatural' – that is, it does not violate deep-seated principles of Universal Grammar. On the contrary, what our discussion suggests is that languages (like Italian) with rich functional systems (e.g. a well developed D-system with a rich system of case inflections, and a well developed I-system with a rich system of agreement inflections) may impose functional licensing and identification conditions on the use of null arguments (since these arguments are themselves functional constituents, being pronominal DPs); whereas a language with few if any functional systems (e.g. a language like Japanese, with no D-system, no case system, and no I-agreement morphology) will allow null arguments to be used 'free' of functional licensing and identification conditions (since the relevant null arguments will be simple non-functional *np* constituents). Given this analysis of the grammar of null arguments, we could argue that early child English falls within the range of languages permitted by UG, precisely because UG specifies that a determinerless, caseless, and agreementless language may allow free use of null arguments (as in the case of adult Japanese). From this point of view, we might argue that young English-acquiring children are not speaking Italian or Chinese (as Hyams claimed), but rather Japanese!

Our suggestion that 'missing arguments' in early child English may have the status of null *np* constituents lacking a D-system has interesting implications for their semantics. If we posit that the D-system is the locus of the binding properties of nominals and pronominals, then it follows that we should expect to find that *np* is free of referential constraints on its use in early child English; and indeed there is some evidence that this is the case. In this connection, it is interesting to note that sentences such as those in (33) below appear to show a systematic ambiguity in early child speech:

(33)   (a)   Want down (Daniel 21)
       (b)   Want open it (Daniel 22)

Thus, these sentences (and others like them) were used by Daniel (on many separate occasions) in two different contexts. For example, (33)(a) *Want down* was used (i) when his brother Wayne was upstairs and he wanted Wayne to come down, and (ii) when he himself wanted to get down off his mother's knee, or off the settee. Likewise, (33)(b) was used (i) when Daniel was himself trying to get the lid off a container, and (ii) when, having failed to get the lid off himself, he then handed the container to the sound recordist and asked *her* to try and get the lid off for him (sometimes adding a tag, as in 'Want open it, please', or 'Want open it, lady'). The dual interpretations assigned to these utterances suggest that they have the respective structures (34)(a) and (b) below (where the first *np* denotes the speaker):

(34)   (a)   *np* want [*np* down]
        (b)   *np* want [*np* open it]

It would seem that in Daniel's speech, *np* can function either like a pronominal (so that the second *np* is disjoint in reference from the first), or like an anaphor (so that the second *np* is coreferential to the first). If this is so, then we might conclude that at this stage null arguments are free of binding constraints on their use, their reference being determined purely pragmatically. It would seem reasonable to account for this by positing that *np* in early child English is a null NP lacking the binding properties associated with the D-system (whereas its adult counterpart *pro* is a null DP with the binding properties of a pronominal DP). Interestingly, it is not just null nominals which seem to be free of referential restrictions in Daniel's speech at this stage: as we noted in chapter 4, overt (pro)nominals would appear to be used in an analogous fashion, and thus can be used in contexts where adults would require a reflexive anaphor: cf. e.g.

(35)   (a)   Kendall see *Kendall* (*Kendall 23, looking at a picture of herself)
        (b)   Want *me*...Want see *me* (Daniel 24, wanting to see himself in a mirror)

In adult English, the italicized (pro)nominals would be interpreted as disjoint in reference from the (overt or covert) subject of the containing clause, and would have to be replaced by a reflexive anaphor (*herself/ myself*) if coreference with the subject were intended. However, the child clearly intends the (pro)nominal object to be coreferential to its subject in both utterances, and this suggests that children have not yet acquired the binding properties of (pro)nominals at this stage. Of course, if the binding properties of (pro)nominals are determined by their D-system, and there is no D-system operating in the child's grammar at this stage, then the absence of binding restrictions on the interpretation of (overt or covert) nominals and pronominals is readily accounted for.

   What we have suggested here is that 'missing arguments' in early child English may be analysed as empty NPs. Because they are NPs, they lack a D-system; and because they lack a D-system, they are not subject to case constraints on their distribution (since case is a property of DP), or binding constraints on their interpretation (since the D-system is the locus of the binding properties of nominals). Accordingly, these empty NPs are free of functional constraints (case constraints, agreement constraints, binding constraints, etc.) on their licensing (i.e. distribution) and identification (i.e. interpretation). Needless to say, the analysis of 'missing arguments' as empty NPs is entirely compatible with the lexical analysis of early child grammars suggested here.

Although we have argued here that the analysis of 'missing arguments' in early child English as null *np* constituents provides a principled account of both their distribution and interpretation, it might nonetheless be objected (in spite of our protestations to the contrary!) that such an analysis violates fundamental principles of Universal Grammar relating to the range of null arguments which UG permits. More specifically, it might be suggested that UG only permits *functional* categories (e.g. DP, and perhaps CP) to be null arguments (not lexical categories like NP), and always requires them to be subject to *functional* licensing/ identification conditions. If this were so, then our analysis of missing arguments as null NPs would be ruled out as 'genetically impossible'.

Given that the various ways we have explored of analysing 'missing arguments' as constituents syntactically projected into the syntax in the form of an empty category of some kind (viz. a null pro(nominal DP), a variable, or a null NP) could all be argued to be potentially problematic in some way, we might feel tempted to explore an alternative (perhaps intuitively more plausible) analysis of 'missing arguments' – namely to suppose that they are literally 'missing' from the syntax. Under this more radical alternative analysis, an utterance such as (25) 'Want' would have a syntactic structure which is both subjectless and objectless, and would be analyseable as a verbal Small Clause (i.e. a VP) containing only the head verb *want* – as represented in (36) below:

(36) $[_{VP} [_{V'} [_V \text{ want}]]]$

At first sight, such an analysis might seem implausible: after all (we might argue), the verb *want* in (25) clearly has an understood thematic subject (= the speaker, Daniel himself) and an understood thematic object (= the chocolate bar), and yet the structure in (36) does not represent this in any way.

However, we can overcome this objection in the following way. Rizzi (1986: 508–9) argues that there are two ways in which the theta-roles assigned by a predicate can be saturated, namely either (i) syntactically, or (ii) lexically. If a given theta-role is *syntactically* saturated, then it is projected into the syntactic structure of the sentence as an *explicit* argument of the predicate concerned, and may take the form of an appropriate filled or empty category. By contrast, if a given theta-role is *lexically* saturated, then it remains *implicit*, in the sense that it is a part of the lexical entry for the predicate concerned which is not projected into the syntax (so that there will be no overt or covert constituent carrying the relevant theta-role in the syntactic structure of the sentence). We can contrast these two different ways of saturating theta-roles in terms of the following pair of examples:

(37)   (a)   John ate *three triple burgers* in the restaurant
        (b)   John ate in the restaurant

(38)   (a)   John devoured *three triple burgers* in the restaurant
        (b)   *John devoured in the restaurant

In (37)(a) and (38)(a) the PATIENT theta-role assigned to the object of *eat/devour* is syntactically saturated, in the sense that the relevant theta-role is discharged onto the italicized complement which is overtly projected into the syntactic structure of the sentence: by contrast, in (37)(b), the PATIENT theta-role assigned by *eat* to its complement is not projected into the syntax, but rather is lexically saturated (in other words, there is no overt or covert constituent in the syntactic structure of the sentence which carries the relevant theta-role). However, we see from the ill-formedness of (38)(b) that the PATIENT theta-role which *devour* assigns to its complement cannot be lexically saturated (and so remain implicit), but rather can only be syntactically saturated (and so must be explicit). Thus, *eat* allows the patient theta-role which it assigns to its complement to be syntactically or lexically saturated, whereas *devour* requires syntactic saturation of the relevant role.

The fact that two close synonyms (like *eat* and *devour*) differ in the mechanisms by which theta-roles may be saturated suggests that there are complex idiosyncratic item-specific restrictions on the mechanisms of thematic saturation. This being so, then we might expect that in the initial stages of acquisition, children will *overgeneralize* both mechanisms, and so allow theta-roles to be freely saturated either lexically or syntactically (overgeneralization is a familiar trait of children's early grammatical development, so this is by no means intrinsically implausible). This would then provide us with an alternative account of 'missing' arguments in early child English – as we can illustrate in terms of the following (hypothetical) paradigm, based on the familiar scenario in which Daniel relentlessly pursues his quest for the elusive chocolate bar:

(39)　　(a)　Danny want bar
　　　　(b)　Danny want
　　　　(c)　Want bar
　　　　(d)　Want

(Although (39) is a hypothetical paradigm, 'real' examples of the relevant structures can be found easily enough: cf. e.g. Bloom 1970: 46.) Let us hypothesize that at this point in his development, Daniel freely allows theta-roles to be either syntactically or lexically saturated, so that any argument of a predicate can freely be either *explicit* (hence projected into the syntax), or *implicit* (hence not projected into the syntax). We might then posit that in (39)(a) both subject and object have been made explicit; in (39)(b) the subject has been made explicit and the object is implicit; in (39)(c), the object is explicit and the subject is implicit; and in (39)(d), both subject and object are implicit. Under this alternative analysis, 'missing arguments' remain *implicit* in the relevant technical sense (i.e. their theta-roles are lexically saturated), and thus are never projected into the syntax at all (Lebeaux 1988 makes a related, though rather different, suggestion). One of the apparent advantages of this analysis is that it provides a natural account of why 'missing arguments' are not subject to syntactic constraints on their use in early child English (e.g. contrary to what Hyams claims, they are not restricted to occurring in nominative/subject positions): if 'missing arguments' are never projected into the syntax, then it follows that they cannot in principle be subject to syntactic constraints on their use. It need scarcely be pointed out that the analysis of 'missing' subjects and objects as *implicit arguments* is entirely compatible with our overall hypothesis that the earliest grammars developed by young children are purely *lexical* in nature. Indeed, we might even argue that the implicit argument analysis is forced on us by principles of Universal Grammar: after all, if UG specifies that explicit (i.e. syntactically projected) null arguments are universally functional categories (viz. DPs) subject to functional constraints on their use, then it follows that languages with purely lexical grammars (e.g. early child English) cannot in principle have explicit null arguments.

The *lexical saturation* analysis of 'missing arguments' offers us an interesting perspective on an intriguing set of data reported in Bowerman (1973). The data which her study provides of Kendall's speech at ages 22–23 months suggest that in subjectless sentences, Kendall would position objects of verbs either *after* the verb, as in (40) below:

(40)　　(a)　Look Kendall ('Look at Kendall')
　　　　(b)　Read...book

     (c)   Bite...finger
     (d)   Open...lotion (Kendall 23)

or before the verb, as in (41) below

(41)   (a)   Doggie sew ('Sew doggie')
         (b)   Kimmy kick ('Kick Kimmy')
         (c)   Kendall pick-up ('Pick up Kendall')
         (d)   Doggie lookit ('Look at doggie')

However, in sentences containing a preverbal subject, the object is always positioned postverbally, never preverbally – as we see from examples such as (42) below:

(42)   (a)   Kimmy ride bike
         (b)   Kendall turn page
         (c)   Kimmy eat hand
         (d)   Mommy pick-up...Kendall

Thus, a Subject + Verb + Object sequence like (42)(a) *Kimmy ride bike* has no Subject + Object + Verb counterpart, so that we don't find **Kimmy bike ride* (on the relevant interpretation). Why should it be that we find preverbal objects only in subjectless sentences?

    One answer which is suggested by the *lexical saturation* hypothesis is the following. Let us suppose that (in Kendall's grammar) only overt arguments are projected into the syntax, and that 'missing arguments' are implicit, and hence not present in the syntax. This means that subjectless sentences like those in (40) have no subject at all, with the consequence that the subject position is available to be filled by (what would otherwise be) the object. If this is so, then sentences like (41) represent structures in which the vacant subject position has been filled by the object (so that what might seem to be a preverbal object is in fact a superficial subject). By contrast, in sentences like (42), the preverbal subject position is filled by the subject, and so cannot be filled by the object. Thus, the assumption that 'missing subjects' are implicit arguments not projected into the syntax, together with the assumption that Kendall's preverbal NPs occupy superficial subject position provides a straightforward account of why we find preverbal objects in subjectless sentences, but not in sentences with an overt subject.

    It might at first sight seem as if we can handle the facts illustrated in (40–42) above equally well in terms of an analysis which assumes that sentences like (41) derive from an underlying structure containing a null thematic subject which is projected into the syntax as an empty category of some kind. For example, we might posit that (41)(a) *Doggie sew* derives from an underlying structure along the lines of (43) below:

(43)   *e* sew doggie

(where *e* denotes the 'understood' AGENT subject, presumably referring to Mommy), with the PATIENT object NP *doggie* subsequently moving into the empty subject position denoted by *e*. However, any such movement of a theta-marked NP into another theta-marked position would be ruled out as impossible by principles of Universal Grammar (in particular, by the *Theta Criterion*, one clause of which requires that 'Each argument bears one and only one theta-role' – Chomsky 1981: 36). The problem is that if the object moves into the empty subject position, then the subject position will be doubly theta-marked, since it carries both the AGENT role assigned to the underlying subject, and the PATIENT role assigned to the preposed object. Thus, I conclude that any analysis of subjectless sentences like (41) which posits that they involve an underlying null preverbal subject projected into the syntax is implausible: more precisely, it is inconsistent with the assumption that preverbal objects actually occupy superficial subject position; and this assumption seems to provide the most plausible account of why preverbal objects occur only in sentences which lack a preverbal subject.

Of course, the analysis proposed here would be considerably weakened if we were able to present a viable alternative to the suggested 'subject' analysis of preposed objects. There would seem to be two main alternatives to the 'subject' analysis. The first is that preverbal objects are in fact objects, and are instances of a mis-setting of the head–complement parameter; the second is that preverbal objects are in fact preclausal topics. However, neither analysis seems to me to account for the key fact that preposed objects occur only in sentences which lack preverbal subjects. Thus, the *object* analysis would provide no principled explanation for why we don't find Subject + Object + Verb sequences – e.g. why (42)(a) has no counterpart **Kimmy bike ride*. Conversely, the topic analysis provides no principled explanation for why we don't find sequences of Topic + Subject + Verb – e.g. why (42)(a) has no counterpart **Bike Kimmy ride*. By contrast, the relevant ordering facts can be accounted for in a straightforward fashion if we analyse preposed objects as superficial subjects; but as we have already seen, this analysis is only compatible with an analysis of 'missing' subjects as implicit arguments not projected into the syntax.

The overall conclusion to be drawn from our discussion is that the Kendall data would seem to favour an analysis of 'missing subjects' as lexically saturated unprojected implicit arguments, rather than as syntactically projected empty categories. Moreover, the *lexical saturation* analysis of 'missing arguments' might also turn out to provide the key for understanding the nature of the child's speech at the single-word stage (as well as providing a basis for seeing continuity of development between the one-word and two-word stages). We can illustrate this in terms of typical single-word utterances such as the following:

(44)   (a)   Dirty (*Allison 16, reaching in bag and pulling out diaper; from Bloom 1973)
        (b)   Gone (*Allison 16, watching bubble as it disappears; from Bloom 1973)
        (c)   Up (*Nicky 16, when going up a step; from Greenfield and Smith 1976)
        (d)   Drop (*Nicky 19, pointing to cups that had dropped on the floor; from Greenfield and Smith 1976)
        (e)   Hot (*Matthew 18, looking at cereal; from Greenfield and Smith 1976)

We might suppose that in examples such as these, the child's utterances are predicates with *implicit* (i.e. lexically saturated) arguments. This is not in any sense a novel idea, as the following remarks about one-word utterances by Grace De Laguna (1927: 98–9) indicate: 'In such a case there is virtual or implicit predication; but the language form is rudimentary. The verbal utterance must be supplemented by some other form of bodily response, like pointing, which serves to indicate the object to which the verbal specification applies.' Her suggestion that what is involved in one-word utterances such as those in (44) is 'implicit predication' can be interpreted within the framework used here as implying that the child's words are predicates with implicit (i.e. lexically but not syntactically represented) arguments which can only be identified on the basis of pragmatic (i.e. contextual) information.

We might then characterize the development of 'missing arguments' along the following lines. At the one-word stage, predicates have lexically saturated (hence syntactically 'missing') arguments. Once children enter the multi-word stage, they begin to learn how to project arguments into the syntax (this involves *inter alia* determining how the principles of categorization and projection are instantiated in the target language the child is acquiring, e.g. setting the various parameters which determine the relative positions of heads, complements, and specifiers). For a while (i.e. during the period of early multi-word speech with which we are concerned here), children freely alternate between lexical and syntactic saturation of theta-marked arguments, so that arguments are sometimes explicit, and sometimes implicit. At a later stage of development (typically from around the age of two years onwards), they begin to master the relevant saturation mechanisms, and thus learn to project arguments which require syntactic saturation into the syntax: generally speaking, syntactically projected arguments will be overt in English, though in specific contexts (e.g. imperative subject position in English), a given argument may be projected into the syntax as an appropriate empty category. Of course, on this alternative view of early child English, there would be no syntactically projected empty nominals in early child grammars of English (e.g. no null (pro)nominals, and no variables), since 'missing arguments' would remain syntactically unprojected (their theta-roles being lexically saturated). In simple terms, the analysis being suggested here amounts to positing that in the earliest multiword speech produced by children (typically between 20–23 months of age), the only syntactically projected arguments in the child's sentence structures are those which overtly surface (i.e. those present in a phonologically non-null form in the surface structure of the child's sentences). Thus, what we are suggesting is a *concrete* analysis of the argument structure of predicates in early child English which eschews the analysis of 'missing arguments' as abstract empty categories.

The *concrete* analysis of 'missing arguments' suggested here offers an interesting perspective on early syntactic development: one of the questions which it raises is whether (in the acquisition of languages like Italian where the adult target language does indeed have syntactically projected null pronominals) children first pass through an earlier stage in which 'missing arguments' are *implicit* before passing on to a later stage of development at which the relevant 'missing arguments' become *explicit* by being projected into the syntax as empty categories: this is a question which clearly falls outside the scope of this present work, but is an important issue for future research to address. What is of more immediate concern to us here is the fact that the suggested concrete analysis is entirely compatible with our overall hypothesis that early child grammars are purely lexical in nature.

Whether or not this concrete analysis will turn out to be defensible is a question which we leave to future research to answer. Certainly, such an analysis is not without posing apparent problems. For example, the suggestion that superficially subjectless child sentences may indeed be syntactically subjectless is seemingly incompatible with the *Subject Principle* discussed at the beginning of this chapter which requires that predicative or clausal structures have a syntactically projected subject position. However, it might be argued that this supposed 'subject requirement' is a mere artefact of a more deep-seated principle which requires the syntactic saturation (or discharge) of obligatory functional features. For example, if we posit that the case features obligatorily assigned by a case assigner must be syntactically saturated (i.e. discharged onto an appropriate constituent projected into the syntactic structure of the sentence), then we can provide an alternative account of the requirement for clauses such as those bracketed below to have an (italicized) 'dummy' subject:

(45)　(a)　[*It* is safe to leave]
　　　(b)　*[Is safe to leave]

(46)　(a)　I don't consider [*it* safe to leave]
　　　(b)　*I don't consider [safe to leave]

We might suppose that the subject *it* is required in these examples in order to receive the nominative case discharged by *is* in (45), and the objective case discharged by *consider* in (46). Looked at from this point of view, there is no 'subject requirement' in adult grammars of English – merely a requirement for certain functional properties (in this instance, *case* properties) to be discharged onto an appropriate syntactically projected constituent. But if subjects are required in the syntactic structure of sentences like (45) and (46) merely to satisfy *case* requirements, then it follows that there would be no such requirement for clauses to have syntactically projected subjects in a caseless language. Since we have argued at some length in the previous chapter that early child English is a *caseless* language, it follows that there cannot in principle be any case requirement for clauses to have syntactically projected subjects in early child English. There would therefore seem to be no reason in principle to object to analysing apparently subjectless sentences in early child English as containing *implicit* (i.e. syntactically unprojected) subjects.

　A second objection to suggesting that 'missing arguments' in early child English are purely implicit is that this would pose apparent problems in accounting for their semantic interpretation, since (as noted in our earlier discussion) children's 'missing arguments' generally have definite reference, whereas implicit arguments are conventionally assumed to have arbitrary reference. However, the assumption that implicit arguments never have a definite interpretation would seem to be called into question by examples such as the following:

(47)   (a)   When I was in trouble, you didn't help
        (b)   When John came to see me, I advised against getting himself involved any further

The implicit object of *help* in (47)(a) doesn't have the same arbitrary reference as 'anyone', but rather can be construed as having the same definite reference as 'me'; likewise, the implicit object of *advised* in (47)(b) doesn't have the same arbitrary reference as 'people', but rather is interpreted as having the same definite reference as 'him'. Thus, it would seem that there cannot be any principle of UG which excludes the possibility of an implicit argument being assigned (perhaps indirectly, through a chain of pragmatic inferences) a definite interpretation. This being so, then the definite interpretation assigned to 'missing arguments' in early child English does not provide an insuperable obstacle to analysing them as *implicit* arguments.

We remarked at the beginning of this chapter that the syntax of 'missing arguments' in early child grammars of English provides a crucial testing-ground for our overall hypothesis that the initial grammars of English developed by young children are purely lexical in character. We then looked at three attempts to characterize the syntax of 'missing arguments' in functional terms (Hyams' *Italian* and *Chinese* IP analyses, and De Haan and Tuijnman's *Dutch* CP analysis), and argued that all three analyses were clearly falsified by the relevant acquisition data: Hyams' IP analyses wrongly predict that 'missing arguments' are only ever found in subject position, whereas De Haan and Tuijnman's CP analysis wrongly predicts that children never produce 'multiple missing argument' sentences; the crucial fact which neither analysis was able to capture is that *any* argument in early child English can be 'missing', and that there is no restriction (in principle) on the number of 'missing arguments' in a given sentence.

In the latter part of this chapter, we have suggested two alternative analyses of 'missing arguments', each of which is entirely compatible with the overall *lexical* analysis of child grammars proposed here. One possibility we suggested was that 'missing arguments' might simply be (unbound) empty NPs, free of functional constraints on their distribution and interpretation (their reference being determined pragmatically). The second possibility which we outlined was that 'missing arguments' might be analysed as *implicit* arguments not projected into the syntax, whose theta-roles are lexically (but not syntactically) saturated. It is far from clear (in our present state of knowledge) which of these alternatives offers a more adequate account of missing arguments in child speech: the central issue of concern from our point of view, however, is that both analyses are compatible with the observed facts, and with the *lexical* analysis of early child grammars of English proposed here.

9

The Overall Structure of Early Child Grammars of English

In this chapter, we draw together the various observations which we have made in the previous chapters, and attempt to formulate a unitary generalization about the observed characteristics of the initial grammars developed by young children acquiring English as their native language. This generalization in turn leads us to formulate a number of hypotheses about the internal organization and structure of grammars of early child English. We'll begin by briefly summarizing the main conclusions reached in our earlier chapters.

In chapter 2, we argued that the earliest one-word utterances produced by young children (typically between one and one-and-a-half years of age) are *acategorial* in nature (so that the child's vocabulary items at this stage have phonological and semantic properties, but no morpho-syntactic properties). The evidence which we adduced in support of this claim can be summarized as in (1) below:

(1) Early child English is *acategorial* in nature, and thus is characterized by:
   (i) nonacquisition of inflections (e.g. plural+*s*, gerund +*ing*, etc.)
   (ii) absence of productive phrasal or clausal structures
   (iii) inability to parse adult sentences correctly (as exemplified by inability to respond appropriately to wh-questions)

In chapters 3–8, we went on to argue that at around 20 months of age (±20%), children typically enter a *categorial* stage of development. We further argued that during the first few months of this stage (i.e. during the period which we referred to as *early child English*, usually associated with children aged 20–23 months, ±20%), the grammars developed by young children show evidence of the development of *lexical* category systems, but no evidence of the development of *functional* category systems. The specific hypotheses and evidence which we put forward relating to the nature of early child grammars of English are summarized in (2–5) below:

(2)   Early child grammars of English show evidence of the acquisition of lexical category systems, and thus are characterized by:

    (i)   acquisition of the four primary lexical categories (N, V, P, A) and their phrasal projections (into N$'$/NP, V$'$/VP, P$'$/PP, and A$'$/AP respectively)

    (ii)   acquisition of a set of lexical inflections (i.e. inflections which attach to lexical categories), e.g. noun plural +*s*, verb gerund +*ing*

    (iii)   cross-categorial symmetry in the internal structure of the N-system, V-system, P-system, and A-system

    (iv)   correct setting of word-order parameters at the *head-/adjunct-/specifier-first* values

(3)   Early child grammars of English have no D-system, and thus there is no evidence of acquisition of:

    (i)   the morphosyntax of referential determiners such as *a, the*, etc.

    (ii)   the morphosyntax of the possessive determiner *'s*

    (iii)   the morphosyntax of case-marked pronominal determiners such as *I/me/my*

    (iv)   the person/binding properties of (pro)nominals

(4)   Early child grammars of English have no C-system, and hence children show no evidence of:

    (i)   acquisition of the syntax of Complementisers

    (ii)   acquisition of the syntax of preposed Auxiliaries

    (iii)   acquisition of the syntax of preposed wh-constituents

    (iv)   the ability to correctly parse wh-questions involving preposed complements

(5)   Early child grammars of English have no I-system, and hence children show no evidence of having acquired the morphosyntax of:

    (i)   infinitival *to*

    (ii)   modal auxiliaries

    (iii)   finite verb inflections $(+s/+d)$
    (iv)   *do*-support
    (v)   copula *be*
    (vi)   progressive *be*
    (vii)   perfective *have*
    (viii)   nominative case-marking
    (ix)   empty categories

Having identified twenty-one specific characteristics of early child English, the obvious task which now faces us is that of *generalization* – that is, of finding a single unifying hypothesis which will account for all of these characteristics in a principled fashion. We have already suggested on a number of occasions that the overall generalization which subsumes the specific points identified in (2–5) is the following:

(6)   Early child grammars of English are characterized by the acquisition of lexical category systems and their associated grammatical properties, and by the nonacquisition of functional category systems and their associated grammatical properties.

We shall briefly show how this unifying hypothesis provides an illuminating account of the salient morphosyntactic characteristics of early child English.

We'll begin by looking at morphological aspects of early English. As we saw in chapter 2, the *precategorial* stage in the child's development is characterized by the lack of any productive use of inflections. However, once the child enters the *categorial* phase of development (typically at around the age of 20 months ±20%), we begin to find productive use of some inflections. Our *lexical* analysis of early child grammars in (6) predicts that children will show evidence of beginning to acquire a set of *lexical* inflections (i.e. the inflections associated with lexical categories) at this stage, but no *functional* inflections (i.e. no inflections associated with functional categories). And indeed, there is abundant evidence that this is so: as we illustrated at length in chapter 2, children at this point are already beginning to make productive use of the noun plural $+s$ inflection and the verb progressive $+ing$ inflection (and may be making limited use of the verb perfective $+n$ inflection). Given the assumption (defended in Radford 1988a: 312–13) that $+ing$ and $+n$ are V-inflections, and that plural $+s$ is an N-inflection (cf. Radford 1988a: 59), the obvious conclusion to draw is that children at this stage have begun to acquire a set of *lexical* inflections (i.e. they have begun to acquire the inflectional properties of lexical categories).

However, there is parallel evidence that they have not yet acquired a set of *functional* inflections. For example, we saw in chapter 6 that children have no productive use of the I-inflections $+s/+d$ at this stage: we likewise argued in chapters 4 and 7 that children have not acquired a system of case inflections, and if we posit that case is an inflectional property of the D-system, then we might equivalently say that children have not yet acquired a set of D-inflections. Since complementizers are uninflected in English, it is clearly inappropriate to ask whether children have acquired C-inflections at this stage (though we saw in chapter 5 that there is no evidence of any C-system in early child English). The upshot of our discussion here is that we have abundant evidence that young children at this stage have acquired a set of N- and V-inflections (e.g. plural $+s$ and gerund $+ing$) but have not yet acquired the corresponding D- or I-inflections (i.e. they have not acquired the morphosyntax of case inflections, or of tense/agreement inflections). The fact that children have begun to acquire lexical but not *functional* inflections clearly provides strong morphological evidence in support of our overall hypothesis that the earliest categorial systems developed by young children are purely *lexical* in nature.

Given the lexical analysis in (6), we should expect to find parallel evidence that children have likewise begun to acquire the *syntactic* properties of lexical (though not functional) categories. We saw in chapter 3 that young children at this stage have indeed begun to acquire the syntax of lexical categories, and show evidence of 'knowing' how to project the four primary lexical categories (N, V, P, and A) into the corresponding phrasal categories. By contrast, in chapters 4–8, we presented considerable evidence that children have no 'knowledge' of the syntax of functional categories at this stage. We argued in chapter 4 that they have not yet acquired the syntax of the determiner system (hence their nonacquisition of the grammar of referential and possessive determiners); and in chapters 7 and 8, we argued that they have not yet acquired a case system (so that there are no case constraints on the distribution of overt or covert nominals or pronominals in early child English). Clearly, the nonacquisition of determiners and case are inter-related phenomena if we posit that case is an inherent property of the determiner system: we could then say that the absence of case constraints on (pro)nominals in early child English follows from the fact that case is a property of the D-system, and early child (pro)nominals have the status of NPs rather than DPs. In chapter 5, we argued that children at this stage have not yet acquired the syntax of the complementizer system (and in particular, have not acquired the syntax of complementizers, preposed auxiliaries, or preposed wh-expressions). In chapter 6, we went on to argue that they have likewise not acquired the syntax of the inflection system (hence their nonacquisition of the syntax of finite auxiliaries or infinitival *to*): in consequence of the absence of an I-system, we find no evidence of acquisition of nominative case-marking (chapter 7), and no functional (case/agreement) constraints on the use of 'missing arguments' (chapter 8). The overall conclusion to be drawn from our discussion is thus that children have acquired a system of lexical categories at this stage, but have not yet begun to acquire functional categories.

At this point, it is interesting to reflect on the overall organization of child grammars of English. A natural question to ask is: 'What is the range of modules operating in children's grammars during the earliest stages of their acquisition of English?' At the one-word stage when the child's speech is *agrammatical* (as we argued in chapter 2), it would seem likely that the only component which is (nonvacuously) operative in the child's grammar is the lexicon: at this point of development, the child is building up a store of lexical items, with each lexical entry comprising a set of phonological and semantic properties. However, given the absence of any morphosyntactic properties for lexical items at this stage, the child's early lexicon is clearly defective in character in comparison with its adult counterpart. It seems likely that other modules of grammar are inoperative (or vacuously operative) at this stage.

We might reasonably suppose that part of the semantic properties of vocabulary items which children acquire during the one-word stage relate to the *argument structure* of predicates. For example, part of what the child has to learn about the meaning of a word like *hit* is that it is a two-place predicate which expresses a relation between an AGENT argument and a PATIENT argument. Since the thematic properties of predicates are an inherent part of their meaning, it seems plausible to suppose that they are early-acquired; indeed, the tacit implication of the research by Greenfield and Smith (1976) is that even as early as the one-word stage, children have begun to master the argument structure of predicates. Some potential support for this claim comes from the fact that a number of comprehension studies (see e.g. Huttenlocher (1974), Sachs and Truswell (1978), and Miller, Chapman, Bronston and Reichle (1980)) have suggested that children at the one-word stage seem able to comprehend multi-word speech which encodes simple predicate + argument structures in which (e.g.) an ACTION predicate has an AGENT or PATIENT argument (e.g. 'Kiss dolly', etc.). The very fact that children at the one-word stage can comprehend simple predicate +

argument structures might lead us to conclude that they have (some) tacit knowledge of the argument structure of predicates. We might hypothesize that one of the reasons why they are able to comprehend but not produce multi-word utterances at this stage is the fact that they have not yet developed a set of morphosyntactic mechanisms which enable them to map (thematic) argument structures into (categorial) syntactic structures: indeed (as we argued in chapter 2), as yet they have no syntactic structures to map argument structures into, since the categorial component of their grammars is not yet operative.

At around the age of 20 months (±20%), children typically enter the *categorial* stage of their development, passing first through a *lexical* stage which generally seems to last for about three or four months. At this stage, we have evidence that they have acquired the four primary lexical categories (N, V, P, A), and that they 'know' how to project these into the corresponding single- and double-bar categories. Thus, it is at this point that the categorial component of the child's grammar becomes (nonvacuously) operative, as is suggested by the structural symmetry in the range of category systems which the child develops (noted in chapter 3). The child's lexicon also comes to have a richer structure, in that lexical entries now contain a specification of the idiosyncratic morphosyntactic properties of items (e.g. their categorial status and their morphological idiosyncrasies).

There are thus two modules which are now (nonvacuously) operative in the child's grammar, viz. the *lexicon* and the *categorial component*. Since the categorial component defines a class of syntactic structures which (*inter alia*) serve to 'express' the predicate–argument structures specified in the lexicon, it is clear that the child's grammar at this point must also contain an *interface* between the lexicon and the categorial component – that is, a set of mechanisms which map (thematic) argument structures into syntactic structures (as was suggested in our discussion at the end of chapter 2). Extending somewhat the use of the term *visibility* found in Chomsky (1981), Rizzi (1986), and Brody and Manzini (1988), let us use the term *visibility mechanism* to denote any mechanism which mediates a mapping from 'invisible' (thematic) argument structures into 'visible' (categorial) syntactic structures (we avoid using the alternative term *projection mechanism* here, since we have used the term *projection* throughout this book to refer to the endocentric relation between phrases and their heads, so that NP is a *projection* of N in this sense). The child's visibility mechanisms will have to determine *whether* and (if so) *how* arguments are made 'visible' by being projected into the syntax.

The question of *whether* a given argument of a given predicate is projected into the syntax or not will be determined by a *saturation mechanism* of some kind: this will specify whether a given theta-role can be *syntactically* saturated (and so projected into the syntax as an 'explicit' argument), or *lexically* saturated (and so not be projected into the syntax at all, remaining 'implicit'). We suggested in the previous chapter that during the period of early multi-word speech, children may freely alternate between lexical and syntactic saturation of theta-marked arguments, so that arguments are sometimes explicit, and sometimes implicit. Of course, the empirical validity of this claim is open to question; but what can surely not be called into question is the hypothesis that early child grammars of English incorporate some kind of saturation mechanism determining which arguments are (or are not) projected into the syntax.

Given that the saturation mechanism specifies only whether a given theta-marked argument can be implicit or explicit, clearly additional visibility mechanisms will be required to determine just *how* an explicit argument is projected into the syntax. The *projection mechanism* in the categorial component provides for two different positions which can be occupied by the arguments of a given head category X. One possibility is that arguments of X can be positioned internally within X-bar, and so function as *complements*; following Williams (1981), we might refer to complements as *internal arguments*. The second possibility is that an argument of X can be positioned externally to X-bar in the specifier position, and so function as a *subject*; in Williams' terminology, we might refer to such a constituent as an *external argument*. Given the assumption that specifiers are unique, then it follows that only one argument of a given predicate can be projected into the syntax as its external argument, and that the remaining arguments will accordingly be projected as internal arguments. Clearly, however, some *externalization* mechanism is required in order to determine which theta-marked argument of a predicate will be projected into the syntax as its (syntactic) external argument; once this has been determined, the remaining arguments of the predicate will be projected into the syntax as its *internal* arguments (i.e. as complements of X contained internally within X-bar). For example, in active transitive clauses containing a two-place predicate with AGENT and PATIENT arguments, it is characteristically the AGENT argument which is externalized (i.e. projected into subject position) in adult English, so that in a sentence such as 'Mary hit John', the AGENT is unambiguously identifiable as *Mary*.

In general, children seem to show evidence of having developed a *thematic* externalization mechanism at the lexical stage of their development (i.e. a mechanism which projects arguments into specific syntactic A-positions on the basis of their thematic function). For example, it is a commonplace observation in the acquisition literature that in simple active transitive structures involving a two-place predicate with AGENT and PATIENT arguments, typical children consistently position the AGENT before the predicate, and the PATIENT after it (cf. remarks to this effect made e.g. by Schlesinger 1971, Brown 1973, Bowerman 1973, Braine 1976, and many others). Examples of AGENT + PREDICATE + PATIENT structures of this type are given in (7) below:

(7)   (a)   *Hayley* draw boat. *Hayley* draw it. *Hayley* read that (Hayley 20)

      (b)   *Mummy* do it. *Bethan* do it. *Me* do it. *Bethan* do that. *Geraint* hit me. *Geraint* push me (Bethan 20–21)

      (c)   *Wayne* taken bubble (Daniel 21)

      (d)   *Helen* do it. *Mummy* do it. *Daddy* do it (*Helen 21)

      (e)   *Mommy* do it. *Baby* do it. No, *Lois* do it. *Kathryn* make this. *Kathryn* no fix this (*Kathryn 21–22)

      (f)   *Mommy* eat cookie. *Baby* eat cookies. *Baby* Allison comb hair. *Baby* open door. *Baby* ride truck. *Baby* drive truck. *Man* drive truck (*Allison 22)

      (g)   *Ashley* do pee...*Ashley* do poo. *Jem* do it with crayons. *Jem* draw orange. *Mummy* smack Jem. *Mummy* thrown it. *Jem* make big plops (Jem 23)

      (h)   *That* take hat (Claire 23: *that* = 'he')

      (i)   *Domenico* pull it. *Daddy* do grass (Domenico 24)

Within the theoretical framework we are adopting here, we can interpret the relevant facts as suggesting that in simple transitive structures, the (italicized) AGENT argument is uniformly externalized (i.e. projected into the syntactic subject position external to V-bar) and the PATIENT argument is uniformly internalized (i.e. projected into a complement position internal to V-bar). If this is so, then it suggeststhat the children concerned have developed a *uniform thematic externalization mechanism* (whereby e.g. explicit AGENTS are always externalized).

    Indeed, it may well be that the relevant mechanism is initially more *uniform* in the child's grammar than it is in adult grammars. For example, functional requirements may override thematic requirements in adult grammars, as we see from examples such as:

(8)   (a)   I broke the window

      (b)   *Broke the window

      (c)   The window broke

In (8)(a), we find the 'normal' pattern of the AGENT nominal *I* being externalized (= projected into subject position), and the PATIENT nominal *the window* being internalized (= being projected into complement position). However, in (8)(b), the AGENT role is lexically saturated, and so not projected into the syntax. In order to satisfy the functional requirement that there be a subject nominal for the nominative case assigned by (the head I of) the finite clause to be discharged onto, the PATIENT *the window* has to be externalized rather than internalized – hence the fact that *the window* is externalized in (8)(c). However, given that there are no functional systems (e.g. no case system) operating in early child English, there would clearly be no requirement in early child grammars for the PATIENT to be externalized in *ergative* structures such as (8)(b). If indeed the child has developed a *uniform* externalization/internalization mechanism at this stage (so that e.g. AGENTS are always externalized, and PATIENTS always internalized), we should expect to find that *ergative* structures for such children will show uniform internalization of PATIENT arguments. One child who may illustrate this phenomenon is Braine's son Jonathan, who at age 24 months produced structures such as the following (from Braine 1976: 34–5):

(9)   (a)   *Mommy* sit. *Daddy* sit. *Andrew* walk. *Daddy* walk. *Boy* walk. *Man* walk. *Daddy* work
       (b)   Hurt *Andrew*. Hurt *fly*. Hurt *knee*. Hurt *plane*. Hurt *hand*. Spilt *bread*. Spilt *raisin*. Bounce *ball*

Examples such as (9)(a) suggest that Andrew uniformly externalizes the italicized AGENT nominals. What is of more direct interest to us here, however, is the fact that in the (agentless) ergative examples in (9)(b), the italicized PATIENT nominal is uniformly internalized by Jonathan. In adult English, the functional requirement for a finite clause to have a subject for nominative case to be discharged onto would mean that the PATIENT argument would have to be externalized, so resulting in structures such as 'My knee hurts', 'The raisins have spilled', 'The ball bounces', etc. However, the child's visibility mechanism is 'blind' to such functional requirements at this stage (for the obvious reason that there are no functional systems operating in early child grammars of English), with the result that PATIENTS are uniformly internalized. The more general point to be underlined here is that the child's externalization mechanism at this stage is 'blind' to the functional requirements which regulate it in adult grammars.

However, it may not be the case that *all* children at the lexical stage of their development have a purely *thematic* externalization mechanism operating in their grammar. Particularly interesting in this respect is Melissa Bowerman's (1973) study of Kendall at ages 22–23 months (which we discussed briefly at the end of the previous chapter). The transcripts of Kendall's speech show that she positions (what in adult terms would appear to be) verbal objects not only postverbally, as in (10) below:

(10)   (a)   Look Kendall ('Look at Kendall')
      (b)   Writing book
      (c)   Break Fur-Book (name of book)
      (d)   Bite...finger

but also preverbally, as in (11) below:

(11)   (a)   Doggie sew ('Sew doggie')
      (b)   Kimmy kick ('Kick Kimmy')
      (c)   Kendall pick-up ('Pick up Kendall')
      (d)   Doggie lookit ('Look at doggie')

Likewise, she positions (what in adult terms would appear to be) subjects not only preverbally, as in (12) below:

(12)   (a)   Kendall bite
      (b)   Kimmy spit
      (c)   Kimmy running
      (d)   Mommy read

but also postverbally, as in:

(13)   (a)   Hug Mommy ('Mommy hugs')
      (b)   See Kendall ('Kendall sees')

(We also find what may be a parallel alternation with nominal complements, which may be either postnominal as in 'picture *Kendall*', or prenominal as in '*Kendall* picture', both structures being glossed by Bowerman 1973: 243 as 'picture of Kendall'.) In consequence, both [NP + V] and [V + NP] sequences in Kendall's speech are ambiguous as between whether the NP functions as a subject or complement – as illustrated by the examples in (14) below:

(14)   (a)   Mommy kiss ('Mommy kisses', or 'Kisses Mommy')
        (b)   Read Kendall ('Kendall reads' or 'Read to Kendall')
        (c)   Kendall hurt ('Something is hurting Kendall' or 'Kendall hurts')

The same pattern is found in structures containing both an overt subject and an overt complement: sometimes we find the order Subject + Verb + Object, as in (15) below:

(15)   (a)   Mommy...sew doggie
        (b)   Kimmy ride bike
        (c)   Kendall turn page
        (d)   Mommy pick-up...Kendall

while on other occasions we find the order Object + Verb + Subject, as in (16) below:

(16)   (a)   Mommy hit Kendall ('Kendall hit Mommy')
        (b)   Picture Mommy see Kendall (?= 'Kendall has seen the picture of Mommy')

The obvious question to ask is what exactly is going on here.

One possible analysis of the relevant facts would be to posit that preverbal 'objects' are actually (mis)positioned in superficial subject position, and that postverbal 'subjects' are likewise (mis)positioned in object position (we use the terms 'subject' and 'object' in inverted commas to denote expressions which would function as subjects/objects in the corresponding adult sentences). The advantage of this analysis would be that it would correctly predict that we always find the 'subject' and 'object' on opposite sides of the verb, so that if the 'subject' is preverbal, the 'object' is postverbal, whereas if the 'object' is preverbal, the 'subject' is postverbal. By contrast, any attempt to analyse preverbal 'objects' and postverbal 'subjects' as dislocated topics would wrongly predict that we should find the orders *Object* + Subject + Verb, and Verb + Object + *Subject* (where the italicized constituents would be dislocated topics). Moreover, such a dislocation analysis would require us to posit that Object + Verb + Subject structures like (16)(a) involve an unnecessarily complex structure containing multiply dislocated topics and multiple null resumptive arguments – a structure which we can represent informally as:

(17)   Mommy$_i$ e_j hit e_i Kendall$_j$

where e is an empty category functioning as a resumptive pronoun (so that (17) is paraphraseable in adult English as 'Mommy$_i$ *she$_j$* hit *her$_i$*, Kendall$_j$'). However, any such *multiple topic* analysis is open to precisely the same objections which we raised in relation to the multiple topic analysis of sentences with 'multiple missing arguments' in the previous chapter: for this reason, a simple *subject/object* analysis seems clearly preferable.

If our proposed *subject/object* analysis is along the right lines, then it follows that an AGENT argument which would be obligatorily externalized by adults in active transitive structures will sometimes be externalized by Kendall (as in (15)(d) *'Mommy* pick-up...Kendall'), and sometimes internalized (as in (16)(a) 'Mommy hit *Kendall*'): likewise, a PATIENT argument which would be obligatorily internalized by adults will sometimes be internalized by Kendall (as in (15)(a) 'Mommy sew *doggie*') and sometimes externalized (as in (11)(a) *'Doggie* sew'). This suggests that Kendall has not developed a *purely thematic* externalization mechanism. It may be that her grammar allows any theta-role assigned by a predicate X to be *freely* projected into any A-position within the maximal projection of X (an A-position being a subject or complement position): however, since most AGENTS are externalized and most PATIENTS internalized in the relevant samples of her speech, this is unlikely. A more plausible alternative is that factors other than thematic function control the externalization of arguments in Kendall's grammar (or can 'override' thematic externalization). One possibility here might be a factor which Fillmore (1977) refers to as the relative *salience* of arguments: it may be that the argument which is perceived to be most *salient* is 'focused' by being externalized. This might then be an overgeneralization of a pattern found in adult English with a restricted class of predicates (cf. alternations such as 'The weight of the snow broke the branches', and 'The branches broke under the weight of the snow'). Another possibility might be that it is the relative *informational content* of arguments which determines their externalization or internalization (e.g. the question of whether a given argument represents 'new' or 'given' information). There seems little point in speculating on what the relevant nonthematic factors might be, for the simple reason that the transcripts of Kendall's speech in the appendices to Bowerman (1973) provide us with insufficient data to decide. What is important from our point of view is that the *externalization* mechanism developed by Kendall does not seem to be a purely thematic one, but rather seems to incorporate some nonthematic mechanism (perhaps serving to 'override' the thematic mechanism which determines externalization and internalization in *unmarked* – i.e. 'ordinary' – structures).

What our discussion so far has suggested is that children at the *lexical* stage of their grammatical development have developed a set of *visibility mechanisms* which map argument structures into syntactic structures. One such mechanism is a *saturation mechanism* which determines whether or not a given theta-role is syntactically or lexically saturated (i.e. projected into the syntax or not). A second such mechanism is an *externalization mechanism* which (for 'explicit' arguments) determines which argument of a given predicate will be projected into the syntax as its external argument (i.e. subject). For most children at this stage, this mechanism seems to be a purely *thematic* one – that is, one which defines a unique mapping between specific theta-roles and specific A-positions in the syntax (so that (e.g.) explicit AGENTS are uniformly externalized). It may be, however, that some children like Kendall allow nonthematic factors to 'over-ride' the normal thematic externalization mechanism, so resulting in structures with non-canonical assignment of theta-roles.

A further type of visibility mechanism which seems to operate in early child grammars is a *linearization mechanism* (i.e. a mechanism which determines the order of arguments relative to their predicate and to each other). Bearing in mind that Travis (1984) and Koopman (1984) have argued that theta-marking is directional in adult grammars, one way of accounting for the relevant ordering facts found in the lexical category systems of early child English would be to posit that theta-marking is similarly inherently *directional* in early child grammars of English. More specifically, we might suggest that lexical heads theta-mark their subjects to the left, and their complements to the right. This would then provide a straightforward account of why specifiers precede and complements follow their heads in early child English (cf. Lebeaux 1988: 274–81 for a parallel suggestion that theta-marking is directional in child grammars). It would amount to claiming that children at this stage develop thematically based linearization principles. We might then say that *linearization* is a further visibility mechanism which operates in early child grammars.

In general, it would seem that the relevant linearization mechanism operates in a *uniform* fashion in early child grammars – hence the fact that in simple transitive structures involving a two-place predicate, we generally find the canonical order AGENT + PREDICATE + PATIENT, as in examples such as (7) above. However, if this is so, then we should also expect to find uniform thematic linearization of constituents in more complex structures containing three-place predicates. Unfortunately, however, there are relatively few examples of children at this stage making productive use of three-place predicate structures – that is, structures in which a predicate has a single external argument and two internal arguments (hence excluding structures like 'Danny want coat on', which contain a two-place predicate *want* whose arguments are the nominal *Danny* and the Small Clause complement [*coat on*]). Examples of potential three-place structures are given below (all but the fourth one have a 'missing' subject argument):

(18)   (a)   Get Mommy juice. Pour Mommy juice (*Allison 22)
        (b)   Give me lorry. Her bringing me more. Give you more
                knickers (Jem 21–23)
        (c)   Giving her drink (Anne 24)

Although the data sample here is clearly too small to base any firm conclusions on, it is interesting to note that the GOAL argument is consistently positioned before the PATIENT argument, suggesting that the linearization of the internal arguments is thematically determined in a uniform way.

The overall conclusion to be drawn from our discussion so far is that early child grammars of English comprise a *lexicon*, a *categorial component*, and a set of *visibility mechanisms* which map argument structures into syntactic structures (i.e. they determine thematic saturation, and the externalization, and linearization of arguments). Indeed, we might suggest that what characterizes the transition from single-word utterances to multi-word utterances is precisely the development of such mapping mechanisms in the child's grammar. The relevant visibility mechanisms might be said to be inherently *lexical* in nature, in the sense that they map argument structures into purely *lexical* syntactic structures (i.e. structures which comprise only constituents belonging to lexical categories).

However, if it is indeed the case that the visibility mechanisms in early child grammars are purely *lexical* in nature, then it follows that these mechanisms differ from their adult counterparts in an important respect, since some of the visibility mechanisms which operate in adult grammars are *functional* rather than lexical in nature. One such functional visibility mechanism which is operative in adult grammars relates to case-marking. For example, in an adult English sentence such as:

(19)   *I* shot *him*

the AGENT is identified as *I* and the PATIENT as *him* (partly) in consequence of the fact that the former carries nominative case and the latter objective case. For obvious reasons, we might refer to case-marking as a *direct* visibility mechanism (in the sense that the thematic role of a DP is directly reflected in its case morphology). Since *case* is a functional property carried by a functional category (= DP), case mechanisms are clearly *functional* in nature. A second functional mechanism by which the thematic function of arguments is made visible (in cases of so-called 'indirect theta-marking') is by the use of 'dummy' prepositions which serve to '*transmit*' a theta-role from a predicate to an argument which it cannot itself directly theta-mark. We can illustrate this second visibility mechanism in terms of a nominal such as that in (20) below:

(20)   the destruction *of* the city

Let us assume (following Emonds 1985) that nouns cannot directly theta-mark their complements, but rather must do so *indirectly* via the use of a preposition. If this is so, then the function of the italicized preposition *of* in (20) would be to 'transmit' the PATIENT theta-role assigned by the noun *destruction* to its complement DP [*the city*], so enabling the noun to theta-mark its complement *indirectly* (via the use of the preposition). In this use, *of* appears to be a 'dummy' preposition, in the sense that it lacks independent semantic or thematic content: this might suggest that *of* (in this use) is essentially a *functor* of some kind (we might assign it to the category K of case particles posited in Abney 1987). In addition to serving the function of transmitting the theta-role assigned by the predicate *destruction* to its PATIENT argument *the city*, the prepositional functor *of* also serves the function of case-marking the latter, so satisfying the functional requirement that a DP like *the city* in adult English must carry case; indeed, we might suppose that the case assigned to *the city* serves to make the thematic role of the latter visible (in an abstract sense). While (as we have seen) English makes use of both *direct* (via case) and *indirect* (via prepositions) functional visibility mechanisms, this does not appear to be true of all languages: for example, in Japanese there would seem to be no use of the case mechanism, with the result that all theta-marking is 'indirect', and involves the use of a postpositional functor of an appropriate kind (e.g. the clitic postposition -*o* serves to transmit a theta role from a transitive verb to its primary internal argument).

However, neither functional visibility mechanism seems to have been acquired in early child grammars of English. Thus, the fact that there is no case system operating in early child grammars of English (as we argued in chapter 7) means that children have not yet developed a mechanism for making theta-marking *directly* visible through case-marking. Moreover, the fact that children use 'bare' (i.e. prepositionless)

NPs as direct complements of nouns and intransitive verbs (so resulting in NPs such as 'picture *mummy*' and VPs such as 'go *shops*', as we also saw in chapter 7) means that they have likewise not developed a mechanism of 'indirect' theta-marking involving the use of the 'dummy' prepositional functors like *of.* On the contrary, it would seem that predicates theta-mark their arguments *directly* in early child English, without the mediation of functional visibility mechanisms. Nor does this seem to be a characteristic solely of early child grammars of *English*. As we noted in chapter 7, numerous studies of other languages have shown that children (roughly) under two years of age typically have no mastery of case-marking mechanisms. Moreover, it is interesting to note that Ito (1988: 51) reports that in the acquisition of Japanese, there is an initial period in which children 'never use' postpositional functors like *-ga* and *-o*: if these postpositions function as indirect theta-markers, what this amounts to (in our terms) is the claim that there is no acquisition of the mechanism of indirect theta-marking in early child grammars of Japanese. Thus, it seems quite likely that our hypothesis that early child grammars of English show no (direct or indirect) functional visibility mechanisms may be of more general validity.

The overall conclusion to be drawn from our discussion here is that children at the lexical stage of their grammatical development make use of purely *lexical* visibility mechanisms – that is, mechanisms which project thematic argument structures into purely lexical syntactic structures (e.g. saturation, externalization, and linearization mechanisms). They have not developed functional visibility mechanisms at this stage (i.e. mechanisms which project argument structures into functional structures), and thus (e.g.) have no case-marking mechanisms for making theta-roles visible: since case is a property of DP, the absence of any functional visibility mechanism for mapping arguments into case-marked DPs follows from our more general hypothesis that early child grammars of English are purely *lexical* in character.

Our discussion here echoes the suggestion made at the end of chapter 2 that the earliest utterances produced by young children are *lexical-thematic* structures: that is, they are simple (and generally uniform) mappings of thematic structures (i.e. structures comprising a predicate and a set of theta-marked arguments) into lexical syntactic structures. If syntactic structures are simple projections of thematic structures at this stage, then it follows that the only elements present in the syntactic structures will be thematic constituents (in the technical sense defined at the end of chapter two). If only lexical categories are purely thematic (in the relevant sense), then it follows that early child syntactic structures will comprise only *lexical* categories.

If our reasoning here is along the right lines, every A-position (i.e. subject or complement position) in the child's syntax is a projection of some theta-marked argument – i.e. every A-position is a *thematic* position. Furthermore, given our arguments in chapter 7 that there is no case system operating in early child grammars of English, all A-positions in child grammars will be *caseless* positions. Now, if A-positions are theta-marked but not case-marked in early child English, then it follows that they are licensed by theta-marking principles, but not by case-marking principles. This in turn means that in early child English, a constituent is licensed to occur in a given A-position only if assigned an appropriate theta-role. Lebeaux (1988: 39) reaches a similar conclusion (by a different route), suggesting that 'Throughout stage I speech, it is direct theta role assignment, rather than assignment of (abstract) case, which is regulating the appearance of arguments'. If constituents are licensed to occur in A-positions purely by theta-marking principles at this stage, then we should expect to find that the only A-positions found in early child grammars are theta-marked positions.

This conclusion has far-reaching consequences, since it means that early child grammars of English differ in important respects from their adult counterparts: the reason is that it is generally held that some classes of lexical predicate do not theta-mark their subjects in English (e.g. *weather* predicates, *raising* predicates, and *passive* predicates). For instance, in structures like (21) below involving *weather* predicates:

(21)   (a)   *It* never snows in Zaire
        (b)   *It* rains a lot in Manchester

the conventional assumption is that the italicized pronominal subject DP *it* is nonthematic (i.e. it is not assigned a theta-role by the weather predicate *snow/rain*), and nonreferential in nature (as we see from the fact that its reference cannot be questioned by *what?*, and from the fact that it cannot be replaced by a referring expression like *the sky*): on the contrary, the pronoun *it* here is a purely *expletive* (i.e. 'pleonastic' or 'dummy') element inserted to satisfy the functional requirement for the nominative case assigned to the subject of a finite clause to be 'discharged' onto a DP (in this case, onto the 'dummy' pronominal DP *it*).

In much the same way, it is generally held that so-called *raising* predicates like *seem* do not theta-mark their subjects (hence the possibility of a 'pleonastic' *it* subject in structures like 'It seems that...'). In consequence of this, the nonthematic subject position with such verbs can serve as the landing-site for a moved theta-marked DP, resulting in structures such as:

(22)   *He* seems [$_{AP}$ --- proud of her]

where the italicized pronominal DP *he* originates as the subject of (and is theta-marked by) the A-bar *proud of her*, and then is 'raised' to become the subject of *seem*: because *seem* does not theta-mark its subject, there is no violation of the requirement imposed by the *Theta Criterion* that 'Each argument bears one and only one θ–role' (Chomsky 1981: 36).

It is generally thought that passive predicates resemble raising predicates in that they likewise do not theta-mark their subjects; this in turn means that passive subject position can serve as the landing-site for a moved thematic DP, so resulting in structures such as that bracketed in (23) below:

(23)   We don't want [*this document* seen --- by anyone]

The italicized DP here arguably originates as the underlying object of (and is theta-marked by) the passive verb *seen*, but can move into the italicized passive subject position precisely because this is a nonthematic position (so that 'passivization' will not result in the moved constituent being doubly theta-marked).

The overall conclusion to be drawn from our (brief and informal) discussion here is that both *expletive* (i.e. 'pleonastic' or 'dummy') subjects and *moved* (i.e. 'raised' or 'passivized') subjects in adult English can occur only in *nonthematic* subject positions. Now, if we are correct in supposing that the only A-positions found in early child grammars of English are *thematic* positions (since an argument in a given A-position is licensed only if appropriately theta-marked), then it follows that we should expect to find that there are no *expletive* or *moved* subjects in early child grammars. It is interesting to note in this respect that Hyams (1986: 63) claims that early child English is characterized by 'a notable lack of...expletive pronouns'. We can illustrate this phenomenon in terms of the following dialogue:

(24)   ADULT: It's raining
        CHILD: Raining (Jenny 22)

We might suppose that the nonthematic expletive pronoun *it* in the adult sentence is required essentially for functional case-marking purposes (e.g. to provide a pronominal DP onto which the nominative case assigned by the finite I heading the clause can be discharged). However, the child has no case system, and so has no need for an expletive subject: indeed, if only theta-marked arguments are licensed to occur in A-positions in early child English, it follows that a nonthematic expletive subject will not be licensed to occur in subject position in the child's sentence, so that the occurrence of a subject is excluded in principle for a predicate which does not assign an external theta-role – i.e. which does not theta-mark its specifier. (Of course, this line of reasoning raises the question of whether the child 'knows' that a weather predicate does not theta-mark its specifier; presumably if the child were to misanalyse adult structures such as 'It rains' as containing a thematic subject, we would expect to find utterances like 'Sky raining', 'Clouds rain' with thematic subjects; the fact that these are not attested – in my own data, at least – might suggest that children may indeed 'know' that weather predicates do not assign an external theta-role.)

As noted above, a second prediction made by our claim that all A-positions in early child English are theta-marked is that there will be no movement of constituents from one A-position to another in early child English, since any such movement will result in multiple theta-marking of the moved constituent (in violation of the *Theta Criterion*). Since both 'raising' and 'passivization' are instances of movement from one A-position to another, we should expect to find that neither type of movement occurs in early child grammars of English. There are two sets of facts which would seem to bear out this prediction. The first is that none of the children in my corpus who were at the 'lexical' stage of development showed any productive use of what might plausibly be analysed as 'raising' or 'passive' structures – nor am I aware of reports in the literature of children at the *lexical* stage of development making productive use of such structures. The second is that data from comprehension experiments (although complex to interpret) suggest that young children at this stage are unable to parse reversible passive structures correctly (cf. e.g. Fraser, Bellugi and Brown (1963); Bever (1970); De Villiers and De Villiers (1973b); Maratsos (1974)). Indeed, such children frequently misparse sentences like 'The lion was chased by the tiger' and misanalyse the superficial subject (*the lion*) as the AGENT: this fact would seem to suggest that they treat passive subject position as a thematic position; and this in turn would bear out our suggestion that all A-positions are *thematic* positions in early child grammars of English.

The more general conclusion to be drawn from the fact that children have not acquired 'passive' or 'raising' structures at this stage would seem to be that there is no A-movement in early child grammars of English (i.e. there are no structures in which a constituent moves from one A-position into another A-position). This conclusion echoes that reached (via a rather different route) by Borer and Wexler (1987: 147), namely that one of the defining characteristics of early child grammars is 'the absence from the early grammar of A-chains'. Within the framework presented here, the absence of A-movement structures in the speech of children at the *lexical* stage of development is a direct consequence of the assumption that all A-positions in the child's syntax are thematic positions: movement from one A-position to another would result in multiple theta-marking of the moved constituent, so leading to a violation of the *Theta Criterion* (as we have seen).

Thus, the lexical analysis presented here provides a principled account of why we find no A-movement constructions like 'raising' or 'passivization' in early child English. However, it would seem that there is a second type of movement operation found in adult English which is likewise not found in early child English – a type of movement which we shall refer to as *F-movement*. By this, we mean movement into an F-position, i.e. a head or specifier position within a functional category system. For example, verbs like *have/be* are raised out of V into I in adult English, but not in early child English; the specifier of VP can be raised into the specifier position within IP in adult English, but not in child English; an 'inverted' auxiliary moves from I to C in adult English, but there is no such 'inversion' in child English; a preposed wh-phrase is moved into the specifier position within CP in adult English, but not in early child English; and possessor phrases are moved from the specifier position within NP into the specifier position within DP in adult English, but not in child English. Why should such F-movement operations be found in adult grammars, but not in early child grammars of English? The answer provided by the *lexical* analysis of early child grammars presented here is that there is no F-movement in early child grammars precisely because there are no F-positions to serve as landing-sites for moved constituents – for the obvious reason that there are no functional category systems in the child's grammar at this stage.

Thus, we are arguing that there is no A-movement or F-movement in early child grammars of English because there are no nonthematic A-positions and no F-positions to serve as landing-sites for movement constituents. It seems clear that the absence of F-positions and nonthematic A-positions are not unrelated facts. Bearing in mind that functional categories are nonthematic and do not assign theta-roles to their specifiers, then it follows that F-positions are intrinsically *nonthematic*.

By contrast, we might hypothesize that the earliest lexical category systems developed by young children are intrinsically *thematic*, in the sense that each constituent within a given lexical category system will theta-mark or be theta-marked by any sister constituent which it has – hence (as we have seen) there are no nonthematic A-positions in early child English. If it is the case that the earliest structures developed by young children are purely *thematic structures*, then this implies (*inter alia*) that the only heads (i.e. word-level constituents) found in early child grammars will be *thematic* heads. Given the assumption that functional heads are nonthematic, it follows that there will be no *functional* heads in early child grammars, hence no D, C, or I constituents. It also follows (e.g.) that the only prepositions which children will use at this stage will be *thematic* prepositions, i.e. those which themselves directly theta-mark their complements (e.g locative *in*, *on*, etc.), and hence which are capable of functioning as predicates in Small Clauses; conversely, it also follows that we will find no evidence of acquisition of *nonthematic* prepositions like 'dummy *of*' (hence the fact that *of* is systematically 'missing' in child structures such as *cup tea*, *drink water*, *picture Mummy*, etc.). The claim that the earliest syntactic structures produced by young children are purely *thematic* in nature also implies that the only A-positions (i.e. specifier/complement positions) found in early child grammars will be theta-marked positions (hence the absence of nonthematic A-positions).

If it is true that the earliest syntactic structures developed by young children are purely *thematic* in nature (a claim implicit in the earlier work on 'semantically based child grammars' briefly discussed at the end of chapter 2), then this means that children's structures will comprise only thematic heads and thematic arguments. Now, given that both A-movement and F-movement are movement into *nonthematic* positions, then the absence of such nonthematic positions in early child grammars provides a straightforward account of the absence of these two types of movement operation. Thus, the analysis of early child syntax as purely thematic in nature seems to have considerable empirical support. (It should be noted that the *thematic* analysis raises some purely technical problems relating to the treatment of adjuncts: however, these can be overcome in a variety of ways which we shall not digress into considering here.)

Now if neither *A-movement* nor *F-movement* operations are found at this stage, then the strongest conclusion which we could reach would be to posit that there are *no moved constituents* at all in early child grammars of English. This in turn would mean that the *transformational module* would be inoperative in early child grammars, with the obvious consequence that all of the structures found in early child English would be base-generated constructions, with no evidence of constituents moving from one position to another: indeed, this assumption is a traditional one which dates back more than two decades, as we see from the remark by McNeill (1966) that 'It is not unreasonable to think of children talking base strings directly'. If the transformational module were inoperative in early child grammars, then this in turn would mean that the *bounding* module (which limits the distance that constituents can move in any single movement) could not be (nonvacuously) operative. Indeed, since we have earlier suggested that the *case* and *binding* modules are likewise inoperative in early child grammars (since the case and binding properties of nominals are determined by a D-system not yet acquired), the overall conclusion we would reach would be that there would only be three components (nonvacuously) operative at this stage, namely the lexicon, the categorial component and an interface between the two (the latter containing, *inter alia*, a set of visibility mechanisms mapping argument structures into syntactic structures).

However, one complication posed by this trimodular conception of early child grammars (implying that there is no transformational component, and hence that there are no movement operations) is that we have to reconcile it with the observation that (as we noted in chapter 5) some children at the (late) lexical stage produce utterances like '*What* daddy doing?' in which the italicized wh-complement *what* might seem to have been preposed into clause-initial position. If such structures involve *movement* of the initial wh-constituent *what* from postverbal position to clause-initial position, then clearly we cannot rule out all forms of movement in early child grammars. However, there are a number of points which need to be noted in this regard (echoing the relevant discussion in chapter 5). Firstly, such structures seem to be *semiformulaic* in nature, so that it is not clear in what sense they are the result of a *productive* syntactic movement rule. Secondly, even if the relevant wh-structures were purely categorial in nature, it is not clear that they would be best analysed as involving *movement*, rather than (as suggested in chapter 5) a base-generated clause-initial topic phrase base-generated as an adjunct to VP, and an empty NP (= *np*) in postverbal object position which has a reprise function (the reference of the empty NP would be potentially unrestricted, but the sentence would clearly receive no coherent interpretation unless the empty NP concerned were construed as 'referring back to' the topic phrase). What makes the 'movement' analysis even more implausible is the fact that although *wh-movement* is an unbounded rule in adult English, there is absolutely no evidence whatever of 'movement' of wh-phrases across a potentially unbounded domain in early child English – such 'movement' as there may seem to be is always clause-internal, and never involves 'movement' across a clause boundary (a fact which might suggest that no movement is involved).

A final query which we might raise about a movement analysis of structures such as '*What* Daddy doing?' is whether or not movement operations of this kind (or indeed of any kind) would be licensed in early child grammars of English. As we noted in chapter 5, if such structures do involve movement, the kind of movement involved is arguably *adjunction* of the moved wh-NP to the overall VP (= verbal Small Clause) structure. Now, while it is clear that the *lexical-thematic* analysis of early child grammars proposed here excludes A-movement and F-movement operations in principle, it might seem at first sight as if it does not exclude in principle operations involving *adjunction* of a moved constituent to a lexical maximal projection – and indeed, Guilfoyle and Noonan (1988) assume that this type of adjunction is licensed as a movement operation in early child grammars of English.

However, there is some reason to suppose that *wh-movement* would not be licensed in early child grammars. For one thing, the trace of a moved wh-phrase is a case-marked variable; and yet, we argued in chapter 7 that there is no case system in early child grammars. More generally, it seems likely that conventional *trace* movement rules (i.e. movement rules which leave behind an empty trace which is coindexed with the moved constituent) would not be licensed in early child grammars of English. The reason is that the indices carried by moved nominals and their traces are referential indices which serve to identify their *binding* properties; yet we argued in chapter 4 that the binding properties of nominals are carried by their D-system, and that children have no 'awareness' of these binding properties at this stage. Thus, if the referential indices carried by moved nominals and their traces are carried by a D-system not yet acquired, then it follows that there can be *no coindexed movement chains at all* in early child English (not even chains resulting from adjunction of an NP to a lexical phrasal category like VP). Now it seems reasonable to suppose that Universal Grammar imposes the strong requirement that all *movement* operations in natural language involve coindexation of the moved constituent and its traces (for the obvious reason that the *Projection Principle* requires a moved constituent to leave a 'trace' behind, and the trace can never be interpreted as referring to any constituent other than the one which has moved). This being so, then it follows from our argumentation here that there cannot in principle be any movement rules of any kind in early child grammars of English, since movement involves assignment of referential indices (to moved constituents and their traces), and these referential indices are arguably a property of a D-system not yet acquired.

Thus, the concluding hypothesis which we have arrived at is that early child grammars of English are direct (and generally uniform) mappings of thematic argument structures into lexical syntactic structures, the mapping being mediated by a set of *visibility* mechanisms (which include mechanisms of *saturation, externalization, linearization,* etc.). If we posit that all A-positions are theta-marked at this stage, then it follows that there cannot in principle be A-movement chains (formed by movement of a constituent from one A-position to another), since this would involve movement from one thematic position to another, and so lead to violation of the *Theta Criterion.* Moreover, given that there are no functional category systems operating in the child's grammar at this stage, it follows for self-evident reasons that there can likewise be no F-movement chains (involving movement into the head or specifier position within a functional category system). More generally still, if we posit that DP is the locus of the binding properties of nominals, it follows from the absence of a D-system in early child grammars that no movement chains whatever can be formed at this stage, since such chains would involve coindexation of the moved constituent and its trace (and the relevant referential coindices are a property of a D-system not yet acquired). In addition, given our earlier hypothesis that case is an intrinsic property of the D-system, it follows that there cannot in principle be case constraints on the distribution of nominals.

Our overall conclusion is that the earliest stage of grammatical development in young children is a lexical-thematic stage in which thematic argument structures are directly mapped into lexical syntactic structures. However, since the ultimate goal of Linguistics is not mere *description* but rather the more daunting task of *explanation,* this raises the question of *why* early child grammars should be purely lexical-thematic systems – a question which we turn to address in our next (and last) chapter.

10

Explanations and Implications

The evidence we have presented in chapters 3–9 has led us to the generalization that early child grammars of English are *lexical-thematic* systems in which thematic argument structures are directly mapped into lexical syntactic structures. If this is so, then the task which now faces us is that of *explaining* the generalization which we have arrived at. In other words, we now need to address the question of *why* lexical-thematic systems should come into operation before functional-nonthematic systems in early child grammars. In this chapter, we shall explore a variety of possible answers to this question, and consider the implications of each of the proposed explanations.

One type of explanation which might be offered is along the following lines. We might speculate that the linguistic properties of items belonging to functional categories make such items more difficult to learn than those belonging to lexical categories: for this reason (we might suppose), functional items are acquired later than their lexical counterparts. If the initial stage of categorial development in child speech involves the categorization (and projection) of the existing items in the child's vocabulary, and if the earliest items which the child learns all belong to lexical categories, then it is clear why lexical category systems develop before functional ones. However, any such proposed 'explanation' of the relative order of acquisition of lexical and functional categories clearly requires us to be able to identify just what are the linguistic properties of functional items which make them more difficult to learn. We might conjecture that both the *formal* (i.e. morphophonosyntactic) and the *semantic* properties of functional items lead to delayed learning.

Consider first how the formal properties of functional items might make them more difficult to acquire than items belonging to lexical categories. We might conjecture that the formal properties of items belonging to lexical categories are more readily identifiable on the basis of limited linguistic experience than those of items belonging to functional categories. However, in order for any such proposed 'explanation' to have potential empirical content, we need to ask what the concrete linguistic correlates are of *identifiability*. One possible factor which might be appealed to here is a *phonological* one: thus (as noted by Abney 1987: 64–5), items belonging to lexical categories generally have a more salient (hence readily identifiable) phonological form than items belonging to functional categories: whereas the former typically contain a potentially stressed syllable, functors by contrast 'are generally stressless, often clitics or affixes, and sometimes even phonologically null' (Abney, ibid.). Now, there have been frequent suggestions in the acquisition literature to the effect that the earliest items acquired by children are those which are most 'acoustically salient': if we follow Gleitman and Wanner (1982: 17) in supposing that the relative acoustic saliency of different items is manifested in *stress* (so that stressed items are more salient than unstressed items), then we should expect to find that stressed items are acquired before unstressed ones (cf. McNeill 1966: 19 for a similar suggestion). If it is the case that items belonging to lexical categories carry (potential) stress, whereas those belonging to functional categories are generally unstressed, then the relative phonological salience of the two classes of item may be an additional factor in accounting for the observed order of acquisition.

In additional to *phonological* factors, it may well be that *morphological* factors also conspire to make items belonging to lexical categories more readily identifiable than those belonging to functional categories. More specifically, we might argue that items belonging to lexical categories generally show greater morphophonological uniformity both in their stem form, and in their inflectional properties. Thus, items belonging to lexical categories typically have a unique stem-form, whereas those belonging to functional categories may have a variable stem-form: for example, the noun 'cat' has the sole allomorph /kat/, whereas the determiners 'a' and 'the' have a variety of allomorphs, so that 'a' may surface as /eɪ/, /ə/, or /an/, and 'the' as /ðə/ or /ði/. Thus, the greater morphophonological stem-uniformity of items belonging to lexical categories might lead us to expect that children acquire lexical categories before functional ones. In a similar vein, we might argue that lexical categories tend to have more transparent (i.e. more readily identifiable) inflectional properties than their functional counterparts. For example, virtually all nouns in English take the plural +*s* or genitive *'s* inflection; and virtually all verbs take the gerund +*ing* inflection. By contrast, functional categories tend to have more *opaque* inflectional properties: for example, the determiners *this/that* have irregular plural forms (*these/ those*), and lack possessive forms (cf. **that's*, etc.): the singular–plural relation (if indeed it is such) is even more opaque in the determiner pair *much/many*; moreover, other determiners like *a/the/some/any* etc. simply don't inflect for number at all. Thus, we might say that lexical categories tend to have a relatively transparent morphological structure, whereas functional categories tend to have an opaque morphological structure. Given that inflectional morphology provides a major clue to the categorial status of items, it would seem reasonable to suppose that children find it 'easier' (from a morphological perspective, at any rate) to identify the categorial status of items with a transparent morphological structure than those with an opaque morphological structure.

A further factor which may make it more difficult for the child to identify the linguistic properties of items belonging to functional categories might be a *syntactic* one, in that functional categories are often subject to complex syntactic restrictions on their distribution which are not applicable to lexical categories. We can illustrate these distributional differences by comparing two different types of nominal premodifier, namely determiners (a *functional* category) and adjectives (a *lexical* category). We find that determiners are typically subject to complex restrictions on the types of nominal with which they can combine: for example, a determiner such as *enough* can combine with a singular noncount noun or a plural count noun, but not with a singular count noun (cf. *enough equipment, enough tools, *enough tool*); conversely a determiner such as *a(n)* can combine with a singular count noun, but not with a singular noncount noun or a plural count noun (cf. *a tool, *an equipment, *a tools*). By contrast, adjectives are not subject to this kind of distributional constraint, as we see from the fact that an adjective like *useful* can combine with all three types of nominal (cf. *a useful tool, useful tools, useful equipment*). Thus, the fact that items belonging to functional (but not lexical) categories may be subject to complex syntactic constraints on their distribution (i.e. on the types of constituent they can combine with) is likely to make them more difficult to acquire than items belonging to lexical categories.

The guiding intuition behind the line of reasoning adopted in the three immediately preceding paragraphs is the supposition that we can explain why functional categories are acquired after lexical ones in terms of the greater formal complexity of functional items. The tacit assumption is that the greater *morphophonosyntactic* complexity of functional items means that their acquisition requires exposure to a far greater body of linguistic experience over a longer period of time than for items belonging to lexical categories. What this amounts to (in simple terms) is the claim that functional items are harder to *learn* because of their greater formal complexity (in particular, their 'irregularity'). However, a *learning* account of the differential development of lexical and functional category systems is problematic both from an empirical point of view, and from a psycholinguistic point of view. From the empirical viewpoint, the obvious problem faced by such an account is the fact that many irregular items in English are early acquired – for example, the verb *go*, or the noun *man*. It is clear that 'irregularity' poses a problem for children, but this does not usually result in a failure to acquire 'irregular' items, but rather an attempt to *regularize* them (so that a noun like *man* will be given an overgeneralized plural form like *mans*). Thus, linguistic irregularity does not automatically result in *delayed acquisition* – a fact which calls into question the viability of attributing the late acquisition of functional items to the supposed 'learning difficulties' caused by their 'irregularity'. In addition to empirical objections to the *learning* account, we can also adduce psycholinguistic objections. As Atkinson (1989: 38) notes: 'Well-known arguments of Fodor (1975, 1980, 1981) militate against this approach. If learning is to be viewed as hypothesis testing, the hypotheses must be available to be tested, and Fodor's conclusion that a "more expressive" system cannot develop out of a "less expressive" one by this mechanism follows.'

However, if it is not entirely plausible to explain the relative order of acquisition of lexical and functional items in terms of their relative *formal* complexity, we might alternatively attempt to invoke their relative *semantic complexity* as an important explanatory factor. In particular, we might suppose that items belonging to functional categories have more complex (and more abstract) semantic properties than those belonging to lexical categories, and in consequence are acquired later. Brown and Fraser (1963) speculated along similar lines: they argued that items can be divided up into two classes on the basis of their semantic properties, namely (i) *contentives* and (ii) *functors*. Contentives (they claim) are morphemes which have a relatively 'concrete' semantic content, whereas functors are items with a more 'abstract' meaning, and which fulfil an essentially 'grammatical' function. They argue that children acquire contentives before functors precisely because contentives have a more 'concrete' meaning which is more readily identifiable by the child. Since, by and large, contentives belong to *lexical* categories and 'functors' to *functional* categories, it follows that we should expect lexical categories to be acquired before functional ones.

In a rather similar vein, Hyams (1986: 82) concedes that relative semantic complexity may be one reason why functional modal I constituents are acquired later than simple lexical V constituents; in this connection, she writes:

> ...Modals are semantically or conceptually more complex than verbs. Although relative semantic or conceptual complexity is not easy to characterise, it seems intuitively plausible that modalities such as obligation (*must*), ability (*can*), futurity (*will*), are more difficult for the child than verbs, which signal actions (*sit*), perceptions (*see*), desires (*want*), etc. To understand the modals, the child must be able to conceptualise possible (or future), but presently non-existing situations... An account along semantic-conceptual lines might provide insight into the late appearance of modals relative to verbs like the above... (Hyams 1986: 82)

If (more generally) it is indeed the case that relative semantic complexity is a major factor in determining order of acquisition of vocabulary items, then we should expect to find that the earliest items acquired by the child will have 'concrete' rather than 'abstract' meanings.

Interestingly, there does seem to be some empirical support for this claim. For example, if we look at the earliest vocabulary items used by Allison Bloom (as reflected in the transcripts of her speech at ages 16 and 19 months), we find that her lexicon comprises (i) items denoting physical objects (*cookie, cow, horse, car, chair*, etc.); (ii) items denoting actions (*tumble, cover, turn, scrub*, etc.); (iii) items denoting spatial relations (*down, up, off, on*, and *over*), and (iv) items denoting attributes (*big, small, dirty*, and *clean*). If we posit that all of the relevant items have a readily identifiable 'concrete' meaning, then it follows that they are *contentives* in the sense of Brown and Fraser (1963). Now, it turns out that *contentive* items of this kind generally belong to the four major lexical categories in adult speech: e.g. items denoting physical objects are typically nouns, those denoting action are typically verbs, those denoting spatial relations are typically prepositions, and those denoting attributes are typically adjectives. Thus, if categorization initially applies to items in the child's existing vocabulary, and if (because of their relative conceptual simplicity) the earliest vocabulary items acquired are contentive items which belong to lexical categories in adult speech, then it is scarcely surprising that the earliest categories which children acquire should be lexical categories. If we appeal to 'semantic complexity' as a factor in determining the order of acquisition of items (and hence of categories), we are implicitly invoking *cognitive immaturity* as the relevant explanatory factor (since we are in effect saying that children lack the cognitive capacity to handle the relevant abstract concepts). However, what weakens this kind of 'explanation' is the absence of any reliable language-independent way of determining empirically the child's cognitive capacity at any given stage of development, the imprecision and vagueness of cognitivist proposals, and the consequent lack of *predictive* power for the associated theory (e.g. existing cognitive theories make no precise predictions about whether the modal *may* will be acquired earlier or later than the determiner *the*). We might be tempted to follow Atkinson (1982: 205) in concluding that attempts to explain aspects of linguistic development in terms of cognitive development have hitherto been characterized by 'a remarkable lack of awareness of the complexities involved in approaching this relationship'.

Given the potential pitfalls of both *learning* and *cognitive* explanations of the development of early child grammars, we might explore the alternative possibility of developing a *teleological* explanation for the child's grammatical development. In other words, we might argue that it is in the nature of the structure of the grammatical system being acquired (itself determined by properties of UG) that some parts of the system must already be 'in place' before others can develop. Within this general line of reasoning, we might argue that it follows from properties of UG that lexical category systems must already be 'in place' before functional category systems can develop. In this connection, it is interesting to consider the inter-relationship between lexical and functional categories in adult English. By way of illustration, consider an adult English nominal such as that bracketed in (1) below:

(1)   I have never seen [*so awful a portrait of the queen*]

Given the arguments in Radford (1989), the bracketed nominal in (1) will have the simplified superficial structure (2) below:

(2)   [$_{DP}$ so awful [$_{D}$ a] [$_{NP}$ [$_{N}$ portrait] of the queen]]

The overall bracketed nominal in (1) thus has the dual phrasal status of an NP contained within a DP. However, there is an intuitive sense in which the bracketed sequence in (1) is one phrasal constituent rather than two (hence the fact that in earlier work the overall bracketed sequence would have been analysed as a single noun phrase constituent). There are a variety of ways of capturing this intuition. One would be to posit that an NP and its containing DP together form a single categorial *supersystem*; and we might posit that the defining characteristic of a *supersystem* is that it comprises both a lexical and a functional projection of the ultimate (lexical) head. This in turn would lead us towards a revised X-bar theory in which any word-level lexical category L would not only permit a lexical projection into L″, but might also permit a functional projection (via a head functional category F) into F″, in the manner schematized in (3) below:

(3)   [$_{F''}$ specifier [$_{F'}$ [$_F$ head] [$_{L''}$ specifier [$_{L'}$ [$_L$ head] complement/s]]]]

We shall refer to the *lexical* projections of a given head as its *l-projections*, and to the corresponding *functional* projections of the head as its *f-projections*. Looked at in these terms, we might suppose that the essential syntactic function of the D-system in adult grammars is to provide an f-projection of NP into DP: likewise, the syntactic function of the I-system is to provide an f-projection of VP into IP; and the syntactic function of the C-system is to provide a further f-projection of VP (via IP) into CP. Now, if it is the case that functional categories serve the role of f-projecting lexical categories into functional categories (i.e. of projecting a lexical category system into a corresponding functional categorial supersystem), then it is clear that in principle children cannot acquire functional categories until they have acquired the corresponding lexical categories (since the former are f-projections of the latter). Thus, the fact that lexical categories are acquired before their functional counterparts (rather than the other way round) may be determined by deep-seated properties of Universal Grammar.

An alternative way of capturing the same intuition that functional categories in some sense serve to 'expand' (and thus presuppose the prior existence of) lexical projections would be to follow Abney (1987) and posit an *Inheritance Principle* whereby functional projections inherit the categorial features of the complement of their head (see Radford 1989 for detailed discussion of this idea). Given this principle, a DP like *the man* would inherit the nominal categorial features of its complement *man*, and thus become an NP by inheritance. On this view, we might argue that since functional projections only acquire their 'true' categorial status by inheritance from their complements, functional category systems cannot in principle come into being until such time as the corresponding lexical category systems are already 'in place' (so that e.g. IP cannot be acquired until VP has been acquired, DP cannot be acquired until NP has been acquired, and so on).

We can represent the specific order of acquisition of the relevant categories predicted by (either variant of) the teleological hypothesis as in (4) below:

(4)   (i)   NP $\geq$ DP
      (ii) VP $\geq$ IP $\geq$ CP

where $\geq$ should be interpreted as 'is acquired earlier than or at the same stage of development as'. In similar terms, we can represent the observed order of acquisition reported on in this book as in (5) below:

(5)   {NP, VP, PP, AP} > {DP, IP, CP}

(where > is interpretable as 'is acquired earlier than'). We might argue that (5) is broadly compatible with (4) (in the sense that (5) falls within the range of possibilities allowed by (4) in respect of the categories mentioned in both schemas), since (5) specifies that NP is acquired before DP (a possibility allowed for in (4)(i)), and that VP is acquired before IP or CP (a possibility allowed for in (4)(ii)).

However, the force of this argument is undermined by the fact that (4) predicts many more possible orders of acquisition than are attested in the present study. For example, (4) allows for the possibility that lexical categories and their functional counterparts (e.g. NP and DP) may be acquired *simultaneously*, rather than *successively*. However, this possibility of simultaneous acquisition is clearly not realized in our present study, given the evidence we have presented that NP emerges before DP, and VP before IP or CP. A second possibility allowed for in (4) but not realized in our present study is that some functional categories may be acquired before some lexical categories: this follows from the fact that the schema in (4) makes predictions only about the relative order of acquisition within specific categorial subsystems (so that within the nominal subsystem, DP will never be acquired before NP, and within the verbal subsystem, IP will never be acquired before VP), and not about the relative order of acquisition of different subsystems (e.g. whether the nominal system will develop before/after/in parallel with the verbal system). Thus, although (4)(i) predicts that NP will never be acquired later than DP, and (4)(ii) predicts that VP will never be acquired later than IP, nothing in (4) precludes the possibility that DP may be acquired before VP, or conversely that IP may be acquired before NP. However, such ordering possibilities are simply not attested in our study, and the teleological hypothesis offers no explanation of why this should be so. We are thus forced to concede that the teleological hypothesis provides no explanation for the essential conclusion in our present study: namely that *all* four major lexical categories are acquired before *any* of the three major functional categories.

Given that the *teleological* hypothesis allows for many more possible orders of category acquisition than are attested in our present study, we might argue that it is too *unconstrained* to serve as an explanatory hypothesis determining the order of acquisition of grammatical categories. In view of the shortcomings of teleological explanations, we might explore the possibility of there being a second way in which properties of UG might play a role in determining why lexical categories are acquired before functional ones. More precisely, we might pursue the possibility of arriving at what Atkinson (1982: 18) refers to as a *language-internal* explanation: this, he characterizes in the following terms: if '*all* the world's languages possess X_1 but only *some* of them possess X_2, then the child learns first exactly what is common to all languages'. If we translate this idea into contemporary terms, it would amount to claiming that we should expect children to acquire first those aspects of language rooted in *universal principles* (because these are innately given, and require no prior experience), and *parametrized* aspects of language later (because these require accumulation of sufficient linguistic experience to enable the relevant parameters to be set at the appropriate values). For obvious reasons, we shall refer to this as a *parametric* theory of acquisition.

In the light of the possibility of developing a parametric theory of acquisition, it is interesting to note the recent suggestion by Chomsky (1988b) that there is no significant parametric variation between languages in respect of their *lexical* category systems, but that there is very significant parametric variation between languages in respect of their functional category systems: more specifically, Chomsky (1988b: 2) suggests that 'Substantive elements (verbs, nouns, etc.) are drawn from an invariant universal vocabulary', so that 'Only functional elements will be parametrized.' What this means is that syntactic variation within languages will be limited to functional category systems (so that it is only the properties of functional systems which have to be learned). It seems possible that there may be parametric variation between languages in respect of both the *range* and *nature* of the functional categories which their grammars make use of.

Variation in the *range* of functional category systems in different languages is illustrated by the fact that although English has both a D-system and a C-system, Japanese appears to have neither: thus, Fukui (1986: 203) claims that Japanese 'lacks the functional category D', arguing that this accounts for numerous properties of nominals, including the fact that the language has no articles; Fukui also claims (1986: 224) that 'there is no syntactic category C in Japanese', arguing that this accounts for why Japanese has no complementizers, and no syntactic wh-movement. Variation in the *nature* of functional categories is illustrated by the fact that different languages appear to have I-systems with different structural properties. Thus, if Pollock (1988, 1989) is correct, French has an *articulated* I-system in which tense (= T) and agreement (= G) head independent phrasal projections into TP and GP. By contrast, a language like Japanese seems to have no G-system (since it lacks agreement inflections), but has a T-system. According to Brody (1989), Old English had an *incorporated* I-system, in the sense that the tense/agreement properties of verbs were base-generated as part of the verbs which carried them. By contrast, if we follow Chomsky's (1986b) *Barriers* analysis, then tense and agreement would be two features of a single I constituent in (Modern) English. What all of this suggests is that the properties of the I-system are parametrized along a number of dimensions. One of these relates to the range of I-properties which are grammatically encoded: for example, the I-system encodes agreement properties in English, French and Italian, but not in Japanese. A second relates to whether I-properties are encoded as *categories* or *features*: thus, Pollock (1988, 1989) analyses tense and agreement as separate *categories* in French, whereas under the *Barriers* analysis of English, they are *features* of the I category. A third dimension relates to whether *featural* I-properties are *functionally* or *lexically* encoded – that is whether they are base-generated as features of functional or lexical categories: thus, if Brody (1989) is right, then tense and agreement were encoded as features of the lexical category V in Old English, but are encoded as features of the functional category I in Modern English. All of this suggests that there is considerable parametric variation in the range of functional properties which are encoded in different languages, and in the ways in which the relevant properties are encoded.

  Now, if it were the case that there is no variation across languages with respect to nature, structure, and properties of the *lexical* category systems which their grammars incorporate, but that there is considerable parametric variation across languages with respect to the range and nature of the functional category systems which their grammars incorporate, then we might suppose that relatively little linguistic experience (and hence relatively little *learning*) is required in order for children to be able to undertake the task of *lexical* categorization (i.e. identifying the set of lexical categories appropriate to the language being acquired, and assigning items to these categories), whereas (in consequence of the extensive parametric variation between languages in respect of the system of functional categories which they employ) children will require considerably more linguistic experience (and hence a greater learning effort) in order to undertake the task of *functional* categorization. It would then follow that lexical categories would be 'easier' (and hence earlier) acquired than functional categories.

This *parametric* explanation of category acquisition offers the obvious advantage over the earlier teleological explanation that it makes the specific prediction that *all* lexical categories will be acquired before *any* functional categories – a prediction which would seem to be borne out by the results of the specific study reported on here. However, one apparent drawback to the parametric explanation (at least, in the general form presented here) is that it would seem to make no predictions beyond this: in particular, it would seem to make no predictions about whether some functional categories are (or are not) acquired before others (e.g. determiners before complementizers). A potentially even more serious drawback is the fact that the fundamental assumption underlying this type of explanation (viz. that functional categories are parametrized, but lexical categories are not) seems to be based on a very flimsy empirical foundation. For example, the suggestion (made by Fukui 1986) that Japanese may lack a C-system is a questionable one in the light of the counterevidence presented in Kanamura (1989). Conversely, the suggestion that lexical categories are not parametrized seems equally questionable: for example, there would appear to be parametric variation in the *range* of lexical categories found in different languages; thus, Schachter (1985: 13) notes that 'While all languages appear to distinguish two open classes, nouns and verbs, only certain languages make a further distinction between these and a third open class, the class of *adjectives*.' And in a similar vein, Stowell (1981: 25) notes that there are languages which have no category of *adpositions* (i.e. no prepositions or postpositions). Moreover, there would seem to be parametric variation in the properties carried by lexical categories in different languages: for example, nouns in Latin inflect for number, gender, and case, whereas nouns in Japanese are not (overtly) inflected for any of these properties. Thus, there is clearly at least *some* parametric variation between languages with respect to the range of lexical categories which they contain, and the grammatical properties which they encode.

Although the *parametric* explanation would clearly be a powerful one if the underlying hypothesis (namely that syntactic parametrization is limited to functional category systems) were empirically substantiated, it has to be admitted that in our present impoverished state of knowledge, it is far from clear precisely how much parametric variation there is in the range and properties of either lexical or functional categories which occur in different languages. Moreover, acquisition data cast doubt on whether Chomsky's parametrization hypothesis can be maintained in its strongest form. Thus, if – as argued here and in Lebeaux (1988) – the ordering of heads, complements, and specifiers in early child grammars is determined by the directionality of theta-marking (a property of lexical heads), then word order variation in early child grammars of different languages (e.g. Subject + Verb + Object in early child English, but Subject + Object + Verb in early child German) clearly reduces to a parametrized *lexical* property (namely directionality of theta-marking), not to any parametric *functional* property.

In view of the uncertain empirical foundations on which the *parametric* account is built, we might seek a rather different kind of explanation for the order of acquisition of categories. One obvious candidate here is the *maturational theory* of acquisition proposed by Borer and Wexler (1987). The essence of the maturational theory is that different principles of Universal Grammar are genetically programmed to come into operation at different biologically determined stages of maturation. Extending the maturational hypothesis suggested by Cinque (1988), we might conjecture that the principles which enable the child to map theta-marked argument structures into *lexical* category systems come 'on line' at around the age of 20 months (±20%). At this stage, the child can 'create' only thematic structures – i.e. structures comprising a theta-assigning head, and a set of theta-marked arguments. Now, we might suppose that the essential function of lexical categories is to directly encode thematic aspects of meaning. This seems to be so for two reasons: firstly, only lexical (not *functional*) heads can theta-mark nominals; and secondly, the range of expressions which can receive a given theta-role is determined by the *lexical* rather than *functional* contents of the expression (as we see from contrasts like *Kill the man/!the stone*, where it is properties of the N *stone* which make it inappropriate as the PATIENT complement of *kill*, not properties of the determiner *the*). Given the obvious interdependence between lexical and thematic structures, it is not surprising that the two come 'on line' together (typically at around the age of 20 months, ±20%). For the next three months, these are the only (relevant) principles which are 'on line', so that all the child's structures at this point are lexical-thematic in nature.

We might conjecture that the next point of maturation in the child's grammatical development is reached (typically at the age of 24 months, ±20%) when the ability to form *nonthematic* structures (i.e. structures which encode *nonthematic* aspects of meaning) comes on line. If this were so, it would lead us to make the following predictions about the child's grammatical development at this point. Since *functional* categories are nonthematic in nature (in the sense that they do not theta-mark nominal complements or nominal specifiers), we should expect to find that it is only at this point that functional category systems can start to develop.

Hence, we should expect to find children beginning to develop an abstract D-system which determines nonthematic aspects of the semantics of nominals (particularly their referential/binding properties): we would also expect to see the emergence of an abstract I-system (e.g. infinitival structures headed by the nonthematic 'particle' *to*), and an abstract C-system (showing e.g. auxiliaries preposed into pre-subject C-position). In addition, we should expect to see children developing what we might call *semi-thematic* structures: i.e. structures involving a head lexical category which has a thematic complement but a nonthematic specifier (viz. so-called 'impersonal' constructions with *expletive* subjects, 'raising' structures, 'passive' structures, and so on).

Thus, given the *maturational* hypothesis suggested here, we should expect to find that children enter the earlier *lexical-thematic* stage at around 20 months ($\pm 20\%$), and progress to a later *functional-nonthematic* stage at around 24 months ($\pm 20\%$). If this were so, then progression to each of these two stages would be marked by a qualitative (and perhaps quantitative) change in the child's speech output. In this connection, it is interesting to note that the onset of the *lexical-thematic* stage seems to coincide with a phenomenon referred to as *vocabulary spurt*. A number of studies (e.g. Smith 1926, Benedict 1979, McCune-Nicolich 1981) have reported that the rate of acquisition of vocabulary items undergoes a sudden rapid increase at around the age of 20 months. For example, McCune-Nicolich's (1981) study shows an increase from a mean figure of 31 words at a mean age of 20 months to a mean of 69 words a month later. Such studies suggest a strong correlation between vocabulary growth and the onset of the *lexical-thematic* stage. One way of explaining this correlation would be in *maturational* terms, by positing that at around 20 months, children reach a 'critical age' – more properly, a 'critical *stage*' – at which they progress to a more advanced (biologically predetermined) stage of linguistic development. We might conjecture that the ability to develop lexical-thematic structures facilitates vocabulary growth, since the development of such structures arguably simplifies the task of identifying the argument structure of predicates (so that e.g. *kill* can be identified as a predicate which takes as its second argument an NP complement denoting an animate entity, and bearing the theta-role PATIENT).

It is also interesting to note that the point at which the child enters the *functional-nonthematic* stage of development (at around 24 months, $\pm 20\%$) seems to correlate with a phenomenon sometimes referred to as *syntax spurt*. In this connection, Anisfeld (1984: 129–30) reports that 'After a period of slow increase in sentence production, there is a period of accelerated growth around the second birthday.' He notes that the number of sentence types which children produce per hour suddenly doubles in the month following the child's second birthday (in broad terms, from around 50 to around 100). It is tempting to suggest that this sudden increase in the number of sentence types may be a direct reflection of the increase in expressivity made possible by the development of functional-nonthematic structures – i.e. by progression to a more advanced (functional) stage of linguistic maturation. It may well be that specific types of language handicap (e.g. language delay, or agrammatism) may be characterized by the late onset of (or loss of) functional-nonthematic modules of grammar.

If the principles which enable the child to form *functional-nonthematic* structures do indeed come 'on line' at a specific point of maturation, then we should expect to find that only *after* children reach this critical point will they start to acquire those aspects of the grammar of English which are essentially nonthematic (or functional) in nature. To be more specific, we should expect to find that only after this critical stage has been reached will the child begin to acquire the following:

(6) (i)   a set of referential/quantificational determiners (*this/that/ the/a/another/some/any/all*, etc.)

(ii)   possessive determiners (as in *daddy's/my/your*, etc.)

(iii)   a set of pronominal determiners (*this/that/it/he/she/they*, etc.)

(iv)   a case-system (cf. the *I/me/my* contrast)

(v)   case-marking principles, and hence (e.g.) the use of dummy case assigners like *of*

(vi)   case constraints on the distribution of nominals

(vii)   referential (e.g. binding) properties of nominals, pronominals, and anaphors

(viii)   functional constraints on the use of empty categories

(ix)   modal, aspectual, copula, and dummy auxiliaries

(x)   infinitival *to*

(xi)   finite verb inflections ($+s/+d$)

(xii)   complementizers

(xiii)   preposed auxiliaries

(xiv)   preposed wh-constituents

(xv)   use of *expletive* nominals

(xvi)   A-movement ('raising', 'passivization')

Items (6)(i–xiv) would involve development of the three primary functional (non-thematic) category systems, namely a D-system (cf. i–viii), an I-system (viii–xi), and a C-system (xii–xiv); by contrast, (6)(xv–xvi) would involve the development of *semi-thematic* category systems, i.e. structures with a lexical head which theta-marks its complement but not its specifier. There is no *a priori* reason to expect that all of the properties specified in (6) should be acquired simultaneously: but if the maturational account is along the right lines, we should clearly expect to find that the relevant properties cluster into significant sets in terms of their relative order of acquisition. In order to determine empirically whether this is indeed the case, we need to undertake a number of fine-grained correlational longitudinal studies of children, starting at the time when they are about to enter the functional-nonthematic stage of development, and continuing until the time when they have acquired (and indeed perhaps *mastered*) the syntax of functional-nonthematic constituents.

Unfortunately, however, there have to date been no satisfactory *correlational longitudinal* studies of the acquisition of a wide set of inter-related functional-nonthematic properties like those listed in (6). Existing studies are simply too narrow in scope: most of them tend to focus on one specific property (as in e.g. the study of the acquisition of passivization in Borer and Wexler (1987), or the study of negation in Weissenborn and Verrips (1989), or the study of null subjects by Valian (1989a, 1989b), or the study of long-distance wh-movement in De Villiers, Roeper and Vainikka (1988) and Roeper and De Villiers (1989), or numerous studies of binding relationships). Studies which are somewhat wider in scope still tend to focus on a particular categorial system (as in the studies of the acquisition of the I-system in Radford and Aldridge (1987), and Aldridge (1988, 1989), or of the C-system in Radford (1987)). They still leave unanswered the key question of whether related nonthematic and functional structures show parallel development.

While (given that our book is limited in scope to characterizing the earlier lexical-thematic stage of child development) we shall not attempt to provide definitive answers to the complex question of the relative order of acquisition of nonthematic and functional structures here, it is interesting to note that for some children at least, a whole range of different nonthematic and functional properties do seem to be acquired within a remarkably short time of the child entering the functional-nonthematic stage of development. We can illustrate this claim with data taken from a single 45-minute recording of the spontaneous speech of Heather at age 26 months (i.e. only a short time after we might expect the principles determining the grammar of functional-nonthematic structures to have come 'on line'). Already, Heather has a well developed D-system. For example, she uses a wide range of referential and quantificational determiners, as we see from the examples in (7) below:

(7)   *that* one; *that* sweetie; *that* candle; *that* little baby; *those* pigeons; *those* dollies; *those* ones; *the* little baby; *a* teddy; *a* vest; *a* little boy; *a* new car; *another* Wispa bar; *another* push-chair; *some* flowers; *some* roses; *some* new shoes; *some* new hair

She also seems to have acquired a wide range of possessive determiners, as we see from examples such as (8) below:

(8)   mummy'*s* chocolate; daddy'*s*; mummy'*s* and daddy'*s*; *your* dolly; *your* hair; *your* sweetie tube; *your* Wispa bar; *my* sweeties; *my* one; *her* cradle; *her* other side; *her* handsome prince

In addition, she makes use of a wide range of pronominal determiners, including those listed in (9) below:

(9)   that; those; these; what; some; I; me; we; you; he; him; she; her; it; they; them

Moreover, she seems to have a well developed case-system, and to be 'aware' of the distinction between nominative, objective, and genitive case-forms – as data like (10) illustrate:

(10)   (a)   *I'll* have that one, shall *I*? *I'm* opening that. Are *we* going on an aeroplane now? You open that, shall *we*? What's *she* saying? *He's* laughing. Isn't *he* beautiful? *They're* my little dollies, aren't *they*?
        (b)   Leave *them* there. I tipped *them* all in there. Can I put *her* in her cradle? You save *me*. You can't get *me*. You open it for *me*. Apples for *me*. I'll get a new car for *him*. There's one for *him*
        (c)   There's *your* dolly. Shut *your* eyes. I want *my* Wispa bar. That's like *my* one. Put her on *her* other side. Matthew has left *his* duck behind

The examples in (10)(a) show nominative pronouns being used in appropriate positions, while those in (10)(b) and (c) show objective and genitive pronouns respectively likewise being used in appropriate positions. This suggests that Heather already has a well developed case-system in her grammar.

    If this is so, then we should also expect to find that Heather 'knows' how to use the 'dummy' (nonthematic) preposition *of* as an indirect case-marker: although there are only four examples in the relevant corpus of structures where adults would require *of* to be used in this way, it is significant that in all four cases, Heather uses *of*: cf.

(11)   all *of* them; one *of* those dollies; two *of* those; bar *of* chocolate

She thus seems to 'know' the principles of indirect case assignment.

Moreover, Heather seems to be (tacitly) 'aware' of case constraints on the distribution of nominals (viz. the requirement that DPs must occur in appropriate case-marked positions). Thus, we no longer find nominals occurring in caseless positions: for example, we no longer find 'Small Clauses' used as independent sentences (i.e. clauses comprising a subject nominal in a caseless position functioning as the external argument of a nonfinite predicate). For instance, in place of earlier Small Clause structures like 'Daddy naughty', 'Mummy in kitchen' or 'Daddy working', we now find IPs with a finite form of *be*: cf.

(12)   It'*s* nice, *isn't* it? It'*s* hard. It'*s* a candle. What *is* that? Where *are* you? What'*s* in there? What'*s* inside your Smartie tube? That one'*s* like yours. I'*m* opening that. I'*m* having one. What'*s* he doing? He'*s* smacking her, *isn't* he? He'*s* laughing. And then we'*re* going shopping

It seems reasonable to suppose that in each sentence, the italicized finite verb form is superficially positioned in I (hence the possibility of preposing it into C, found e.g. in '*Isn't* he beautiful?'): but if this is so, then the subject of the italicized V will be in a case-marked position (viz. a position assigned nominative case by the finite I), so that the requirement that DP must occur in an appropriate case-marked position is satisfied.

We might go further and argue that there are signs that Heather is beginning to master the referential properties (e.g. the person properties) of the D-system. For example, she seems to 'know' that (indeterminate) nominals are intrinsically third person forms, and so not used to refer to either speaker or addressee, except in vocatives: she consistently uses first person pronouns to refer to herself (never her own name), and second person pronouns to refer to addressees (never their names): e.g.

(13)   (a)   *I'll* have that one, shall *I*? Can *I* have it? Not when *I'm* eating *my* sweeties. Shall *I* close it? *I* like *my* Wispa bar. *I'll* be sick soon. *I'll* get *my* Smarties, shall *I*?

         (b)   Did *you* want that one? Do *you* like that one? *You* put it on. *You* eat it. Would *you* like a sweetie? I'm opening *yours*

By contrast, she uses names either non-vocatively to refer to a person who is neither the speaker nor the addressee (as in the (a) examples below), or vocatively to refer to the addressee (as in the (b) examples):

(14)   (a)   I want *Alice*. I'll get some new hair for *Rapunzel*. There's *Rapunzel*. There's *Sleeping Beauty* again. I like *Super-Ted*. I've given those to *Daddy* for when he comes back. *Matthew* has left his duck behind

        (b)   I got some presents for you in there, *Lisa*. *Alice*, where are you? Thank you, *Lisa*. Be ever so careful, *Mummy*. Hello, *Dick*. Fine thank you, *Dick*

It would thus seem that Heather already 'knows' a considerable amount about the person properties of nominals and pronominals.

In addition, Heather also seems to have some (tacit) 'knowledge' of the functional constraints on the use of empty categories in English. Thus, she never uses a null pronoun in an objective position, but rather (like adults) uses an overt objective pronoun – e.g.

(15)   I tipped *them* all in there. Can I have *it*? I'm opening *that*. Can I do *that*? I did *it*. I'll open *it*. Can I put *her* in her cradle? You put *those* on. I'll get *her* from down there. Leave *them* here. Cut *it* off. I like *it*. I'll fix *it*

Likewise, in nominative positions where adults require an overt subject, she uses an overt rather than a covert subject, for example:

(16)   Do *you* want that one? Can *I* have it? Shall *I* close it? Are *we* going on an aeroplane now? It's nice, isn't *it*? I'll get my Smarties, shall *I*? He's smacking her, isn't *he*? They're my little dollies, aren't *they*? What's *she* doing? What's *he* got? Not when *I'*m eating my sweeties. When *I* was a little baby. Because *she*'s laughing. I think *that*'s a ball. I've given those to Daddy for when *he* comes back

However, Heather is clearly 'aware' of the possibility of having a null (second person, nominative) subject in imperative sentences, as the following data indicate:

(17)   See what's inside it! Put them in! Put these on! Shut your eyes! Leave them here! Open it! Cut it off! Be ever so careful, Mummy! Wait till that starts! Don't get my trousers on, will you!

She also seems to be 'aware' of the possibility of '*clipping*' a main clause subject (sometimes along with its auxiliary) in casual speech in adult English (resulting in 'clipped' sentences like 'Have to work harder', 'Don't really know', 'Can't help you', 'Doing anything tonight?', 'Feel like a drink?', etc.): this is illustrated by examples such as the following:

(18)   Have to lie it down like that. Be nice if I call her Helen. Got some dollies in there as well. Got a new dress for you. Having one. Can't. Don't know. Don't like it. Don't want my Wispa bar back. Isn't! [contradicting 'It's a cold day today']. Would! [contradicting 'You wouldn't like it really']

What is interesting here is that she seems to 'know' that the subject cannot be 'clipped' if preceded by overt material in the same sentence – hence she never clips subjects in the italicized positions in (16). Her apparent acquisition of the complex conditions governing the use of 'missing subjects' is truly astonishing in a child of only 26 months.

Just as we have clear evidence that Heather has a well developed D-system, so too we also find evidence of a highly developed I-system. For example, Heather has acquired various kinds of auxiliary, as we see from data such as (19) below:

(19)   *Do* you like that one? *Did* you want that one? That *does*. I *do* laugh. I *don't* know. *Can* I have it? I *can't*. I *couldn't* know. *Shall* I close it? I*'ll* have that one, *shall* I? You *will* save me. It *might* not. *Would* you like a sweetie? I*'ve* got some new shoes. Matthew *has* left his duck behind. What *have* you got? I *haven't*. I*'m* opening that. He*'s* smacking her, *isn't* he? *Are* we going on an aeroplane now? It*'s* nice, *isn't* it? They*'re* my little dollies, *aren't* they?

She also seems to have command of the use of the infinitival I constituent *to*: cf.

(20)   Have *to* lie down like that. You suppose *to* put it on your knees. That used *to* be mine. I used *to* have one with seats. I'm going *to* have one of those dollies. I'm going *to* get my sweeties. He has *to* leave it there now. Do you want *to* have that one?

And in addition, she appears to be 'aware' of the tense/agreement inflection system found with finite verbs: cf.

(21)   Wait till that *starts*. It *tastes* nice. I *tipped* them all in there. That *does*. *Did* you want that one? *Is* her cradle in there? I*'m* opening

that. *Are* we going on an aeroplane now? Alice, where *are* you? They'*re* my little dollies, *are*n't they? When I *was* a little baby. What *have* you got? Matthew *has* left his duck behind

Overall, then, there seems little doubt that she has a highly developed I-system operating in her grammar.

In much the same way, there is parallel evidence that she has a well developed C-system. For example, we find that she makes productive use of preposed auxiliaries: cf.

(22)   *Did* you want that one? *Do* you like that one? *Can* I have it? *Can* I do that? *Shall* I close it? *Is* her cradle in there? *Isn't* he beautiful? *Are* we going on an aeroplane now? *Wasn't* that a shame?

(and there are numerous examples of sentence *tags* showing a similar Auxiliary + Subject order). Given the (not unreasonable) assumption that pre-subject auxiliaries are positioned in the head C position of CP, this would suggest that Heather has developed a C-system. Significantly, she also positions preposed wh-phrases in pre-Auxiliary position (i.e. in the specifier position within CP), as we see from examples such as the following:

(23)   Alice, *where* are you? *What*'s she saying? *What*'s she doing? *What*'s that teddy doing? *What*'s that little baby doing now? *What*'s he doing? *What*'s he got? *What* have you got? *Why* was he gone?

Overall, then, we find that all three of the primary functional category systems (the D-system, the I-system, and the C-system) seem to be extraordinarily well developed in Heather's grammar. Moreover, all three systems seem to have a broadly symmetrical structure, involving a head, a following complement, and a nonthematic specifier position which can serve as the landing-site for moved constituents (viz. for a moved possessor phrase in the case of DP, for a moved subject in the case of IP, and for a moved wh-phrase in the case of CP).

Given that Heather has developed a nonthematic *functional* specifier position, the obvious question to ask is whether she has likewise developed a nonthematic *lexical* specifier position (i.e. whether she has developed *semi-thematic* structures in which a lexical head theta-marks its complement but not its specifier). There is some evidence that she has done so. For example, she produces a number of structures which arguably involve 'raising' or 'passive' predicates (italicized in the examples below) – structures such as the following:

(24)   You *suppose* to put it on your knees. That *used* to be mine. I *used* to have one with seats. I'm *going* to have one of those dollies. I'm *going* to get my sweeties. He *has* to leave it there now. That one might be *called* Dick. And that might be *called* Helen

It is interesting that Heather appears to misanalyse the passive predicate *supposed* as a raising predicate *suppose*: since both passive and raising predicates in structures like '*You* (are) suppose(d) to + VP' would appear to involve movement from a thematic specifier position in a subordinate VP to a nonthematic specifier position in a superordinate VP, the misanalysis is understandable. What is more significant, however, is the fact that data like (24) suggest that Heather may have developed *semi-thematic* structures alongside *nonthematic* structures (although it obviously has to be conceded that many alternative analyses could be envisaged for such data).

If Heather has indeed developed semi-thematic structures of this type, then we should expect to find her using structures with *expletive* subjects: and indeed, we do find a number of examples of potential expletive structures – e.g.

(25)   *There* are some dollies there. *There* are some sweeties in there. *There*'s some flowers on the back. *There*'s a pram in there. *There*'s one for him. *It*'s surprises in my postbag

Of course, it is impossible to be certain that *there* has an expletive (rather than a locative) function in such cases, so that the data are suggestive rather than conclusive. It is interesting to note that Heather appears to have used the 'wrong' expletive pronoun in the last example, so that in place of '*There* are...' she says '*It*'s...'.

Although the evidence which we have drawn upon in order to assess Heather's competence is limited to a single 45-minute speech sample, there can be no doubt about the vast repertoire of nonthematic/ functional structures which Heather seems to have at her command by the age of 26 months. She is clearly well on the way towards acquiring all of the key nonthematic properties identified in (6) above. When her speech output is compared to that of children just a few months younger (i.e. children at the earlier lexical-thematic stage), the nature of the linguistic development which has taken place during that short period of time is nothing short of astounding. What is particularly striking is that the development is *cross-categorial* (i.e. it isn't just the D-system, or the I-system which has evolved, but rather a whole range of different functional and nonthematic structures have developed together). This cross-categorial developmental parallelism would seem to provide a strong *prima facie* case for suggesting that maturational factors may be at work.

The purpose of providing this brief (and inevitably superficial) characterization of Heather's competence is not (of course) to imply that all children should be expected to have attained the same level of competence as Heather at roughly the same age (26 months): this would clearly be an absurd claim, since some children at 26 months are still at the earlier lexical-thematic stage of development. On the contrary, the purpose of our discussion of Heather is to raise the possibility that once children start to develop nonthematic structures (whether at 24 months, 26 months, 28 months, or whenever), a whole range of different functional and nonthematic properties will start to be acquired together, and thus will show broadly parallel development. If there is indeed just such a *developmental parallelism* in the 'growth' of functional and nonthematic structures (as the maturational theory would lead us to expect), then this would lead us to predict that we will never find any normal child at any stage of development who has (say) a fully developed I-system, but no D-system or C-system: this prediction can, of course, be tested by a suitably large corpus of detailed cross-sectional studies of appropriate children (e.g. children aged 2–3 years). The hypothesis of *parallel development* would also lead us to predict that there will be no children who (say) develop an I-system at 24 months, a D-system at 30 months, and a C-system at 36 months: this prediction can in turn be tested by fine-grained longitudinal studies of children in the relevant age groups. Any serious attempt to evaluate the maturational theory of acquisition clearly requires the development of a large-scale research programme aimed at putting these predictions to the empirical test.

Although it falls outside the scope of the present book to undertake such an enormous task, we shall briefly point to data from other children of Heather's age which seem to exemplify the predicted pattern of parallel development. For the sake of brevity, we shall not attempt to illustrate all sixteen aspects of development highlighted in (6) above; rather, we shall concentrate simply on showing that the children concerned have already acquired the three major functional category systems (DP, IP, and CP). The structures produced by the children in the examples below are plausibly analysed as DPs in the case of the (a) examples, IPs in the case of the (b) examples, and CPs in the case of the (c) examples:

(26)   *Elizabeth at 26 months*
   (a)   Which side? That side. That one. This one. All those things. All these. A lot. A bottle. A round one. A nice time. The freezer.

The ten little ducks. Any of my presents. Some sellotape. Any more. Andrew's. My little rabbit. My little teddy. My pretty frock. My cup of tea. Our eyes. Her mouth. His ball

(b) I'm not on that one. I'm drinking my cup of tea there. There I am again. But I don't want it. I don't like her. He didn't find it. We can see now. You can see yourself. He can't find them. They're not in there, he said. She'll have to lie on my lap. We won't have that one. One of these broke off. And it winds up. It hasn't got a key on, to wind on. I want to sit here

(c) Have I got it? Aren't I in here? Is that where I was at Nanny's? Is any more in there? Is it a polly? Does this one open? Shall I go fetch it? Have you got it off? What are you saying? What's that you sayed? What are all these doing, mummy? What am I doing here, mummy? What have you got there?

(27) *Jem at 26 months*

(a) The red one. The lovely water. The lovely little room. A red lovely car. A little sheepy. A little piece of chocolate. A bit of chocolate. What a mess! That big spider. Some smarties. Jem's car. Jem's mummy. Mummy's nosey. Daddy's finger. My bag. Their webs

(b) I'll get up on the car. I can't see it. Jem can't go down. You won't, mummy. I've got it. We saw the lighthouse. Jem wanted to see Moon. We goed somewhere. There was Aunty Ann. Jem goes in that big spider. Jem has some. Jem's hungry. They're talking to each other. I want to do sleepy-byes on the cushion

(c) May Khadija say it? Can Jem go out? Where's the world? Where's the bus?

(28) *Adam at 26 months* [Note: *them* behaves like *those* in his dialect]

(a) That tape. That button. That one. That little pig. This tape. This one. This other one. These words. All these. Them shoes. Them big holes. Some water. Some more. Another one. A wire. A button. A pig. An elephant. A big aeroplane. A big hole. The other man. Daddy's. My bottom. His hands

(b) I can mend this. He can't go in. I'll take my shoes off. It does. It doesn't work. Them might burn my feet. Them are guns. I knocked Man down. Something broke. That's come out of my box

(c) Can I open these? What are these? Where's that shoe gone? Where's the book? Where's it in there?

(29)   *Rebecca at 26 months*
   (a)   That one. Those two. This one. This dog. These two faces. The fridge. The drawer. The other man. The other one. The other two ones. The orange one. A mirror. A boy. A sad face. A black sheep. Another one. Two mans. Two ones. All the green faces. Granny's dog. Their heads
   (b)   I'm having this. We've lost him. We're making a boat. It's fallen off. He's granny's dog. It's having a walk. He's having a boatride. This is a light. I'm not. It's off now. This is green. I want to put this in now. Cos I do
   (c)   Can I see him? Can I see out the window? Is this one in the kitchen? What's this got? What's it got on? What's that man doing? Where is the other man? Where are your fingers?

(30)   **Helen at 26 months*
   (a)   That one. That other one. That piece. This big piece. This one. These bits. Some bulbs. Some pieces. A bed. A box. A little one. A big one. The big piece. My best shoes
   (b)   This can build this one on there. I can do. I can't find it. That won't fit in there. No, don't do that! Cos I do. They're red. No, t'isn't red. I've been playing all the day. He's looked. I want to do it. That fell down
   (c)   Mummy, can you do these? Medicine...can I have? Where's it gone? What's Tommy doing? What's Mamma doing? What's that doing? What's mummy making? What's mummy maked?

(31)   *Robert at 26 months*
   (a)   This way. This one. That one. Another one. Another Snoopy watch. The handbag. Some more toys. A smurf. A Snoopy watch. A tiny care-bear. A good-luck bear. Grandad's. My bedroom. My finger. My birthday
   (b)   I don't want it on. I don't know. You can hook it up. We haven't got one. We've been. I saw it on telly. He fell off. You muddle it up, you do. Timmy does. It's too heavy
   (c)   Can I have some more toys? Mum, what are you doing? Where's Timmy? Where's Grandad?

(32)   *Hannah at 26 months*
   (a)   Two wheels. Two pictures. The slide. The little boy. A boy. A little kitten. A little girl. That cat. That one. That way. These ones. Hannah's one. My ribbon

(b) The little boy's fallen down. There's a doggy. That's a boy. Those are apples. Mummy made these ones

(c) Did that happen there? Does that go in there? Is that Victoria? Are toys over there? What's that cat doing? Where's my ribbon?

Each data-set in (26–32) above is taken from a single recording of a child aged 26 months (i.e. a child who has only just entered the *functional* stage of development). Yet each set of examples shows evidence of a well developed D-system, I-system, and C-system – thus suggesting that these three functional systems do indeed develop in parallel.

Moreover, the same pattern of symmetrical simultaneous development of functional category systems is also found in the Bristol corpus, as the following (limited) set of data will suffice to illustrate (since the Bristol children were recorded at three-monthly intervals, the first recording which shows clear evidence of the development of functional category systems is generally that at 27 months for most of the children; hence the children discussed below are a month older than those discussed above):

(33)   +*Jonathan at 27 months*

(a) Those jeans. That one. The door. The dustman. The red one. The green one. The big one. The plate. A green one. A brown one. A good boy. Every single one. Daddy's plate. My pants. Your hands

(b) I will be a good boy. I'll let you have one. Bonny won't eat it. I want to come see Jonathan. I'm trying to wriggle it. I am going to eat the beans in there. I'm making you one. They were jeans. I was frightened to death. I did catch my boat. I don't like them

(c) Is it Uncle Billy and Auntie Pat's trousers? Can I put one in my mouth? Can you put them in for dinner time please? What are you doing? Where did you find it?

(34)   +*Tony at 27 months*

(a) This way. This boat. That thing. That man. That blue one. The man. The moon. A big plane. Noddy's car. Arlene's one. That lady's name. My blue lorry. Your turn

(b) I don't like it snowing. I didn't do it on purpose. I can't find it. Later I will need it. That won't go up. I won't do it. That blue one is Arlene's one. I've got in bed now. It's raining. I runned down. He splashed me. I want to buy this boat. I want to see the moon outside

(c) Can I see the moon outside, mummy? What am I saying? Why have you got it shut? Why is Noddy's car dirty?

(35)   +*Penny at 27 months*
  (a)   This one. That radio. The machine. A bus. A green one. A cup of tea. A lot of pens. Some toys. Some bricks. Some more sauce. Roy's car. Daddy's bedroom. Daddy's and my mummy's. My rag dolly. My yellow dolly. My other dolly
  (b)   Because it might break. I can't hear you. I'll wipe your bum. Paul, don't play with that, will you? You're too big for that. Because you're going out now. No, I am not. Jean wants a green one. I want to go through. I want to sit up there, Ma
  (c)   Can I come in? Can I have one, Dad? Will you come down? Have you done? Why don't you buy me a new one? Where are you going, Dad?

(36)   +*Olivia at 27 months*
  (a)   A bit more. A little one. A bath. The gravy. The flannel. The handbag. Two ones. This way. That one. Another one. Mummy's dress. Mummy's tights. My door. My other money. Your door
  (b)   I can't do a bit more. I'm going to eat it. I'm going to get the gravy. I'm going potty. I'm put my boots on. I'm having the flannel. You'll get a cross. I don't want dinner. I've finished. That's my door, isn't it? I'm busy making sweets. I tipped up my bag. And I did!
  (c)   Will you wash my mouth? Can I have my chocolate? Is it going down in my belly? Where has my hat gone? What have you got there?

(37)   +*Benjamin at 27 months*
  (a)   Those shoes. That birthday. That one. These colours. This one. A sweet. A wee. A birthday. The paint. My ball. My hand. My car. Your car. Yours
  (b)   I'm going to do a wee. I'm going to get wood. I'm bringing my car. I've got a birthday. I don't like that. This one doesn't work. I do like to use purple. It won't work. But this one will. You wanted those shoes. Daddy gives me lots of money
  (c)   Where's the paint gone? I don't know where my car – where my car is. Where's my bone?

The fact that all three functional category systems have been acquired by age 26/27 months strongly suggests that the systems do not develop independently of each other, but rather in parallel. The striking developmental parallelism here is precisely what we might expect to find if the course of language development were determined by maturational factors. However, as noted above, a large-scale research project involving dozens of fine-grained longitudinal studies is needed in order to provide a sterner empirical test of the *developmental parallelism* predicted by the maturational hypothesis.

Our research in this book has been concerned primarily with the nature of the *initial* grammars developed by young children: there are three reasons for this. Firstly, the 'early patterned speech' period is the point at which children's sentences are maximally different from their adult counterparts, and so (in some intuitive sense) represents the most intrinsically interesting stage of development. Secondly, an investigation of children's initial grammars is the logical starting point for any serious investigation of the acquisition processes by which children develop successive grammars of their native language. Thirdly (and perhaps most importantly), this is the point at which the hypothesis that different principles of Universal Grammar come 'on line' at different stages of linguistic maturation can most obviously be tested.

The research reported on here has led to a number of interesting findings. From a theoretical and descriptive point of view, perhaps the most important result is that the Government-and-Binding (GB) model offers us a particularly insightful perspective on the nature of early child grammars. Within this framework, characteristics of early child speech which might otherwise seem to be unconnected (e.g. the nonacquisition of tense/agreement inflections on verbs, the nonacquisition of determiners, and the nonacquisition of wh-preposing) turn out to be intricately interconnected, and reducible to a single postulate – namely that early child grammars are purely *lexical-thematic* systems. The GB model enables us to ask genuinely interesting questions about the nature of grammatical development, and offers the prospect of enabling us to provide some genuinely interesting answers (though we are clearly a long way away from being able to claim that the answers we are currently able to offer provide *explanations* of the observed phenomena).

From a psycholinguistic point of view, the main interest of our work is that it provides an apparent challenge to the traditional *continuity hypothesis*, under which all the various modules of the child's grammar are hypothesized to be 'in place' from the very beginning, requiring only a limited amount of experience to 'activate' them: as we have seen, such an account provides no convincing explanation for why lexical-thematic systems uniformly develop before functional-nonthematic ones. Our findings would appear to be more directly consistent with a maturational approach under which UG makes different types of principles available to the child at different stages of maturation (hence the sudden 'spurt' of grammatical development at around 20 months, and a later 'spurt' at around 24 months). As we have noted, the maturational theory makes significant predictions about the course of future development after the lexical-thematic stage: it predicts that we should expect to find broadly *parallel growth* in the various functional and nonthematic structures which the child acquires. Thus, our present research paves the way for a future research programme tracing the development of nonthematic and functional systems in child grammars. The central aim of the projected future programme must be to test the key prediction of parallel growth made by the maturational theory: the pilot study represented by the data in (7–37) above suggests that the prediction is likely to be borne out.

A further topic for future research relates to the question of precisely how the transition from *lexical-thematic* to *functional-nonthematic* grammars takes place, and what is the nature of the children's grammars in this crucial transitional phase of development (a period when children often appear to alternate between apparently *lexical-thematic* structures like 'Me want have ball', and apparently *functional-nonthematic* structures like 'I want to have the ball'). The acquisition literature has occasionally suggested that children at a given stage of grammatical development G_j may produce structures which are the output of an earlier grammar G_i. Is it really plausible to posit that two different grammars (e.g. a lexical-thematic one and a functional-nonthematic one) could both be operative *at the same time* within the same child, so that the child is *bigrammatical* (and hence, in a sense, *bilingual*)? Or is there an alternative *monogrammatical* account of the phenomenon of apparent *reversion* to earlier structures?

An additional question for future research is that of the extent to which the grammatical development of children acquiring languages other than ('standard') English (especially languages with markedly richer or poorer functional category systems than English) is (or is not) parallel to that of children acquiring Standard English. If the maturational theory is correct, then we should expect to find that the two-stage model of early grammatical development suggested here (in which an earlier *lexical-thematic* stage precedes a later *functional-nonthematic* stage) will be applicable not just to English, but to other languages as well. Although we are beginning to accumulate quite a large body of observational data about the acquisition of a variety of languages (e.g. Slobin 1985), there have as yet been remarkably few theoretical studies which address this crucial developmental question (though Platzack (1989) argues that early clause structures in Swedish are purely lexical structures which lack functional categories). This is clearly an area where a great deal of future research is needed. It is not inconceivable that the pattern of acquisition for *independent* functional systems may prove to be rather different from that for *incorporated* functional systems (recall the suggestion in Brody (1989) that in Modern English, the I-system is independent of the V-system, whereas in Old English the I-system was incorporated into the V-system). Given that our study here has been limited to the acquisition of a language (viz. Modern English) with independent functional systems, this clearly underlines the need for research into the acquisition of languages with incorporated functional systems.

We have now reached a stage in our understanding of the process of language acquisition where we can begin to ask interesting questions, and define interesting areas for future research: it is to be hoped that the time will not be too far away when we can begin to provide genuinely interesting answers.

Bibliography

Note: Where a work is shown as having been reprinted, the page references in the text are to the reprinted version.

Abney, S.P. (1987) *The English Noun Phrase in Its Sentential Aspect*, PhD diss., MIT

Akmajian, A. and Heny, F. W. (1975) *An Introduction to the Principles of Transformational Syntax*, MIT Press, Cambridge Mass.

Akmajian, A. and Wasow, T. (1975) 'The constituent structure of VP and the position of the verb BE', *Linguistic Analysis* 1: 205–45

Aldridge, M. (1988) *The Acquisition of the Inflection System*, PhD diss., University College of North Wales, Bangor

Aldridge, M. (1989) *The Acquisition of INFL*, Indiana University Linguistics Club

Anisfeld, M. (1984) *Language Development From Birth to Three*, Erlbaum, London

Atkinson, M. (1982) *Explanations in the Study of Child Language Development*, Cambridge University Press, Cambridge

Atkinson, M. (1985) 'How linguistic is the one-word stage?', in Barrett, pp. 289–312

Atkinson, M. (1989) 'The logical problem of language acquisition: representational and procedural issues', MS, University of Essex

Bar-Adon, A. and Leopold, W.F. (1971) *Child Language: A Book of Readings*, Prentice-Hall, Englewood Cliffs NJ

Barrett, M.D. (ed.) (1985) *Children's Single-Word Speech*, Wiley, New York

Benedict, H.E. (1976) *Language Comprehension in 10–16 month old infants*, PhD diss., Yale University

Benedict, H.E. (1979) 'Early lexical development: comprehension and production', *Journal of Child Language* 6: 183–200

Berko, J. (1958) 'The Child's Learning of English Morphology', *Word* 14: 150–177

Berman, R. (1988) 'Word Class Distinctions in Developing Grammars', in Levy et al., pp. 45–72

Beukema, F. and Coopmans, P. (1988) 'A Government-Binding Perspective on the Imperative', MS, University of Utrecht

Bever, T. (1970) 'The cognitive basis for linguistic structures', in J.R. Hayes (ed.) *Cognition and the Development of Language*, Wiley, New York, pp. 274–353

Bloom, L. (1970) *Language Development*, MIT Press, Cambridge Mass.

Bloom, L. (1973) *One Word at a Time*, Mouton, The Hague

Bloom, L., Lightbown, P. and Hood, L. (1975) *Structure and Variation in Child Language*, Monographs of the Society for Research in Child Development, vol. 40

Bloom, L., Lightbown, P. and Hood, L. (1978) 'Pronominal-Nominal Variation in Child Language', in. L. Bloom (ed.) *Readings in Language Development*, Wiley, New York, pp. 231–238

Borer, H. (1984) *Parametric Syntax*, Foris, Dordrecht

Borer, H. (1986) 'I-Subjects', *Linguistic Inquiry* 17: 375–416

Borer, H. and Wexler, K. (1987) 'The Maturation of Syntax', in Roeper and Williams, pp. 123–172

Borsley, R.D. (1984) 'Missing NPs in Welsh', MS, University College London

Bowerman, M. (1973) *Early Syntactic Development*, Cambridge University Press, Cambridge

Braine, M.D.S. (1963) 'The Ontogeny of English Phrase Structure: the first phase', *Language* 39: 1–13

Braine, M.D.S. (1971) 'The acquisition of language in infant and child', in C.E. Reed (ed.) *The Learning of Language*, Appleton-Century-Crofts, New York, pp. 7–95

Braine, M.D.S. (1973) 'Three suggestions regarding grammatical analyses of children's language', in Ferguson and Slobin, pp. 421–429

Braine, M.D.S. (1976) *Children's First Word Combinations*, Monographs of the Society for Research in Child Development, vol. 41

Brody, M. (1989) 'Old English impersonals and the theory of grammar', *Working Papers in Linguistics*, University College London, 1: 262–294

Brody, M. and Manzini, M.R. (1988) 'On implicit arguments', MS, University College London

Brown, R. (1968) 'The Development of Wh Questions in Child Speech', *Journal of Verbal Learning and Verbal Behaviour* 7: 279–290

Brown, R. (1970) *Psycholinguistics*, Free Press, New York

Brown, R. (1973) *A First Language: The Early Stages*, George Allen and

Unwin, London

Brown, R. and Bellugi, U. (1964) 'Three processes in the child's acquisition of syntax', *Harvard Educational Review* 34: 133–51 (reprinted in Bar-Adon and Leopold, 1971, pp. 307–318)

Brown, R. and Fraser, C. (1963) 'The Acquisition of Syntax', in C. Cofer and B. Musgrave (eds) *Verbal Behaviour and Learning: Problems and Processes*, McGraw-Hill, New York, pp. 158–201

Brown, R., Cazden, C. and Bellugi, U. (1968) 'The Child's Grammar from I to III', in J.P. Hill (ed.) *Minnesota Symposium on Child Development*, vol. 2, pp. 28–73 (reprinted in Bar-Adon and Leopold, 1971, pp. 382–412)

Bruner, J. (1983) *Child's Talk*, Oxford University Press, Oxford

Bühler, K. (1922) 'Vom Wesen Der Syntax', in *Idealistische Neuphilologie: Festschrift für Karl Vossler*, Carl Winter Universitäts Verlag, Heidelberg, pp. 54–88 (extract reprinted in Bar-Adon and Leopold, 1971, pp. 52–56)

Burzio, L. (1986) *Italian Syntax*, Kluwer, Dordrecht

Cazden, C. B. (1968) 'The acquisition of noun and verb inflections', *Child Development* 39: 433–448

Chiat, S. (1982) 'If I were you and you were me', *Journal of Child Language* 9: 359–379

Chiat, S. (1986) 'Personal Pronouns', in Fletcher and Garman, 1986, pp. 339–355

Chomsky, N. (1965) *Aspects of the Theory of Syntax*, MIT Press, Cambridge Mass.

Chomsky, N. (1977) 'On Wh-movement', in P.W. Culicover et al. (eds) *Formal Syntax*, Academic Press, New York, pp. 71–132

Chomsky, N. (1981) *Lectures on Government and Binding*, Foris, Dordrecht

Chomsky, N. (1982) *Some Concepts and Consequences of the Theory of Government and Binding*, MIT Press, Cambridge Mass.

Chomsky, N. (1986a) *Knowledge of Language: Its Nature, Origin, and Use*, Praeger, New York

Chomsky, N. (1986b) *Barriers*, MIT Press, Cambridge Mass.

Chomsky, N. (1988a) *Language and Problems of Knowledge*, MIT Press, Cambridge Mass.

Chomsky, N. (1988b) 'Some Notes on Economy of Derivation and Representation', MS, MIT

Cinque, G. (1988) 'Comments on D. Lightfoot', MS, University of Venice (to appear in *Behavioural and Brain Sciences*)

Clahsen, H. (1984) 'Der Erwerb von Kasusmarkierungen in der deutschen Kindersprache', *Linguistische Berichte* 89: 1–31

Clark, E.V. (1978) 'From gesture to word: on the natural history of deixis in language acquisition', in J.S. Bruner and A. Garton (eds) *Human Growth and Development*, Oxford University Press, London

Clark, E.V. (1981) 'Lexical innovations: How children learn to create new words', in Deutsch, pp. 299–328

Clark, E.V. (1982) 'The young word-maker: a case study of innovation in the child's lexicon', in Wanner and Gleitman, pp. 390–425

Clark, R. (1974) 'Performing without competence', *Journal of Child Language* 1: 1–10

Cook, V.J. (1988) *Chomsky's Universal Grammar*, Blackwell, Oxford

Crystal, D. (1986) *Listen to Your Child*, Penguin, Harmondsworth

De Haan, G. and Tuijnman, K. (1988) 'Missing subjects and objects in child grammar', in Jordens and Lalleman, pp. 101–121

De Laguna, G. (1927) *Speech. Its Function and Development*, Yale University Press, New Haven (reprinted by Indiana University Press, Bloomington, 1963)

De Villiers, P.A. and De Villiers, J.G. (1973a) 'A cross-sectional study of the acquisition of grammatical morphemes in child speech', *Journal of Psycholinguistic Research* 2: 267–78

De Villiers, P.A. and De Villiers, J.G. (1973b) 'Development of the use of word order in comprehension', *Journal of Psycholinguistic Research* 2: 331–341

De Villiers, J., Roeper, T. and Vainikka, U. (1988) 'The Acquisition of Long-distance Rules', MS, University of Massachusetts

Deutsch, W. (ed.) (1981) *The Child's Construction of Language*, Academic Press, New York

Dore, J., Franklin, M., Miller, R.T. and Ramer, A. (1976) 'Transitional Phenomena in Early Language Acquisition', *Journal of Child Language* 3: 13–28

Dunn, C.J. and Yanada, S. (1973) *Japanese*, Teach Yourself Books, London

Ede, J. and Williamson, J. (1980) *Talking Listening and Learning*, Longman, London

Elliott, W.N. and Wexler, K. (1986) 'A principle theory of categorial acquisition', MS, University of California at Irvine

Emonds, J.E. (1985) *A Unified Theory of Syntactic Categories*, Foris, Dordrecht

Ervin-Tripp, S.M. (1964) 'Imitation and structural change in children's language', in. E.H. Lenneberg (ed.) *New Directions in the Study of Language*, MIT Press, Cambridge Mass., pp. 163–89

Ervin-Tripp, S.M. (1973) *Language Acquisition and Communicative Choice*, Stanford University Press, Stanford

Farmer, A.K. (1984) *Modularity in Syntax: A Study of Japanese and English*, MIT Press, Cambridge Mass.

Fassi Fehri, A. (1988) 'Generalised IP structure, Case, and VS word order', in Fassi Fehri et al., pp. 189–221

Fassi Fehri, A., Hajji, A., Elmoujahid, H. and Jamari, A. (eds) (1988) *Proceedings of the First International Conference of the Linguistic Society of Morocco*, Editions OKAD, Rabat

Ferguson, C.A. and Slobin, D.I. (eds) (1973) *Studies of Child Language Development*, Holt Rinehart and Winston, New York

Fillmore, C.J. (1977) 'The Case for Case Reopened', in P. Cole and J.M. Sadock (eds) *Syntax and Semantics*, Academic Press, New York, vol. 8, pp. 59–81

Fletcher, P. (1985) *A Child's Learning of English*, Blackwell, Oxford

Fletcher, P. (1987) 'Language Acquisition and Linguistic Theory', *Linguistics Abstracts* 3: 1–9

Fletcher, P. and Garman, M. (eds) (1979, 1st edn) *Language Acquisition: Studies in First Language Development*, Cambridge University Press

Fletcher, P. and Garman, M. (eds) (1986, 2nd edn) *Language Acquisition: Studies in First Language Development*, Cambridge University Press

Flynn, S. and Lust, B. (1980) 'Acquisition of Relative Clauses: Developmental Changes in Their Heads', *Cornell University Working Papers in Linguistics*, 1: 33–45

Fodor, J.A. (1975) *The Language of Thought*, Crowell, New York

Fodor, J.A. (1980) Contributions to M. Piattelli-Palmarini (ed.) *Language and Learning: The Debate Between Jean Piaget and Noam Chomsky*, Routledge and Kegan Paul, London

Fodor, J.A. (1981) *Mental Representations*, Harvester, Hassocks

Fraser, C., Bellugi, U. and Brown, R. (1963) 'Control of grammar in imitation, comprehension, and production', *Journal of Verbal Learning and Verbal Behaviour* 2: 121–135

Fukui, N. (1986) *A Theory of Category Projection and its Applications*, PhD diss., MIT

Gathercole, V.C. (1985) ' "He has too much hard questions": the acquisition of the linguistic mass–count distinction in *much* and *many*', *Journal of Child Language* 12: 395–415

Gelman, S. A. and Taylor, M. (1983) 'How 2-year old children interpret proper and common names for unfamiliar objects', *Child Development* 55: 1535–40

Georgopoulos, C. (1984) 'On Beluan Islands: a study in agreement morphology', in C.Brugman et al. (eds) *Proceedings of the Tenth Annual Meeting of the Berkeley Linguistics Society*, University of California, Berkeley, pp. 76–86

Gleitman, L. (1981) 'Maturational Determinants of Language Growth', *Cognition* 10: 103–114

Gleitman, L. (1989) 'The structural sources of verb meaning', text of keynote address to the Stanford Child Language Conference, April 1989

Gleitman, L., Gleitman, H. and Shipley, E. (1974) 'The emergence of the child as a grammarian', *Cognition* 1: 137–64

Gleitman, L. and Wanner, E. (1982) 'Language acquisition: the state of the state of the art', in Wanner and Gleitman, pp. 3–48

Goodluck, H. (1989) 'The Acquisition of Syntax', MS, University of Ottawa

Goodluck, H. and Behne, D. (1988) 'Development in Control and Extraction', prepublication draft of paper to appear in *Theoretical Studies in Language Acquisition: Papers from the Berlin Workshop*, edited by J. Weissenborn, H. Goodluck, and T. Roeper, Erlbaum, New York

Gordon, P. (1985) 'Evaluating the semantic categories hypothesis: the case of the count/mass distinction', *Cognition* 20: 209–42

Greenberg, J.H. (1966) 'Some Universals of Grammar with Particular Reference to the Order of Meaningful Elements', in J.H. Greenberg (ed.) *Universals of Language*, 2nd edn, MIT Press, Cambridge Mass.

Greenfield, P., Reilly, J., Leaper, C. and Baker, N. (1985) 'The structural and functional status of single-word utterances and their relationship to early multi-word speech', in Barrett, pp. 233–267

Greenfield, P.M. and Smith, J.H. (1976) *The Structure of Communication in Early Language Development*, Academic Press, London

Grimshaw, J. (1981) 'Form, function and the language acquisition device', in C.L. Baker and J.J. McCarthy (eds) *The Logical Problem of Language Acquisition*, MIT Press, Cambridge Mass.

Grosu, A. (1988) 'On the distribution of Genitive Phrases in Rumanian', *Linguistics* 26: 931–949

Gruber, J.S. (1967) 'Topicalisation in Child Language', *Foundations of Language* 3: 37–65

Gruber, J.S. (1973) 'Correlations between the Syntactic Constructions of the Child and the Adult', in Ferguson and Slobin, pp. 440–445

Guilfoyle, E. (1984) 'The Acquisition of Tense and the Emergence of Lexical Subjects', *McGill Working Papers in Linguistics*, McGill University, Montreal

Guilfoyle, E. and Noonan, M. (1988) 'Functional Categories and Language Acquisition', text of paper presented to Boston University conference on language acquisition

Guillaume, P. (1927) 'Le dévelopement des éléments formels dans le langage de l'enfant', *Journal de Psychologie* 24: 203–229; translated as

'The development of formal elements in the child's speech', in Ferguson and Slobin, 1973, pp. 240–251

Gunji, T. (1987) *Japanese Phrase Structure Grammar*, Reidel, Dordrecht

Hale, K. (1981) *On the Position of Warlpiri in a Typology of the Base*, Indiana University Linguistics Club

Hale, K. (1982) 'Preliminary Remarks on Configurationality', in J. Pustejovsky and P. Sells (eds) *Proceedings of the North-Eastern Linguistics Society*, vol. 12, pp. 86–96

Hale, K. (1983) 'Warlpiri and the Grammar of Nonconfigurational Languages', *Natural Language and Linguistic Theory* 1: 5–47

Harris, Z.S. (1951) *Structural Linguistics*, Chicago University Press

Hawkins, J. (1983) *Word Order Universals*, Academic Press, London

Hellan, L. (1986) 'The Headedness of NPs in Norwegian', in P. Muysken and H. Van Riemsdijk (eds) *Features and Projections*, Foris, Dordrecht, pp. 89–122

Hill, J. A. C. (1983) *A Computational Model of Language Acquisition in the Two Year Old*, Indiana University Linguistics Club

Hoekstra, T. (1984) *Transitivity: Grammatical Relations in Government-Binding Theory*, Foris, Dordrecht

Horvath, J. (1985) *FOCUS in the Theory of Grammar and the Syntax of Hungarian*, Foris, Dordrecht

Huang, J. C.-T. (1984) 'On the distribution and reference of empty pronouns', *Linguistic Inquiry* 15: 531–574

Huttenlocher, J. (1974) 'The origins of language comprehension', in R. Solso (ed.) *Theories in Cognitive Psychology*, Erlbaum, New York, pp. 331–368

Hyams, N. (1986) *Language Acquisition and the Theory of Parameters*, Reidel, Dordrecht

Hyams, N. (1987a) 'The Theory of Parameters and Syntactic Development', in Roeper and Williams, pp. 1–22

Hyams, N. (1987b) 'The Setting of the Null Subject Parameter: A reanalysis', text of paper presented to the Boston University Conference on Child Language Development

Hyams, N. (1988) 'The Acquisition of Inflection: a parameter-setting approach', MS, University of California at Los Angeles

Hyams, N. (1989) 'The Null Subject Parameter in Language Acquisition', in O. Jaeggli and K. Safir (eds) *The Null Subject Parameter*, Kluwer, Dordrecht, pp. 215–238

Ingram, D. (1989) *First Language Acquisition: Method, Description, and Explanation*, Cambridge University Press, Cambridge

Ito, T. (1988) 'Sentence Production: From Before to After the Period of Syntactic Structure', *Mita Working Papers in Psycholinguistics* 1: 51–55

Jackendoff, R. (1972) *Semantic Interpretation in Generative Grammar*, MIT Press, Cambridge Mass.

Jacobs, R.A. and Rosenbaum, P.S. (1970) *Readings in English Transformational Grammar*, Ginn and Co., Waltham Mass.

Jacobsen, B. (1977) *Transformational-Generative Grammar*, North-Holland, Amsterdam

Jaeggli, O. (1982) *Topics in Romance Syntax*, Foris, Dordrecht

Jaeggli, O. and Hyams, N. (1988) 'Morphological Uniformity and the Setting of the Null Subject Parameter', MS, University of California at Los Angeles

Jaeggli, O. and Safir, K. (1987) 'The Null Subject Parameter and Parametric Theory', MS, University of Southern California

Jespersen, O. (1922) *Language: Its Nature, Development and Origin*, Macmillan, New York

Jordens, P. and Lalleman, J. (eds) (1988) *Language Development*, Foris, Dordrecht

Kanamura, A. (1989) *A Comparative Analysis of the Complementiser Phrase in English and Japanese*, diploma dissertation, University College of North Wales, Bangor

Karmiloff-Smith, A. (1979) *A Functional Approach to Child Language*, Cambridge University Press

Katz, B., Baker, G. and Macnamara, J. (1974) 'What's in a name?', *Child Development* 45: 269–273

Kayne, R.S. (1983) 'Chains, Categories External to S, and French Complex Inversion', *Natural Language and Linguistic Theory* 1: 107–139

Kayne, R.S. (1984) *Connectedness and Binary Branching*, Foris, Dordrecht

Kazman, R. (1988) 'Null Arguments and the Acquisition of Case and INFL', text of paper presented at University of Boston conference on language acquisition

Klima, E.S. and Bellugi, U.(1966) 'Syntactic Regularities in the Speech of Children', in J. Lyons and R. Wales (eds) *Psycholinguistic Papers*, Edinburgh University Press, pp. 183–207

Koopman, H. (1984) *The Syntax of Verbs*, Foris, Dordrecht

Kuczaj, S. (1977) 'The acquisition of regular and irregular past tense forms', *Journal of Verbal Learning and Verbal Behaviour*, 16: 589–600

Kuroda, S-Y. (1987) '(D')Accord ou Pas Accord: quelques idées générales concernant une grammaire comparée de l'anglais et du japonais', *Recherches Linguistiques* 14–15: 189–206, Vincennes

Lalleman, J. (1988) 'The study of child language acquisition: a survey and a discussion of some recent developments', in Jordens and Lalleman, pp. 1–28

Lebeaux, D.S. (1987) 'Comments on Hyams', in Roeper and Williams, pp. 23–39

Lebeaux, D.S. (1988) *Language Acquisition and the Form of the Grammar*, PhD diss., University of Massachusetts

Lefebvre, C. and Muysken, P. (1988) *Mixed Categories: Nominalisations in Quechua*, Kluwer, Dordrecht

Levy, Y. (1983) 'It's frogs all the way down', *Cognition* 15: 75–93

Levy, Y. (1988) 'The Nature of Early Language: Evidence from the Development of Hebrew Morphology', in Levy et al. 1988, pp. 73–98

Levy, Y. et al. (eds) (1988) *Categories and Processes in Language Acquisition*, Erlbaum, London

Lust, B. (1986, 1987) *Studies in the Acquisition of Anaphora*, Reidel, Dordrecht (2 vols)

Macnamara, J. (1982) *Names for Things: a study of child language*, MIT Press, Cambridge Mass.

MacWhinney,B. (1978) *Processing a first language: the acquisition of morphophonology*, Monographs of the Society for Research in Child Development, vol. 43

MacWhinney, B. (ed.) (1987) *Mechanisms of Language Acquisition*, Erlbaum, London

Maratsos, M. (1974) 'Children who get worse at understanding the passive: a replication of Bever', *Journal of Psycholinguistic Research* 3: 65–74

Maratsos, M. (1979) 'Learning how and when to use Pronouns and Determiners', in Fletcher and Garman, 1979, pp. 225–240

Maratsos, M. (1981) 'Problems in categorial evolution: Can formal categories arise from semantic ones?', in Deutsch, pp. 245–261

Maratsos, M. (1982) 'The child's construction of grammatical categories', in Wanner and Gleitman, pp. 240–266

Maratsos, M. (1988) 'The Acquisition of Formal Word Classes', in Levy et al., pp. 31–44

Maratsos, M. et al. (1979) 'Some empirical findings in the acquisition of transformational relations', in W. A. Collins (ed.) *Minnesota Symposia on Child Psychology*, Erlbaum, Hillsdale.

Maratsos, M. and Chalkey, M.A. (1980) 'The internal language of children's syntax: The ontogenesis and representation of syntactic categories', in Nelson, pp. 127–214

McCarthy, D. (1954) 'Language Development in Children', in L. Carmichael (ed.) *Manual of Child Psychology*, Wiley, New York

McCloskey, J. (1986) 'Inflection and Conjugation in Modern Irish', *Natural Language and Linguistic Theory* 4: 245–281

McCloskey, J. and Hale, K. (1984) 'On the syntax of person-number inflection in Modern Irish', *Natural Language and Linguistic Theory* 1: 487–533

McCune-Nicolich, L. (1981) 'The cognitive bases of relational words in the single word period', *Journal of Child Language* 8: 15–34

McNeill, D. (1966) 'Developmental Psycholinguistics', in Smith and Miller, pp. 15–84

Menyuk, P. (1969) *Sentences Children Use*, MIT Press, Cambridge Mass.

Miller, J.F., Chapman, R., Bronston, M. and Reichle, J. (1980) 'Language comprehension in sensorimotor stages V and VI', *Journal of Speech and Hearing Research* 23: 284–311

Miller, J.F., Klee, T.M., Paul, R. and Chapman, R.S. (1981) *Assessing Language Production in Children*, Edward Arnold, London

Miller, M. (1979) *The Logic of Language Development in Early Childhood*, Springer-Verlag, New York

Miller, W.R. and Ervin, S.M. (1964) 'The Development of Grammar in Child Language', in U. Bellugi and R. Brown (eds) *The Acquisition of Language*, Monographs of the Society for Research in Child Development, vol. 29, pp. 9–34

Mulford, R. (1985) 'Comprehension of Icelandic pronoun gender: semantic versus formal factors', *Journal of Child Language* 12: 443–53

Nelson, K.A. (ed.) (1980) *Children's Language* (vol. 2), Gardner Press, New York

Nishigauchi, T. and Roeper, T. (1987) 'Deductive Parameters and the Growth of Empty Categories', in Roeper and Williams, pp. 91–121

Painter, C. (1984) *Into the Mother Tongue*, Pinter, London

Park, T-Z. (1981) *The Development of Syntax in the Child with special reference to German*, AMOE, Innsbruck

Peters, A. (1983) *The Units of Language Acquisition*, Cambridge University Press

Peters, A. (1986) 'Early syntax', in Fletcher and Garman, 1986, pp. 307–325

Phinney, M. (1981) *Syntactic Constraints and the Acquisition of Embedded Sentential Complements*, PhD diss., University of Massachusetts

Piattelli-Palmarini, M. (1989) 'Evolution, selection and cognition: from "learning" to parameter setting in biology and in the study of language', *Cognition* 31: 1–44

Pinker, S.(1982) 'A theory of the acquisition of lexical interpretive grammars', in J. Bresnan (ed.) *The Mental Representation of Grammatical Relations*, MIT Press, Cambridge Mass., pp. 655–726

Pinker, S. (1984) *Language Learnability and Language Development*, Harvard University Press, Cambridge Mass.

Pinker, S. (1987) 'The Bootstrapping Problem in Language Acquisition', in MacWhinney, pp. 399–441

Platzack, C. (1989) 'A grammar without functional categories: A syntactic study of Early Swedish Child Language', MS, Lund University

Pollock, J-Y. (1988) 'Sur la syntaxe comparée de la négation de phrase en anglais et en français', in Fassi Fehri et al. (eds), pp. 107–127

Pollock, J-Y. (1989) 'Verb Movement, Universal Grammar, and the Structure of IP', *Linguistic Inquiry* 20: 365–424

Postal, P.M. (1970) 'On So-called Pronouns in English', in Jacobs and Rosenbaum, pp. 56–82

Radford, A. (1985) 'The Development of Clauses in early child speech', paper presented to the *Psychology Colloquium*, University of Wales

Radford, A. (1986) 'Small Children's Small Clauses', *Research Papers in Linguistics* 1: 1–38, University College of North Wales, Bangor

Radford, A. (1987) 'The Acquisition of the Complementiser System', *Research Papers in Linguistics* 2: 55–76, University College of North Wales, Bangor

Radford, A. (1988a) *Transformational Grammar*, Cambridge University Press, Cambridge

Radford, A. (1988b) 'Small Children's Small Clauses', *Transactions of the Philological Society*, 86: 1–46 (revised and extended version of Radford 1986)

Radford, A. (1989) 'The Syntax of Attributive Adjectives in English: Abnegating Abney', paper presented to the Colloquium on Noun Phrase Structure, University of Manchester, September 1989

Radford, A. and Aldridge, M. (1987) 'The Acquisition of the Inflection System', in W. Lörscher and R. Schulze (eds) *Perspectives on Language in Performance*, G. Narr Verlag, Tübingen, pp. 1289–1309

Ramer, A. (1976) 'Syntactic Styles in Emerging Language', *Journal of Child Language* 3: 49–62

Rizzi, L. (1982) *Issues in Italian Syntax*, Foris, Dordrecht

Rizzi, L. (1986) 'Null objects in Italian and the Theory of *pro*', *Linguistic Inquiry* 17: 501–557

Rodgon, M. (1976) *Single Word Usage: Cognitive development and the beginnings of combinatorial speech*, Cambridge University Press, Cambridge

Roeper, T. (1987) 'The acquisition of implicit arguments and the distinction between Theory, Process, and Mechanism', in MacWhinney, pp. 309–343

Roeper, T. and De Villiers, J. (1989) 'Ordered parameters in the acquisition of Wh-questions', MS, University of Massachusetts

Roeper, T. and Williams, E. (eds) (1987) *Parameter Setting*, Reidel, Dordrecht

Rom, A. and Dgani, R. (1985) 'Acquiring case-marked pronouns in Hebrew: the interaction of linguistic factors', *Journal of Child Language* 12: 61–77

Rothstein, S.D. (1983) *The Syntactic Forms of Predication*, PhD diss., MIT

Rouveret, A. (1980) 'Sur la notion de proposition finie: gouvernement et inversion', *Recherches Linguistiques* 9: 76–140, Vincennes

Rouveret, A. (1989) 'X-bar theory and barrierhood in Welsh', MS, University of Paris VIII

Rouveret, A. and Vergnaud, J-R. (1980) 'Specifying reference to subject: French causatives and conditions on representations', *Linguistic Inquiry* 11: 97–202

Rudin, C. (1988) 'On Multiple Questions and Multiple Wh Fronting', *Natural Language and Linguistic Theory* 6: 445–501

Sachs, J. and Truswell, L. (1978) 'Comprehension of two-word instructions by children in the one-word stage', *Journal of Child Language* 5: 17–24

Saito, M. (1985) *Some Asymmetries in Japanese and their Theoretical Implications*, PhD diss., MIT

Schachter, P. (1985) 'Parts-of-speech systems', in T. Shopen (ed.) *Language Typology and Syntactic Description*, Cambridge University Press, Cambridge, pp. 3–61

Schaerlaekens, A. (1973) *The Two Word Stage in Child Language Development*, Mouton, The Hague

Schieffelin, B.B. (1981) 'A developmental study of pragmatic appropriateness of word order and casemarking in Kaluli', in Deutsch, pp. 105–120

Schlesinger, I.M. (1971) 'The production of utterances and language acquisition', in D.I. Slobin (ed.) *The Ontogenesis of Grammar*, Academic Press, New York, pp. 63–101

Schlesinger, I.M. (1982) *Steps to Language: Toward a Theory of Native Language Acquisition*, Erlbaum, Hillsdale NJ

Slobin, D.I. (1966) 'The Acquisition of Russian as a Native Language', in Smith and Miller, pp. 129–148

Slobin, D.I. (1979, 2nd edn) *Psycholinguistics*, Scott Foresman and Co., London

Slobin, D.I. (ed.) (1985) (2 vols) *The Cross-Linguistic Study of Language Acquisition*, Hillsdale NJ

Smith, F. and Miller, G.A. (eds) (1966) *The Genesis of Language: a Psycholinguistic Approach*, MIT Press, Cambridge Mass.

Smith, M. (1926) *An Investigation of the development of the sentence and the extent of vocabulary in young children*, University of Iowa Studies in Child Welfare, vol. 3 no. 5

Smith, M. (1933) 'Grammatical errors in the speech of preschool children', *Child Development* 4: 183–90

Smith, N. (1973) *The Acquisition of Phonology: A Case Study*, Cambridge University Press, London

Sportiche, D. (1988) 'A Theory of Floating Quantifiers and Its Corollaries for Constituent Structure', *Linguistic Inquiry* 19: 425–449

Stern, W. (1928) 'The chief periods of further speech development', in Bar-Adon and Leopold, 1971, pp. 45–52

Stowell, T. (1981) *Origins of Phrase Structure*, PhD diss., MIT

Tanz, C. (1980) *Studies in the Acquisition of Deictic Terms*, Cambridge University Press

Tavakolian,S.L. (ed.) (1981) *Language Acquisition and Linguistic Theory*, MIT Press, Cambridge Mass.

Tracy, R. (1986) 'The acquisition of case morphology in German', *Linguistics* 24: 47–78

Travis, L. (1984) *Parameters and Effects of Word Order Variation*, PhD diss., MIT

Valian, V. (1986) 'Syntactic Categories in the Speech of Young Children', *Developmental Psychology* 22: 562–579

Valian, V. (1989a) 'Children's production of subjects: competence, performance, and the null subject parameter', to appear in *Papers and Reports in Child Language Development*, Stanford University

Valian, V. (1989b) 'Null subjects: a problem for parameter setting models of language acquisition', to appear in *Cognition*

Valian, V., Winzemer, J. and Erreich, A. (1981) 'A "Little Linguist" Model of Syntax Learning', in Tavakolian, pp. 188–209

Van der Geest, T. (1977) 'Some interactional aspects of language acquisition', in C. Snow and C. Ferguson (eds) *Talking to Children*, Cambridge University Press, Cambridge

Wanner, E. and Gleitman, L. (eds) (1982) *Language Acquisition: the state of the art*, Cambridge University Press, Cambridge

Weissenborn, J. and Verrips, M. (1989) 'Negation as a Window to the Structure of Early Child Language', MS, Max-Planck-Institut, Nijmegen

Wells, G. (1979) 'Learning and using the auxiliary verb in English', in V. Lee (ed.) *Language Development*, Croom Helm, London, pp. 250–270

Wells, G. (1985) *Language Development in the Pre-school Years*, Cambridge University Press, London

Williams, E. (1981) 'Argument Structure and Morphology', *The Linguistic Review* 1: 81–114

Xu, L. (1986) 'Free Empty Category', *Linguistic Inquiry* 17: 75–93

Index